The West End Front

The Wartime Secrets of London's Grand Hotels

MATTHEW SWEET

faber and faber

First published in 2011
by Faber and Faber Ltd
Bloomsbury House
74–77 Great Russell Street
London WC1B 3DA
This paperback edition first published 2012

Typeset by Faber and Faber Ltd

Printed and bound by CPI Group (UK) Ltd, Croydon, CR0 4YY

A CIP record for this book
is available from the British Library

ISBN 978-0-571-23478-3

FSC
www.fsc.org
MIX
Paper from
responsible sources
FSC® C101712

4 6 8 10 9 7 5 3

The West End Front

Matthew Sweet presents *Night Waves* and *Freethinking* on BBC Radio 3, and is the summer presenter of *The Film Programme* on Radio Four. He is the author of *Inventing the Victorians* and *Shepperton Babylon*, which he adapted as a film for BBC Four. His TV programmes include *Silent Britain*, *A Brief History of Fun*, *The Age of Excess*, *Truly, Madly, Cheaply* and *The Rules of Film Noir*.

Further praise for *West End Front*:

'Scandalously enjoyable . . . delightfully gossipy and often moving, it shines an affectionate search-light on an entirely forgotten chapter of World War Two.' Mark Gatiss

'Glamour and seediness jostle for our attention while Sweet combines nostalgic whimsy and gossipy flourishes with impressive sleuthing.' *Daily Express*

'There's something magical about London's grand hotels . . . Matthew Sweet has tapped this glamour to tell tales of the human dramas the hotels hosted during the second world war . . . Strange people, strange times. Check yourself in for a good read.' Mark Mason, *Spectator*

'Very good fun, sympathetic to victims as well as bosses, and full of amusing peculiarities' Andrew Motion, *Guardian*

'Sweet has had the clever idea of uncovering the bizarre, grotesque and often rather seedy wartime experiences of the great hotels. His book is, in many ways, a counterblast to the idea that we British all pulled together in adversity, with everyone, high and low, behaving with impeccable restraint and fortitude. Sweet writes with the enthusiasm of an obsessive: he has been on the prowl for stories about these hotels, on and off, for 15 years.' Craig Brown, *Mail on Sunday*

'Superb . . . While this book is about grand hotels, it is also partly about the high end of the underworld that frequented them – a subject of enduring interest.' Simon Heffer, *Standpoint*

'Sweet turns a quizzical eye on the London socialites determined that their high life should continue undisturbed. The ambivalences and ambiguities of their conspicuous self-interest during a national emergency is exposed in gloriously gossipy stories.' *The Times*

'Sweet is a master at uncovering the unlikely . . . his witty and evocative book brings it to life.' *Word* magazine

---

by the same author

Inventing the Victorians
Shepperton Babylon

To Connie

Contents

List of Illustrations

Victor of the Ritz

A bird's been flapping in the chimney
All the day long.
Smoked salmon instead of eggs for breakfast
Something must be wrong.
An Egyptian waiter has kissed a girl
In room number four–two–three
(Why the hell did she make such a fuss
Instead of calling for me?)
The Ritz may be falling like London Bridge
And I be a bloody fool
But in a hotel where Victor ceased to rule
I would not wish to be.

It's hot as hell and the windows won't open,
All the day long.
It's freezing cold and the heating's off.
Something must be wrong.
A Yank's been phoning all night to New York
In room number four–two–three.
Why the hell won't he wait till morning
Instead of awakening me?
The Ritz is falling like London Bridge
And I am a bloody fool
But in a hotel where Victor ceased to rule
I would not wish to be.

I wait for the breakfast I ordered at seven
All the day long.

Though the tea will be black and the toast will be soggy
Something must be wrong.
They've chilled the claret and heated the Perrier
Ordered by room four–two–three.
And I quite forget what I asked them to bring.
It's a far-off dream to me.
The Ritz has fallen like London Bridge
And I'll weep like a bloody fool
But in a hotel where Victor ceased to rule
I would not wish to be.

Graham Greene

Introduction

Ritzkrieg

The night before the lights went out, Victor Legg was the lone-liest man in London. He clocked off in the early hours of the first day of September 1939, but he did not go home. Instead, he walked. He went east, past Fortnum & Mason, where the windows were already crossed with sticky tape and the walls banked with sandbags. He struck out across Piccadilly Circus, through the insomniac streets of Soho and into Covent Garden, where he found an all-night Italian café; one of those places where signs on the walls warned customers that they were not permitted to sleep on the premises. He sat. He smoked. He ordered bacon sandwiches and coffee. And he waited for the world to know what he knew.

The West End was brighter that night than it would be for a decade. On the canyon wall of hoardings above Piccadilly Circus, the vanishing pleasures of peacetime were described in light. A neon Austin Morris motored on an open road of glow-ing lines. A burning sign proclaimed the superiority of the Ekco television set – the best receiver for a service that was doomed to go dark the following lunchtime. Above them all, the Guinness clock measured out its last few illuminated hours. And on the grand Edwardian building from which Victor had begun this solitary journey the bulbs also glowed, picking out its name in blackout blue.

Victor Legg joined the nocturnal population of the Ritz in late 1935. He turned up at the back door of the hotel in search of work and, much to his surprise, was ushered into the presence of the assistant manager, a hard-headed Swiss named

Edouard Schwenter. Schwenter asked him if he had any experience of hotels. Victor replied that he had worked behind the reception desk of the Berkeley, a smaller, older establishment on the other side of Piccadilly – but omitted to mention that he had been given the sack. Schwenter enquired whether he could operate a telephone switchboard. Victor confirmed that he could, which was not quite a lie. Schwenter then asked if he could speak French. Here, the truth was unavoidable. The assistant manager made a show of disappointment, then gave him the job on the spot. It was only when he began his first shift that Victor understood the nature of this generosity. Schwenter had a lover who often called the hotel. French was the language of their adultery. The new telephonist was quite unable to understand its breathless details.

Every evening at seven o'clock, Victor went to the topmost floor of the hotel and took his place in a hot little room a few doors down from the resident hairdresser. Here, lights pulsed insistently, operators demanded attention and, with a Bakelite headset clamped to his ear, he slotted jacks into sockets and connected the callers to the called. At ten o'clock on the last night of August 1939, a brisk military voice asked to be put through to the Grill Room. Victor obeyed, transferring the call to Kaneledis, the basement cloakroom attendant – but kept the switchboard key in the forward position, allowing him to eavesdrop on the conversation. The caller asked if Randolph Churchill was in the building. Kaneledis had little trouble confirming his presence. Churchill was the son of one of Britain's most prominent politicians – and so notorious for his foul-mouthed intolerance of hotel staff that waiters bribed each other in order to avoid serving him.[1] 'He's in the bar,' replied the attendant. 'May I ask who is calling?' The voice on the end of the line gave a sharp response: 'You may not.' A few moments later, Churchill had the receiver in his hand.

'Randy?' asked the caller.

'Yes?'

'The Germans bomb Warsaw tomorrow morning. Nine o'clock.'

The significance of this exchange was not lost on Victor. It was as good as a declaration of war; confirmation that Neville Chamberlain's policy of Appeasement had reached its endgame; a signal that history had clicked back round to 1914. As soon as Churchill had rung off, Victor put through a call to a friend who worked at the BBC. Before he could communicate the news, however, he heard another voice on the line. 'Operator,' it said, 'I'd be careful what you repeat.' The line fell silent. Victor followed suit. He spent an uneasy night in that hot little room at the top of the Ritz, reflecting on this unfriendly warning and wondering when the security services had begun tapping the phones. At the end of his shift, he was relieved to step out into Piccadilly, walk through the quiet West End streets, settle himself at his favourite table at Elena Giacopazzi's café near the Theatre Royal and work his way through several pots of coffee and a packet of Craven 'A'. At 10.30 he walked out to the newspaper stand by Covent Garden tube station and bought a copy of the morning edition of the *Star*. The headlines carried no news of any bombardment. He flipped to the back page, which bore a gloomy announcement about the cancellation of Saturday's races at Northolt Park, and scanned the list of the runners and riders scheduled to churn the turf in Manchester that afternoon. Two, he noted, were the property of the Aga Khan, the millionaire Imam, diplomat and Ritz resident, on whose horses the hotel staff placed loyal bets. The *Star* kept the right-hand column of the page blank to list the names of last-minute withdrawals from the field. But the international crisis had obliged its editor to stop the press in acknowledgement of something graver than a waterlogged course or a bruised fetlock: a line cabled by a reporter from the British United Press agency, confirming that at nine o'clock that morning, ninety minutes before the *Star* hit the stands, the outskirts of Warsaw had felt the impact of a rain of Luftwaffe incendiaries. Half an hour later, the story had already migrated to the front page: 'Danzig proclaims return to the Reich,' boomed the paper. 'Germans bomb Polish town.'

By the time I met Victor Legg, two years before his death in 2007, his name had become synonymous with the Ritz. It was an institution to which he had given half a century of his life – three years on the switchboard, the rest behind the desk in the circular vestibule, mostly in the revered position of head hall porter. His devotion to the place was so profound that his wife, on several occasions, had advised him to take his bed and sleep there. ('It was like a drug,' he conceded. 'A disease.') He had retired in 1976, but his conversation remained thickly populated with plutocrats and earls and novelists and monarchs. He showed me a letter from Jackie Onassis, thanking him for rescuing her son from a makeshift bed on a bench in Green Park, and lending him the money for an air ticket to Amsterdam. He produced three typewritten pages by Graham Greene – one a three-stanza elegy commemorating Victor's long service to the hotel, the other a letter complaining about the quality of the sausages. He spoke of nights spent gambling in the casino with a prominent Israeli arms dealer; singing nonsense songs with the economist J. K. Galbraith; gassing with the Queen Mother. The story of this sleepless night in 1939 was one of his stock anecdotes. He had probably told it a thousand times. And yet, almost seven decades after the event, his beady blue eyes still betrayed the impact of that triple shock: a prediction of war, a mysterious reprimand and a prophecy fulfilled beside a list of the runners in the 2.30 at Castle Irwell. 'It frightened the life out of me,' he admitted. 'How could the War Office have known it all in advance, so precisely?' Two days later, Chamberlain sat in front of a BBC microphone and issued the news that most people had been anticipating for months: Britain was at war with Germany. 'When we heard the announcement, we thought that was that,' recalled Victor. 'What use is the Ritz in the middle of a war?'

By 1939, London's grand hotels had evolved their own distinctive culture of luxury. The pattern had been established in 1889, when the impresario Richard D'Oyly Carte opened the Savoy, a seven-storey, all-electric, glazed-brick pleasure palace on the Thames Embankment. Seventy of its 268 rooms had en suite baths; all had hot and cold running water. (George Holloway, the builder assigned to the project, asked Carte if the hotel was intended to house amphibians.) Speaking-tubes could be used to summon room service at any hour of the day or night. ('Please command anything from a cup of tea to a cocktail,' enthused the brochure, 'and it will come up in the twinkling of an Embankment lamp.'[2]) Six hydraulic lifts made the building's height a source of interest rather than exhaustion. A subterranean power-plant and a 500-foot artesian well gave the hotel an independent source of energy and water. These systems were triumphs of British engineering, but the ethos of the Savoy was a foreign import. Two men were responsible for ensuring that it survived the journey. The first was the general manager, César Ritz, the thirteenth child of a Swiss shepherd and a veteran of the 1870 siege of Paris – during which he learned to cook with rat-meat and made blood pudding from the elephants in the city zoo. As head of kitchen services, Ritz appointed the Frenchman Georges Auguste Escoffier, a blacksmith's son who wore high heels to enable him to see into the pans at the back of the ranges. Ritz flattered his guests with subdued lighting and roseate tablecloths, gave them wine in Baccarat crystal glasses, and filled the restaurant with music to give diners a reason to linger. Escoffier reorganised the preparation of food along military lines, drilled his brigades of cooks in the preparation of ortolans, terrapin and snipe, and refused to learn English on the grounds that it might have an adverse effect on the quality of his cooking. Together, these men created the ambience that persuaded the plutocracy and the aristocracy to do something to which they were unaccustomed – eat, drink, smoke and dance in public. For this, the Savoy's board celebrated Ritz and Escoffier as artists and heroes, until the day they discovered that these star employees were defrauding the company to the tune of £19,137. A private detective was hired to investigate allegations of bribery, profiteering, embezzlement and the mysterious disappearance of enormous quantities of cigars, wines, spirits and eggs. In March 1898, both men were dismissed.

The Savoy suppressed the truth of the affair, which left Ritz and Escoffier free to profit from a boom in the construction of luxury hotels that lasted until the beginning of the Great War. By 1897 D'Oyly Carte had rebuilt Claridge's, a collection of discreet townhouses on Brook Street, in the seven-storey image of the Savoy. The Hotel Russell rose the following year – a heap of Gothic terracotta with sculpture queens and prime ministers on sentry duty. The Carlton, a vast confection of mansard roofs and domed cupolas, was raised at the corner of Haymarket and Pall Mall in 1899: Ritz supplied managerial advice and Escoffier took charge of the kitchens, where, it is claimed, he employed a young Vietnamese *entremettier* who later led a Communist revolution under the name of Ho Chi Minh.[3] Ritz's revolution, however, went on without him: in 1901 he suffered a devastating mental breakdown, brought on, it seems, by logistical headaches caused by the postponement of Edward VII's coronation. The investiture was rescheduled, but Ritz's melancholia failed to lift. He was utterly disengaged from the process of planning and building the hotel on Piccadilly that bore his name, and failed to attend the opening in May 1906. (Today, the wall of the general manager's office bears the note of congratulation Ritz sent in his place – a desultory, almost illegible thing.) César Ritz died just before Armistice Day in an asylum near Lucerne, by which time London had gained a battalion of grand hotels, and his name had become an adjective – one that stood for wealth, superiority, luxury and extravagance.

A certain kind of behaviour went with that word. You could

have observed it on the June night in 1905 when the American financier George Kessler arranged to flood the courtyard of the Savoy, fill it with swans, surround it with twelve thousand fresh carnations, four thousand lamps and a canvas simulacrum of Venice – and dine with his guests on a large silk-lined gondola moored at its centre. (The blue dye in the water killed the swans, but there was compensation in the form of a performance by Caruso, a phalanx of Gaiety Girls bearing bottles of Moët & Chandon, and the appearance of a baby elephant with a five-foot birthday cake strapped to its back.) You could have seen it in 1906, when the fountain at the Savoy gushed with champagne in honour of the German arms manufacturer Gustav Krupp – or on one of those lunchtimes in the 1930s when Viscount Castlerosse, the aristocratic gossip columnist of the *Daily Express*, pulled off his sable-lined overcoat and settled himself down in the Savoy Grill to consume three chump chops, an entire ham and six lobsters. George Hayim, a plutocrat's son who knew the bars and restaurants of London in the late 1930s, recalls roaring up to the Grosvenor House Hotel in the sleek car of an equally privileged young friend, who pressed a half-chewed stick of American gum into the white-gloved hand of the valet.[4] 'People of a certain class did things like that and it didn't occur to them to be ashamed or embarrassed,' he told me. 'It makes me shudder now to think of it.'

It took a deep economic recession and another war, however, to produce a British electorate ready for the state to nationalise the industries that had created the individuals who enjoyed such amusements – and, in effect, to abolish the glittering world that had been their playground.

*

When war checked in on the morning of 3 September 1939, the guests of London's grand hotels began to check out, in anticipation of some species of Apocalypse. Since the 1920s, government departments had been crunching numbers for a putative Second World War, attempting to estimate the likely death-toll and the repairs bill from data on the Zeppelin raids of the Great War, from new advances in German aviation technology and – latterly – from casualty statistics from General Franco's bombing raids on Barcelona. The strategists predicted that Hitler would launch a 'knock-out blow' against London, that the first fortnight of bombardment might produce half a million deaths and serious injuries, and that the next casualties would be public order and public health. 'We must expect that, under the pressure of continuous air attack upon London, at least 3,000,000 or 4,000,000 people would be driven out into the open country around the metropolis,' theorised Winston Churchill in 1934. 'This vast mass of human beings, numerically far larger than any armies which have been fed and moved in war, without shelter and without food, without sanitation and without special provision for the maintenance of order, would confront the Government of the day with an administrative problem of the first magnitude, and would certainly absorb the energies of our small Army and our Territorial Force.'[5]

The threat of poison gas was uppermost in the minds of those who remembered the Western Front – though this time, the shells were expected to burst over civilian areas. Newspapers printed cut-out-and-keep guides to help their readers differentiate between flavours of chemical weapons, exhorting them to remember that phosgene smelled like musty hay; lewisite like geraniums; mustard gas like garlic. A decontamination centre for the West End was set up at the Marshall Street baths in Soho, where nurses in respirators and oilskins practised procedures involving bleach powder, petrol and hot soapy water. The Ministry of Health issued one million burial forms. London Zoo executed its venomous snakes. The capital was emptied of its children. Scrubbed and ticketed, they assembled at railway stations and war memorials to begin their journey to billets in areas unlikely to be seen through a Stuka bombsight. Herbert

Morrison, the leader of the London County Council, jollied them into exile: 'Keep a cheerful British smile on your face . . . as many of your fathers used to do, sing "Pack Up Your Troubles in Your Old Kit Bag".'[6] It is hard to imagine that they found this particularly encouraging.

Hoteliers, too, were in need of comfort. Waiters stood idly in deserted restaurants and grills. Desk clerks spiked room reservations. Banqueting managers placed newspaper advertisements announcing the cancellation of formal functions. Bandleaders and musicians went to bed early. Glamorous architecture disappeared under banks of sandbags, disfiguring buildings and creating a magnet for rough sleepers. (One unfortunate man was found dead underneath the sandbags behind the Strand Palace Hotel, having crawled into a gap to warm himself at an air-vent.[7]) The day after Chamberlain's declaration of war, the Savoy concluded that the risk of bombardment had transformed the atrium of the restaurant from an asset into a death-trap. The doors were shut. Two days later, the Ritz management elected to close the Grill Room for lunch and the restaurant for dinner. Along with the Savoy and the Dorchester, they also locked their uppermost floors and draped the furniture in dust-sheets. (Conversely, the Charing Cross Hotel simply reduced the price of its top-floor rooms, allowing fearless guests to acquire a place in the middle of town at peppercorn prices.) At the Savoy, John Hansen, the mountainous Danish doorman, walked into the front hall of the hotel to discover that the glass in the revolving doors had been painted a dark blue and that the desk in his cubby-hole office had lost the board displaying the arrival and departure times of the great passenger liners – a sign that the hotel had abandoned the established practice of despatching porters to the docks to collect new arrivals and their luggage. A concrete observation post was sunk into the roof of the Savoy: seventy employees who had trained as ARP wardens took turns watching for enemy aircraft scudding above the Thames. (The oldest volunteer, William Lawes of the Works Department, protected himself from the cold with a 200-guinea raccoon-fur coat from Lost Property.)

But the most potent indicator of change, as far as the staff was concerned, was the relaxation of the strict sartorial laws, signalled in the moment that Sir George Reeves-Smith, managing director of the Savoy, exchanged his silk top-hat and frock coat for a bowler and a lounge suit. A year later, such revisions of protocol were identified as a significant cultural shift: 'I have a feeling', pronounced the novelist W. Somerset Maugham, 'that in the England of the future evening dress will be less important than it has been in the past. I think it will be a more democratic England. I think there will be no more rich people and I hope there will be no more poor people.'[8] The Savoy's official historian recorded the shock of Reeves-Smith's initiative: 'The reception clerks followed him with looks of dismay and returned incredulously to their books.'[9]

More dismay followed. September 1939 was the blackest month in the history of the hotel business. George Cross, the owner of a number of small residential hotels in London, augured the collapse of the entire sector. 'I warn the faint-hearted and the powers that be', he declared, 'that unless immediate steps are taken scarcely an hotel will be available to accommodate naval and military officers and others whose business will sooner or later take them to the Metropolis.'[10] Cross chose to close his establishment in Marble Arch, but others were simply obliged to hand over their keys to the authorities. The War Office claimed the Hotel Victoria and the Metropole on Northumberland Avenue. The Army requisitioned the Great Central at Marylebone. (One floor soon became the domain of MI9, the secret department charged with aiding Allied troops trapped behind enemy lines.) Across the country, the pattern was repeated. The managing director of the Buxton Palace Hotel protested that his workplace had been 'invaded by a horde of arrogant officials ruthlessly marking with a label everything they thought they might possibly need, from beds to

the safe in the office'. He was particularly galled by the seizure
of his entire canteen of cutlery, commandeered by the occupiers for use in their snack bar: 'Expensive lobster forks', he
raged, 'do not seem suitable for cheap sandwiches!'[11] Words
like 'ruthlessness' and 'tyranny' echo through these complaints.
'I ask despairingly', exclaimed one manager, 'whether nothing
can be done to prevent our homes and businesses being ran-
sacked and destroyed, as though we, and not the Nazis, were
the enemy.'[12] By the end of the first month of the war, twenty
thousand hotel workers had been dismissed from their posts,
and George Reeves-Smith, in his capacity as vice-chairman of
the Hotels and Restaurants Association, issued a public warning about the 'paralysis of a great industry'.[13] It was a paralysis
that seemed to presage something more terminal.

Slowly, however, the guests and the diners returned. After
eleven days of darkness and silence, the Dorchester ballroom re-
gained its dancers. 'Night-life', reported the diarist of the *Daily
Express*, 'is just beginning to glisten faintly again behind our
dark doors.'[14] The following week, the band struck up again at
the Berkeley. ('After all,' said a representative of the hotel, 'what
is the use of sitting looking at each other during dinner?'[15])
By December, the shiny papers were reporting a phenomenon.
'Most of the big hotels have discovered, and smartened up,
some previously unconsidered place lurking somewhere in their
depths,' reported the *Tatler*, merged, for the sake of the war
economy, with the *Bystander*. 'Here their night life flourishes,
while the grand grills, restaurants and lounges preserve an eerie
emptiness. But everyone knows that something pretty purpose-
ful is going on somewhere. Long, deserted passages – perhaps
a sinister hotel servant directing you along them – stairs down,
sudden bits of naked brick wall, and grubby little doors giving
on to goodness knows what. Then, suddenly, there is a burst of
music, and there everybody is, making merry just as usual in the
new quarters where, perhaps, provisions used to be stored.'[16]

The Savoy restaurant was reincarnated in the form of a subterranean banqueting room, reinforced with scaffolding. The Ritz reopened its underground spaces: a notice on the ground floor advertised 'a seasonable novelty – a snack or full meal in an air-raid shelter'.[17] As the war approached its second month, 'Chips' Channon, Conservative MP for Southend, informed his diary that the Ritz had become 'fantastically fashionable', concluding confidently, 'Ritzes always thrive in wartime.'[18] The following year, he made a similar report from the Dorchester: 'London lives well. I've never seen more lavishness, more money spent or more food consumed than tonight; and the dance floor was packed. There must have been a thousand people.' Before he departed for Belfast, where he was stationed with the Royal Signals Corps, Victor Legg watched the visitors return to the gilded spaces of the Ritz. 'We thought the war would kill the place,' he recalled. 'But once people got comfortable with the blackout and all the restrictions, they came back. And it seemed more lively than it had been for years.'

Instead of vanishing into history, London's grand hotels became more prominent in the cultural and political life of this country than ever before. They were the homes of Cabinet ministers and military leaders, plutocrats and aristocrats. At lunch tables and in smoking rooms, decisions were made that affected the progress of the war. Hotel apartments became the retreats of governments-in-exile, diplomatic missions and the deposed monarchies of occupied Europe. Journalists filed articles from makeshift offices carved from the carcasses of once-expensive suites. Con-artists and swindlers, invigorated by the opportunities brought by war, hunted for victims among the potted palms. Illegal abortionists, profiting from the wartime increase in unwanted pregnancies, conducted their business behind locked hotel-room doors. Writers, poets, artists, musicians and prostitutes haunted bars and lobbies. Below the pavement of Piccadilly, a flourishing homosexual subculture worked its way through the Ritz's stock of gin and Angostura bitters. Cooks tested the limits of the rationing law and their own ingenuity, confecting dishes from acorns and turnips and eels, and cooking on electric radiators when the bombs deprived them of gas: it was their recipes that the nation followed. Spies and spymasters made rooms above Park Lane, Piccadilly, Brook Street and the Strand into thriving centres of espionage, using quiet suites for debriefings and interrogations, picking at the plasterwork for hidden microphones, and despatching agents of the secret state to loiter in the coffee lounges and listen for treachery. The Dorchester, the Savoy, the Ritz and Claridge's: each was a kind of Casablanca.

*

It was engineering that made all this possible, though it did its work discreetly. Walk into the Ritz today and you feel as if you have entered some alternative universe in which the guillotine has never been invented, where rococo remains fashionable, and where liberty, equality and fraternity have never quite caught on. Through its revolving doors, beyond the fumy air of Piccadilly, might be a world full of pomaded types in periwigs. This is the trick of the Ritz: it appears to have existed for ever. Since its opening night in 1906, the hotel has been seducing wealthy patrons with the same illusion. The Palm Court might be the personal arboretum of Louis XVI. Beyond the glass ceiling, however, is nothing but a rack of low-watt light bulbs and the floorboards of the first-floor rooms. And these are not the only feats of legerdemain performed by the architects, Charles Mewes and Arthur Davis. Every way you look in the Ritz, the view recedes into the distance. You feel as if you could drive around the place in a carriage without scuffing so much as an architrave. But this is a conjuring trick performed with paint, plaster and mirrored glass. Despite the eye's insistence, the Ritz is a little strip of a building; a piffling place compared with most grand hotels. The exterior is just as much a sham. The façade appears to be carved from stone, but some smart work with a pickaxe would soon expose the steel skeleton of a skyscraper, something more like the innards of the Flatiron Building than the Palace of Versailles.[19] This is the reason why war did not silence the Ritz.

The details had already been reported at great length in Edwardian engineering and architectural journals: glowing paragraphs about rafts of reinforced concrete and two-layer grillages of steel beams that complied with 'the latest standards for steel-framed office buildings in America'.[20] In October 1939, the *Réunion des Gastronomes*, a body representing hotel and restaurant proprietors, urged its members to report them again, and woo back lost patrons with reassuring words about sturdy joists and girders. The Ritz reminded the public of the existence of its metal frame – omitting to mention that the steel had been imported from Germany. The Dorchester boasted of the sturdy concrete roots that it had put down deep under Park Lane. The Waldorf ballyhooed its alloy bones. The structures of the Savoy and Claridge's were rather less resilient, but that did not stop the publicity manager from using the hotel's official New Year cards to celebrate the impregnability of the Savoy's reinforced restaurant. 'This room is provided with special protection from blasts and splinters,' she declared. 'The inner wall is fourteen inches thick. The outer wall, five feet distant, is nine inches thick. The brick joints in each wall are strengthened with steel mesh, and the two walls support each other by sixteen connecting steel rods.' Looking back on these days from the vantage point of the 1950s, the woman who supplied this copy claimed to have believed her own propaganda: 'I felt a warm pride steal over me that I was part of this world,' wrote Jean Nicol, 'a world as self-contained as a walled city of bygone days, where perfection of service was the rule whether the chandeliers glinted on the sheen of satin, or, like tonight, an oil-lamp swayed above the khaki and blue serge of uniforms.'[21]

Here is the ambivalence upon which this book turns. The nature of a reinforced luxury fortress in the West End is depend-

ent on the position of the observer. For many, the indestruct-
ibility of the social life of London's grand hotels was evidence
of Britain's indomitable nature, proof that Hitler was not sufficiently powerful to disrupt the rituals of cocktail hour. 'People
must eat some time or other even if there is a war on,' wrote
the gossip columnist of the *Tatler*, 'and thank goodness "we hae
meat and can eat – and so the Laird be thankit". It is not so in
another country which is involved in this conflict, whatever the
Liar-in-Chief may want us to believe.' For Society magazines,
made skinny by war but still printed on glossy rotogravure
pages, this was 'the West End Front', where socialites defied
Hitler by lunching for England.[22]

More radical opinion saw something else entirely – and the
satirist Michael Barsley had a word for it. *Ritzkrieg*, a counter-
attack by the wealthy in defence of their pre-war privileges
– and in hope of turning the conflict into a crusade against
Communism: 'stale-mate, followed by Stalin-mate, and an attack on the USSR'. In a series of sketches for the *Tribune* and
the *New Statesman*, Barsley used deft cartoons and diabolical
puns to summon up the leaders of this assault: Colonel Bogus,
a military man 'of the type who formed an alliance between
the Nouveau Riche and the Nouveau Reich'; Lucy Rolls-Voyce,
who owes her appointment to the Intelligence Department to
string-pulling by her father, Lord Damson. ('P'raps', she trills,
'that's why I get the plum jobs.') Barsley imagined these articles
as a stack of secret documents stashed inside a hollow volume
of Gibbon's *Decline and Fall* – an upper-class relation of the
Protocols of the Elders of Zion. 'The Ritzkrieg,' he wrote, 'unlike its more famous predecessor, the *Blitzkrieg*, was a plan
of Inaction and Reaction. It was, in a word, the Old Guards'
Private War, fought by private means.'[23] Today, Barsley's book
makes a somewhat tiresome read, but his point is clear: the inhabitants of the Ritz were fighting the war for themselves.

*

The germ of this book grew from an encounter with the son of the most notorious wartime resident of the Ritz. I met him in Tirana in May 1997, while reporting on his campaign to restore the Albanian monarchy. King Leka of the Albanians, as he styled himself, was a white-haired, bespectacled, six-foot-eight arms dealer who chain-smoked Rothman's cigarettes. His father had been Albania's first and last royal ruler: Ahmet Muhtar Zogolli, who led a 1924 *coup d'état* against the government from which he emerged as President. In September 1928, Zogolli went one better and crowned himself King Zog I of the Albanians, swearing an oath of allegiance on the Bible and the Koran, and presiding over celebrations in which sheep were ritually slaughtered outside the royal palace, Italian planes bombed Tirana with confetti and the letter 'Z' was scorched into hillsides. A Zogist salute was incorporated into the business of civic life: a chop to the heart from the right forearm, highly influential upon the directors of low-budget science fiction.[24] Observers of the royal court of Albania compared what they saw to the kind of preposterous Balkan states often seen in musical comedies.[25] When Kemal Atatürk, the founder of the modern Turkish nation, asked if there was an operetta going on in Tirana, Zog is said to have abandoned his most Ziegfeldish official uniform – a white-and-gold number with a plumed fur hat.

The reign of Zog was brief. The King funded electrification and road-building projects with financial assistance from Italy. In April 1939, however, Mussolini called in the debt, and sent troops marching down the asphalt roads for which his government had paid. The royal family fled the country: Zog, his wife Queen Geraldine, their three-day-old baby Prince Leka, the King's six sisters, three nephews and two nieces, and a twenty-strong party of advisers, courtiers and bodyguards. Their flight across Europe ended at the Ritz, where the Albanian party occupied much of the third floor of the hotel and immediately became the subject of newspaper gossip and official suspicion. The Foreign Office kept Zog at arm's length. They declined formal diplomatic contact and expressed private disgust at his attempt to claim compensation for some items of luggage lost at Dover. Journalists, however, were more interested in the dozens of suitcases that did make it to Piccadilly. ('They do say', noted Rex North of the *Sunday Pictorial*, 'that a van drew up outside the Ritz Hotel loaded up with two million pounds' worth of gold bars.') Press and politicians, however, were united in their belief that Zog had arrived in London with a large amount of dirty money. Special Branch detectives monitored his financial transactions, and observed his sister, Princess Seneji Abid, exchanging thousands of dollar bills at a branch of the Westminster Bank. 'He is understood to have a bill for some $80,000', they reported, 'and cases of bullion at the Ritz Hotel.'[26]

In the spring of 1997 Albania declared a state of emergency, instituted when two-thirds of the population lost its savings in government-backed pyramid investment schemes. A dusk-to-dawn curfew was enforced. UN tanks rumbled along the roads. Guns, looted from the state armouries by an angry population, were everywhere. In a modest villa on the outskirts of Tirana, King Leka reminisced about his father's years of exile. 'We'd eat dinner at eight and he'd go to bed immediately after, and I'd join him in the bedroom. The conversation would last until midnight or one in the morning, and we'd cover the Balkans, naturally, and Albania in particular – in every aspect of politics, history, geography and human nature.' Zog had his only son memorise population figures, geographical statistics and the GDPs of every country in the world. 'It was a tremendous education,' he recalled, glowing with pedagogic nostalgia. 'I've met a lot of great men in my life, and he was the greatest.' I asked him whether it was true that his father had paid his hotel bills with gold bullion. 'Certainly not,' he said, drily.

I joined Leka and his entourage of seedy-looking foreign mercenaries as they took their campaign to Vlora, an Adriatic port under the control of a rebel committee headed by a former cigarette-smuggler named Albert Shite. An unruly crowd of five thousand was waiting for us. Perched on the edge of a massive marble monument commemorating Albania's 1912 declaration of independence, Zog's son took up his megaphone and attempted to make a speech about 'brotherhood, peace and unity'. Nobody wanted to listen. 'Where's the money?' demanded one man. 'Has he brought any money with him?' Leka's royal guard began to look sweaty and nervous. Leka, drowned out by hecklers, cut his losses and struggled back to his limousine. A gang attempted to hijack one of the royal cars with a stick of dynamite – but was obliged to be content with its hub caps. Peals of gunfire rang out above our heads. Then, with a screech of brakes, we were off down the pitted backstreets of Vlora. The royal visit had lasted twenty minutes. After half an hour, the cars drew up at a roadside café. 'That was . . . interesting,' reflected the King, settling down in a white plastic chair and splitting the seal on a new packet of Rothmans. 'My presence seems to ignite the spark. I just hope I'll work out as a stabilising factor.' I asked him about the anger of the crowd; their demands for financial compensation for the collapse of the pyramid schemes. 'I'm not sure that was what they meant,' said Leka. 'I think they were talking about my father's luggage. The communists loved that story.' Everybody laughed. The bodyguards handed out cans of fizzy drink. We toasted the house of Zog with blood-warm Fanta. The back-slapping, the laughter and the automatic weapons put me in mind of wartime press reports about Zog's bodyguards, their all-night poker games, their habit of patrolling the third floor of the Ritz with sawn-off shotguns. I tried to imagine Leka and his cronies on the Palm Court of the Ritz.

*

Most social histories of the Home Front have dealt with the experiences of 'ordinary' people – the Land Girls, the Tommies, the evacuees, the diligent correspondents who filled out their Mass Observation diaries each night before they went to bed. Their emphasis is on collective suffering, pleasure and struggle: how Britons endured separations from husbands, wives, families, lovers; how they strove to make edible food from swedes and offal and desiccated egg; how they survived the physical and emotional shocks of total war. As 1939 edges closer to the limits of living memory, our appetite is for accounts of the Second World War that emphasise the shared experiences of the conflict. This is why so many books about the war have the words *We* and *Our* in their titles, though they deal with events that are beyond the experience of anyone under the age of eighty. This is why, since 2000, when one of the few surviving originals was put on display in the window of a second-hand bookshop in Alnwick, a little-known wartime propaganda poster that exhorted Britons to 'Keep Calm and Carry On' has been reproduced on thousands of postcards, mouse mats, coasters, tea towels, duffle bags, deck-chairs, notebooks, cufflinks and hoodies. In the space of a decade, the phrase has gone from archival obscurity to a mantra of middle-class self-pity. In 2010, a British tabloid gave it away on prints and mugs, as if it believed that enduring the final months of Gordon Brown's government were an equivalent experience to being firebombed by the Luftwaffe. It is a peculiar cultural shift: the same generation that tried not to look bored when their grandparents started banging on about coupons and rocket-bombs and blackout blinds is now putting up wartime propaganda posters in its kitchens and office cubicles, in sentimental solidarity with the people of Churchill's Britain.

Observing the Second World War through the experiences of those who stayed and worked at the Savoy and the Ritz might seem an eccentric way of disrupting the customary narratives of the Home Front. Hotels are not home – indeed, they are sometimes used for doing the things we dare not do at home, and would rather remained unseen by those who know us best.

But the public and private worlds underwent many strange and sudden revisions in the rooms and corridors of the wartime grand hotel – as did the social structures that shaped them. In these years, chambermaids nudged aristocrats awake for snoring in the air-raid shelter; Communists disguised as lunching ladies ripped off their fur-wraps to reveal banners that declared, 'Ration the rich!'; revered head waiters were marched from restaurant floors and into prisons and internment camps; crownless kings sat mournfully in their suites and contemplated lives of exile and despair; Trotskyist agitators exhorted chefs and chambermaids to join the revolution.

I have spent much of the last few years talking with those who were part of these events: Joe Gilmore, the Savoy barman who mixed fruit cocktails for George Bernard Shaw and kept Churchill's secret bottle of whisky under the bar; Crown Prince Alexander of Yugoslavia, born in an illusory patch of his homeland conjured into being in Suite 212 at Claridge's; Joyce Stone, who spent each midnight of the Blitz in the marbled halls of the Dorchester, while her husband conducted the band; Gilbert Bradley, for whom the Lower Bar of the Ritz was the place he was picked up by a sourly beautiful Tory MP with an artificial leg and wife and son in Sussex; Max Levitas, the last known survivor of a brigade of Communist protestors who, as London burned, marched into the air-raid shelter of the Savoy and ordered tea and bread and butter. I have pursued others, too, who have lived with the consequences of scenes played out in suites and lounges seventy years ago: the sons of a celebrated writer who left his lover to die in a room at the Mount Royal Hotel above Oxford Street; the family of a con-man who preyed on impressionable young men in the bar of the Charing Cross Hotel; the friends and relations of a suspected Nazi agent who was installed at the Waldorf by her handlers from MI5, who proved quite unable to cope with her frank attitude to sex. ('Much of Mrs Lonsdale's conversation', asserted one informer, 'cannot possibly be submitted in a report owing to its indescribably filthy nature.') All are gathered here, under the roof of this book, assembled because their stories have obsessed me for the last five years – and because most of those stories refuse to fit the version of the life on the Home Front upon which we seem, as a culture, to have agreed.

I have said that Michael Barsley's *Ritzkrieg* is not a very funny book. Perhaps it never was. But it is a book that imagines looking back on the war from a future Britain transformed by the experience of that conflict – the country that we now occupy. 'It will be seen', he wrote, 'that as far as rations are concerned, the Old Guard scarcely altered their lives or their eating capacity. As far as luxurious living is concerned, we leave the reader to judge for himself. It may be that social historians of the future will cast a not very friendly eye on this peculiarly wasteful and decadent activity of society.'[27] Let us put that assertion to the test.

I

Aliens

On 20 August 1940, Dr Harry Beckett Overy, a member of the Royal College of Surgeons and personal physician to Winston and Clementine Churchill, went to visit Loreto Santarelli, the restaurant manager of the Savoy Hotel. Instead of taking a cab to the Strand from his office in Lowndes Square, Beckett Overy headed for the outskirts of Ascot. He drove until he reached a cluster of single-storey brick buildings and canvas bell tents: the winter quarters of the Bertram Mills Circus. No elephants or llamas or tigers were in evidence. In their place, Beckett Overy found watchtowers, Bren guns, a bank of electric floodlights and a double girdle of barbed wire. On the other side of the fence he found Loreto Santarelli, on the brink of lunacy: 'His tongue and fingers are tremulous,' observed the doctor. 'He has aged considerably, and his heart's action is quickened. With re- gard to his mental condition the change is very great . . . if he remains in confinement at the Camp suffering from its minor discomforts, added to his intense feeling of injustice, he will be- come a complete nervous and physical wreck and likely to be certifiable.'[1]

Loreto Santarelli was born just before Christmas 1885 in Amatrice, a small town on the Via Salaria. He was the eighth child of Pietropaolo Santarelli, a wine merchant whose business had made him rich enough to buy a palazzo from the town's decaying aristocracy. Pietropaolo's education had been minimal and he did not want the same to be true of the next generation. At the age of ten, Loreto was enrolled in a seminary, where he began training for the priesthood – a training against which he eventually rebelled. He left home and found lodgings in Rome, where he took a job peeling potatoes at the Grand Hotel – which had been opened in 1894 by César Ritz. In 1909, Santarelli crossed Europe and joined that force of decorous Italian labour upon which the British hotel trade depended. He scooted between tables at Claridge's and the Berkeley with beatific grace, butlered in a household near Chepstow and ministered to diners at the Royal Automobile Club – where he courted the receptionist, Gertrude Richley, a nautical optician's daughter from Cardiff who knew her own mind and rolled her own cigarettes. They married in Paris in the spring before the Great War, when Gertrude's waist size exactly matched her years. Then, a few months after the Armistice, the Savoy Hotel took over their lives.

Santarelli joined the waiting staff at a weekly salary of forty shillings – but his Vatican manners ensured his swift and stately progress through the hierarchy and, in September 1926, the 'News in Brief' column in *The Times* announced his elevation to restaurant manager – the youngest ever incumbent of the job. He was in no doubt that he held the most distinguished office in the hotel – far more distinguished, certainly, than the job of Benito Manetta, his opposite number at the Grill. Arnold Bennett used Santarelli in his novel *Imperial Palace* (1930), as a model for Mr Cappone, the restaurant manager who is obliged to 'know the names and private histories and weakness and vanities and doings of every regular customer' and 'to look romantic and be exquisitely polite'.[2] The cartoonist Autori sketched him as a long lean line of a man with glamorous dreamy eyes. The gossip columnist of the *Daily Mirror* relied upon him for stories.[3] When the movie producer Alexander Korda required a technical adviser on the set of *Service for Ladies* (1932), he sent for Santarelli. (The film starred one of his regular customers, Leslie Howard, as a grand-hotel waiter who passes for one of his own customers.) When the Maharajah of Rajpipla wired the Savoy restaurant to book a table for a party of one hundred, Santarelli found space for them by dragging a set of smaller dining chairs out of the lumber room – then procured an Indian elephant in purple and cream garlands. The general manager, Albert Gilles, refused to allow the animal through the door, but the Maharajah recognised Santarelli's efforts with a diamond-studded solid-gold cigarette case. Perhaps Gilles was the only person impervious to his charm. George Reeves-Smith declared Santarelli to be the 'best known and most popular restaurant manager in Europe'. The actor-manager Seymour Hicks believed that his 'charming ways could make skim-milk masquerade as cream if ever he felt it necessary to do so'.[4] During the war years it was said 'he could persuade a duchess that she would rather eat a powdered-egg omelette than the roast beef that had just been crossed off the menu'.[5]

Santarelli's working hours were long, but there was always the lucre. City Croesuses passed him their juiciest share tips. A jammy arrangement with his employers gave him tuppence on every shilling cup of coffee drunk in the hotel. His bank account never slipped into the red. He paid his income tax and supertax with diligence. He flew his wife, Gertrude, to Paris for weekends. He invested over £4,000 in Savoy stocks and saved enough to buy an enormous villa in Streatham – in which he installed Gertrude and their children, Anna and Peter. He enjoyed an exalted position within London's community of expatriate Italians, who struck a medal to recognise his charitable services to émigrés whose careers had proved less prosperous. But he also made sure to signal to the authorities where his loyalties lay. In 1932, he applied to become a naturalised British citizen, and attended an interview at the Home Office at which he was handed two paragraphs of text snipped from the papers. One he copied out in his elegant menu copperplate. The other he declaimed to an official of the Ministry: 'Fears that the British government is about to act with dangerous haste in granting a constitutional government to India have not been allayed by the speech of Lord Willingdon, the Viceroy, at the opening of the annual session of the Chamber of Princes in Delhi to-day.' And with that, Loreto Ottavio Santarelli was no longer an Italian.

The security services, however, took a different view. MI5 had been keeping Santarelli under observation since December 1935, when an informer identified him as the head of a Fascist cell in London, asserting that he was on a £1,000-a-year retainer from Rome. The informer claimed to have flashed a Fascist Party membership card at Santarelli and received a brotherly welcome. The restaurant manager, it was claimed, headed 'a small group of Italian Fascists in London who would form a good nucleus for anything the Duce might require'.[6] In May 1939, a wire-tap on the phones at the official London headquarters of Mussolini's party had picked up a request from the Italian consulate for information regarding Santarelli. In wartime, no such person could be permitted to remain at the Savoy. Claude Dansey, the deputy chief of the Secret Intelligence Service, lunched in the restaurant almost every day and used a quiet table to interview potential recruits. Guy Liddell, MI5's director of counter-espionage, conducted meetings over midday cocktails in the American Bar. Intelligence officers hired rooms in the building to carry out the politer kind of debriefing and interrogation. Dusko Popov, a valuable double agent codenamed Tricycle, lived on the premises – when he was not in Lisbon, listening to the clatter of the roulette wheel. So Santarelli was arrested. Special Branch came for him on the afternoon of 25 June, just as high tea was being served. Two policemen searched his rooms, confiscated his passport, declared him a 'person of hostile association' and marched him from the Savoy to a cell at Brixton Prison. They also came for Fortunato Picchi, the Savoy's assistant banqueting manager, a dedicated Arsenal fan who despised Mussolini but bore an uncanny resemblance to the man. They came for Picchi's immediate superior, Ettore Zavattoni, who, conversely, adored Mussolini and kept a stiletto and a fresh-ironed black shirt in his bureau drawer. They came for waiters and wine butlers and cooks and restaurateurs across London and delivered them, without criminal charge, from hot kitchens and mirrored dining rooms into police cells and holding camps across the country.

*

Wartime Britain was not a democracy – and its treatment of residents born in enemy nations was an index upon the kind of society it had become. In the first six months of the conflict, Westminster busied itself in the dissolution of the peacetime state, the work given impetus by rumours of an imminent German invasion. The Emergency Powers Act suspended the normal processes of legislation. Habeas Corpus went with them, under the weight of the Act's Regulation 18B – which made provision for the detention of suspects without trial. Tracts of England's south-east coast were militarised; razor wire was unrolled across sand and shingle; seaside hotels were requisitioned; machine guns were mounted on Admiralty Arch. Downing Street decreed the evacuation of nineteen locations in Kent and East Anglia, warning regional Civil Defence Commissioners that civilians sufficiently foolhardy to remain would not be permitted to leave the battle zones until the fighting was over. 'Only trustworthy persons should be left in the towns, and [. . .] all who are suspect should be removed.'[7] Identifying the untrustworthy became an urgent pursuit. A five-foot pile of reports on the activities of suspected Fifth Columnists tottered in the office of Vernon Kell, the director general of MI5: accounts of strange marks daubed on telegraph poles, nuns with hairy arms and Hitler tattoos, municipal flowerbeds planted with white blooms to direct planes towards munitions factories; pliant Home Counties Quislings preparing to seize power as soon as the Germans made landfall at Dover. Britons with German or Austrian backgrounds had been objects of suspicion since the Munich Crisis – but by the spring of 1940, as Mussolini's involvement in the conflict became increasingly likely, hostility against Britain's Italian population also blossomed. The *Mirror* howled that Italian communities within British cities were furnaces of 'Black Fascism . . . Hot as hell'.[8] Spaghetti houses and coffee shops and delicatessens pinned hopeful signs in their windows declaring their proprietors to be Swiss. An organ-grinder in Leeds displayed the notice, 'I'm British and the monkey is from India.'[9] The Labour MP Ernest Thurtle demanded of the House of Commons, 'In the interests of national security, will the Home Secretary look into the case of the Savoy Hotel, which is staffed with anti-British Italians and where highly placed officers frequently dine?'[10] In MI5's temporary HQ in Wormwood Scrubs, employees combed the index-card system – an immense gazetteer in which the names of suspicious persons were archived – and declared that there were 1,500 Italian Fascists walking the streets of Britain, all of whom might be potential Fifth Columnists. ('Desperate characters' is the expression used in official documentation: the same used in pulp fiction to denote the swarthy criminal types felled by a swift right hook from Sexton Blake.) Vernon Kell plumped for a code word by which chief constables up and down the country would know when to handcuff these blacklisted individuals: ARRITFAS. However, before the mass arrests began, MI5 had already begun to move against those whom they suspected of being part of a Fascist secret army – and their first target was one of Santarelli's colleagues within the Savoy Hotels company.

On 24 April 1940, Ferruccio Cochis, the general manager of Claridge's, received a letter from his employers requesting him to vacate his quarters in the eaves of Brook Street. Cochis had worked for the hotel for twenty-one years. He was offered a month's pay in lieu of notice, but he refused to go quietly. Richard D'Oyly Carte, chair of the Savoy group, told him that the anti-British stance of the Italian press made the position of all Italian employees problematic, but Carte's deputy George Reeves-Smith was more honest: Scotland Yard, he said, suspected Cochis of being a link between Fascist elements in London and the government in Rome – and that consequently, he had been blacklisted and scheduled for internment the moment that Mussolini entered the war. Those suspicions about Cochis may have been nurtured by his colleagues at Claridge's, where his volcanic temper endeared him to few. He was particularly disliked by the clerks at reception, one of whom, in the months before the war, telephoned the general manager's office and, in a plausibly refined German accent, booked an entire floor for a secret visit by Adolf Hitler and his staff. Cochis had begun a tornado of spring-cleaning and the procurement of several hundred new cushion-covers before a second call came through, cancelling the proposed visit. Cochis was sharp enough to notice the youngest clerk on the reception desk emerging from one of the telephone boxes in the entrance hall. 'It was', noted an observer, 'one of the few occasions when the calm oasis of the hall was shattered.'[11]

The specific reason for the dismissal of Cochis only became clear sixty years later, when the diaries of Guy Liddell, MI5's director of counter-espionage, were declassified. According to Liddell's account, the fate of Ferruccio Cochis was sealed in March 1940 when Sumner Welles, the US Under Secretary of State, arrived in London on a secret diplomatic mission that was, in the words of the *Washington Post*, 'as secret as a Hollywood divorce'. One of the aims of the mission was to drive a wedge between the Axis powers in the hope of dissuading Italy from entering the war on Germany's side. However, a few days after Welles's arrival in London, the American embassy relayed intelligence that the Under Secretary of State's suite at Claridge's had been bugged by agents from Rome. The source, an exiled Italian foreign minister, was considered reliable. This was a potentially disastrous lapse: when Welles got roaring drunk – which was often – he had a habit of propositioning butlers and railway porters.

Guy Liddell had Welles's suite searched by an expert from

the Post Office, who concluded that taking a claw-hammer to the plasterwork was the only way of ruling out the presence of hidden microphones. Miles Thornewill, the Savoy board member who let in the spooks with his master-key, prized the decor above the personnel. He told Liddell's men that he would be only too pleased to dismiss Cochis and that he was 'prepared to sack the whole staff rather than lose American custom'.[12] Sumner Welles packed his suitcase and moved into the Dorchester. (A cover story insisted that this was in order to allow him to be closer to one of the guests, the Foreign Secretary, Lord Halifax.) The general manager of Claridge's received his notice seven weeks later, his sacking timed to coincide with the conclusion – and, predictably, the failure – of Welles's mission. A Belgian named Van Thuyne, vetted by the security services, was installed in his place, and remained there until 1968. Cochis, however, was relatively fortunate. His fate was decided before Winston Churchill took power.

By May 1940, officials from the Home Office had formulated an internment policy that aimed to distinguish between citizens of enemy countries who were a danger to the British state and those who posed no threat. On his first day as Prime Minister, Churchill rejected their plans in favour of his own, less complex idea, expressed in three simple words: 'Collar the lot.' Much misery was created by the attempts that were made to comply with this order – attempts that continued even when it became clear that no hidden army of saboteurs existed. MI5 had committed itself to a figure of 1,500 prime suspects. However, when the Home Office requested a list of their names, the intelligence agency could only cough up 750. Italian names, they bluffed, had many variant spellings. Keen to fulfil the quota, MI5 beefed up the list by including Italian residents who had no known connections with Fascism. Perversely, some of them were dedicated anti-Fascists – men such as Decio Anzani, secretary of the Italian league of the Rights of Man.[13] 'Every bureaucracy', wrote Harold Laski, while these arrests were being made, 'contains foolish men to whom no price is too high for unity in ideas, who are prepared, therefore, rather to suppress than to persuade.'[14] Britain's wartime internment policy was shaped less by legitimate security concerns than by panic, bureaucratic fastidiousness and the xenophobia of men who had spent too much time hugger-muggering in well-upholstered London clubrooms. And that is how Loreto Ottavio Santarelli was swallowed up by the internment system – that, and the fact that his wife had grown to hate him.

*

Joan Lambert is probably the only person alive who knew both Loreto and Gertrude Santarelli. When asked to describe them, she talks about Loreto's lucent blue eyes, his towering height, his easy manners; Gertrude's dark good looks, fiery temper and preternatural ability with a needle. She also talks of the blazing rows that the couple were quite happy to conduct in front of their relations. Joan's father, Robert, was Gertrude's youngest brother – one of a battalion of Richley children who grew up performing nocturnal flits from rented accommodation on both sides of the Irish Sea, and thus acquired a necessary talent for survival. Joan is the historian of the family. She has tracked its movements, recorded its stories and pondered its mysteries – the greatest of which is the fate of Gertrude's father, John Richley, an unsuccessful retailer of nautical equipment, who vanished from his children's lives in the 1890s. (The most popular hypotheses are that he had run off with a lover or made an accidental beery descent into the water of Cardiff docks.)

The Richley girls had grit. The eldest sister, Agnes, nursed her way through Serbia during the First World War, but learned self-preservation squirrelling away the small change that her father would toss drunkenly down the stairs every Friday night – a practice that allowed the family to eat until the following Thursday. The third sister, Lily, ran a milliner's shop in Chelsea where she led customers to believe that their hats were resized with the stretching machine in the back room – rather than the brute force she applied with her fists and knees. The sixth sister, Hannah, married Armand Zoro, a French pastry chef who made confectionery for Whitelaw Reid, the American ambassador, and followed Santarelli to the kitchens of the Savoy. Joan's branch of the family was not so prosperous, which is perhaps why she remembers her childhood encounters with Loreto and Gertrude so clearly. She can recall the ritual Christmas visits to the smart flat that her aunt and uncle maintained in Chelsea; the family meal in the Streatham villa that was plunged into chaos when Peter Santarelli thundered down the hallway pushing a trolley laden with plates of soup, and kept control of the trolley, but not the soup; the £5 note Peter gave her to persuade her to call him 'Uncle'. ('Later, of course, we told him that if he gave us another five pounds, we'd stop calling him it.') She also recalls how the war scattered and transformed the family. Peter joined the Army, anglicised his surname to Blair-Richley and served in the Far East until the hatch of his tank came crashing down on his fingers. (Wartime family photographs show him standing with his left hand placed carefully out of sight.) Joan and her twin sister were evacuated deep into the Wiltshire countryside. Gertrude, Joan recalls, spoke occasionally of 'Poor Loreto' – though the fact of his imprisonment was never discussed.

*

A few remain, however, who stared at the same coils of barbed wire, shared the same rations, and know how it felt to be declared an enemy of their adopted state – and through their memories, Loreto Santarelli's experiences of internment can be reconstructed. Robert Rietti, a teenage actor under contract to ENSA, was arrested in his dressing room in July 1940. Before they locked the police cell door the officers confiscated his shoelaces, his belt and his umbrella. The next morning, he re-members, the umbrella had gone mysteriously missing. 'I don't know why I was so angry about this,' he ponders. 'But I made such a scene that they gave me a new one from lost property.'

Seven decades after the event, Ettore Emanuelli could still recall the knock on the door of his family home; the plain-clothes policemen who turned over his bedroom looking for evidence of treachery. 'They told my mother that they were tak-ing me away for questioning,' he reflected, when I visited him on an unseasonably warm day in February 2008. 'She didn't see me again for two and a half years.' His father, who owned an ice-cream business in Staffordshire, was not taken. His brother Luigi, who was a driver in the Eighth Army, was not taken. But Ettore had been in Italy on the day that Chamberlain declared war on Germany. A sales rep from the firm that supplied the family business with wafers and cornets had offered to obtain him a place on an educational summer camp in Rome, and Et-tore had agreed enthusiastically. 'I thought we would be going to museums and art galleries,' he said. 'But instead we did lots of marching through the streets with wooden rifles.' A search of his bedroom in Tunstall produced the cadet's jacket with which he had been issued in Rome. 'They regarded me as a person in possession of an enemy uniform,' he remembered. 'After that was written on my record, I don't suppose I stood much of a chance. They called us Nazis. But we were just shopkeepers and waiters and café proprietors.'[15]

Emanuelli is a slight, gently spoken man, whose voice still bears the rich trace of his early boyhood in South Wales, where his parents sold tutti-frutti to the miners. A few years ago he began to lose his sight. When he showed me the reliquary of his period of detention, he checked over each artefact with a powerful electronic magnifier. We sat on the maroon leather sofa in his immaculate sitting room in a suburb of Stoke-on-Trent, and examined these materials. Here was the masthead he designed for a newspaper he had hoped to launch in the Ascot internment camp. Here was a photograph of the Italian football team formed at the camp at Peel, on the Isle of Man, to which he was transferred in May 1941. (He designed the poster for their fixture against a team from the Metropolitan Police, who were brought in to keep order in the camp after the inmates staged a riot.) Here was the red rectangle of cardboard that was fixed to the cell door in his first place of confinement, a frowsty archipelago of HM Prison Walton, where he, Robert Rietti, Loreto Santarelli and a large band of Anglo-Italians, Mosley men and pacifists were locked up under the terms of Regulation 18B. When he rattled off the number on the card, he did not use his magnifier.

*

Walton's D Wing had not been occupied since Lady Constance Lytton and a gang of hunger-striking suffragettes were housed – and force-fed – in its cells. The internees' first task was to scrape away the thumb-deep stratum of pigeon guano and carcasses that had accumulated in the years since 1910. Rietti and Emanuelli can recall the mouse-droppings they fished from the watery morning porridge; the makeshift candles they fashioned from the fat that deliquesced on their evening mug of cocoa; the boom of German incendiaries raining down on Liverpool docks. They can recall the nineteen-hour days of solitary confinement, the mesh stretched over the stairwells to discourage suicide attempts; the fact that the little red card on each cell door identified the prisoner by religion as well as name, alerting the Fascist inmates to Rietti's Jewish background. ('Let's do him, the swine,' he heard a British Union detainee mutter in the middle of the night.)

It was here that Rietti and Emanuelli heard the first whispered accounts of one of the great disasters of the war: the sinking of the *Arandora Star*, a transatlantic liner commandeered for the transportation of enemy aliens to camps in

Canada. She sailed from Liverpool docks on the first day of July 1940, with a cargo of almost 1,300 German and Italian internees. Among them was Carlo Ravetto, a wine butler who had worked at the Ritz since 1917, and his brother Ludovico, head waiter at the same hotel. Their boss, Cesare Maggi, was also on board, along with Italo Zangiacomi, the horse-racing-obsessed general manager of the Piccadilly Hotel, and Ettore Zavattoni, the pro-Fascist Savoy banqueting manager celebrated for his lavish sense of occasion. (He had once used a £60 sheet of artificial turf to transform one of the hotel's private dining rooms into a replica of Epsom racecourse.) Armando Ermini, head waiter at the Savoy Grill, who had fought for Britain in the Great War, was also on board. At 7 a.m. on 2 July, as the *Arandora Star* was passing north-west of the Bloody Foreland of County Donegal, a German U-boat holed its hull with a torpedo. Water flooded into its carcass. Six hundred and eighty-two lives were lost. The first reports in the British press focused not on the injustice of this tragedy, but on accounts of German and Italian prisoners struggling, with undignified violence, for places on the liner's lifeboats. In the years since 1940 there have been many acts of remembrance for the dead of the *Arandora Star*. One of the most obscure and poignant is in the ledgers that record the comings and goings of the staff of the Ritz. In the column that registers the reason for an employee's departure, a single spidery word has been entered next to the names of the Ravetto brothers: 'Drowned.'

On the last day of July 1940, Walton's freight of waiters, shopkeepers, troublemakers and Fascists was packed into a train and despatched southwards to the winter quarters of the Bertram Mills Circus in Berkshire. The circus had an intimate relationship with the secret state: Cyril Mills, son of the founder, was a senior member of the committee that oversaw the control of double agents, and this connection ensured that garish circus vans were frequently used to deliver MI5 staff and equipment, and circus employees from enemy nations remained untroubled by the threat of internment. The Ascot camp was served by a branch line that allowed prisoners to be shunted right up to the gates. Just before embarkation, however, a little drama was played out on the platform at Lime Street. One of the Anglo-Italian detainees persuaded a flustered young recruit to let him pay a visit to the toilets. The prisoner was Darby Sabini, a member of the racetrack gang immortalised in Graham Greene's *Brighton Rock*. Darby and his brother 'Harryboy' Sabini had a two-decade history of intimidation, extortion and grievous bodily harm, effected with knuckle-dusters, billiard cues, razor blades, butcher's knives and the jagged ends of broken pint pots. Both were interned under Regulation 18B. Darby Sabini's Home Office file describes him as 'a drunkard and a man of most violent temperament, with a heavy following and strong command of bullies of Italian origin and other undesirables . . . a dangerous gangster and a racketeer of the worst type and one whom it is most likely enemy agents would choose as a person to create and lead violent internal action against this country'.[16] He did not come back from the gents.

The British Fascists who recorded their arrival in Ascot that day claimed that the guards had treated them with leering brutality; that they had laid the death-threats on thick. Ettore Emanuelli remembered no bruises from rifle-butts – just the dizzying heat and the unorthodox nature of the roll-call taken once every train compartment had disgorged its human cargo. 'We were all lined up in the field and made to strip naked,' he recalled. 'Even the old men.' Almost a lifetime later, his embarrassment was palpable. When the coffee was finished, he produced a bottle of whisky. We drank a couple of generous measures, and Ettore chivvied his memory into summoning some more images from the camp: Battle of Britain planes 'like little silver fish in the sky'; Carlo Rossi, proprietor of the Beacon Hotel in Bristol, lolling on his bunk with a novel by Rafael Sabatini; the words 'Great Britain' stretched reproachfully across the broad back of Vercelli, an Olympic high-diver who walked around the camp in his team shirt; the sight of Quentin Joyce, a civil servant interned on the grounds that he was the brother of Lord Haw-Haw; the cowed figure of Joe Beckett, Oswald Mosley's personal bodyguard and a former British heavyweight boxing champion, who sobbed himself to sleep every night.

I was curious about the relationship between the Italians – detained because of official assumptions about their secret allegiance to brutal corporatist governments – and the British Union detainees – confined because of their noisy adoration of brutal corporatist governments. Robert Rietti could not conjure any hatred for the Mosleyites, despite having been set upon by a gang of them in the shower block – one of whom might have succeeded in throttling him had it not been for the violent intervention of Darby Sabini, returned to captivity after a week on the lam. Rietti's generosity, I sensed, was partly due to his close relationship with an 18B detainee at Ascot, whom he always referred to as 'Jim' – a Catholic Dubliner whose parents had taught him that Jews were what happened when black Aboriginals had sex with camels. 'He clung to me like a limpet,' he recalled. 'We were so close that others nicknamed us "the twins". It was an odd relationship.' I suspected it might have been a romantic one, too, as far as Jim was concerned. When he learned that Robert was Jewish, he suffered a kind of breakdown. 'A brainstorm, I'd call it,' said Rietti. 'He didn't eat or sleep for days.'

Ettore Emanuelli, too, had no axe to grind against the Fascists. To prove the point, he showed me two surviving pages from an autograph book that he passed among his fellow internees. The first was by Frederick Bowman, who used his page to declare himself as editor of the *Talking Picture News* and president of the Animal Service Association – and illustrate himself as a stick-man hanging from the gallows, beside a reference to 'Ascot Concentration Camp'. Emanuelli's chief memory of the man was the daring escape attempt he made from Brixton

Prison in 1943: when a Catholic bishop came to visit the inmates, Bowman very nearly succeeded in escaping captivity by improvising a purple cassock and making for the gate in a plausibly clerical manner. The archive reveals a little more: Bowman regarded himself as a martyr for peace – in 1940, he had attempted to prevent Italy and America from entering the war by bringing the Italian and American consuls in Liverpool in touch with the Marquess of Tavistock's Peace Party. The Liverpool police, however, who put him under surveillance, regarded him as a Nazi sympathiser and 'the type of man who would attach himself to any organisation, subversive or otherwise, out of which he could obtain financial benefit and notoriety', as well as 'a moral pervert' who had 'been practising flagellation with women friends'. Bowman protested against his imprisonment by going on hunger strike, then compounded his offence by greedily consuming prodigious quantities of hospital milk and Marmite. Once he was released, he hatched a plot to spring a pair of 18B detainees on a visit to a dentist beyond the prison walls. Despite this, MI5 and the 18B Advisory Committee regarded him as 'an unimportant and unintelligent and vociferous Pacifist'.[17] Emanuelli chuckled at the harsh judgement. 'We treated these people as friends,' he said. 'There was no animosity.'

He produced another page of his autograph book: a sketch of the hallway of a cosy house in the Surrey village of Ewell – a memory of home bearing the signature of Leigh Vaughan-Henry. Seventy years on, I was able to fill Ettore in on the details of Dr Leigh Vaughan-Henry's peculiar career: how he spent the First World War interned in Ruhleben POW camp, giving lectures on Debussy and mounting productions of Shakespeare comedies; how he composed the national anthem of the uninhabited Caribbean island of Redonda ('O God Who Gave Our Island Soil'), wrote a badly received play about the organist John Bull, and supplied ballet pieces for the Annea Spong Dancers; how he became musical director of the British Union of

Fascists and exchanged letters with Ezra Pound on the horrors of 'Bloomsbuggery', as he wooed the poet into writing articles on economics for *Blackshirt* magazine.[18] Aside from his BUF connections, MI5 had three reasons to intern Vaughan-Henry: he had claimed to run a network of pro-Nazi 'sergeants' who would assume control after the collapse of British civil defences; he was believed to have played a minor part in the affairs of a Nazi spy named Anna Wolkoff; and evidence existed, apparently, that he had developed a notation system through which coded messages could be embedded in pieces of music and broadcast to Germany. He was busted on 10 June 1940. Later, he claimed that the men from Special Branch hurled abuse at him and threatened him with cocked revolvers. They denied it, but did admit to snorting over the stash of snaps of Mrs Vaughan-Henry posing in the nude, and noting the whorl of dog turd on his bedroom floor.

*

Under international law, Camp Seven at Ascot was illuminated at night – so it became a useful navigation marker for Luftwaffe raids on London. Robert Rietti recalled that when the German planes scudded over, the Mosleyites would wave their arms in the air and shout, 'Come on and bomb this rotten country to hell!' But in those first few months at Ascot there was little unity among the Fascist inmates – only grim, bitter arguments on obscure ideological points. Most argumentative was Arnold Spencer Leese, founder of the Imperial Fascist League and author of *The One-Humped Camel in Health and Disease* (1928). Leese was appalled to discover that he had been billeted with members of the British Union – whom he deplored for the half-heartedness of their anti-Semitism. Leese spent much of his time in Camp Seven propounding his theory that MI5 was run by Jewish conspirators of the sort prominent in the pages of *The Protocols of the Elders of Zion*. (Curiously, Leese's enthusiasm for such ideas did not preclude *Country Life* magazine from commissioning him to write articles about the dos and don'ts of camping.[19])

Those with a more ecumenical approach to ultra-right-wing politics eventually managed to make peace between the various splinters. The day-to-day administration of the camp was left to its inmates – and this soon acquired a distinctly totalitarian flavour. A Fascist bureaucracy and disciplinary system was established under 'Tommy' Moran, acting leader of the BUF, who had been bloodied in the Battle of Cable Street. A Fascist newspaper, *Unity*, was bashed out on pilfered office stationery. Charlie Watts, British Union district leader for Westminster and St George's, started a group known as HMAFEA – 'Hail Mosley and Fuck 'Em All.' The authorities even permitted the Fascist internees to commemorate the eighth anniversary of the foundation of the British Union with a celebratory dinner in the camp's main hall – a large brick building in which Miss Priscilla Kayes had once rehearsed her lion-taming act. 'We, the representatives of National Socialism in this miserable camp, can do our bit,' declared one of the celebrants. 'Let us live as National Socialists even within the camp as an example to people.'[20] They did – they ensured that the Anglo-Italians were allocated all the worst jobs. Camp Seven at Ascot was a little Fascist paradise surrounded by pine trees.[21]

Loreto Santarelli fared better than most. He was appointed head of the catering facility, where he made the most of meagre materials. (For the first week, salted herrings formed the principal ingredient of every meal.) Working under him was a man who had been head chef at Reece's restaurant in Liverpool and a master baker named John Charnley, a Fascist from Hull, who had been detained after he was caught squeezing plastic resin through the keyholes of Jewish Yorkshiremen and hurling sandbags through their windows, marked 'A present from Haw-Haw'. (He had also been accused of painting a swastika on the roof of his family home, to indicate the pro-Nazi sympathies of its occupants and save them from the attentions of the Luftwaffe.) Kitchen life was complicated by the committed corruption of the camp adjutant, Alfred Braybrook, who paid profits from the canteen into his own private bank account, confiscated the valuables of internees and stored them at his home. When, after his transfer to a camp in York, the authorities acted on their suspicions, they discovered a stash of 1,040 safety razor blades, one hundred gold sovereigns, a £1,000 package of jewellery, a cine camera, two typewriters and compelling evidence that Braybrook had turned the canteen into a system for laundering the money he stole from internees.[22] Keeping his head down in the corner of the kitchen, with a flat knife and a block of margarine, was Ettore Emanuelli. 'They gave me the job', he recalled, 'because I was good at spreading margarine very sparingly, so it went further.' He mimed the action with his hands. Even today, butter lasts a long time in his house.

*

As Santarelli made lunch for Fascists in a concrete hut in Berkshire, George Reeves-Smith was orchestrating a campaign to spring him from captivity. The secretary of the 18B Advisory Committee received a barrage of testimonials from some of the Savoy's most respectable clients. Lord Southwood, a former errand boy who had become a muscular press baron, relayed Santarelli's negative remarks about Mussolini. H. Fothergill, managing director of the Contrafto Engineering Company, offered to put up £500 surety for Santarelli's good behaviour in the event of his release. 'At one time,' asserted Sir Guy Hambling, another admiring plutocrat, 'he discussed with me the advisability of purchasing from me one or two pedigree Tamworth pigs, as I happen to breed them. I only give this as a small example of how British his outlook was.'[23] The accused added his voice to the protest. 'This detention has given me great shock and pain that I am sure it will effect [sic] my health in time,' he wrote. 'I can swear on God's name that I am an innocent man, that I have never done anything [w]rong against England.'

In the event, however, it was the medical evidence upon which his case turned. The committee had mixed feelings about the report on the state of Santarelli's health by Dr Harry Beckett Overy, which had advised his subject's immediate removal to a nursing home. The committee was aware that Beckett Overy had the ear of Winston Churchill – and had occasionally poked about in it with an otoscope. He was sufficiently close to the family to have been entrusted with the translation of a Latin document from the Blenheim archive – a prescription written for John, first Duke of Marlborough, advising him to treat his gout by injecting his penis with turpentine.[24] Not all his connections were so auspicious: Beckett Overy had also been personal gynaecologist to Unity Mitford, who went to him for advice on contraception, principally because of her delight in his surname. The committee were also aware that Beckett Overy was the brother of Santarelli's solicitor, and therefore unlikely to offer an impartial opinion. Their doubts were dispelled only when the medical officer at Camp Seven produced a similarly gloomy prognosis, noting the ominous bagginess of Santarelli's clothes and his state of weepy depression, concluding: 'I fear that if confinement in a Camp is continued then he will become a permanent melancholic.' So in the first week of September 1940, the former restaurant manager of the Savoy was given temporary discharge from Ascot on one condition – that he should spend every night of freedom under the roof of an expensive private nursing home in South Kensington, pending his appearance before the Advisory Committee. And that might have been the end of the story, had it not been for the intervention of his wife.

*

Whoever met Santarelli at the gates of Ascot, it certainly wasn't Gertrude. She learned of his discharge three weeks later, in a letter from the Home Office. In the eyes of the law, if not their mutual God, the Santarellis' marriage was already extinct. It had been made so by Loreto's affair with a professional dancer, Rene Kite, who, in the years before the war, hoofed her way around the Savoy ballroom as part of a double act called Barry and Bingham. Gertrude resented the sexual betrayal, of course – but she also found it difficult to accept the subsequent reduction in her circumstances; the excommunication from the rich and rarefied world in which her husband moved. That may help to explain her reaction when, on 7 October, she received an unexpected phone call from a woman who claimed to be her husband's former lover and the mother of his illegitimate child.

The caller had news of Santarelli: he was not living at Miss Williams's Nursing Home on Collingham Gardens but cohabiting with Rene Kite at Forset Court, a block of flats on the Edgware Road. At 12.30 that day, Loreto's daughter, Anna Santarelli, answered the telephone to her father. She asked him why he was not staying at the nursing home. She was told to mind her own business. Once her father had rung off, Anna instructed the operator to make a note of the call's origin. Ambassador 2782, she declared, was the phone number of a 'dangerous alien at large'. To ensure that the information was conveyed to the correct authorities, Gertrude fired off a letter to Scotland Yard, declaring that her husband had breached the terms of his release. The letter has been preserved with the government files relating to Santarelli's internment, and it is a document written in the spirit of hot vengeance. It enumerates the incriminating details, informs the authorities where Santarelli might be found and concludes, 'I feel it is my duty as an Englishwoman to inform you of these facts.'

A few days later Sergeant Albert Webb of B Division rolled up at Collingham Gardens to question its principal about Santarelli's movements. Miss E. J. Williams was painfully evasive. Her employees, however, were not so reticent. Santarelli, they said, had not slept at the home for nearly a month – and they had seen very little of him except the occasional breakfast visit. 'It is obvious', reported Webb, 'that it is not considered by members of the staff that his health has anything at all to do with his stay at the nursing home.' Webb's next port of call was Forset Court, where he bent the ear of the concierge who was, fortuitously, a retired member of the Kent constabulary. The former manager of the Savoy restaurant, it emerged, was so firmly established as a resident in the block that he had begun to receive parcels and complain about the lateness of the milk.

'Santarelli', concluded Webb, 'does not really reside at No. 5 Collingham Gardens at all. His alleged ill-health and his supposed residence at the nursing home appear to be nothing more than a plot to circumvent the Defence Regulations under which he was originally detained.' When confronted with these accusations, Santarelli produced a written defence: two pages of sophistry, concocted under the supervision of his solicitor, through which he attempted to explain his movements across London in terms of anxiety rather than love. At Collingham Gardens, Santarelli insisted, the air-raids had exerted a disturbing influence upon his nervous system from which the concrete corridors of Forset Court had provided secure sanctuary: 'I had no other object in going to Forset Court except to be able to obtain sleep which was essential in view of the state of my nerves,' he insisted. 'I will henceforth continue to sleep at 5 Collingham Gardens although I fear that this will have a disastrous effect on my health.' The Home Office invited him to pull the other one: Santarelli's arguments, its officials concluded, 'would not deceive a child, and should be rejected indignantly'; his claims to require medical treatment were 'farcical'; the supportive manoeuvrings of his solicitor 'sharp practice' – all this, with the hearing before the Home Office Advisory Committee yet to come. 'If the Secretary of State's orders under Defence

Regulations are not to be regarded as capable of evasion with impunity, the logical course is to re-arrest Santarelli and detain him.' Gertrude, it seemed, was going to have her revenge.

*

The head of the committee appointed to consider appeals by internees against detention under Regulation 18B was Norman Birkett, a barrister who had made his name in a divorce case involving a colonel accused of ameliorating his financial problems by encouraging his wife to sleep with a Hungarian nobleman, a Polish major, a Spanish bullfighter and a high-ranking English Army officer.[25] Birkett heard the cases against British Fascists, whom he considered to be 'a pitiful procession of ill-educated folk'.[26] The Anglo-Italians were dealt with by his colleague Percy Loraine, the former British ambassador to Rome who had received Mussolini's declaration of war. It was deeply unrewarding work – not least because there was no fee. Colonel MacLeod of the War Office liked to ring up committee members and shout down the phone that the hearings were 'a monstrous waste of public time'.[27] The Sunday papers claimed that prominent 18B detainees such as Oswald and Diana Mosley drank champagne and conducted bridge parties behind bars. Oswald Hickson, an auk-like libel expert with bloodshot eyes who was solicitor to the Mosleys and a gaggle of prominent Fascists, bombarded Birkett with protests about 'secret trials'.[28] Vernon Kell's office applied pressure from the other side of the argument. 'MI5 of the secret service', reflected Birkett in a rueful letter to his cousin written on Christmas Day 1940, 'want everyone interned.' Toiling for the 18B Committee was, he admitted, a 'thankless task' – which is, perhaps, why, to those caught up in the system, its decisions lacked consistency and coherence.[29]

Robert Rietti remembered the dismay felt by the inmates at Ascot when the Sabini brothers became the first to be released from detention. (Declassified government files suggest that the Brighton constabulary were responsible, as they regarded Darby and Harryboy with the sentimental indulgence that the police often reserve for age-mellowed racketeers and extortionists.) Rietti's own release came soon after: but it was a release into poverty and anxiety. He continued to write to his friend Jim, who remained behind the barbed wire, though letter after letter remained unanswered. (Thirty years later, Jim's sister found these letters carefully packed in a suitcase in her brother's house, and contacted Rietti to tell him that Jim, who had trained as a priest after the war, had been killed by an IRA bomb while visiting the home of a parishioner.)

Ettore Emanuelli recalled that for him, the process of appeal was painful and protracted. At his hearing, the members of the committee glanced at the glowing character testimonial furnished by his parish priest – and immediately dismissed its contents when they realised the priest was from neutral Ireland. Ettore was eventually discharged in late 1942. 'I was a complete bag of nerves when I came out. I was afraid to walk down the street. I thought everyone was staring at me. It was almost like having a breakdown.' He tried to enlist in the RAF, but – in common with many former internees and prisoners of war – he was put on the Directed Labour scheme. He was assigned to work in the kitchens of the Arden Hotel in Birmingham, where he moulded meat paste into the shape of pork chops and worked small wonders with the packets of dehydrated ice cream passed to him by GIs stationed in the city. The manager of the Arden, he recalled, was a conscientious objector. 'He had his wedding at the hotel and draped over the table was a huge Union Jack.' Ettore and his colleagues were disgusted by such patriotic displays at an event organised by a man who had refused to fight. 'It rankled with us,' he said. 'We didn't think that was right.'

Those who had worked in the most prestigious establishments found such humiliations hard to bear. Albert Pam, a

Venezuelan businessman who made a fortune from Marmite, recalled making a wartime visit to the factory of the Pressed Steel Company in Cowley, and realising that the man struggling to run the secondary works canteen was a former deputy manager of the banqueting room of a fashionable London hotel. 'Poor man,' he mourned, 'I don't know what became of him; his experience and his special abilities were of no use in war conditions, and there must have been a hundred like him.'[30]

There were greater injustices. In January 1941, Santarelli's colleague Fortunato Picchi was released from internment on the Isle of Man in order to take part in Operation Colossus, a mission to blow up a concrete aqueduct that spanned the Tragino gorge in southern Italy. He and his men were parachuted into position, did their work with dynamite, and were captured. As he was the only Italian national in his party, Picchi was singled out for brutal treatment. He was tortured, tried and executed, probably by firing squad, on Palm Sunday 1941. His landlady in London, Florence Lantieri, heard a sneering report of his demise on an Italian radio station, and was moved to announce his death in *The Times* – much to the annoyance of the military. As the press saluted a 'hero of the New Italy' and at least one film producer sought permission to dramatise his career, the War Office and the RAF exchanged a more dismal correspondence: 'Although Picchi was an idealist,' sniffed the commanding officer at the airbase from which the men of Colossus were despatched, 'he was also, after all, a traitor to his country and it seems rather difficult to make him out a hero.' Even in death, it seemed impossible for an Anglo-Italian to be entirely above suspicion.

Loreto Santarelli's hearing took place on 23 October 1940. The committee questioned him about his investments in Italy: he professed that he had inherited his father's house, nothing more. They pressed him about his donation to a social club on the Charing Cross Road administered by the Italian Fascist Party: he said that he had written the cheque because he was told that Gracie Fields had done the same. The hearing failed entirely to discuss the subterfuge over his place of residence – so he knew nothing of the official huffing and puffing recorded in the written summaries of his case: the remarks about his 'unsavoury domestic issues' and 'the fact that he grossly abused his conditions of release'. The committee decided it had no authority to use Regulation 18B to penalise Santarelli for his progress from Collingham Gardens to Forset Court. They revoked the order against him – with the proviso that he remain subject to the maximum restrictions that the law would allow: weekly appearances at his local police station and a ban on leaving the London area or owning a car or a camera.

Santarelli would never again peer through the wrong side of a barbed-wire fence. He was almost a free man – but he was not the man he was. When he returned to his job at the Savoy, the old assurance was gone. His hands trembled as he poured from a wine bottle or a coffee pot. He no longer possessed the 'soft triumphant smile' of his fictional alter ego, Mr Cappone. Perhaps he was anxious because he knew that some of the staff had petitioned their employers to prevent his return; that Hugh Wontner, the Savoy's managing director, had been obliged to hold long meetings with the objectors in order to prevent a walk-out. (The revolt was led by Mr Webber from the accounts department.) Or it might simply have proved impossible to smooth away the effects that internment had wrought upon Santarelli. His profession was dignity, and he had been robbed of his dignity. Wontner formed his own conclusions. 'He became . . . distorted,' he told an interviewer in the 1980s. 'He died a dejected man.'[31]

On 11 October 1944, while treading the carpets of the Savoy, Santarelli suffered a fatal heart attack. His requiem mass at St Mary's church in Cadogan Square was attended by hundreds of clients and colleagues – and by a figure described by the reporter from the *Sunday Dispatch* as 'the lone woman in black'. The allusion was to the mysterious veiled mourner who, in 1944, was still making her yearly pilgrimage to the grave of Rudolph Valentino in the Hollywood Memorial Park. The veiled woman of Cadogan Square, however, was only too happy to reveal her identity to the man from the *Dispatch*. She was Rene Kite, Gertrude's hated rival. 'He was a very kind and generous man and I adored him,' she said. 'Three years ago he and his wife were divorced, and a year later we became engaged.'

Joan Lambert, reflecting upon the last years of her uncle's life, recalls the explanation that Gertrude gave for his decline. It was, she insisted, the shock of hearing about those drowned colleagues on board the *Arandora Star* that shattered Santarelli's health. 'She always said that it broke his heart,' Joan reflects. Perhaps that event was responsible for some of the cracks – by 1944, the bitter details of the disaster had been exposed by the press, by a government inquiry and by rumour. Santarelli would have heard accounts of how internees had run in bare feet through the dark and glass-strewn labyrinth of the capsizing ship; how their progress was impeded by sealed doors and barbed-wire blockades; how soldiers fired on prisoners who attempted to board a lifeboat reserved for military use; how one man hanged himself rather than jump into the sea. It must have been difficult to hear such details. The threat of imprisonment, however, is as hard to bear as bad news – and Gertrude had attempted to prolong that imprisonment. Little wonder that she blamed her former husband's early death on the aftershock from a German torpedo.

One incident in the wartime history of the Savoy suggests why Santarelli might never have felt free of anxiety, even in the dining room he had ruled for a quarter of a century. Each lunchtime a discreet table in the restaurant was occupied by Claude Dansey, the deputy chief of the Secret Intelligence Service. Dansey, known to his agents as 'Colonel Z', was recorded by those who knew him as 'an utter shit . . . crude, incompetent, but with a certain low cunning'; a man 'consumed by hate [whose] hates were legion'. He worked from an office near St James's Park that bore a brass plaque marked 'Minimax Fire Extinguisher Company', but he preferred to use the Savoy restaurant to interview potential recruits. One of these, James Langley, described his experience of meeting Dansey for the first time. Langley had lost an arm at Dunkirk, escaped from a German military hospital at Lille, then found his way back to England: a good audition piece for anyone hoping to join Dansey's network of operatives. He was told to go to the front hall of the Savoy and make himself known to a man with a folded copy of *The Times* under his arm and a red carnation in his lapel. When Langley arrived, Dansey liked what he saw – and immediately asked about what species of honour he might like as a reward for joining the service. Langley was told that he was entitled to an MC, an OBE or the Order of Stanislaus. ('I call it Pologna Prostituta,' Dansey enthused, 'as it is immensely popular with the women.') Although they ate in the restaurant – Santarelli's domain – Dansey insisted on being served by the manager of the Grill, Benito Manetta. Manetta was famed at the Savoy for the index-card system he had collated, which documented the tastes and preferences of every significant guest – a benign version of the MI5 index of suspicious persons. Langley remembered that as Dansey spoke to Manetta, he taunted him about his colleagues held in the internment camps, forgetting, perhaps, that Manetta's head waiter, Nemo Ermini, had drowned on the *Arandora Star*. 'I like them to think I was responsible and if I am not well looked after they will follow,' Dansey explained. 'Manetta says he has some excellent steak and a fresh Stilton, I hope they will be to your liking.'

It is the last part of his speech I find chilling: 'Of course I never would dream of taking any action,' he said, 'however poor the food.'[32]

2

Reds

There were forty of them. There were eighty. There were a hundred. They marched. They sauntered. They were angry. They were bewildered. They came with two dogs and they came with none. Theirs was a daring act that saved thousands of lives. Or it was a pretty piece of propaganda, gift-wrapped for the Führer. What happened beneath the Savoy Hotel on 14 September 1940, the eighth night of the Blitz, depended on the position of the observer: whether she or he was Red or anti-Red; East Ender or West Ender; dreaming of revolution or restoration. That Saturday night, when those forty or eighty or a hundred arrived at the doors of the hotel – with their dogs, or dogless – a small army of journalists was on the premises for a briefing by the Ministry of Information. Few, however, wrote about their uninvited fellow guests until the war was safely over. The government also maintained a public silence on the story, despite the urgent Cabinet discussion held the following Monday morning – a discussion with sinister undertones. But old comrades, years later, made that West End outing into a famous victory, a second Battle of Cable Street. It worked its way into plays and novels, into the mythology of the British Left. And though no horses charged and no batons swung, the Savoy Hotel invasion was the most serious political demonstration of the war – and dramatic evidence that conflict with Germany did not bring the class war to an end.

Max Levitas has spent most of his long life on the front line of that conflict. He was part of the famous human barricade that halted the Blackshirts' progress through the East End in

October 1936. He stood his ground at Brady Mansions during a twenty-one-week rent strike – brought to an end only by the government's decision to freeze rents for the duration of the war. He was one of the dozen Communist councillors elected to the Borough of Stepney in 1945, during that giddy moment when the electorate could still see the avuncular side of Joe Stalin. He was there in 1991 when the Communist Party of Great Britain voted for dissolution and secured victory in the long war of attrition against itself. He was there, too, on that Blitz-struck Saturday night in 1940, shouldering the red banner of the Stepney Young Communist League as his group of demonstrators marched from the Embankment towards the silvered canopy of the Savoy. They marched for better air-raid shelters in the East End. They marched against the myth that the Luftwaffe had brought equality of suffering to Britain. And they received their marching orders from a series of urgent editorials in the Communist newspaper, the *Daily Worker*: 'If you live in the Savoy Hotel you are called by telephone when the sirens sound and then tucked into bed by servants in a luxury bomb-proof shelter,' the newspaper asserted. 'But if you live in Paradise Court you may find yourself without a refuge of any kind.' And above these words, in thick bold print: 'The people must act.'

Max Levitas nods in agreement when I read the article back to him. 'The surface shelters protected you from shrapnel, from flak, but not much else,' he reflects. 'If a bomb fell on one of those it would collapse and kill everybody in it. The Communist Party argued for deep shelters. But the National Government wouldn't listen. They wouldn't even open the Underground. It was easy to ignore that message if you were sitting in the basement of a very nice hotel. So we decided to march on one.' I ask him why they chose the Savoy. Max Levitas smiles a tolerant smile. 'It was the nearest.'

I meet Max Levitas at the Idea Store, a gleaming cultural institution planted in the East End to compensate locals for the assimilation of their much-loved public library into the Whitechapel Art Gallery. He is a small, cloth-capped nonagenarian, wrapped tightly in a raincoat and muffler. Standing on the studded purple rubber floor of the foyer, he looks like a preserved fragment of the old Stepney. It is a chilling morning in February, and he can spare me an hour before he goes for his Turkish bath – a weekly ritual since the 1920s, when his father took him to the long-vanished Schewik steam rooms on Brick Lane. We catch the lift to the top-floor café, secure two cups of tea and a table with a view of the bristling City skyline, and he tells the story of his association with the area: how his parents fled the Lithuanian pogroms in 1912 and made landfall in Dublin, where Max was born three years later; how his father took the family first to Glasgow, and finally to Stepney, where work could be found among a supportive community of Jewish exiles. History radicalised those members of the Levitas clan it did not destroy: Max's Aunt Sara and her family were burned to death in the synagogue of the Lithuanian shtetl of Akmian; Max's father became a leading member of the distinctly Semitic, distinctly Red-tinged International Tailors and Pressers' Union; Max's elder brother, Maurice, fought against Franco's forces in the Spanish Civil War; Max gave his youth to the Communist Party of Great Britain and was name-checked by Oswald Mosley in a speech denouncing the enemies of British Fascism.

The organisers of the Savoy invasion shared a similar ideological background: they were all revolutionaries. 'And they're all dead,' Max sighs. 'Some were clothing workers. Some were bootmakers. Some were dockers.' It is an inventory of lost trades. The first names he sifts from his memory are two stevedores, Ted Jones and Jack Murphy, veterans of pre-war campaigns for unemployment relief. The rest comprise a knot of men from the Stepney Tenants' Defence League, which organised rent strikes against slum landlords in the East End: George Rosen, its bullish secretary, known as 'Tubby'; Solly Klotnick, a furrier and a veteran of the Battle of Cable Street; Solomon Frankel, a clothing worker who took a bullet in Spain that robbed him of the use of his right hand. Michael Shapiro, a wiry young academic from the London School of Economics and author of *Heartbreak Homes: An Indictment of the National Government's Housing Policy* (1935), was the intellectual of the group and unofficial legal adviser to the Communist Party: owlish and prematurely bald, he combined his devotion to theoretical Marxism with a passion for the quickstep, and once smuggled a ticketless girlfriend into a dance at St Pancras Town Hall by yanking her up through a window. At the head of the group stood Phil Piratin, Communist councillor for Spitalfields, chief spokesperson of the invaders, and the author of the most widely read account of their night at the Savoy. His memoir *Our Flag Stays Red* (1948) puts seventy in the hotel lobby, among them a number of children and pregnant women. Max's memories are different. 'There were forty of us,' he affirms. 'I'm sure of that.' I ask if there were any dogs. He shakes his head. 'No dogs,' he says. 'It was the Savoy.'

September 1940 was a difficult month to be a Communist in London. Stalin and Hitler remained entwined under the terms of the Molotov–Ribbentrop Pact. Directives from the Comintern insisted that the war was an imperialist misadventure; one that might conclude with the happy event of the collapse of European capitalism. Not every marcher, however, carried the Party card. On the night preceding the invasion, Max and his fellow activists toured the air-raid facilities of the East End, arguing, in the words of their leader, that 'what was good enough for the Savoy hotel parasites was reasonably good enough for Stepney workers and their families'. Some recruits came from the public shelter in Brady Street, a few from the cellar of the Mann, Crossman and Paulin brewery on the Whitechapel Road, where Solomon Frankel was the air-raid marshal. More were collected at the Tilbury shelter, a railway warehouse on Commercial Road that had acquired an enormous unofficial nocturnal population and all the sanitary horrors inevitable when ten thousand people share four earth-box toilets. An

American journalist who made the same tour a week later claimed that most shelterers were unsympathetic to Max and his comrades, and had quotes to prove it: 'Fellow came in 'ere the other night, Communist 'e was, and wanted them all to go up to the Savoy and make a row. Laughed at 'im, they did.'[1] Max Levitas recalls only enthusiasm and congratulations – and suggests that if anyone thinks that forty is a modest number for a protest march, they should remember what was raining out of the sky during the second week of September 1940.

In that week, German incendiaries turned the docklands into a scene from Dante. The goods in each warehouse generated their own particular inferno. Rum barrels exploded like fifty-gallon Molotov cocktails. Spice stores bombarded the air with stinging particles of hot pepper. Burning sugar caramelised on the surface of the water. To many occidental observers, it appeared that a second sun was setting in the east. Two thousand people were killed in the first night of bombing alone. 'London', wrote the American journalist Ernie Pyle, 'was ringed and stabbed with fire.'[2]

At eight o'clock on that Saturday evening, the demonstrators gathered in Embankment Gardens and waited for the air-raid sirens to begin. Once the warning had sounded, they pulled banners from under their coats, formed themselves into a tight group and began moving towards the revolving doors of the hotel. Max Levitas remembers that as they entered the lobby, he saw Lund Hansen, the doorman, signal to the concierge, who picked up the desk telephone and called the police. The panic button under the desk was also pushed – illuminating an insistent flashing light in the office of the assistant general manager, Willy Hofflin, a tall, soldierly Swiss noted for his chilling briskness. Phil Piratin made a short speech: 'These men, women and children, many of them homeless, have come from Stepney to seek shelter – the newspapers have widely advertised the comfortable shelter facilities that exist in the West End hotels.' A small crowd of patrons gathered to watch the show. The Liberal MP Sir Archibald Sinclair, the Secretary of State for Air, peered at the red banner on his way to dinner. A gang of hacks descended from the American Bar: among them was Drew Middleton, a plump, football-loving Associated Press reporter with a gut dislike of Communism. By the time an inspector, two sergeants and six constables had arrived from Bow Street, the scene was set for a bruising skirmish in the class war.

'The manager . . . found himself in a most embarrassing situation,' recounted the American-born novelist Constantine FitzGibbon in *The Blitz* (1957). 'Although there were no bombs falling as yet, he could hardly eject all these people into the street without seeming excessively callous. On the other hand, his first responsibility lay with his clients. His shelter had sufficient accommodation for them, but if it were thrown open to the public, it was obvious that within a night or two it would be completely filled with people who had no connection with the hotel at all. In that case the hotel might just as well go out of business. Furthermore, were not the pilots and other people who sought an evening's relaxation at his hotel entitled to it?'[3]

'The guests thought that we were going to take over the hotel,' recalls Max Levitas, 'and we went there expecting some kind of opposition. But the general manager was extremely sympathetic.' Seventy years on, Max still seems surprised. A reporter from the *Daily Worker* recorded Hofflin's conciliatory speech: 'There is no reason why these people should not have the same shelter as the Savoy's guests.' If these were truly the words used, it was a simple statement of legal fact – all shelters were obliged to accept visitors during a raid. However, according to Max, the police, eager for an opportunity to repel the invaders back towards the Thames, were visibly disappointed. 'They were there to clear us out,' he says, 'but they couldn't do that without the manager asking them to – and he didn't.'

Not every report of that night agrees with the Levitas version. Standing on the margin of this tableau, Drew Middleton claimed to have seen something else entirely – the demonstrators 'pushing the pregnant woman in front of them'; the manager taming a 'voluble Communist' with his professional tact; the policemen grinning to themselves on their way out into the night; the anger of a belligerent group of East Enders defused by West End good manners.[4] This was the plot followed by most reports made by writers who possessed such manners themselves. Basil Woon, a screenwriter and socialite who had spent the 1930s writing one-liners for Jean Harlow, reflected that 'even people with double-barrelled names and crisp white notes in their pockets have been known to pause and straighten their ties before braving the gold lace and gimlet eyes of the minions on guard at the Savoy, so it is just possible that the faithful band from the Arches [had] a moment of uncertainty as they step[ped] from the noisy darkness into the bright lights of the lobby'. 'The demonstrators', claimed Constantine Fitz-Gibbon, 'were so awed by the Chaldean splendours of the hotel that they soon forgot to shout their slogans, despite the promptings of their leaders.'[5] Communism had been neutralised by the Savoy's air of grace. 'It was a very damp squib of a demonstration,' FitzGibbon concluded, 'arranged and carried out by [Hitler's] Communist allies.'[6]

Just as Cable Street and Marx and the struggle against Fascism are reflected in the words of Max Levitas and Phil Piratin and the *Daily Worker*, the Savoy invasion held a mirror to the loyalties of those whose sympathies lay elsewhere. For Drew Middleton, the American correspondent, Piratin and his band were little better than Fifth Columnists. ('This, of course,' he reflected in his memoirs, 'was before this man and his followers discovered that the Germans were "fascist hyenas".'[7]) Basil Woon's account in *Hell Came to London* (1941) was less hostile – probably because he knew what it was to be poor. As a child, he had received a grant from a charity that aided 'children of those who have once moved in a Superior Station of Life' – later, he bummed around North America, following the fruit harvest and 'lived with the down-and-outs in a dime lodging-house'.[8]Constantine FitzGibbon, whose principal source of information was the manager who admitted the demonstrators to the shelter, had the most potent mix of motives. At the age of seventeen, with a headful of Marx, Lenin and John Strachey's *The Coming Struggle for Power* (1932), he applied, unsuccessfully, to go to Spain to fight with the International Brigades. By twenty-three he had renounced left-wing politics and become a staff officer in American military intelligence. In the late 1940s he became convinced that Communism was 'an extremely dangerous and well-organised anti-social movement, dangerous even to the British both as an external and as an internal threat'[9] – and fleshed out the idea in a dystopian novel about a Kremlin-funded English revolution, in which the Labour Party establishes concentration camps in Hyde Park and the last hope for democracy is an American general holed up at the Savoy. *When the Kissing Had to Stop* (1960) made him a hate-figure for the British Left, in acknowledgement of which he published a collection of political journalism called *Random Thoughts of a Fascist Hyena* (1963). Drew Middleton would have appreciated the joke.

*

Despite these contending points of view, there is little dispute about what the new arrivals found when they were admitted to the subterranean part of the hotel. The Society press had already described its inhabitants and mapped out its topography: a padded, cavernous space with a dance floor on one side and a dormitory on the other; separate sleeping quarters for single men, single women and couples; mattresses and camp beds with matching sheets and pillows in green and pink and blue; a curtained recess behind which lay a recumbent Duke and Duchess of Kent; sandbags packed against scaffolding poles painted in the colours of the Union Jack; a 'snore warden' making a discreet patrol of the huddled masses of the upper ten thousand. ('As one is quietened', he complained, 'another starts.'[10]) The Savoy's publicity managers, Richmond Temple and Ronald Tritton, had permitted such images to percolate into the press before a single bomb had fallen. On the first night of the war, the photojournalist Marvin Breckinridge went below the hotel to snap a line of dressing-gowned Savoyards, each with a white respirator case settled on their lap, like a box of lime creams with which they might have endured a punishingly long German opera. *Life* magazine printed a shot of two American notables, one from the Illinois Railway Company, the other a celebrated Virginian huntsman, bedding down on a barricade. Temple and Tritton even allowed *Life* to document the shelter's operating theatre, where uniformed nurses – led by Greta Hofflin, the wife of the assistant general manager – stood ready to extract hot shards of shrapnel from the flesh of paying guests.

For some readers, these pictures demonstrated the implacability and nerve of London's residents: if Hitler could not disrupt the business of dinner, then what chance did he have against shipping or heavy industry? For others, however, those images had a less patriotic resonance. The nurses aroused particular resentment, partly because there were no medical facilities in most public shelters; partly because their immaculate hair and make-up suggested that they belonged to another profession entirely. 'To 'Arry and 'Erbert and Maudie and Mary,' observed Basil Woon, 'sleeping on their sodden newspapers in foul dens substituting for bombed homes, these pictures – which occasionally reached them via the fried fish merchant – seemed, to say the least, unreasonable . . . 'Arry and 'Erbert and Maudie and Mary feel more than a mild stirring of resentment at the spectacle of people apparently making a game of the war that to them has meant only discomfort and misery.'[11] Woon was patronising, but he was right. To the eyes of the real people beneath his cockney stereotypes – the interviewees of this chapter among them – London's grand hotels had become a locus of resentment; proof that all were not equal under fire. Some businesses were celebrated for their ability to keep calm and carry on. When the grand hotels practised that same policy, it represented something less attractive: the tenacity of privilege during wartime.

*

During the Phoney War, voices to the left of the Labour Party called for the requisition of the Savoy, the Dorchester, the Ritz and Claridge's. 'Before there is the slightest thought of cutting down the consumption goods of the masses of the people,' declared Willie Gallacher, the sole Communist MP in the Commons, 'every luxury hotel and wealthy house in the country must be closed down.' But the incongruity of these institutions also troubled more mainstream commentators. When Peter Howard, diarist of the *Sunday Express*, reported that fourteen ladies and twenty-three lords were being accommodated at the Dorchester, he did not write them up as heroes, despite his own anti-socialist sympathies. 'A man and his wife can live for a year in comfort at a first-rate hotel for £3,000,' he noted. 'It may be described as community living, though hardly as Communism.' As the bombs began to fall, ambivalence began to invade reports of bomb-proof bolt-holes in West End hotels: the Popote restaurant beneath the Ritz, with its comic mural of the First World War trenches; Grosvenor House, so thickly insulated from the sounds of war that the diners were informed of the end of an air-raid by the band singing 'All clear, all clear' to whatever tune they happened to be playing. In the *Daily Worker*, that doubt was distilled into something more potent. The poet Randall Swingler described how London families were turning the Underground platforms into unofficial shelters in defiance of government policy. '"Civilisation!" says one man to me. "It's enough to make you cry. And then think of them that's dancing at the Savoy to Carroll Gibbons' band – enjoying themselves – while this is going on. It's all wrong – the whole thing's wrong."[12]

*

Phil Piratin, the leader of the Savoy invaders, read those words on the morning of the invasion. He had been hearing – and declaiming – similar ones since the summer of 1938, when air-raid provision became a matter of national debate. As the possibility of war grew concrete, Britons gave serious consideration to how they might protect themselves from the anticipated barrage of German high explosive and phosgene gas. Luxury respirator cases went on sale in Selfridges. Shallow trenches were dug in public parks and slowly filled with rainwater. Four weeks after Chamberlain landed at Croydon Aerodrome with that piece of paper flapping in his hand, he installed Sir John Anderson behind a new desk at the Ministry of Civil Defence – and invited him to come up with a plan to prevent the incineration of the largest number of British people at the lowest possible cost. Anderson's answer was the surface shelter that would bear his name: a small apron of corrugated iron that was planted into thousands of wartime British lawns. A grander design, however, had already been put on the table in August – a plan that involved the construction of steel tunnels seventy feet below ground, in which swaths of the urban population might take refuge from gas attacks. Its author was J. B. S. Haldane, a biologist whose habit of using his own body as an experimental subject earned him the nickname of 'the world's most daring scientist'.[13] Investigating the deaths of ninety-nine personnel on board the submarine HMS *Thetis*, Haldane suffered convulsions brought on by oxygen starvation and the effects of deep-level pressure, and fractured a vertebra. Researching the efficacy of air-raid precautions, he inhaled mustard gas, shut himself inside a gas-proof box made of galvanised steel, and volunteered to expose the shortcomings of the Anderson shelter by sitting inside one and allowing the RAF to bomb him. The Air Marshals declined his offer, just as the Home Office rejected his plans for deep-level shelters. That he was regarded by MI5 as 'a leading figure in extremist politics' did not encourage them to favour his proposals.[14]

Cost was the principal official argument against the design. A pamphleteer from the Royal Institute of British Architects also doubted whether it would be possible to prevent the suffocation of the occupants. Sir John Anderson, however, believed that the creation of massive underground spaces would nurture a 'deep shelter mentality'; that civilians who took refuge in such places would simply refuse to emerge. Haldane suspected that the state had a more sinister motive for favouring small surface shelters: it feared that subterranean bomb-proof structures would become strategically important in the event of insurrection; that they would shield rebels from any 'police bombing' that might be used to subdue a revolution. He claimed to have heard a prominent British supporter of Franco declare that he 'relied on the Air Force to deal with socialism in England if it ever became a danger'.[15] Nothing on the record suggests that this remark was more than clubroom bluster, but by the time Haldane published the allegation, air-raid protection had become an ideological subject. There were many, suggested the professor, who believed that it was 'better to die under capitalism than live under socialism'.[16]

The principal advocates of the deep-shelter campaign were a band of activists who believed precisely the opposite. The National Unemployed Workers Movement was founded in 1921. It was led by Donald Renton, a Stepney resident and flame-haired veteran of the Spanish Civil War, and Wal Hannington, a soft-spoken, bespectacled toolmaker with a killer left hook and a genius for the consciousness-raising stunt. (His audition piece for the NUWM was a protest at the Slough Motor Transport Depot in 1920, for which he persuaded striking workers to dress up as choirboys and process behind a giant white cloth elephant that represented the cadaver of capitalism.) During the last winter before the war, as the number of jobless men hovered at the two million mark, Hannington and Renton mobilised their supporters with the aim of placing two policy ideas on the public agenda: an increase in the winter allowance for the un-employed and a scheme to put men to work in the construction of deep-level concrete bomb-shelters. In mid-December 1938, a hundred activists flopped down in unison at Oxford Circus, stopping the traffic and shaming the shoppers tottering home with Christmas gifts. Another group gatecrashed a dinner of the Wine and Food Society at the Albion Hotel in Brighton and de-clared, 'You feast while we starve.' In February 1939, J. B. S. Haldane took eighty protestors on a fishing expedition to the waterlogged trench shelters on Primrose Hill, bearing placards that read: 'Bring Anderson to Eel – Give us work on ARP.'[17]

The most headline-grabbing turn of the campaign, however, occurred a few days before Christmas 1938, when Hannington, Renton and a fifty-strong group of supporters, dressed in the best clothes they could reclaim from the pawnbroker, arrived at the Ritz Hotel before the eyes of a throng of forewarned journalists. They processed into the Grill Room, where Renton made an impromptu speech. 'We thought the Ritz management would like to help a few unemployed men by giving them a Christmas dinner – the same kind of dinner that they will give the other kind of workless gentlemen who will doubtless visit them later this evening.'[18] Hannington added that the propriet-ors of East End cafés always had a civil welcome for privileged types who came on 'slumming' jaunts to the Whitechapel Road. Flash-bulbs popped, and the following day, the front page of the *Daily Mirror* belonged to the Communists.[19]

So when, twenty-one months later, Phil Piratin, Max Levitas, Tubby Rosen, Michael Shapiro and their supporters settled themselves on the deck-chairs, armchairs and unoccupied floor space of the Savoy shelter, they were not simply performing a one-off publicity stunt; they were bringing the Haldane campaign into the heart of the West End. And to show they meant business, they ordered tea.

Eight years after these events, Phil Piratin recorded the night at the Savoy in his autobiography. He remembered someone looking around the room and declaring, 'Shelters . . . why, we'd love to *live* in such places!'[20] He remembered that as they settled down for the evening, some of his comrades began to unpack their sandwiches from tin boxes and paper bags – and that it was at this point that he asked the waiters for tea and bread and butter. This order came with a caveat that Piratin borrowed from the demonstrators who had occupied the Ritz. Although the Savoy exacted a minimum charge of 2s 6d, Piratin announced that he and his colleagues would pay twopence per head, the same price displayed on the menu at a Lyons Corner House – and the same price that Renton and Hannington had proposed to the acting manager of the Grill Room in December 1938. The men from the NUWM, however, had not received their tea. 'Due to a mistake,' confessed one of the demonstrators, 'we had overlooked the fact that the Grill was never open in the afternoons, only in the evenings.'[21] Its acting manager, Edouard Schwenter, declined to serve them with tea, bread, butter or anything else.

In September 1940, Phil Piratin did not make the same error. 'Three or four of the waiters went into a huddle, with one in particular doing the talking,' he wrote in *Our Flag Stays Red*. 'He was evidently convincing the others. How they convinced the chef and management, I do not know, but within a few minutes, along came the trollies [sic] and the silver trays laden with pots of tea and bread and butter.' Perhaps the Communist insurgency had thawed the customary formality of the Savoy. Perhaps the war had done some of the work for them. 'The waiters were having the time of their lives,' Piratin recalled. 'They were obviously neglecting their duties, standing around, chuckling and playing with the children.'[22] Children were not a common sight in the West End at the end of 1940, though not quite as rare as working-class customers at the Savoy.

*

Phil Piratin is a forgotten figure – ignored, even, by many histories of British Communism. For me, he has become a symbol of necessary ambivalence towards the institutions at the heart of this book, a warning about falling too deeply for the romance of the grand hotel. Piratin was the son of a Fournier Street furrier, against whose wishes he married another young radical, Beatrice Silver, in 1929. The night of 7 June 1934 confirmed his political allegiances, when he witnessed a group of Blackshirts beating up a demonstrator and heard a senior policeman declare, 'Get back to your slums, you Communist bastards.' Piratin was a pragmatist, a strategist and a pugilist. Those who knew him speak of his mastery of the soapbox speech; recall that his physical power added phantom inches to his five foot eight; that he could halve an apple with a twist of his hands. Alf Minto, who took his advice as a student activist in the 1950s, remembers him as 'a bit of a flash Harry, but warm-hearted. You could just picture him working Petticoat Lane.' Alice Hitchin, who knew him when she was a member of the Young Communist League, caught more heat than warmth. 'I was terrified of him,' she told me. This was not an unorthodox response. To Michael Shapiro, Piratin was 'arrogant and autocratic, with little or no theory and principles, but plenty of bossy determination to be obeyed'. To the Special Branch informer who reported on his movements, 'he couldn't distinguish between people and machines'. As a leader, Piratin demanded absolute loyalty. 'If you didn't carry out the decisions of the Party you'd get a hell of a ticking off,' recalls Max Levitas. 'I once had one from him. It was the first time I ever cried in my life.' Even in his nineties, Max Levitas seems as tough as tanner's apron. It's hard to imagine him in tears.[23]

Those closest to Phil Piratin felt the same fear. 'My father was a disciplinarian,' Piratin's son, Malcolm Lee, told me, over tea and biscuits at his kitchen table in Wanstead. 'He never laid a finger on me, but he didn't need to. He would freeze and his voice would become very precise.' He looses a squeaky laugh and stirs a spoonful of honey into his tea. 'He could frighten the shit out of me.' Malcolm Lee is a retired lawyer with a passion for the jazz trumpet, married to a cellist who once made her living playing in a string quartet at the Savoy. He was radicalised from the cradle. Beatrice and Phil Piratin turned their home into a political meeting room and encouraged their son to participate in the debates – any adult Communist who interrupted his observations about the progress of the Spanish Civil War was quickly silenced. Even Michael Shapiro, the acknowledged intellectual of the group, was obliged to defer to his short-trousered comrade. The war in Spain nurtured Malcolm's musical as well as his rhetorical abilities. The Piratin household was a receiving station for the personal effects of fallen members of the International Brigade. Among these Malcolm discovered a battered bugle, which he taught himself to play, giving little thought to the circumstances of its owner's death.

War broke the Piratin family apart – but the fractures occurred along fault-lines established before September 1939. The separation between Malcolm's parents was not friendly. 'My father could do very unkind things,' he recalls. 'And he wasn't overgenerous. My mother had to work very hard to keep going.' Her desperation is recorded in the letter she sent to the Ministry of Labour, imploring them to issue her husband with call-up papers, so that she might receive the weekly allowance paid to the wives of servicemen. (The letter betrays no knowledge of Piratin's rejection for military service.) As his parents' marriage collapsed, Malcolm was evacuated from London. In November 1939 his mother slipped a navy blue balaclava on his head and put him on the train to High Wycombe in Buckinghamshire. He was nine years old. He lodged in a boarding house in the tiny village of Downley, run by an old Italian Communist with a dog called Garibaldi. Here, he was toughened by fist-fights with country lads, for whom an East London Jew was a figure of threatening exoticism, and bullied by the wife of his host. His state of mind was not improved by the rumour that went around Downley declaring that his mother had been arrested as a German spy on the platform of Marylebone Station.

In fact, it was his father who had been put in handcuffs. In June 1940 Phil Piratin was arrested at a rally in Hyde Park, after the men from Special Branch had listened to his analysis of the Dunkirk evacuation. 'Our men have been killed,' he declared. 'They are running away because the whole of the army has been brought into chaos.' The price was a night in the cells, and another page added to his MI5 file. During these months he made half-hearted visits to his workplace, the stockroom of Leonard Perry's Gown and Mantle manufacturers, but put most of his energies into Party activities and his relationship with a new partner, a comfortably wealthy divorcee named Cecilia Gresser. Beatrice received little financial help from her estranged husband. Malcolm received subscription copies of the *New Statesman*, which remained unread. An authorised biography of Stalin was more welcome, as were occasional visits, during which Phil Piratin would regale his son with stories of his political activities and take him out on cross-country expeditions that were somewhere between fun and preparation for joining the Partisans in the event of a German invasion. 'If I had to say one word about him,' concludes Malcolm Lee, 'it would be that he was patriotic. I began laughing about that by the age of fourteen. He thought anything British was good. He adored Winston Churchill. He used to weep whenever he saw the White Cliffs of Dover on the Ferry back from France.'

'An East End communist', wrote Basil Woon, 'can still shout "God Save the King" – and mean it.'[24] And yet, Phil Piratin believed in the overthrow of capitalism and thought that the war might bring it about. When he made statements such as 'no revolution would be successful without arms' or he declared his view that 'when time for action came the new rubber knobs on the underground trains should come in useful', it was written down and underlined in the red ink of official disquiet. This was why MI5 lavished him with such intense interest, why his telephones were tapped throughout the war, why officers from Special Branch kept diligent records of the daily business of his life: his views on the sweet ration; his visits to the Royal National Throat, Nose and Ear Hospital on the Grays Inn Road; his coffee in a Lyons Corner House with 'a coloured man of Negroid appearance'. Eventually, he became so familiar with the plain-clothes officers assigned to tail him that he occasionally paid their bus fares when they found themselves without sufficient money for a ticket.

*

How long did the Communist tea party under the Savoy last? Even this is open to argument. Constantine FitzGibbon states that fifteen minutes after Piratin and his followers settled in the shelter, the all-clear wailed over the rooftops of the Strand, signalling the end of the bombardment and of the hotel's obligation to its East End visitors. The Stepney Communists retreated to Embankment Gardens, where they waited for the next alert to justify their return. 'However,' wrote FitzGibbon, 'by the time it sounded arrangements had been made, and Piratin, Rosen and their flock were escorted to another shelter, a deep public one some hundred yards away.' Basil Woon's account follows the same narrative. In *Hell Came to London* the demonstrators are dispersed 'before they can make real inroads into the sandwiches'.[25] Max Levitas, however, insists that he and about twenty from his group stayed the entire night. He also has a strong memory of having breakfast at the hotel's expense. 'Two eggs. Ham. Plenty tea. Plenty toast,' he enthuses. 'I'd had a good night's kip there, too. It was a good night's work.' At seven o'clock, with a warm belly, he left the hotel and walked back through the glass-strewn streets to his tailor's shop on Brick Lane. Seventy years on, his satisfaction is palpable.

Max also refutes the incident that serves as an epilogue to Basil Woon's version of the Savoy invasion – and which appears in many second-hand accounts of that night. With present-tense urgency, Woon describes Piratin's group making their way, uncertainly, to the doors of the hotel. 'They feel, somehow, that matters have not gone according to plan. Their leader, especially, is feeling baffled and a trifle cheated. A gesture is needed, evidently, but what? There is a whispered consultation. Someone has an inspiration. A cap is passed around. And as the visitors from the Arches pass out into the night their leader approaches the dignified and awesome Head Porter. "'Ere, my man," he says – and pours into the functionary's hand a stream of coppers.' It is an action that erases the power of their protest; suggests that 'Arry and 'Erbert and Maudie and Mary are in thrall to the occult power of class difference as much as the natural clientele of the Savoy; argues that in England, social embarrassment is a more powerful force than social radicalism. It also replays the moment of paralysing awkwardness with which the NUWM protest at the Ritz was said to have ended. On their way from the Grill Room, Renton, Hannington and their supporters passed the group of patrons taking tea on the Palm Court. Among them was the romantic novelist Barbara Cartland. 'The people having tea just sat there, still, looking upper class,' she recalled, half a century later. 'There was an uncanny silence.'[26]

*

Constantine FitzGibbon described the Savoy invasion as 'a curious and rather sad little event which, though much talked about at the time, was not fully reported in the English papers.' He was certainly right about the coverage. The BBC ignored the story, as did most of the British press. Predictably, the *Daily Worker* was the only indigenous newspaper to give it front-page treatment. Another left-leaning title, the *Sunday Pictorial*, gave tacit support to the protestors by sending its reporter, Bernard Gray, to the air-raid shelters of London's grand hotels, disguised as a member of the proletariat. Gray slipped into a pair of old flannel trousers, a two-shilling scarf and a raincoat 'borrowed from a respectable working-class friend', and failed to get into Claridge's. ('I should get badly pulled over the coals if I let you in,' the doorman confessed.) The American correspondents, many of whom had been drinking in the Savoy that night, looked the other way, or worse. James Reston of the *New York Times* asserted, quite wrongly, that the demonstrators had been 'rushed out by the police', though his article offered a fairly sympathetic account of the Communist campaign for deep shelters. The press had their own narrative to follow, prescribed by their patriotism, by their feeling of solidarity against Germany, and by the Ministry of Information. There was no space in that story for the suggestion that bombing was exposing, not closing, the divisions within British society. When George Orwell heard of the Savoy invasion, he identified it as a sign of greater upheavals to come: 'When you see how the wealthy are *still* behaving, in what is manifestly developing into a revolutionary war, you think of St Petersburg in 1916.' The thought seems never to have made it any further than his diary.[27]

No such reticence was necessary, of course, in Germany. The Nazi daily *Völkischer Beobachter* fell upon the story with enthusiasm. 'For ten days now eight million people have flown into the air raid shelters and the subway,' crowed its editorial. 'Londoners have become cave dwellers. Life has stopped. The working population is fleeing from the east and south of the city to the West End. Desperate men and women have stormed the luxurious Savoy hotel. Only police have been able to evacuate them. The question comes into one's mind . . . whether at all and for how long the English population will follow Churchill on this path . . .' The Savoy was also high on the agenda of Workers Challenge, a German propaganda radio station broadcast from Berlin and run by National Socialists masquerading as international socialists. A pair of British prisoners of war delivered a script by William Joyce, in which images of plutocrats drinking their way through the Blitz were amplified by authentic effing and blinding: 'Strike me bloody pink!' raged one of his amateur actors. 'Things must be in a pretty queer state if they start blocking the workers like that.' Old ladies in Brighton and Eastbourne, it was said, tuned in eagerly to hear the swearing. MI5 was more concerned about how the station had received such swift news of the demonstration. ('The complaint of the Communists', sniffed Guy Liddell, 'is that the rich eat omelettes at the Savoy, while the poor can only buy one egg a fortnight if they can afford it.'[28])

When the War Cabinet met on Tuesday 17 September, Churchill opened business with some dark reflections on the Savoy invasion: the official minutes of the discussion tick with phrases that sound like euphemisms for state violence. Sir John Anderson, Home Secretary since the war's outbreak, asserted in the House that these protestors were not ordinary members of the public, but a small, organised unit. 'He agreed with the Prime Minister that it would be necessary to take strong action to prevent demonstrations of this kind, which if allowed to grow, might easily lead to serious difficulties' – which sounds like Parliamentary code for the use of force. Anderson dismissed a suggestion by Lord Beaverbrook, the Minister of Aircraft Production, that the basements of banks in the East End and the City could be opened during air attacks. 'The fire risk must be taken into consideration,' he insisted – and also, presumably, other risks incurred by allowing groups of Marxists free entry to the vaults of London's financial institutions. As the bombing continued, however, thousands of Londoners broke the law by occupying the corridors and platforms and booking halls of the Underground system. It was often a member of the Communist Party who exhorted the staff of London Transport to keep the gates unlocked or, if that failed, to supply a crowbar to open them again – but the participants were far more populous and less ignorable than the Stepney comrades. On 21 September, exactly one week after Phil Piratin, Solly Klotnick, Max Levitas, Michael Shapiro and George Rosen ate their subterranean bread and butter, London Transport killed the electricity at Aldwych, the Underground station nearest to the Savoy. The tracks and the suicide pits between the rails were boarded over. Chemical toilets were installed. Three hundred and twenty yards of Piccadilly Line tunnel were transformed into a refuge for 2,500 people. The shelterers shared the space with the Elgin Marbles – which, unlike the local population, had been enjoying the protection of the tunnels for the previous three weeks.

When Sir John Anderson had addressed Parliament on the deep-shelter issue in June 1940, he made a remark that would come back to haunt him: 'I do not want to be controversial,' he told the Commons, 'but looking back I must say frankly that I am devoutly thankful we did not adopt a general policy of providing deep or strongly protected shelters. Had we done so, we should at this moment have been in a far worse position, looking at the problem as a whole, than we are today.' He did not remain in office long enough to eat these words. At the beginning of October he was bumped from his position by Herbert Morrison, the Minister of Supply, in a reshuffle necessitated by the terminal ill-health of Neville Chamberlain. Morrison's objections to Communism were as vehement as any Tory diehard. ('Herbert Morrison hated my father,' says Malcolm Lee, 'and he hated him back.')

Perversely, however, the new Home Secretary began his tenure by doing the Communists a series of unintentional favours. One of Morrison's first acts was to relieve Stepney Borough Council of responsibility for the civil defence of its own territory – a humiliating blow for the local Labour leadership, and precisely the opposite for the East End Communists.[29] Out went Stepney's ARP controller, Morris Davis – much to the relief of the many ratepayers who believed that in addition to failing in his war duties, he had accepted bribes, sold municipal contracts and embezzled money from a charity for tubercular children.[30] Dan Frankel, the incumbent Labour MP, was also damaged by the affair. Thanks to the efforts of Piratin and his colleagues, the shortcomings of the Stepney shelters had become a public scandal. An angry crowd massed at the gates of the Borough's ARP Control Centre. Public figures made unannounced visits to Brady Street and the railway arches on Commercial Road, and phoned through lists of complaints to the Home Office: Marie de Rothschild, the wife of a prominent Tory banker, and Clementine Churchill were among this battery of self-appointed scrutineers. The Zionist campaigner Lady Dugdale ventured east at the behest of the Home Intelligence Department, and filed a report with inevitable allusions to Dante.[31]

*

Improvements were instituted with extravagant haste and the Stepney Communists took the credit. Some were even willing to give it to them. 'The Savoy had no ground for complaint when Mr Rosen and his friends called and demanded shelter there,' asserted the *New Statesman*. 'Their best reply would have been to welcome their visitors into the shelter with open arms. It is clear that people who don't want extreme doctrines to grow in the East End must remove the scandals, not curse those who expose them.' The article would have pleased at least one subscriber, even if his son failed to remove the magazine from its wrapper.

The reversal of policy was not quite sufficient to dissuade other protestors from targeting the Savoy. With Herbert Morrison in the Home Office, there was little prospect of an official entente with the Communists. On 21 January, the new Home Secretary closed down the *Daily Worker*, the newspaper that had carried the most critical reports of the National Government's ARP policy, the most detailed accounts of the Savoy invasion, and a suspiciously decoy-like news story that, two days before Piratin's protest, suggested that the demonstrators were preparing to march on the Dorchester. In the first week after the ban, a second Communist intervention occurred at the Savoy, with the aim of influencing American attitudes to the war, and disrupting the flow of stirring stories being cabled home by the US foreign correspondents. On 26 January 1941, the former presidential candidate Wendell Willkie landed in England to make his own assessment of British morale, and to canvass opinion on the proposed Lend-Lease agreement, Roosevelt's strategy to finance the war effort with American money. Willkie's itinerary incorporated the inspection of a public air-raid shelter in the East End, a meeting at Downing Street and visit to the House of Commons. The following day he lunched with a cabal of businessmen at the Savoy, among them Robert Kindersley, president of the National Savings scheme and Harry McGowan, the chairman of the ICI chemicals company. Shortly before they arrived, a group of twenty-nine well-dressed women entered the restaurant and threw off their furs to reveal banners protesting against the government's food policy and began to chant, 'More food for workers.' Willy Hofflin, newly promoted to general manager, deployed the porters to block their progress. Hugh Wontner ordered the doors of the restaurant closed, splitting the demonstrators into two groups. Realising that the management intended to remove them by force, the women began using their scarves to tie themselves to chairs and stair-rails. According to the hotel's official historian, it was the head porter, Hansen, who persuaded the protestors to leave. 'With Majestic firmness he convinced the ringleaders that they must either leave or be forcibly removed, and the rank-and-file departed after assaulting some of the hapless porters who yet managed to keep their self-control.' A photographer from *Life* magazine snapped them on the pavement of Savoy Court, their mouths open in noisy protest, their banners declaring, 'Ration the Rich', 'Our Children Must Not Starve' and 'Omelettes for the Rich – One Egg a Week for Us'.[32] Willkie, arriving as the last of the women were being ejected from the building, declared that if such a demonstration had occurred at the Waldorf-Astoria in New York, those responsible would have been dispersed by riot police and tear gas.[33]

It took another man in uniform to remove the Savoy from the cross-hairs of protest. On Sunday 22 June 1941 Hitler launched Operation Barbarossa, sending thousands of troops into Russian territory and opening a second front in the east. With that act, he terminated the Molotov–Ribbentrop Pact, put Britain and the Soviet Union on the same side, and allowed British Communists to support the war with a clear conscience. Churchill and Joe Stalin stood shoulder to shoulder, on the posters at least. Red flags flew together with Union Jacks. British Communists who had never been comfortable with Moscow's insistence that the war was a kind of Ragnorok for the old gods of imperialism found themselves returned to the bosom of the Party. Harry Pollitt was restored to the position of general secretary of a newly respectable political movement. Although the men from Special Branch continued to tail Phil Piratin through the tube system and maintain the ban on his membership of the armed forces, there was a thaw in the relationship between the Stepney Communists and the state. In 1943, the Ministry of Labour made enquiries about employing Phil Piratin and Michael Shapiro to write official propaganda material in a sphere 'where their technical qualifications could be utilised and their views do less harm'. Two years later, they both had something better than the indulgence of Whitehall. They had power.

*

In the summer of 1945, democracy returned to Britain. The General Election that brought Clement Attlee his landslide victory also gave the Savoy invaders cause to celebrate. The Stepney Communists campaigned for improved housing developments and on their record of resistance against the British Union of Fascists. But voters in the East End also remembered how they had argued for deep shelters; knew that fewer of their neighbours would have died in the fire and falling masonry if the National Government had listened to their demands. A reward came at the ballot box. Twelve Communists took their seats on Stepney Borough Council. Among them were Michael Shapiro, Tubby Rosen, Solly Klotnick and Max Levitas. Phil Piratin was elected MP for Mile End. Press photographs show him being carried through the blasted streets on the shoulders of his supporters, a hero amid the rubble. On his first day in Parliament he joined Willie Gallacher, the only other Communist MP in the Commons, in a rousing chorus of the Red Flag – much to the embarrassment of the remaining Conservatives and the intense annoyance of Herbert Morrison. Piratin, however, was under no illusions about having nurtured a deep love of Marxist-Leninism in the population of Stepney. He was fond of explaining his electoral success with the story of a constituent who had voted for him because of his exertions to get her a new dustbin. There was nothing dialectical about that kind of materialism, but a vote was a vote. His mandate, however, proved impossible to sustain. The wartime depopulation of Mile End and the smallness of the constituency had helped him into office – both these advantages were removed by the time the electorate went to the polls again. Neither was he helped by the publicity that arose after his fist-fight in the Commons cafeteria with Tom Lucy, a journalist from the *Daily Telegraph* who sounded an ugly note of anti-Semitism in the lunch queue.

Piratin's generation of Communists were secular East End Jews who looked to the Party as a means to build a society that would banish pogroms and poverty into history. That Party, and its mother institutions in Moscow, did not always respect that aspiration. In the 1950s, Russian foreign policy in Hungary and domestic policy towards its indigenous Jewish population ensured that few of Stepney's Communists escaped agonies of conscience. Phil Piratin followed the Moscow line and tried not to think too deeply about its contradictions. Some left the Party behind. Others searched elsewhere in the world for purer forms of ideology. Michael Shapiro looked eastwards towards China. He learned Mandarin. He read Mao. From his soapbox at Speaker's Corner and on Communist holiday camps in the New Forest he enthused about the battle against the Kuomintang. In 1950 he left England to work as an adviser to the state news agency in Peking. After his departure, few of his friends and family ever saw him again. In 1955 his name appeared in a Ministry of Defence report on the treatment of British prisoners of war in North Korea. Two witnesses claimed to have encountered him as he toured the prison camps under the protection of the Chinese People's Liberation Army. One, a sergeant in the Royal Ulster Rifles, alleged that Shapiro had threatened to have him executed by firing squad. The charge was never substantiated, but the damage was done. Unable to return to England, Shapiro started a family in the serviced bungalow provided by the Peking government, wrote articles applauding his hosts and became a shadowy presence in hostile accounts of China in the British press. In the 1950s a *Daily Express* reporter clocked him at an official banquet in Peking and dismissed him as an 'ingratiating, even obsequious figure [who] trotted about eagerly, trying to make friends, or at least acquaintances with the British visitors'.[34] In 1967 he was named as one of a number of expatriates who were reported to have demonstrated their loyalty to the Cultural Revolution by sacking the British embassy in Peking – an act for which the Chinese authorities rewarded him with five years of detention without trial.[35] Shapiro was fortunate, however, in that he was rehabilitated without being killed first: when he died in 1986, Deng

Xiaoping hailed him as 'a staunch international soldier and sincere friend of the Chinese people'.[36]

Max Levitas speaks of Shapiro as if he had been lost at sea, long ago. The last known survivor of the Savoy invasion has his feet firmly planted in the cement of Stepney. It's impossible to imagine him going to China for ideological reasons. He has lived in the Borough for almost nine decades, and an hour sitting with him in the café of the Idea Store is enough to demonstrate his importance to the community that surrounds him. As we talk, our conversation is punctuated by interjections from other users of the library, a crowd of slightly younger regulars who come to shake his hand, pat his back, pay their respects to this quiet man in a muffler and cloth cap, an ambassador from the twentieth century. And this is his declaration: 'We went to the Savoy to show the class position; to show how the rich lived with a great mass of stuff while the ordinary working man and woman had to live on the coupon books. And because of what we did, the Underground was opened, and people had somewhere to shelter from the bombs. I'm very proud of the part that I played.'

The Savoy invasion was not a Potemkin mutiny, not a scene from the Odessa Steps – but neither was it the sad little event described by writers who regarded Communism as a peril to the state. When those forty or eighty or one hundred demonstrators moved from the darkness of the Embankment into the electric light of the hotel lobby, they obliged the National Government to examine its conscience – or to confront the fearful consequences of not doing so. They created the circumstances in which London would elect its first Communist MP and a dozen Communist councillors. Enough, I think, to earn that night under the Strand a place in our collective memory of the Second World War – and to persuade us to consider what the second half of the twentieth century might have been, if Britain's shift to the left had gone further than Attlee and Morrison and the National Health. In some alternative world where Phil Piratin's victory was the first step on the road to a Soviet England, a rosy image of that night beneath the Savoy is surely on the back of the banknotes: East End children in scuffed shoes and utility knitwear; Brylcreemed waiters abandoning the rules of the house; Phil Piratin, Max Levitas, Michael Shapiro and their allies, negotiating tea and bread and butter for all.

3

Players

A few days before Hitler invaded Poland, Sir Norman Kendal, head of both Special Branch and the Criminal Investigation Department of the London Metropolitan Police, cancelled a trip to Berlin; a fact-finding mission that was scheduled to include a lecture on policing methods by SS-Gruppenführer Reinhard Heydrich, a tour of Dachau concentration camp and a talk by Heydrich's deputy, Artur Nebe, on 'New Ways of Researching the Criminal Personality'.[1] Kendal sent his regrets by post. 'I am more sorry than I can tell you to miss seeing you and all my other friends,' he wrote, 'but it cannot be helped and we must hope for better luck some other time.' Nebe was equally sorry. 'I sincerely hope that your wife and daughter will come to Berlin and spend a few enjoyable days with us,' he replied, as German troops mobilised on the Polish border. It is not quite clear how Sir Norman would have put this knowledge to use once he was back behind his desk at Scotland Yard, but, six months into the war, he had become painfully frustrated by the security policy of the government to whom he was answerable. One of his strongest sources of anxiety was a huge building on Park Lane: an eight-floor, 300-bedroom reinforced-concrete citadel populated by garrulous and undisciplined Cabinet ministers, suspected German spies, doubtful aliens and inexperienced MI5 agents. 'The whole place', he declared, in a despairing confidential memo, 'is crawling with foreigners.'[2]

The Dorchester, however, was built for just such an infestation. Its co-founder, Sir Francis Towle, was also the inaugurator of the Come to Britain Movement, a coalition of business leaders, sponsored by the Foreign Office, who argued that international tourism should be a source of mutual understanding as well as hard currency. His contribution to the brochure published to mark the Dorchester's opening was an essay in which he augured that the ocean liner, the aeroplane and the dirigible would establish a new, peaceful, cosmopolitan world: 'It is now recognised that the encouragement of travel in this country by visitors from overseas is a most important form of invisible export, and a habit which, if developed, has a far-reaching effect for good in international relationships and business undertakings. It is with this responsibility in mind that my colleagues and I have built this great hotel.'³ These were the ideals of the Come to Britain Movement: 'It cannot but be good', observed Lord Derby, Towle's fellow campaigner, 'for John Bull at home to learn that there may be another point of view than his own, and that the stranger is a fellow much like himself.'⁴

Seven years after the Dorchester began to accept bookings, Europe was at war and Towle's idealistic internationalism had been supplanted by Norman Kendal's culture of suspicion – the same body of ideas that had proved so catastrophic for Loreto Santarelli, Ferruccio Cochis and the passengers on board the *Arandora Star*. Security files were opened on guests – with special attention paid to the high number of Swiss and Hungarians. English members of staff were encouraged to inform on foreign colleagues. The MI5 officer Guy Burgess ran two spies on the premises, and played lover and recruiting officer to both. The older of the two was Eric Kessler, the press attaché to the Swiss embassy, who took the codename Orange and passed on diplomatic gossip from his own colleagues and his Polish counterparts. The junior partner was Peter Pollock, a painfully handsome nineteen-year-old whom Burgess had met at Cannes during the summer of 1938, while on holiday to restore his morale after he was accused of indecency in the gents at Paddington station. (Burgess insisted that he had not been passing obscene notes between the cubicles, but merely sitting on the lavatory, re-reading a chapter of *Middlemarch*.) During 1940, Pollock lived at the Dorchester, where he drank cocktails, nibbled salted almonds and ingratiated himself with just the kind of foreign guest that fired the anxieties of Norman Kendal. Eventually Burgess's man had ten targets on his watch-list, mainly homosexual Magyars who were charmed by his unfingermarked good looks.[5]

Kendal's informers, however, identified the hotel's managing director as the principal security risk – Anton Bon, scion of a dynasty of St Moritz hoteliers, and nicknamed 'the Major' by the Dorchester's staff. Kendal's spooks saw something more sinister in his military manner and were convinced that his political sympathies were with the Nazis. The same suspicion was entertained of Gaston Kung, a Swiss waiter who had been assigned to the most sensitive position in the hotel – serving in the rambling fifth-floor suite that had been occupied since November 1939 by the Foreign Secretary, Lord Halifax.

*

The presence of Edward Halifax in the hotel may help to explain Kendal's concerns. Waiting on the Foreign Secretary would have been a plum appointment for any German spy. Halifax had been one of the chief architects of Chamberlain's policy of Appeasement; after its collapse he took responsibility for investigating the possibility of a negotiated peace with Germany – inquiries that he sometimes pursued without the knowledge or consent of the Cabinet or the intelligence services. Among the visitors to the Foreign Secretary's suite in the year of his occupation was an impecunious Etonian adventurer named John Lonsdale Bryans, whom he despatched on a private mission to meet German contacts in Zurich. ('The Bryans case would make a sensational reading for the *Daily Mirror*,' remarked the MI5 agent assigned to monitor the affair.[6]) Halifax also used the Dorchester apartments for his meetings with a married lover, Alexandra 'Baba' Metcalfe – a tireless adulterer who was conducting a parallel romance with Dino Grandi, Mussolini's representative in London. Metcalfe's pillow-talk included lobbying Halifax to support an end to the internment of Oswald Mosley, another line on her sexual curriculum vitae. (The affair had earned her the nickname 'Baba Blackshirt'.) In addition to these potential sources of compromise, Halifax also had the habit of leaving confidential Foreign Office telegrams in the lavatory; scattering the carpet of his sitting room with secret intercepts; standing in the public areas of the hotel and talking cheerfully and loudly about matters of state with people whom he hardly knew. Anyone standing next to him in the lift would hear more news about British foreign policy than *The Times* was permitted to print. His colleagues believed that this was legacy of his tenure as Viceroy of India. 'In India no-one was allowed to come anywhere near him who had not been most carefully seeded,' noted the Foreign Office private secretary Gladwyn Jebb, 'and he therefore got into the habit of thinking that he could speak freely to all within reach.'[7]

The Dorchester, however, was not the Viceroy's Palace. It was a building in which the respectable and the dubious mixed by the thousand, knocking back cocktails and indulging in careless talk. The photographer Cecil Beaton made an inventory of its inhabitants: 'Cabinet ministers and their self-consciously respectable wives; hatchet-jawed, iron-grey brigadiers; calf-like airmen off duty; tarts on duty; actresses (also); *déclassé* society people; cheap musicians and motor-car agents.'[8] German spies made appointments to meet in the coffee lounge. Their British counterparts patrolled the marble floors. At the front of the hotel, General Eisenhower plotted the progress of the war behind a concrete barrier installed for his protection. At the back of the hotel, the Park Lane prostitutes known collectively as the Hyde Park Rangers warmed themselves on an air-vent they nicknamed 'the hotplate'. And in the ballroom and the Gold Room, uniformed men and women moved to dreamy, intoxicat-

ing rhythms of the dance-band. This was 'the Dorch'. A palace
of intrigue in the heart of Mayfair.

*

Joyce Stone has good reason to remember the atmosphere and
the sounds of the Dorchester. Between the summers of 1940
and 1942, she spent most of her evenings at a table on the
hotel's long internal promenade, watching the comings and goings of the night people, listening to the boom of the ack-ack
guns in Hyde Park and the music in the vast mirrored ballroom next door. Here, her husband, Lew, a prominent British
bandleader of the war years, marshalled his modest gang of musicians, kept the dancers foxtrotting and bunny-hugging over
the parquet, and calmed nerves when the noise of the bombardment penetrated the compressed-seaweed soundproofing of the
Dorchester's walls. 'Incendiaries normally came down in sticks
of seven or eight,' Joyce explained, when I visited her in the
spring of 2006. 'But Lew worked out something to stop everyone from panicking.' After the second blast, he had the band
strike up the first bars of the Anvil Chorus from *Il Travatore*.
The musicians played every other note, timing the gaps to allow
the detonating bombs to complete Verdi's line. 'It happened so
often', Joyce recalled, 'that they became very good at it.' And,
banging the arm of her chair with her hand, she demonstrated.

The music with which Lew Stone filled the Dorchester was
not for jitterbuggers. It was smoky, soft, romantic, insinuating:
the most important component of a wider experience that was
also conveyed in the light from the chandeliers; the bubble of
conversation; the sparkles of the glass studs set into the ballroom's mirrored walls; the miasma of expensive cigarettes. Its
popularity ensured that Joyce Stone was present at the hotel
on 16 September 1940, when a land-mine blew out the windows on the Hyde Park side of the building. (True to stereotype,
she said, the foreign waiters came running first, followed by

British patrons walking with exaggerated insouciance.) On the night of 8 March 1941 she was copying out sheet music under the usefully bright lights of the Dorchester first-aid room, when casualties poured in from the bombing of the Café de Paris. (A former member of her husband's band, the Trinidadian sax player Carl Barriteau, was caught in the explosion: Joyce recalled him telling her that on his way into the club that night, a man had touched him for the price of a drink – the same man who, hours later, hauled him from the burning wreckage of the club to the Charing Cross Hospital.) On 4 September 1941, Joyce was present when Winston Churchill arrived at the Dorchester to attend a party that marked the passage of two relations into the Auxiliary Territorial Service. (The staff and guests rose to their feet and applauded as the Prime Minister passed through the building.) From her table on the promenade, she felt the impact of the fall of France and the collapse of the Molotov–Ribbentrop Pact; listened to the note of desperation in late-night conversations before America entered the war. 'We knew we were behind in our armaments,' she reflected. 'We knew that our country was on the brink of being destroyed.' Lew Stone shared these doubts and was prepared to voice them in public – an act of conscience that was not without its price. Throughout all this, however, the band kept on playing.

The future Mrs Stone was fifteen when she fell in love with the West End and its music. It happened at the Savoy in the year of the General Strike, where the glitter of the River Room and the rhythm of Fred Elizalde's house band conspired to make her a lifelong devotee. She was Ethel Newman in those days, the bright young daughter of a well-to-do Gloucestershire family that had made its fortune from the foundries and furnaces of Stroud. Her great-grandfather had been chief engineer on the Sebastopol Docks and remained on good terms with the Romanovs, because he had supplied Tsar Nicholas I with parcels of West Country cheese. Her father was a large cog in the works of Smith's Motor Accessories, a prosperous manufacturer of speedometers and fuses and cockpit instruments. Joyce, however, was an uneasy member of this privileged county set. For her twenty-first birthday she took a gang of friends to the Monseigneur, an opulent playroom under the pavement of Jermyn Street, where the waiters wore blue velvet and the music came soft and sweet. The eleven-piece band was led by a gifted musical arranger named Lew Stone, whose recent displacement of his predecessor, Roy Fox, had provoked tremors in the small world of British dance-band music. (Fox returned from a stay in a Swiss sanatorium to find that his services were no longer required.) Vocals were supplied by Al Bowlly, a cherubic crooner adored for his romantic, full-throated style. Both performers seemed exotic to Joyce and her friends: Stone was a working-class East End Jew who had grown up as Louis Steinberg on the Boundary Road Estate in Bethnal Green; Bowlly had been born in Mozambique to Greek and Lebanese parents who brought him to Johannesburg, where he worked for a time in his uncle's barber shop. In defiance of the freezing November weather, Joyce requested 'We're Having a Heatwave' and watched her friends flirt energetically with Bowlly. Thinking back on the night three-quarters of a century later, it seemed significant to her in two ways: it was, of course, the moment at which she met her husband, but it was also a memorable demonstration of English social hypocrisy. 'Inside the Monseigneur they flirted with Al,' she reflected. 'But they would never have been seen dead with him outside.'

Joyce was both the victim and the beneficiary of such intolerance. In the early years of their marriage, Lew urged his wife to harden herself to the stings of casual British anti-Semitism. (Joyce did, though she still has recall of a charity coffee morning at which one of the guests suggested that German Jews had brought their troubles upon themselves.) It was, however, the indeterminacy of Stone's social position that allowed their relationship to develop. One of Joyce's birthday guests secured an appointment to audition for the bandleader at his flat in Regent's Park – which, as readers of the *Melody Maker* knew, was a converted coach house with a glass-roofed bedroom that allowed its owner to sleep under the stars. Hilda Allen, however, was the daughter of the high sheriff of Gloucestershire, and so afraid of her father's reaction to the meeting that she broke the arrangement and asked Joyce to convey her apologies – giving the messenger an opportunity to pursue Lew for herself. (Joyce's clinching strategy was to help him copy the orchestration for a new arrangement, using the skills she had acquired as a piano student at the Royal College of Music in London.) The couple kept their relationship secret for two years, not least because Joyce's parents were under the happy impression that she intended to marry her fiancé – a presentable young man with £30,000 in the bank and an impressive position in a firm of cash-register manufacturers. Joyce and Lew were married, with the minimum of fuss, at Marylebone Registry Office in May 1937. After the ceremony, Mrs Newman went home to Gloucestershire and cried herself to sleep. Mrs Stone moved with the beat of the band, became more or less nocturnal, and inhabited a world of which she would become one of the last survivors. 'The West End I knew is gone,' she reflected. 'I don't know whether that's good or bad. But sometimes it's almost a physical ache in me, I want it back so much.'

*

Seven decades on, the figures of this night-time world were strong in Joyce's memory, and during the course of our conversation, she invited each one to rise for a solo: Gerald Bright, formerly the relief pianist at the Palaseum Cinema on the Old Kent Road, who acquired the Latinate pseudonym of Geraldo and waggled his hips as leader of the Savoy's Gaucho Tango Orchestra; Tiny Winters, a taciturn double bassist whose singing voice was so high that many of his fan letters were addressed to 'Miss Tiny Winters'; Harry Berly, a preternaturally gifted viola player who threw himself on the electrified track at Oval Underground station in March 1937. (The papers said he was 'jazz-weary' and lovesick for a solicitor's daughter from Rickmansworth; Joyce was sure that it had more to do with being denied the honour of being the first to record William Walton's Viola Concerto.) We discussed the goggle-eyed, nine-stone clarinettist Harry Roy, who led the band at the Embassy night-club and created a sensation by marrying the daughter of the Rajah of Sarawak, the colonial ruler of a province of north-west Borneo where headhunting remained a popular pastime. 'Are you a married man?' Joyce asked, mischievously, before telling me how Roy once scandalised the Stones by bragging about his affair with his own mother-in-law.

The war ensured that many hotel dance-bands were immediately disbanded. Sydney Lipton, a violin prodigy whose hopes of a solo career were dashed by an accident involving a deck-chair and the tip of his left index finger, found that there were no musicians to lead from his podium in the ballroom of Grosvenor House. The bandleader at the May Fair, Bert Ambrose – a hopeless gambler who rejected requests written on the back of any banknote smaller than a fiver – lost four of his best players to the RAF. He reduced his orchestra to an octet and accepted help from America – in the form of his lover Evelyn Dall, a rumbustious peroxide broad from the Bronx who was billed as 'the original blonde bombshell', despite having stolen the soubriquet from Jean Harlow. The pair planned to marry, but found their enthusiasm unreciprocated by Ambrose's wife, who refused to be party to a divorce. Dall compromised by taking the band's manager as her husband, securing a work permit and a reason to be wherever Bert Ambrose went – the May Fair ballroom, the mess halls at RAF bases, the all-night poker games in hotel basements.

Lew Stone's residency at the Dorchester was a result of the intransigence of his immediate predecessor, Maurice Winnick, a rail-thin Mancunian who had perfected a sleepily melodic style of dance music modelled on the work of the Canadian Guy Lombardo. In early 1940, Winnick expanded the size of his band without consulting the hotel's entertainments manager, who declined to pay the wages of the new members. Lew Stone was more prudent. As chair of the Dance Band Director's Association, he knew that most of the best musicians were disappearing into the armed forces and that a full complement of talented professional players would be hard to maintain. Although no member of his slimmed-down seven-man outfit was fit to fight, Stone was confident that they were capable of making music that would fill the ballroom. Technology also helped, in the form of the Novachord, a new American-made keyboard instrument, filled with tube valves and oscillators and resistors, and now recognised as the world's earliest example of a polyphonic synthesiser. The machine weighed as much as two pianos, required a weekly visit from the maintenance man of the Hammond Company and produced a sulphurous smell of room-clearing intensity whenever it blew a valve. It could, however, also provide a passable imitation of a clarinet or a euphonium or a piano, allowing a small band to produce a big sound – and, arguably, making the Dorchester ballroom the birthplace of British synth-pop.

For the Stones, a gig at the Dorchester would always be followed by supper in the courier's room beside the kitchen. There was, Joyce remembers, a feudal aspect to the catering arrangements. She and her husband would be served chicken legs by a liveried floor waiter from the restaurant. The musicians, however, would be seated at a separate table and receive something less exciting – an omelette, perhaps – from a waitress. Pudding was usually glacier-hard ice cream straight from the freezer: they gave it the nickname 'orange pneumonia' and took to carving their names in it to see if anyone else was eating the stuff. Food like this, however, became increasingly precious: the Stones were once involved in a traffic accident in central London in which their car was overturned. Joyce's principal memory of the event is of her husband combing the wreckage for the paper-wrapped cut of spring chicken he had received that evening from the Dorchester's chef.

Occasionally, they would risk a meal elsewhere: Joyce re-collected an invitation to a café on Brook Street where the Dorchester fire-watchers ate after their shift. The manager had an unexpected surplus of bacon and smoked kippers, and asked the band to assist in its after-hours demolition. 'As soon as we got inside, a time-bomb came down just outside the place. We all rather lost our appetites.' They abandoned the food and re-treated to the basement. There they waited, expecting death, hoping that the bomb-disposal squad would do their work in time. Fortunately, they did. Lew Stone and his band ran back to the concrete bosom of the Dorchester. 'I beat them all back to the hotel,' Joyce recalled. 'And I was in high heels. That's how brave I was.'

*

The Dorchester was conceived as a symbol of progressive in-ternationalism. Its internal structure, however, suggests that it was built for war. When it opened in 1932, Francis Towle's business partner, Sir Malcolm McAlpine, declared the building 'bomb-proof, earthquake-proof and fireproof'. It was as if the architects had absorbed the images of the aerial wars of the future described in the fiction of H. G. Wells and cut their concrete accordingly, creating an armoured behemoth in which tomorrow's rich might sit out the firestorms. If so, they chose well. The IRA considered trying to blow the building up, but the miniaturised pen-bombs they had been promised by their American allies failed to materialise, and they were obliged to content themselves with an incendiary at the Park Lane branch of the Midland Bank. The Luftwaffe proved unable to do more than break some of the hotel's windows. 'The Dorchester', declared the gossip columnist Bridget Chetwynd, as German bombs rained on London, 'is its own little self-contained and fairly bomb-proof world, where people can dine and dance, sleep, and then have breakfast without exposing themselves to the hazards of the night.' In his private diary, the Canadian diplomat Charles Ritchie concurred: 'I simply cannot believe that bombs would dare to penetrate this privileged enclosure or that they could touch all these rich people. Cabinet ministers and Jewish lords are not killed in air-raids – that is the inevitable illusion that this place creates.'[9]

The hotel's site, a triangular sliver of land on the edge of Park Lane, had been the location of Dorchester House, a vast Italianate palazzo built in 1853 by the art collector Robert Stayner Holford. In 1905, the American ambassador, Whitelaw Reid, acquired the tenancy; during the Great War the building was refitted as a hospital for wounded servicemen; by the 1920s, it was an architectural curiosity open to the public on written application. (As a child, Joyce Stone was taken there for tea and a tour of the arboretum: she recalls her mother's fury when she informed the butler that she did not eat margarine on her bread.) In September 1929, a syndicate of developers led by McAlpine and Towle reduced Holford's mansion to a 20,000-ton heap of disarticulated bricks, lead pipes, marble slabs and steel girders. Once the land had been cleared, three subterranean levels were sunk deep into the earth of Mayfair and sealed with a three-foot-thick raft of reinforced concrete. Above this, two thousand miles of steel rods were woven, shaped and embedded within another fifty thousand tons of concrete. 'If anyone could be equipped with eyes of X-ray penetration,' enthused McAlpine, 'to him the building would appear as one huge birdcage of interlaced steel rods, and it is interesting to know that it would be a more difficult task to take this building down than it has been to build it.'[10]

War rendered X-ray vision unnecessary. The solidity of the Dorchester was evidenced by the wealth and rank of the names in its booking ledger. Claridge's, a relatively fragile establishment, had rooms to spare: the future BBC newsreader Kenneth Kendall, then a young cadet officer in the Coldstream Guards, remembers that he was able to spend his leave in a pleasant thirty-five-shilling room overlooking Brook Street. A night on Park Lane, however, was beyond his means. The Indian novelist D. F. Karaka was obliged to secure accommodation at the Dorchester by bribing the receptionist: a packet of nylon stockings bought him a camp-bed in the banqueting suite.[11] Even Cecil King, the editorial director of the *Sunday Pictorial* and the *Daily Mirror*, struggled to find a berth – and perhaps not only because his newspapers were gunning for Edward Halifax. 'Apparently', he noted, 'a lot of jittery people, who do not regard their own houses as very stable, have moved in there.'[12] (Among them was his cousin, Esmond Harmsworth, his opposite number at the *Daily Mail*.)

Many of these bed-blockers were the bodies of the British Establishment most despised by the *Mirror* and the *Pictorial*: wealthy Cabinet ministers, dowager duchesses, plutocrats, bit-players from the court and social column. The undeserving rich. King wrote an article for the *Pictorial* on the subject, 'Grand Hotel 1940' – which was sufficiently sceptical in tone to earn him a dressing-down from Malcolm McAlpine. King was not alone in his opinion. Four weeks before the article ran, the diplomat Charles Ritchie cast an eye around the hotel and saw 'a luxury liner on which the remnants of London society have embarked in the midst of a storm . . . a fortress propped up with money bags'.[13] Cecil Beaton employed the same imagery: to him, the Dorchester was 'reminiscent of a transatlantic crossing in a luxury liner, with all the horrors of enforced jocularity and expensive squalor'.[14] If Claridge's catered to the royal and ministerial diaspora of Europe and the Savoy to the stars of show business and the fourth estate, the Dorchester, too, had its own constituency. They were the rich: *nouveau* and *ancien*; influential and marginal; landed and stateless; titled, untitled and unentitled. They had nothing in common but wealth, or a cherished history of wealth.

Perversely, many of these figures lived on the premises at the 'duchess' rate – a concessionary tariff extended to guests whose presence was calculated to increase the hotel's prestige. Halifax paid only £23 a week for his enormous suite, a policy which ensured that the highest echelon of Dorchester society conducted its business at Cabinet level. Joining the Foreign Secretary on the register was Oliver Stanley, Minister for War from January 1940, and one of the few Cabinet members who had raised his hand against the Munich Agreement. Stanley was accompanied by his wife, Lady Maureen, who had a more complicated relationship with Appeasement: as the daughter of Lord Londonderry, one of Hitler's most enthusiastic British cheerleaders, she carried the taint of Munich in her blood. In other suites above Park Lane dwelt the aristocratic pin-up Lady Diana Cooper and her faithless husband, Duff, Minister for Information; Oliver Lyttelton, president of the Board of Trade; Charles Portal, the air chief marshal; the Conservative MP Victor Cazalet, a director of the Dorchester Hotel group and liaison officer to General Sikorski's Polish government-in-exile, which resided in the hotel; Duncan Sandys, Churchill's son-in-law and Financial Secretary to the War Office, not yet known for being the likely owner of the penis at the compositional centre of the most notorious Polaroid photograph in British cultural history. (The woman in the picture, snapped on a camera borrowed from the War Office, was Mrs Margaret Sweeny, who moved into the Dorchester in April 1940, in order to give birth to her son, and stayed five years.)

Air-raid provision at the Dorchester reflected the social rank of its guests. The communal shelters in the basement, despite the partitions of yellow and pink satin, were rather too communal for some of the hotel's inhabitants. Pamela Churchill, the woman unfortunate enough to be married to Randolph Churchill, slept in the reinforced vestibule of the apartments of

the Australian Premier, Robert Menzies. Victor Cazalet converted the hotel's subterranean gymnasium and Turkish baths into
a bomb-shelter, where he slept beside his most elevated friends:
Sir George Clerk, the former British ambassador to France; Diana and Duff Cooper; Dorothy and Edward Halifax, and –
when domestic diplomacy permitted – his mistress, Alexandra
Metcalfe. 'Very quiet and safe as can be,' Cazalet recorded in
his diary; possibly because he was unaware of the sound that he
and Duff Cooper made while they were unconscious.[15] ('They
went through the whole scale of snores,' grumbled Metcalfe,
'bass, falsetto, bubbles like a boiling kettle and the swallowing
kind.'[16]) The safety of 'the Dorm', as it was nicknamed, was
also debatable: it lay beneath the drive in front of the main entrance, and was therefore utterly unprotected by the concrete
body of the building. Halifax, an observant Anglo-Catholic, imported an altar and crucifix into this small space, though this
does not seem to have been a direct response to the thinness of
the tarmac. The bombs, in any case, failed to bother him: after
three minutes of noisy yawning, he fell into a deep slumber that
the Luftwaffe could not disturb.

Around these governmental stars circulated satellites of the
most extreme variety. Sworn enemies lived inside the Dorchester's steel-and-concrete shell. Most strikingly, the wartime
Dorchester was the home of the leaders of the Zionist movement, and also to a cabal of upper-class British anti-Semites. If
you had settled yourself in the lobby on a night in 1940, you
might have spotted Margaret Greville, the red-haired illegitimate daughter of a millionaire Scottish brewer, unrestrained in
her enthusiasm for Hitler or anyone else who took a dim view
of Jews, trundling across the marble in her wheelchair. Conversely, you might equally have encountered Chaim Weizmann,
the president of the British Zionist Federation, who turned Suite
210 into a Yevisha where his supporters discussed how to persuade the National Government to establish an official Jewish
Fighting Force in Palestine. A spy at the keyhole would have

seen that Weizmann's most zealous admirers were Gentiles of distinguished stock: Lord Balfour's niece Lady 'Baffy' Dugdale and a British Army officer named Orde Wingate, a brilliant but unstable figure with a taste for raw onions, violence and nudity. (Quite self-consciously, Wingate positioned himself as the agent who would do for the Jews what T. E. Lawrence had done for the Arabs – an ambition in which he was supported by General Ironside, the Chief of the General Staff.) Jew-baiters and Zionist radicals – these people would have encountered each other in the public spaces of the hotel on a daily basis.

The paradox is explained partly by the inclusive nature of the grand hotel, and partly, I think, by the political colours of the Dorchester's directors – the men who were empowered to reduce or waive the bills of their most favoured guests. Lord and Lady Portal owed their £5-a-week third-floor semi-suite to their friendship with Sir Louis Greig, a Gentleman Usher in Ordinary to George VI and a member of the January Club, a genteel adjunct to the British Union of Fascists. Chaim Weizmann's easy terms were the work of the accommodating Victor Cazalet, who – despite being a founder member of a pro-Franco pressure group called the Friends of National Spain – was a passionate Zionist who spoke repeatedly for the cause in British public life, and a man who could hear the background buzz of anti-Semitism in the table-talk of his contemporaries. 'One knows so well,' he told the Commons in March 1940, 'people who start a conversation by saying, "Of course, I have [*sic*] a great many Jews, intimate friends who I admire and like very much, but . . ."'[17]

In the war years, that 'but' remained unedited from conversation. As Juliet Gardiner has argued, 'Anti-Semitism, a regrettably prevalent feature of thirties Britain, was not diminished by the shared threat of the blitz, nor by reports of Nazi persecution of the Jews . . . All the old smears about Jews on the make, Jews and sharp practice, were given a bitter wartime topicality.'[18] The evidence was recorded by the Mass Observation project –

in the words of the Birmingham woman who described Jews as 'parasites who live on mugs like us'; the Edinburgh man who thought them 'a scourge to mankind' that only the atomic bomb could neutralise. No such sentiments appeared in the print media or the published diaries of respectable commentators, but there is, I think, the whisper of them in some accounts of the Dorchester and its cosmopolitan clientele. For some, the hotel was too populous, too diverse, too teeming with those whose spiritual and ideological loyalties might lie somewhere beyond the broad mass of the British people. Cecil King looked upon the hotel's nocturnal inhabitants and pronounced them 'an extraordinary mixed grill'. Cecil Beaton tasted a 'mixed brew'. Charles Ritchie reflected: 'In the Dorchester the sweepings of the Riviera have been washed up – pot-bellied, sallow, sleek-haired nervous gentlemen with loose mouths and wobbly chins, wearing suede shoes and checked suits, and thin painted women with fox capes and long silk legs and small artificial curls clustering around their bony, sheep-like heads.' Ritchie knew Victor Cazalet and did not like him. ('His overbearing flouncings nonplus me,' he wrote.) The diplomat was, however, also an intimate of the biologist Miriam Rothschild, whose family he considered part of '*haute juiverie* . . . the best educated aristocracy the world had ever seen.' In the published version, at least, no 'but' appeared.[19]

Another whisper: at the end of October 1940, the press became excited by the winningly sleazy story of Josephine Green, a seventeen-year-old who, at the beginning of the war, had married a Russian businessman called Eduard Epstein. During the first year of the marriage Mr Epstein induced his bride to go to bed with an Army captain at the Grosvenor House Hotel, and to seduce a wealthy old man in the Dorchester, who provided the teenager with at least £3,000 in cash, £1,000 worth of jewellery, a fast car and a furnished flat in Mayfair. 'I am going back to a quiet family life, and shall do my best to forget what has happened in the past,' Green told the *Daily Mirror*, which pictured her sitting on the sofa of her parents' home on Park Lane. The copy-editor chose to pull out, underline and embolden four words from the story – 'Rich Jew of 75' – a phrase calculated to invoke the disgust of the reader. The three other most prominent elements on the page were a photograph of a Red Cross nurse tending a casualty on a rubble-strewn pavement, a portrait of a blond seven-year-old pulled from the ruins of a bombed house, and a report from Glasgow about a pair of convicted war profiteers with the un-Hibernian names of Max Schönbach and Benjamin Brazil.[20]

An anecdote by the poet Stephen Spender amplifies the phenomenon. In 1999, recalling the early years of the war in an article for the *Guardian* newspaper, he described the fortnight in 1940 when he became a favourite of one of the most forceful plutocrats resident in the Dorchester: Emerald, Lady Cunard, an American heiress with ash-blonde hair and a fiery tongue, who kept a three-room suite on the seventh floor, stuffed with Brobdingnagian furniture rescued from her bomb-struck townhouse at 7, Grosvenor Square. ('It made the eyes boggle,' declared Diana Cooper.) In these rooms, behind heavy brocade curtains, Buhl cabinets and marble sphinxes declared war on Sèvres urns and bookcases stuffed with leather-bound volumes of Balzac, and Cunard declared war upon her guests; whom she delighted in goading into outbursts of resistance or tears. The clutter created an obstacle course for the Dorchester's waiters and limited the hostess to a modest octet of diners, a shifting cast that incorporated Cecil Beaton, Ernest Hemingway (whom she judged 'androgynous'), Cyril Connolly, editor of the literary magazine, *Horizon*, and Spender, a shock-haired poet who had fought in Spain, where Harry Pollitt had urged him to die in order to furnish British Communism with 'a Byron'.[21]

Spender was a contributor to *Horizon* and a volunteer in the Auxiliary Fire Service. The former, not the latter, inspired Cunard's interest: she became intensely irritable when his firefighting duties frustrated her desire to have him as her poet-in-residence. Spender recalled her summoning him to the Dorchester to dine in the rooms of another resident, Daisy Fellowes. 'When we sat down to dinner,' recalled Spender, 'I took an immediate dislike to our hostess who informed me that she was suing a neighbour for £2,000 because his or her dog had shit on her carpet. Daisy Fellowes then went on to tell me how much she hated her own daughter. After this a fellow guest, Sir Joseph Addison, formerly British Minister in Prague, informed the table that he succeeded that day in preventing his Club (the Travellers) from electing as a member "a dirty little Czech Jew", by threatening to resign.'[22] Fellowes was the cocaine-bibbing heir to the Singer sewing-machine company, and well known for dismissing her third child as 'the result of some horrible little man called Lischmann'; Addison was an enthusiast for the dismemberment of Czechoslovakia, who, when once asked if he had any Czech friends, replied, 'Friends! They eat in their kitchens.'[23] Spender spent the rest of the evening trying and failing to formulate a witticism that might convey his disapproval of his fellow diners. Instead, he rose to leave the table as coffee was served, explaining that he was obliged to take the Underground back to his Fire Station. 'Well,' declared Addison, 'I hope you're not squashed to death by a crowd of Yids.' The following morning Cunard telephoned him to say that he was right to leave the party. She did not, however, invite him to another.

Most accounts of Emerald Cunard's social gatherings celebrate them as colourful bursts of eccentricity in the gloom of the wartime blackout. A litany of her enjoyably outrageous remarks has survived on the published record, and many are rightly retold. ('What do you think about incest?' she once asked a dull American businessman, before serenading him with the finale to Act One of *Die Walküre*, in which Siegmund and Sieglinde declare their forbidden love.) Isaiah Berlin, a regular at the same table, said that the most malicious game an Englishman could play was to speculate who would have collaborated if the Nazis had invaded. I find it difficult, however, not to suspect that a German victory would have left the conversation in Cunard's suite relatively unchanged – nor to contrast that suspicion with the ideas that inform the most frequently repeated anecdote concerning the Jewish inhabitants of the wartime Dorchester.

Here's how the story goes. Chaim Weizmann is in the air-raid shelter beside the Labour peer Victor Rothschild, the brother of Miriam and a scientific adviser to MI5. Rothschild is failing to reassure his three terrified young children, who are howling their way through the bombardment. Weizmann asks him why he has not despatched them to America. 'Because of their blasted name,' he replies. 'If I sent those three little things over, the world would say that seven million Jews are cowards!'[24]

Gentile or Jew, war put the wealthy in an awkward position. It wrapped their servants in khaki. It closed down their households. It restricted their movements. It placed their property at the service of the state. It required them to demonstrate their loyalty to the country or be suspected of the opposite. It compelled them to justify their existence. 'Defeatists', muttered one magazine columnist, 'pervade our "upper classes" in London like a stinking blight.'[25] The security services, though composed mainly of members of this class, put much of their energy into sniffing them out, and opened files on many of the Dorchester's best customers. Captain Leonard Plugge, for instance – owner of Radio Normandy, Conservative MP for Chatham and chair of the Parliamentary Science Committee – was identified as a potential traitor. His name is memorialised in the word still used to describe brazen commercialism in the media, and it was his interest in money that made him an object of suspicion. ('He doesn't care a damn about this country', snapped Guy Liddell, 'and is merely concerned with filling his own pockets.'[26]) A watch was also put on Plugge's wife, Gertrude, who was mistrusted for her hazardously close friendship with their neighbour, the Egyptian ambassador, Dr Hassan Nachat Pasha, a man rumoured to have gone bear-hunting with Göring before being posted to London.[27] A Society lady – Norma Dalrymple-Champneys, an expert in antiquarian books and manuscripts – was the MI5 agent assigned to report upon their activities.[28]

It was on the pages of the shiny magazines – the ones that had reported on their peacetime hunt balls and spaniel-breeding activities – that privileged Britons sought to prove their usefulness to the wartime state. Honourables and viscounts and duchesses were photographed in their service uniforms or superintending the tea-urn in refuges and reception centres. Dr Pasha let the photographer from the *Bystander* snap him as he rolled back the carpet at the Egyptian embassy for 7 a.m. rapier practice.[29] Others presented the maintenance of their pre-war social lives as a form of war-work: they lunched for England, eating modestly in grand restaurants and tolerating the smallness of the omelettes to demonstrate that Hitler was too impotent a force to disrupt the social rituals of the West End. They held fashion shows and gala nights in aid of refugees and troops; auctioned the star exhibits of their wardrobe for military charities; transformed grill rooms and cocktail bars into theatres of patriotic self-advertisement.

Let us revive one act among many. On the last Saturday of the peace, Princess Stephanie von Hohenlohe lunched alone in the restaurant of a grand hotel. The daughter of a Viennese dentist, she had married into the Austrian aristocracy and become, despite her Jewish origins, a trusted confidante of Adolf Hitler. MI6 considered her to be 'the only woman who can exercise any influence on him', and Lord Rothermere, proprietor of the *Daily Mail*, came to the same conclusion. He put her on an annual retainer of £5,000 to carry letters from London to Berlin and advance his bizarre ambition to see his son, Esmond Harmsworth, ascend the Hungarian throne. Von Hohenlohe spent much of the 1930s living at Rothermere's expense in a suite at the Dorchester, supplied at a reduced rate by the manager, Anton Bon, who was keen to have as many princesses as possible under his roof. From here she proselytised Nazism to the British aristocracy and involved herself with a dubious American banker who was hungry to secure the contract to supply the RAF with parachutes – all of which caused her security file to bulge inside its foolscap wallet. By the summer of 1939, however, Rothermere had stopped his cheques, the head porter of the Dorchester was blabbing to the War Office about the Princess's activities, and at least one of her friends felt compelled to write a letter to Scotland Yard excusing their decision to have lunch with her at the hotel. ('I am telling you this', wrote the correspondent, whose letter survives as a censored government document, 'in case some interested person might say, 'What is xxxxx doing in the Princess's company?'[30]) War had placed Von Hohenlohe beyond the pale. Her symbolic expulsion from Society was enacted in the restaurant of the Ritz and reported across the world.

'Before Princess Hohenlohe could be shown to her seat,' noted *Time* magazine, 'a murmur went up among the fashionable ladies, and a voice was heard, loud & clear above the hushed room: "Get out, dirty spy."' The command – which was ignored – came from a battery of lunching ladies who included Lady Maureen Stanley, Loelia, Duchess of Westminster, and Jean Norton, the wife of Richard Norton, a baronet's son who managed Alexander Korda's production company, London Films. 'Imperturbably, the Princess sat down,' continued the *Time* correspondent, 'and the ladies went on with their lunch. But as they departed, Mrs. Norton stopped long enough to warn the head waiter that if the Princess was not kept out of the Ritz from then on, Mrs. Norton and titled friends would go somewhere else to eat.'[31] It was the Princess who shifted: by the end of the following month, the cocktail menus of New York were absorbing her attention. Norton received her reward from fate in the form of the death of her father-in-law in his suite at the May Fair. She spent her first day of life as a Baroness scrubbing the toilets in a munitions factory.

One of the most enduring expressions of pro-war upper-class

solidarity blossomed in the Dorchester ballroom in the spring-time of the Phoney War, though its roots went back to the Great one. The Officers' Sunday Club existed to save the pipped and brocaded servicemen of the Second World War from the danger-ous consequences of their own boredom. ('An ordinary Sunday afternoon in London', pronounced Padre Bowyer, the chaplain of the RAF, 'would drive a saint to drink – if he could find one.') It was the creation of the Dowager Marchioness of Townshend, the powdered and pomaded relic of one of the most bizarre leg-al scandals of the Edwardian era. The former Gwladys Sutherst was the daughter of a radical barrister whose campaigns for the rights of shop assistants and transport workers juddered to a halt in 1898, when he was declared bankrupt. Thomas Sutherst attempted to remedy his financial woes by brokering a mar-riage between his daughter and the Marquess of Townshend, an aristocrat of doubtful mental stability, who agreed to take the hand of Gwladys under the impression that it came attached to a dowry of £3,000. When it became clear to Townshend that his new father-in-law was equally broke, the Marquess sent a pair of private detectives truffling for dirt on his bride, and Tho-mas Sutherst responded by calling in a pair of doctors to declare Townshend insane. The lawyer convinced the newly-wed that his evident derangement was a result of the sinister mesmeric influence. Weirdly, Gwladys's union with Townshend survived these painful hostilities – unlike Thomas Sutherst, who went down with the SS *Lusitania* in May 1915. As her husband des-cended into lunacy, Gwladys resuscitated the Townshend family fortunes by producing marketable romantic fiction, volumes of catchpenny epigrams, and a series of screenplays for the Cla-rendon Film Company, with plots that incorporated hypnotism, industrial disputes, fraud, madness and other aspects of her family history. She also developed an interest in philanthropy. On Sundays during the Great War, the Marchioness entertained groups of wounded officers at the Knightsbridge Hotel with hot drinks from the kitchen, high-kicks from Nijinsky and a closing number from the West End attractions Phyllis and Zena Dare.

When a new World War broke out, Gwladys Townshend was keen to give Allied officers an alternative to loitering in parks and cinemas, and convened a meeting at the Dorchester to lay out her plans: tea, cake, sandwiches and a dance-band every Sabbath afternoon in the ballroom between 3.30 and 7 p.m. A great crowd of Society ingénues and their older married relations were drilled into squads of hostesses, scouts and usherettes – co-ordinated by the Marchioness with a military precision that suggests her talents might have been put to better use in the Cabinet War Rooms. On arrival, an officer reported to the Control area and paid his three-shilling fee. From here he would be escorted to a table in the ballroom, at which he became the responsibility of a member of the Club's Senior Committee. These were Establishment females of the first water: political spouses such as Clementine Churchill and Maud Hoare; Edna Bigio, the consort of a Syrian shipping magnate; Eva Sherson, whose husband was enormous in Malayan rubber; Mrs Horace Farquharson, an experienced Society fixer who arranged expensive coming-out parties that ensured the confident launch of the dreariest debutantes; the Marchioness of Queensbury, a Royal Academician who designed the futuristic uniforms worn by the airmen in Korda's 1936 movie version of *Things to Come*. Between these tables moved their daughters and the daughters of their friends, who ensured that every officer, even those without any English, spent some time careering around the dance floor on the arm of an attractive young woman. Cabaret artists performed. Races were held, in which the first prize was an onion presented on a velvet cushion. 'Something had to be done for these thousands of lonely officers,' reflected Sylvia Schweppe, a stalwart of the Club's committee. 'They were far from their homelands and friends, and far from their loved ones, too.' In the Dorchester ballroom, they narrowed that distance – with certain restrictions. In June 1940 a committee member requested that the 'Boomps-a-Daisy' should be struck from the playlist, 'owing to the fact that so many officers were now carrying revolvers in their hip pockets'.[32] Pictures of the event demonstrate how high the body count might have been: hundreds of dancers packed the space like waltzing veal calves. As one sweaty naval captain commented, 'There were masses of lovely women but very hot dancing.'[33]

The *Tatler*, that weekly bestiary of the British Establishment, ballyhooed the club on its glossy pages. The inaugural event was captured in a spread of photographs of notable Society women attempting to show their assigned partners a good time. Emerald Cunard, caught in the middle of a laugh that gives her the appearance of someone being gassed, is pictured with a young Army captain. An older officer gazes encouragingly at the constipated features of Lady Maureen Stanley, 'a warm supporter of anything benefiting the soldier-man'.[34] (Perhaps she is thinking of her unrepentant father, sitting at home in County Down with his porcelain stormtrooper – a gift from Joachim Ribbentrop – steadfast on the drawing-room mantelpiece.) Below them, a gap-toothed naval lieutenant named Leslie Clarke seems to have drawn the long straw in the form of Lady Howard of Effingham, a luminous Hungarian beauty known in her former life as Miss Maria Gertler. 'If there had been anything in way of an Armada to defeat this time, a Howard of Effingham would have had a hand in it,' cooed the *Tatler*, betraying no knowledge of her place on the MI5 watchlist, or the financial arrangement upon which the Howard marriage was founded. (In 1938 the bankrupt peer Mowbray Howard received a lump sum of £500 and weekly allowance, paid from the bank account of his bride's real partner – Edward Weisblat, a notorious Polish arms dealer who had made a fortune selling guns to Franco during the Spanish Civil War.[35])

The *Tatler* photographer also snapped the honorary secretary of the Officers' Sunday Club, Brigadier-General Reginald Kentish, as he breathed all over the seated figure of another

Dorchester resident, the actress Diana Napier. The presence of Kentish, a veteran of the Boer War and the Somme, founder of the National Playing Fields Association and a member of the International Olympic Committee, was not a consequence of the Dorchester's wartime militarisation. He had been part of the ballroom furniture since 1932, when, during a period of financial embarrassment, he had accepted a curiously vague job from the syndicate that owned the hotel. He was supplied with his own office, a large suite and a generous allowance – though his real work was conducted, nocturnally, in the public areas of the hotel, where he smiled benignly from his table, did his best to persuade the most affluent guests to hold their private parties on the premises, and took a paternal interest in the Dorchester's resident cabaret attraction, an eight-strong line of high-kicking teenage chorines imported to Park Lane from California. The precise nature of his responsibility towards 'Les Girls', as they were billed, was the inevitable subject of gossip. The poet Robert Graves was once accused of having written to Sir Malcolm McAlpine to denounce Kentish as 'procurer to the Dorchester Girls'.[36] Kentish himself recorded that an Indian maharajah staying at the hotel had once passed him a copy of the floor-show programme, with the performer of his choice indicated by a note in the margin. (He returned the booklet with a further addition: '*Votre Altesse, je suis un Général, mais pas un Procureur-Général.*'[37]) It remains possible, however, that Kentish played some small diplomatic role in the nuptials of the cabaret dancer Rosalie Fromson and Marcus Sieff, the future chairman of Marks and Spencers, and in the marriage of Rozelle Rowland (an artiste known for her gold-painted nudity) to a Belgian industrialist, who whisked her away to his faux-Moorish palace by the Pyramids.

The dancing girls left the Dorchester with Maurice Winnick, who took them on a tour of the English provinces. However, the nudging and winking that occurred around Reginald Kentish persisted – partly due to the publication, in late 1939, of a

gleefully saucy novel by John Paddy Carstairs, in which a character called 'the Old Colonel' oversees the cabaret dancers of
a Park Lane hotel and professes his desire to 'sleep with each
and every one of them every night of the week and the whole
year round'. The gossip columnist Viscount Castlerosse told
Kentish that he had been 'libelled on every page' of *Vinegar
and Brown Paper*, and encouraged him to sue the publishers for
£5,000. Once Kentish had obtained a copy, however, he only
felt flattered by the caricature. 'To be quite honest,' he admitted,
'the thought that anyone should think that at my age – I was
over 60 at the time – I should desire and apparently be able to
perform such a physical feat, gave me a feeling of pride more
than anything else!'[38] Carstairs' novel does, however, offer an
explanation as to why Kentish was hired. 'The Colonel smiled,
sipped his champagne. It was a Veuve Cliquot '26, so he smiled
again; paused a moment to wonder how on earth he'd got the
appointment, sighed and dismissed the thought, not realising
how nice his name looked on the hotel stationery.'[39]

Joyce Stone giggled at the mention of the name of Reginald
Kentish. Her abiding memory of the man was of a portly,
balding figure in khaki, gingerly picking his way around the
ballroom in the small hours of the morning, collecting empty
wine glasses and loading them onto a tray. One of the house-
keepers, she recalled, informed her that the Brigadier-General
was not doing this to be helpful. Kentish mistrusted the strength
of the ceiling in the Dorchester gents. During air-raids, he found
the hotel glassware a convenient alternative.

*

Lew Stone declined to perform at the Officers' Sunday Club, although he did not forbid his players from appearing on its platform. For him, voluntary work for some of the richest people
in Britain did not exert a strong appeal. He also had misgivings
about the war that would have made him an uncomfortable

presence in a ballroom packed with uniformed Allied officers – particularly in the spring of 1941 when he found himself black-listed by the BBC on the grounds that 'no individual holding any views contrary to the national effort or with conscientious objections to military service should use the microphone'. He was in distinguished company: the trumpeter and arranger Phil Cardew, the bandleader Sydney Lipton, the composer Alan Bush and the actors Michael Redgrave and Ursula Jeans were also banned from the airwaves. The cause of the Corporation's displeasure was their support for the People's Convention, a vigorous but short-lived political campaign backed by the Communist Party of Great Britain, and founded by the rebel Labour MP D. N. Pritt. The Convention argued for 'defence of living standards, defence of trade union and democratic rights, adequate air-raid precautions, deep bomb-proof shelters and re-housing of victims, friendship with the Soviet Union, a people's government and a people's peace'.[40]

Some interpreted Pritt's arguments as a form of revolutionary defeatism: George Orwell considered that 'the supporters of the People's Convention came near to claiming that willingness to resist a Nazi invasion was a sign of Fascist sympathies'.[41] In January 1941 he went around London tearing down the posters advertising the group's first large public rally at the Royal Hotel in Bloomsbury. Despite his efforts, over two thousand delegates attended and the Convention quickly became a focus for popular dissatisfaction with the progress of the conflict, resentment about the continued presence in government of those who had supported Appeasement, and the suspicion that the war was being prosecuted for the benefit of a wealthy minority – 'a small group of rich and powerful controllers of our banks, our finances, our industries, our trade, our land – the men who are determined to maintain both the capitalist system and their own control of this country'.[42] Just the sort of people whose wives officiated at the Officers' Sunday Club.

Michael Redgrave gave his support to the Convention's six-point plan because it seemed 'a sound socialist document'. Phil Cardew's motives were more complex. Although he was a member of the Communist Party, a subscriber to the *Daily Worker* and a founder member of the Musicians' Union, Cardew always travelled first class and employed a bodyguard to protect him from importunate members of the public. 'My construction on his behaviour', his nephew, Seth Cardew, told me, 'was that he somehow believed that a violent revolution was coming to England from the Soviets, and he wanted to establish credibility as a long-time sympathiser.' Lew Stone presented his involvement with the Convention as serendipitous: 'A number of us in the show business were sitting in a café over our coffee when we were approached by somebody who explained the objects of the People's Convention and read to us the six points,' he told a reporter. 'We all agreed to the thing in principle.'[43]

For Joyce Stone, the decision was a continuation of the left-wing radicalism that she and her husband had evinced in the 1930s. 'We all knew that war, or something like it, was coming,' she explained. 'It started with Franco in Spain.' Describing her political awakening, she spoke regretfully of a friend who had died for the Republican cause – the young mathematician David Haden-Guest, the son of a Labour peer, shot down by a sniper as he read his newspaper. She spoke of her work for the Spanish Medical Aid Society. She spoke of the dance lessons she gave for the children at the Dalgarno Road community centre in west London, where some of the pupils turned up barefoot or knickerless. 'Sometimes I would go to the working men's college in Camden and play to the unemployed,' she recounted. 'They used to sit with their feet up on the table because their shoes were just pieces of corrugated paper. It was that bad. And then there was the other side, the very wealthy who would come to the Embassy Club or the Monseigneur or the Dorchester every night. It was a very synthetic world.'

The BBC managers who removed Lew Stone from the airwaves were quick to congratulate themselves on their efficiency.

'There can be no doubt', affirmed the Controller of the Home Service, 'that this is public non-adherence to the national war effort.'[44] The Corporation received warm support from Duff Cooper and from the *Sunday Express*. 'If a man is not whole-heartedly with us he is against us,' thundered the newspaper, 'and must be prepared to accept the consequences.'[45] Everyone else, however, seems to have found the business sinister, or ridiculous, or both. The Archbishop of York saw 'the action of the BBC as tyrannical and calamitous'. The novelist E. M. Forster, speaking of a conductor blacklisted along with Stone and Cardew, declared, 'They have treated him exactly as Hitler would have treated a musician who was a Jew.'[46] Support also came from less expected causes. Cassandra of the *Daily Mirror* had little respect for the political views of showbiz people: 'The latest Gallup survey', he scoffed, 'has shown that of all the actors and actresses who joined the People's Convention, 83 per cent thought it was a new Bridge Club.'[47] The columnist cared even less, however, for political vetting, declaring that the Corporation had treated Lew Stone and his fellow artists with 'dictatorial impudence'. ('Isn't this ban', he asked, 'part of the same wretched suppressive game that we despise so much in Germany?'[48]) A week later, Winston Churchill entered the argument, raising a few easy laughs in the Commons by suggesting that pacifist musicians should not be silenced unless they intended to broadcast 'a very spirited rendering of *Deutschland über Alles*'. That bolt of sarcasm killed the policy. It was music to the ears of Stone and his listeners – but was quickly followed by news of the worst kind: the death of Al Bowlly, killed by an enemy parachute-mine in the early hours of 17 April, as he slept in his flat on Jermyn Street. The blast blew out the windows and doors of his apartment block. Bowlly was killed by the impact of his own bedroom door.

Lew Stone's voice returned to the BBC on 21 June, with a live concert broadcast carried by Forces radio. The following day, Germany invaded Russia, an event that turned one of the six points of the People's Convention into government policy. 'Friendship with the Soviet Union' was now a theme quite suitable for the Home Service. Neither Stone nor the Officers' Sunday Club, however, remained at the Dorchester. In July 1941 the Club relocated to the Great Room of Grosvenor House, the largest banqueting suite in Europe. The following year, the band, swelled to its pre-war size, exchanged the Gold Room on Park Lane for the air bases and Army camps of Britain – where the Ministry of Labour considered them better deployed. They visited thirty-nine venues in forty-two days: through East Anglia to Lincolnshire, then Yorkshire and Scotland, as far north as Inverness. 'We never knew where we were going,' said Joyce. 'It was all top secret. If we travelled by train, they'd send a bus to pick us up from the station, which would take us down country lanes through the blackout. It was all very hush-hush.' The long tour ended in Southampton. They were rehearsing in a hotel ballroom when Churchill declared Victory in Europe. It was a raucous, joyous, unforgettable evening: the ships' sirens brayed and hooted all night in Southampton Water. Joyce woke up on the first morning of the peace and watched the gardener picking discarded condoms from the rose bushes.

*

Just as in the cases of the wine waiters and banqueting managers arrested under Regulation 18B, anxieties about the Dorchester's complement of wealthy cosmopolitans, doubtful foreigners and Communist fellow travellers eased as the fears of a German invasion abated. State paranoia does not account for every doubt expressed about the inhabitants of the concrete fortress on Park Lane. In September 1940, Vera Schalburg, a Siberian alumnus of the Folies-Bergère with a heroin habit and a political allegiance to Germany, waded out of the Moray Firth in the company of two male co-conspirators, ready to start life in Britain as a Nazi agent. Her party did not get very far – a member of the public clocked the suspicious dampness of their suitcases, which, when opened, were found to contain German sausage and a list of RAF bases. The two men were executed and Schalburg vanished, never to emerge, into the machinery of the secret state. Before that silence fell, however, the captured spy revealed that the Dorchester was her ultimate destination: she had arranged to meet a contact in the hotel to hand over a wireless transmitter, then planned to troll the lounges in the hope of extracting information from Allied officers on leave.

I have only heard, however, one story of a successful Nazi in-filtration of the hotel, and its provenance is not sound. It was told to me at the bar of the Special Forces Club, a discreet little joint tucked behind Harrods, and attributed to a recently de-ceased member of the Special Operations Executive, the secret army that conducted sabotage and subversion behind enemy lines. It concerned the Frenchman Raymond Couraud, a former gangster who had earned the *croix de guerre* in the battles of Narvik, and was training, under the auspices of the SOE, a six-man assassination squad that aspired to eliminate Rommel and other leading members of the Wehrmacht. One drunken night, Couraud got into an argument with a British colleague about the relative merits of French and English hospitality. The opin-ion of an unbiased third party, they concluded, would settle the argument. They found one patrolling a beach on the coast of Normandy: a German soldier whom they bundled into the back of a small boat, transported across the Channel and de-posited in the ballroom of the Dorchester, where, disguised in an Allied uniform, he was taken dancing and became the will-ing receptacle for a torrent of cocktails. Twenty-four hours later this accidental tourist was returned, with a blinding hangover, to the beach from which Couraud and his colleagues had ab-ducted him. The story does not record who won the bet.

I asked Joyce Stone if she thought that she had ever en-countered a genuine German spy in the coffee lounge of the Dorchester. She replied by remarking on the volume of careless talk that she had overheard – particularly from one of de Gaulle's lieutenants. Norman Kendal's suggestion that Anton Bon was a Nazi sympathiser produced a burst of derision. 'Mr Bon was a lovely man,' she insisted. It was, she said, his idea that she spent her nights in the hotel rather than alone at home; his idea to move the nightly dances from the ballroom to the safer subterranean space of the Gold Room. She also recalled his generosity to the Dorchester's staff: the bakers whom he permitted to sleep on the flour bags in the warm zone by the hotel's ovens; the fire-watchers whom he visited on the rubble-strewn roof during air-raids. 'He didn't have to go up there and do that,' she said. 'The idea that he was a supporter of Hitler is simply ridiculous.'

And to illustrate the point, she tells me the story of the day she spent in the company of a real Nazi. In the summer of 1935 she went on holiday to Bavaria with the man whom her parents wanted her to marry. They visited the Munich beer hall in which Hitler had begun his political career, a hot space full of drunken Brownshirts. They stopped for a young hitch-hiker, a bright-eyed, blond-haired member of the Hitler Youth named Kurt. The boy became their companion for the day. They gave him lunch. They photographed him with their box camera. They stopped by Lake Walchensee, rented a boat and rowed it out to the middle of the lake. At the calm centre, Joyce's fiancé asked Kurt what he thought of Hitler. Kurt looked around, as if he feared the presence of underwater eavesdroppers. 'My father has been in work for the first time since 1918,' he said. 'But we don't approve of what Hitler's been doing to the Jews.' Joyce remembers repeating these words to her parents on her return home, and listening to their dismissive reaction. And today, when she hears it said that nobody in Britain was aware of the persecution of the Jews until after the war, she tells the story of Kurt, and repeats the words that she heard in that rowing boat on Lake Walchensee in 1935. She kept the photograph of Kurt, smiling into the camera in his Hitler Youth uniform, propped on a shelf in the study. 'We knew,' she insisted. 'We just didn't want to open our eyes to it.'

Dachau concentration camp opened for business in 1933. This was not an obscure fact. Heinrich Himmler, the head of the SS, had convened a press conference to announce the opening of 'a concentration camp for political prisoners'. Reinhard Heydrich had already declared his commitment to violence: 'We must be hard on our opponents, even if we run the danger of perchance harming an individual opponent and of possibly being decried as unrestrained ruffians by a few no doubt well-meaning persons.'[49] In the years before the war, the cruelties visited upon Dachau's population of Communists, social democrats and Jews were hardly unknown. Official material produced in Germany boasted that it was possible for prisoners to appeal against the policy of forced castration. In the first months of the war, even the *Tatler* detailed the tortures carried out in the camp. War robbed Sir Norman Kendal of the chance to inspect its razor wire, to have coffee with Heydrich and Artur Nebe. In 1998, documents were released that demonstrated that at least one person had raised an objection to the visit: Denis Nowell Pritt, the Labour MP who would found the People's Convention, who, in his capacity as chair of the Howard League for Penal Reform, wrote to the head of the CID to suggest that Reinhard Heydrich was not the kind of man from whom the Metropolitan Police should be taking advice. Pritt received a curt reply. 'You are', pronounced Kendal, 'imputing sinister motives where no such motives exist.'

On the first day of September 1939, a few days after this letter was written, the BBC broadcast a report of an attack on a radio station in the town of Gliwice, on the German-Polish border. 'The German News Agency reports that the attack came at about 8.00 pm this evening when the Poles forced their way into the studio and began broadcasting a statement in Polish. Within quarter of an hour, say reports, the Poles were overpowered by German police, who opened fire on them. Several of the Poles were reported killed, but the numbers are not yet known.'[50] The attack, which became the pretext for Hitler's invasion of Poland, was a fake. The bodies recovered from the scene were concentration-camp inmates dressed in the uniforms of Polish soldiers. The SS guards who murdered them referred to the bodies as 'canned goods'. The man who supervised the operation was Reinhard Heydrich.

4

Brigades

In *Miss London Ltd* (1943), a larky comedy about an incompetent escort agency, there is a scene in which a couple endures the miserable business of dinner for two in a blacked-out West End hotel. The film's star, Arthur Askey, a spiky, garrulous Liverpudlian in horn-rimmed specs, is disguised as Romero, an excitable Italian waiter at the Hotel Splendide. 'Please forgive the potatoes being so black,' he trills, through a false moustache. 'It is a mark of respect for our head waiter. He died this morning.' When the gentleman of the party, pondering the menu, announces that he could eat a horse, Askey suggests the fricassee of beef. 'There's no need to take me literally,' comes the reply. That same year, Jean Kent, a former Windmill girl and one of the misses of *Miss London Ltd*, suffered a similar experience. The company, she recalled, was bad – a faintly lascivious Jack M. Warner, son of the film-studio founder, and a few years yet away from reading in *Variety* that his father had given him the sack. The food, however, was worse. 'I ordered something called Chef's Surprise,' she recalled. 'I should have known better. When it came it was a puff pastry case with turnip inside.'[1]

Four years into the war, most diners had lost their capacity for surprise. They had grown accustomed to eating the kind of vegetables once considered the proper diet of pigs and cows; learned to eat moussaka made with chunks of dehydrated mutton. They were blasé when confronted by dishes based on ingredients from the poacher's peacetime larder, their humble origins occluded by fancy French names. The Savoy offered *le rable de lièvre à la crème*, a saddle of hare in a creamless white-wine sauce; Grosvenor House supplied Rabbit Campagnarde ('with mushrooms if available'). Woodcock grew popular; rook less so. For Nancy Mitford, pigeon pie became such a potent symbol of wartime life that she named a novel after it. In addition to game, unfamiliar quadrupeds also laid down their lives for the table. The Savoy served roast kid with a gratin of Jerusalem artichokes. In 1942, Pierre Louis Ruette, the chef at the Waldorf, took delivery of 78lbs of horseflesh. He insisted that this meat was destined solely for the stomachs of foreign staff who had no qualms about eating it, either because this was true, or because he knew that heavy fines were imposed upon establishments that used horse, undeclared, in pies, casseroles and tournades.[2] The hotel kitchen, with its heat, its noise, its strict hierarchies and its cosmopolitanism, was not the most penetrable of professional environments.

In *Meet Me at the Savoy*, an account of the hotel written by its formidable public relations officer, Jean Nicol describes entering the kitchens of her workplace as though she had just discovered a foreign country under the foundations. 'The noisy chatter of many tongues broke round my ears and through the steam I saw the bobbing of white chefs' caps and the waving of gesticulating hands. Opposite me, through an open door, I saw a coloured man plucking chickens, the soft feathers floating down to mingle with the sawdust on the floor. Beside him a slim Chinese methodically sliced carrots into glowing discs. A group of *commis* chefs argued loudly in French as they jostled before a notice-board hung with the orders of the day.'[3] It is an exotic realm of good-natured clamour, and as true as any copy for a press release. The memoirs of a trainee chef at the wartime Dorchester, however, provide a sardonic corrective. For Clement Freud, grandson of the psychoanalyst, propelled below Park Lane in 1941, the hotel kitchen 'was a hell-hole of a huge dark dank building built regardless of inconvenience to staff'. Here, apprentices were routinely locked inside fridges, storerooms were used for assignations with waitresses, a full-time cockroach-killer slept under his desk by day and scooted about on kneepads by night, and the senior *chef de légume* was an elderly French alcoholic who garnished vegetable dishes by stuffing his mouth with chopped parsley and spitting over them. ('This was particularly effective with new potatoes,' reflected Freud, 'where the evenness of his aim made the dish look impressive.') These memoirs provide a rich, vivid, uproarious picture. Unfortunately, its author is no longer around to reveal how much it resembles historical reality.[4]

For nothing but the truth, I was obliged to ask a policeman. Leslie Amos can claim the rare distinction of having worn both Claridge's whites and Scotland Yard blue during the course of his career. Now in his mid-eighties and living in retirement on a pebbly stretch of the East Sussex coast, he is an interviewee of unimpeachable veracity. In anticipation of our meeting on a rain-lashed day in February 2007, he made detailed notes, just as he might have done in preparation for a court appearance. 'I want to get this right,' he said, flipping the pages of his notebook. 'I don't want to tell you a load of old toffee.'[5]

For Leslie Amos, the hotel trade was the family business. His father, George, was head luggage porter at Grosvenor House, and organised the convoys of cars to transport suitcases and hatboxes from Southampton docks to Park Lane. 'He used to love it there,' his son reflected. 'The palatial surroundings. All those weird and wonderful people.' The Amos family home – a modest council house in Charlton, south-east London, could not compete. 'He just used to come home to sleep.' Leslie shows me the watch that his father received on his retirement in 1959 – an engraved reward for carrying bags, marshalling portmanteaus and doffing his cap from the Wall Street Crash to the Cuban revolution.

Leslie was sixteen when he first walked through the Claridge's staff entrance on Brook's Mews – past the little office of the house detective, who was posted by the door to spot suspicious bulges in the clothes of his fellow employees. The year was 1942 and the job was a prize: each year, the top three pupils at the Westminster Technical Institute graduated straight from the classroom kitchens in Vincent Square to the tiled underworld of Claridge's. Here, in the heat that roared from banks of anthracite-fuelled stoves and the scalding steam that surged from the pressure cookers, presided Marcel Percevault, *maître chef des cuisines* – an agile, immaculate Frenchman who had known Escoffier and lost an eye in some undisclosed incident that was possibly military, possibly culinary. Percevault became Leslie's mentor, but other figures from this Mayfair Hades were still bright in his mind: the huge Italian *plongeur* who used his bare hands to scour copper pans with a mixture of sand and vinegar; the sly old-timer who asked the new recruit to hide a couple of eggs under his tall white hat, then encouraged a colleague to smack him over the head; the pastry chef who took five shillings from greenhorn staff, promising to exchange the coins for a £20 note if they could eat six of his sponge fingers without a glass of water. (Leslie managed two and a half.)

Like all large hotel kitchens in the West End of London, Claridge's followed the Brigade system founded in the 1820s by Marie-Antoine Carême and refined by Auguste Escoffier at the Savoy. The system divided kitchen staff into parties, each responsible for a different aspect of food preparation, from soup (generally considered the least auspicious) to sauces (an elite corps who understood the complexities of velouté and béchamel). Leslie was assigned to the larder, the division that prepared salads, canapés, terrines and cold *hors d'œuvres* in a cool chamber separated from the main body of the kitchen. Orders in emphatic French were issued through a speaking-tube from the work station of the *aboyeur*, whose instructions were acknowledged with a chorused reply specific to each partie. (Leslie remembers that the kitchens of Claridge's resounded to groups of men and boys shouting 'Balls!' and 'Wa-haeey!') In response to these commands, Leslie scooted over the floor in his regulation wooden clogs, coaxed lobsters from their shells, sculpted flowers from carrots, slipped the scales from salmon and embedded the naked fish in green aspic jelly. Upstairs was an unknown world to him, but he knew that when he was required to construct a Dagwood – a towering club sandwich nicknamed after a gluttonous American cartoon character called Dagwood Bumstead – that the finished product was taken on a silver tray and into the presence of the film star Douglas Fairbanks Junior, who often stayed in a suite occupied by the MGM producer Irving Asher. (Fairbanks had been a Claridge's regular since 1938, when he had conducted an affair on the premises with Marlene Dietrich and gained a necessary familiarity with the fire escape.[6])

To combat the sizzling temperatures, the management provided each member of the kitchen staff with a pint of shandy, sipped, customarily, from a heat-impervious silver sauceboat. This was one of the few concessions to comfort. 'The working conditions were awful,' Leslie admitted. 'There was shouting all the time. Bad tempers. Burns. Injuries.' He holds up a hand to show me a knife-scar still visible after seven decades. 'There was no going to hospital. They bound it up and you carried on working. Nobody sued in those days. There was no health and safety.' His kitchen colleagues could be sadistic: 'If the other chefs wanted to upset you they would throw a handful of pepper on the stove that flew up and burned your eyes.' But the waiters were worse. 'Waiters', pronounced Leslie, 'are the natural enemy of chefs' – particularly the temporary ones who came to the hotel to make up staff numbers for banquet, and would, if not watched, steal lobsters from Leslie's station and smuggle them from the building in the long pockets of their tailcoats. Nor was Leslie enamoured of the split-shift system, which gave kitchen and waiting staff a 9 a.m. start, an 11 p.m. finish and four hours off in the middle of the day, obliging him to spend winter afternoons killing time in the newsreel cinema, and the summers rowing a skiff across the Serpentine.

This arrangement did nothing to alleviate the fatigue of his war duties with the Home Guard, which first deployed him on a battery of rocket projectors on Blackheath, then at Shrapnel Barracks on Woolwich Common, where he joined the eleven-strong crew of a heavy anti-aircraft gun. The projectors fired six-foot shells packed with metal debris – broken bike chains and old razor blades – which were loosed skywards with the aim of disrupting the flight of bombers swooping upriver to the docks and the West End. The big guns aimed to bring German planes burning to the ground. It was exhausting, filthy work. 'Sometimes there wasn't time to go home and change,' he reflected. 'I'd turn up at work in uniform, with my hands all cut and covered in cordite.' In December 1943 Gunner Amos got out of the kitchen and joined the Navy. For three years, his home became the broad steel back of the aircraft carrier HMS *Implacable*. He braved an Arctic storm that put the ship in dry dock for three months, went searching in the Scapa Flow for the German battleship *Tirpitz*, raided the coast of Japan, and became used to a phenomenon of which he remembered having seen very little at Claridge's. Rationing.

*

In a total war, the supply of food exerts as much influence over the outcome as the supply of guns. More people died of starvation during the Second World War than were felled by bullets. Both Allies and Axis were aware of this possibility long before the first shot of the conflict was fired and shaped their policies accordingly, remembering how food had become a determinant of victory or failure between 1914 and 1918. The Great War offered a culinary warning from history. In Germany, rioters demanded bacon, potatoes and meat. Coffee disappeared from the smart cafés and restaurants of Berlin and was replaced by a substance synthesised from roasted nuts and coal tar. By the end of the war, the pigs were eating the nuts and the coffee was being made from turnips. In desperation, German food manufacturers pursued experiments to extract protein from dragonflies and render fat from rats, crows and cockroaches. With these memories of hunger still strong, the Nazis put national food production and dining habits on a martial footing long before the first shot of the Second World War was fired. National Socialist agricultural policy aimed for self-sufficiency. Propaganda celebrated the wholesome German apple over the decadent banana and orange. In 1938, cream cakes were outlawed.[7]

Although not nearly so savage or prolonged, Britain also endured deprivations during the Great War. In the spring of 1917, a relentless U-boat campaign against merchant shipping reduced food supplies to critical levels. Meat became scarce. A queue of three thousand people was recorded outside a grocer's on the Walworth Road. Legislation was passed to limit the number of courses in hotel and restaurant meals, but there was much scepticism about their supposed universality. In November the *Daily Herald* ran a story entitled, 'How They Starve at the Ritz', an account of the improperly long, luxurious and smoked-salmon-filled meals being eaten on Piccadilly.[8] When rationing was introduced the following spring, the lateness of the measure increased public resentment of the ubiquity of margarine and turnips.

When war came again in 1939, millions of ration books had already been printed and 1,200 local food offices summoned into being. Sugar, butter, bacon and ham became controlled substances on 8 January 1940. Meat followed in March, then tea, cheese, margarine, lard, jam, sweets and chocolate. The coupons entitled every adult to the same minimum weekly amount, regardless of circumstances or occupation – whether they were hacking coal under the Rhondda or shuffling papers within lunching distance of a West End hotel. For the Ministry of Food, this was the blindness of justice. 'Fair shares all round' was the mantra of Lord Woolton, appointed Minister for Food in April 1940. Hungry dockers and labourers and miners who came home every night to a modest dinner – supplemented, probably, by some of their wife's share – saw it differently. Meals eaten out were not included in the ration: guests at the Savoy and the Dorchester could eat handsomely without being obliged to surrender a single coupon. Although patrons of cheaper establishments also benefited from this rule, that did little to allay the popular suspicion that, within expensive restaurants and grand hotels, the rationing laws were in miraculous abeyance. 'Restaurants, and particularly the more luxurious ones,' Woolton later recalled, 'were popularly supposed to have all the food their clientele demanded. It was not true: but it was a political issue which, with all the egalitarianism of rationing, could not be ignored.'[9]

Alan Lascelles, the King's equerry, identified the Minister for Food as 'the only man in the Government at whom I have never heard anybody express the desire to throw a brick'.[10] But Woolton's words of denial invite some kind of missile. The clientele of London's grand hotels did not always need to make demands. Customers with country estates might arrive with their own produce: salmon fished from their own rivers; venison shot on their moors. The Savoy had its own poultry farm, which ensured that rehydrated egg was not as salient a feature of its menu as that of the Lyons Corner House across the road. Although there are accounts that mention the 'vile' powdered-egg omelettes served at Claridge's, the yolk under Leslie Amos's hat suggests that eggs were plentiful enough on Brook Street.[11]

Black-market food was available to modest West End diners – a café in Covent Garden market supplied egg-and-bacon sandwiches to customers who asked for a 'biscuit' – but such transactions attracted less opprobrium than their dinner-dressed equivalents on the Embankment. The perceived transgressions of luxury establishments were made unignorable by popular journalism. Under the celebrated pseudonym of William Hickey, Tom Driberg, the Labour MP, Communist informer and connoisseur of the gentlemen's conveniences of London, conducted a campaign against his fellow diners on the Strand

and Park Lane through his column in the *Daily Express*. In the first fortnight of the war he mocked the red-inked addition to the menu of the Ritz, which warned, 'Owing to heavy increase in cost, caviar can no longer be included in fixed price meals and will be charged at an extra 9/– per person.'[12] The following year he detailed his easy procurement of rationed products from the staff of the Savoy. (The hotel protested, but the mud stuck.) In November 1942 he posed a Parliamentary question to the Minister of Fuel and Power, asking him 'whether he will state the names and addresses of the owners of the private motor-cars whose registration numbers are HPD 849, FYL 480, GKE 465, GGO 280, COW 648, EYR 248, FOJ 373, GPL 892, EOV 524, HVW 440 and JPD 713, all of which vehicles were between 1.30 p.m. and 3 p.m. on Friday, 16 October, outside the Savoy Hotel, a place readily accessible by public transport'.[13] Cassandra, his opposite number at the *Daily Mirror* joined the offensive. 'If you have money,' he declared, 'you can say "To hell with rations", laugh at food coupons – and eat as much RATIONED FOOD as you wish.' The front page was a report of heroic consumption: 'Within five days I have eaten at least seven times my weekly meat ration, five times my bacon ration, nearly half a pound of butter, and have had so much sugar that I couldn't eat it all. Not content with this debauch, I have swallowed saddle-of-hare in wine sauce, lobster thermidor, the inevitable (if you live that way!) caviare, Hungarian pork goulash, quails-in-aspic and truffled goose livers. In addition, I have climbed outside two dozen oysters and a considerable quantity of fish, ranging from smoked salmon, by way of tunny, sardines and anchovies, to an enormous Dover sole.' Much to the distress of Jean Nicol, George Reeves-Smith and their colleagues, the Berkeley and the Savoy hotels were the only institutions mentioned by name. Aghast, Nicol rushed around the kitchens of the Savoy, took notes on the soup being brewed from fish-heads and the canapés cut from unglamorous vegetables, and circulated them to journalists. But according to Clement Freud, Cassandra's scepticism was common below stairs in the very hotels that he had criticised. 'When your weekly salary was what they spent on a portion of grilled lamb cutlets with Broad Beans à la Crème and allumette potatoes, the feeling that we were part of the same human race flew out of the window,' he wrote. 'We hoped the bombs would kill our customers.'[14]

Official sensitivity to such feelings may explain why the Ministry of Food developed the habit of launching its new initiatives at West End hotels, as if to demonstrate that the food of the rich was as proscribed as that of the poor. Thirty days before bacon went on the ration, the Ministry invited journalists to the Savoy Grill for a taste of its official substitute, which was scheduled to go on sale that week; cured mutton jiggered into dark, streaky rashers in the smokehouses of T. H. Wall and Son, the nation's favourite purveyors of pork sausages and vanilla ice cream. Over brunch, Cecil Rodd, Wall's public relations man – the genius who coined the slogan 'Stop me and buy one' – led the cheers for the product, describing how the company's cooks had conducted tests with sheep carcasses and produced meat in both rasher and ham form. A cooking demonstration was given by Miss M. Baron Russell, who marshalled slices of the stuff around a grill pan and informed her audience that the longer it sizzled, the better it tasted. However, the true *éminence grise* of the state-sponsored wartime mutton rasher – and of the Savoy event – was Frederick Alexander Macquisten, the squeaky-voiced Conservative MP for Argyllshire who had first proposed its mass production. 'We read that the devil entered into swine,' he pronounced, 'but we never heard of the devil entering into sheep.'[15]

In his long and peculiar career on the backbenches, Macquisten had campaigned for lighter taxes on the whisky industry; for the abolition of Gretna Green marriages; for the criminalisation of lesbian sex. He also led a one-man crusade against pasteurised milk, which he believed was destroying the fertility of British women. ('Give it to rats and they fail to reproduce their species,' he averred. 'It is a form of birth control.') Few of his proposals were entertained by Parliament until November 1939, when he had the good fortune to make one that coincided with an unannounced government policy. Most of the bacon consumed in Britain was imported from Denmark and Canada, but increasing domestic production during wartime was a risky strategy, owing to the similarity of the human and porcine diets. As sheep do not compete with people for grain and potatoes, the Ministry of Supply had already decided that mutton might provide a palatable alternative to bacon. When Macquisten advanced the same argument in the Commons, Alan Lennox-Boyd, the Chancellor of the Duchy of Lancaster, was forced to concede that 'an experimental cure' was being arranged. 'Is the Honourable Gentleman aware that I have eaten the product,' trilled Macquisten, 'and that if his bacon people cannot make it, any farmer's wife in Perthshire will tell them how to do it?' To the intense annoyance of those working on the project, the Member for Argyllshire also gave the product a name. 'That fool Macquisten nearly spoilt the market by calling it "macon", which sounds silly,' raged Tom Johnston, Regional Commissioner for Scotland. Mutton-bacon sounds much better.'[16] But the name stuck.

Early samples of the product were supplied to the Savoy, the Dorchester and Grosvenor House, whose chefs conducted their own tests under the gaze of photographers. 'West End Chefs try their art on Macon,' exclaimed the *Daily Express*, as it recorded their responses. 'Marvellous,' cooed Oscar Muller, *sous-chef* at the Savoy. 'You can hardly tell the difference.' (Ruebens Richard, *maître chef* at the Dorchester, was less enthusiastic: 'Hmm,' he rumbled. 'Faint taste of sausage about it.'[17]) The Savoy maintained its enthusiasm by lending a chef to cook strips of home-cured macon sent in by readers of the same newspaper. Macquisten, inevitably, was the judge, but the Savoy's man agreed that Wallace Cheney from Littlehampton had produced something 'almost as good as Wiltshire bacon'.[18]At the first secret Commons debate of the war – a seven-hour discussion of supply problems – the press was permitted only to report that Members of Parliament had sustained themselves by eating sixpenny packets of macon-filled 'Secret Sandwiches for Secret Sessions'.[19] The following week, the Grand Hotel in Scarborough held a 'macon-and-egg supper' to raise money for the local hospital – and wangled themselves an extension of the licensing hours, on the grounds that it was 'much more salty than pig bacon'.[20] By the time of the official launch at the Savoy, the term was irremediably attached to the product. 'I do not pretend to know where the name came from,' said Cecil Rodd, disingenuously, to the reporters gathered in the Grill. 'It just happened.'[21]

The Savoy's endorsement failed to save macon's bacon. Government-funded production was halted after less than two months. At the end of February an official from the Ministry of Food conceded that he 'did not think there was really any demand for it'.[22] It is impossible to know what effect this had on the Member for Argyllshire, whose name had become suddenly synonymous with an unloved meat product. Three days after the government abandoned his idea, however, Frederick Macquisten died at his home in Walton-on-Thames, felled by a severe haemorrhage that occurred during a bout of bronchial pneumonia from which he had been expected to recover. 'Macon MP is dead,' said the obituaries.[23]

*

The Savoy's involvement in a second Ministry of Food campaign was much more successful. Not many people actually liked Woolton Pie – 'Fit for the pig pail,' said one unhappy consumer – and even fewer may have deigned to put one in their own oven. Ordering it in restaurants, however, and pretending to enjoy it, seems to have provided middle-class diners with a way of making a public demonstration of virtue. Even Lord Woolton, after whom it was named, was suspected of feigning enthusiasm on the many occasions he was photographed chewing his way through a portion. 'There may have been those who were not convinced by the smile, the look of relish directed at the morsel on the fork,' reflected an editorial in *The Times*, 'but they were of that obstinate and sceptical breed who, when faced with the medicine of childhood, refused to believe in the sleight-of-hand tricks of such parents as Mr Darling, tricks designed to show that they themselves found it delicious.'[24]

The recipe was devised by François Latry, the Savoy's short-legged, foul-tempered *maître chef des cuisines*. Latry had worked under the Strand since 1919, during which time he developed a reputation for conceiving dishes of insane finesse and complexity. For a naval officers' reunion dinner, he concocted a salad from chrysanthemum petals and spiced oil. For Arthur Conan Doyle and Hilaire Belloc, he filled crayfish with foie gras and braised a turbot in a kettle of vintage burgundy. For two French friends and their newborn baby, he cast an Easter egg large enough to enclose a full-sized cot. For a wealthy German industrialist, he constructed a smaller chocolate egg that, by use of minute hooks and pulleys, caused it to hatch out a diamond pendant. Woolton Pie, by contrast, was a confection of stewed swede, turnip and cauliflower concealed beneath a lid of short-crust pastry or mashed potato. Steak and kidney pie without the steak or the kidney. Although it instantly became a byword for anything indigestible – the radio critic of the *Listener* dismissed George Bernard Shaw's play *Androcles and the Lion* as 'the saddest piece of Woolton pie that we have had from the microphone for many weeks' – Latry's pragmatic creation became a fixture of the menu at communal canteens, at hotel restaurants, and at the Savoy, where it was served with *cabbage à la Woolton*.[25] It was the equality of suffering, conjured in root vegetables – though some establishments took it more seriously than others. 'I had some Woolton Pie this week in a

London hotel, but it had taken on French airs and was called "Le Woolton Pie",' revealed the Cassandra column of the *Mirror*. 'Maybe that's fine, but it can't stand on its own legs as the backbone of a meal in this particular hotel. When I ordered it, the waiter anxiously asked what I was going to have as the main course.'[26]

The dawn of Woolton Pie was strictly timed. In went on the menu in March 1941, just as the Food (Restriction on Meals in Establishments) Order came into force, capping the price of a three-course restaurant dinner at five shillings. Luxury foods, however, escaped regulation. Those that could afford the surcharge were not denied their lobsters and oysters and caviar – though the Ritz, at least, took pains not to embarrass their less wealthy patrons, by supplying a menu denuded of the premium items. Occasionally, however, small acts of redistributive justice did occur under the chandeliers. For the New Year's Eve party of 1941, the management of the Dorchester printed a novelty menu on pieces of cardboard no larger than a postage stamp – which gave, in a minuscule typeface, an account of turtle soup, beluga caviar, fillets of sole, *tournades de bœuf*, *poires Belle Hélène* and Stilton. Clement Freud, promoted from subterranean drudgery into the twinkling overworld of the restaurant, calculated that most of the diners at his table would be incapable of reading these words, and neglected to supply one of the courses. As a chorus of 'Auld Lang Syne' rang through the public areas of the hotel, he retired to a storeroom and ate his way through ten portions of beluga.[27]

As it had for Macquisten, François Latry's work with the Ministry of Food became his epitaph. 'Woolton Pie creator dies' was the headline in *The Times* when he expired in 1966.[28] He may not have resented this. Although his instinct was for extravagance, Latry did not regard the war simply as an inconvenient restraint upon his artistry. According to Stanley Jackson, 'Although he might well sigh, "*Où sont les sorbets neiges d'antan?*" he had no sympathy for dowagers who mourned

Lapsang Souchong or businessmen in reserved occupations cajoling for extras.'[29] He instructed his waiters: 'Tell them it's steak or ships.' This was not an abstract patriotism. Latry's son, Roger, was a British agent who fought with the Maquis, was captured and tortured by the Gestapo and despatched to the Bergen-Belsen concentration camp. Belsen was not conceived as a place of extermination. Until the end of 1944, it was one of the few camps in which the prisoners received a food ration above starvation levels. In the spring of 1945, however, that policy was terminated. In the last few weeks of the war, a thousand inmates were dying each day from the effects of disease and hunger. When the camp was liberated by British troops in April 1945, they found the ground littered with decomposing corpses. Roger Latry was not among them. He had survived those final foodless weeks. He also claimed to have survived a more literal sentence of death. The date for his execution had, apparently, been set for 17 April 1945. The British arrived on the 15th.

5

Cons

Who notices the Charing Cross Hotel? Hidden above the heads of London's commuters, it is as prominent and unregarded as the purloined letter in the Poe story. The first-floor coffee lounge, with its terrace in white and green wrought iron, commands a view of the Strand and Trafalgar Square – but nobody returns its gaze. The lounge is the perfect place for an off-the-record briefing. On 22 May 2002, the BBC reporter Andrew Gilligan met the former United Nations weapons inspector David Kelly to hugger-mugger over the British government's case for war in Iraq. They ordered Coke and Appletiser, and began a conversation that would result in the sacking of Gilligan and the suicide of Kelly. At the Ritz, someone from MI5 might have clocked them.

The Charing Cross is emphatic in its separation from the station below. It has extended an arm across Villiers Street to an annex on a separate site: a steel pseudopodium in the Italianate style. Only the lobby – a space of floral-patterned armchairs and inoffensive contemporary art – deigns to make contact with the ground. Life on the concourse of Charing Cross is hardly polite. The appetites of its inhabitants are focused on pleasures other than tea and sandwiches in a place with a carpet: the commuter husband trying to stuff a sly Bacon Double Cheeseburger without besmirching his tie with incriminating lard-spots; the shambolic smack addict cadging his fare home; the hare-eyed cottager biding his time by the cash machines opposite the gents. Above them, the Charing Cross Hotel keeps its nose in the air and stares steadily towards the bell-tower of St Martin's.

It has, however, no business to be so squeamish. The South Eastern Railway Company built the place in 1865, to serve the needs of its passengers. Some of the rooms had balconies overlooking the concourse: the spectacle of steam and coal-smuts was as good as a sunset. In its early years, demand for beds outstripped supply – which discouraged the employees from treating their guests as anything more than an encumbrance. The place became so notorious for the incivility and incompetence of its personnel that the management was forced to cull the worst offenders from the register, simply to bring an end to an embarrassing series of letters in the newspapers.[1]

Seventy years later, this bloody-mindedness was directed against the Germans rather than the guests. Instead of retreating to the basement shelters, Betty Hughes, a young waitress from Port Talbot, used the wail of the air-raid sirens as a cue to escape her duties in the first-floor coffee lounge and take a hot bath on the firm's time. She took a long soak on the night of 17 April 1941, the heaviest night of bombardment that the Luftwaffe had yet inflicted on London. The building received a direct hit. On the Hungerford Bridge, Lieutenant Ernest Gidden watched the hotel burn as he attempted to defuse an unexploded parachute-mine that had become fused to a live electric rail under the main signal gantry of Charing Cross station. Walking the Strand, Allan Nevins, a visiting American academic, saw the flames thrash over the roof of the hotel. Above them both, Betty Hughes' attic room was completely destroyed. In the communal bathroom at the end of the corridor, however, the waitress, her towel, her dressing gown and her washbag survived unscathed. To settle her nerves, the management slipped her a cheque for £40 – the biggest tip of her career.[2] Lieutenant Gidden – after flipping a lump of molten metal from the casing of the mine and chiselling out the clockwork fuse – received the George Cross.[3]

If, historically, some of the hotel staff had taken a sceptical view of their responsibilities, neither were the guests above reproach. Like the concourse of the station below, the public areas of the hotel supported a thriving criminal ecosystem of scavengers, opportunists and predators. Perhaps it still flourishes – though I have loitered here and seen nothing more suspicious than a forgetful tourist who left without paying her bill. Among those bagged by the police among the potted palms were Francis Scaivé, a former police surgeon who made a second career of pawning umbrellas lifted from the reading room, and Rudolph Lamprecht, an engineer who practised a scam with the use of a forged document claiming that he had been awarded a contract to supply the French government with automated pillar boxes.[4] Others escaped justice: in 1872, the smoking room was searched for Russian anarchists when an official from the City of Moscow Gas Works vanished from his room, apparently under intense pressure from some shadowy political organisation. (Before he disappeared, R. J. Bauer posted an enigmatic and mendacious note to a colleague: 'Having no choice left but either to do things against which my whole soul revolts, and which I find utterly impossible to do, or to die myself, I have chosen death, and shall die some hours hence.'[5]) A pistol in the mouth was the preferred exit strategy for a bigamist and fraudster who, as the Great War began, went from Charing Cross to the morgue under one of his many aliases – the retired American major Henry Cecil Fitzgerald. (Although he had genuine combat experience in the Spanish-American War, the bogus major's most valorous battles were fought against the cashiers of Europe's casinos.[6])

*

The Second World War brought a formidable old beast prowling through the coffee lounge: Sir Curtis George Lampson, an impecunious baronet of American descent, and the most aristocratic con-artist of his generation. His grandfather, Curtis Miranda Lampson, had been ennobled for his part in the laying

of the Atlantic cable; his father had put his energies into producing twelve illegitimate children. Being the first male child born
in wedlock, Curtis was destined to collect the Lampson baronetcy, which apparently inspired a murder-plot against him in his
first days of life – concocted by his eldest sister Nina, whom
he regarded as 'the most venomous and vitriolic of the illegitimate children'. Although he was only nine years old when he
inherited his title, Curtis quickly learned to appreciate its occult
power. At Charterhouse, he recalled, 'boys, who had embarked
upon mild bullying, sought my company. Masters became almost respectful. I was taken to garden parties and local bazaars
to be led around, like a peke on a chain, and introduced to hosts
and hostesses, with due emphasis placed on the prefix to my
name.'

He would spend the rest of his life attempting to spin such
snobbery into gold. When working for a firm of telephone san-
itisers, his title ensured that a cold call was put straight through
to the managing director – who was usually willing to flip open
the diary on his command. When employed by Thomas Cook
to guide American tourists around London, his title guaranteed that his charges hung on every word. When engaged as
a sales rep for Thomas Beecham, farmers were fascinated to
discover that a baronet had come to the gate to declare that
Vacho was the most effective treatment for bovine mastitis.
When convalescing from the effects of dysentery and malaria,
the Lampson baronetcy gave him the opportunity to endorse a
health tonic called Dr Paulin's Vitamina. ('I appear to be normal
again,' he enthused in a testimonial printed next to a photograph that appeared to depict him using a boa constrictor as a
chest-expander.[7])

These manipulations were, of course, perfectly legal. The police had no interest in whether Sir Curtis used his heritage
to persuade readers that a patent nerve tonic could remedy
'loss of Vitality, Insomnia and terrible stomach trouble'. They
did, however, express curiosity about another of his business

strategies: his decision to spend the first few months of the war sitting in the first-floor coffee lounge of the Charing Cross Hotel, telling credulous young men that a commission in one of the less bullet-pocked parts of the armed forces could be theirs – for a few fat envelopes of used oncers.

*

Sally Milwidsky knows her grandfather was a reprobate – a figure whose irrepressible energies found few legitimate outlets and produced little genuine success. Sally saw the best and the worst of Sir Curtis, and althought she shares no fund of fond anecdotes about the time they spent together during her childhood, she is perfectly capable of discussing him without a shudder. She recalls him with the air of sneaking admiration that is often reserved for the black sheep of an otherwise respectable family, and even shows signs of high amusement as she recounts family stories about his rackety life: his enthusiasm for Jazz Age parties at which guests turned up naked with evening dress painted onto their bodies; his dealings with the blood-drinking libertine Aleister Crowley, whom he encountered at the Café Royal; his habit of ignoring bills sent by his daughter's school, which obliged Sally's mother, Sophy, to wave goodbye to newly made friends at the end of each term.

Sally is my point of contact with the Lampson family. I hoped to talk face-to-face with Sophy, too – but after reading a copy of a police report on her father's activities, she changed her mind about giving an interview. ('I'd be afraid of what I might say,' she told me.) With Sally, I find myself enthusing about Sir Curtis like a wet-eyed fanboy. 'Your grandfather was a rogue,' I suggest. 'I think', she replies, 'there was more to him than that.' Proving the point, she hands me a thick sheaf of dog-eared typescript. Its pages are dense with handwritten corrections – and bookmarked, I notice, with small ads clipped from the columns of British newspapers in the 1960s, several of which bear line drawings of topless women. This is *A Pot-Pourri of Thoughts and Deed* – Sir Curtis's unpublished autobiography. Sally puts the kettle on, leaving me to puzzle over its eccentricities and improprieties.

*

The life of Sir Curtis Lampson was a project of intoxicating oddness. He took a film crew from Senegal to Timbuktu. He took cocaine in Paris. He endured accidental castration at the hands of the NHS. He endured financial ruin when he sank his savings into *Gentle Shepherd*, an opera that closed after fourteen performances in Scotland. In his youth he campaigned for the rights of working women – particularly good-looking ones in crisply ironed uniforms. Late in life, he campaigned for the accurate labelling of bust-enlargement cream. He was an explorer, journalist, playboy, soldier, bank-teller and television playwright. When making one of his regular visits to the criminal courts, he gave his profession as 'lecturer' – but his talks attracted rather less attention than his public appearances as a bankrupt, bilker and bill-dodger. His course of lectures on *Life in Latvia*, for instance, was a dismal failure: 'The public did not support them', he explained, 'owing to the wireless and other attractions.'[8] But he was no Professor Moriarty. His form suggests that he was a man who, rather than joining the queue at the Labour Exchange, preferred to employ his aristocratic background in the pursuit of small-time swindles. His most extravagant crimes were committed in Prohibition-era Washington, where he supplied sly bottles of bootleg liquor to a thousand thirsty clients – two of whom were high-ranking types at City Hall.[9] Once Sir Curtis had resettled in England, however, the recorded offences became more prosaic: attempting to use a platform ticket to ride a train from Victoria to Folkestone; drink-driving in Sevenoaks; stinging a Birmingham businessman for £75 by promising to help him peddle cut-price cigarettes to the stately homes of England; fined for being drunk and disorderly in the Edgware Road, declaring, '*Heil Hitler!*' and 'Down with the Jews!' The generosity of the victim kept his most ambitious crime of this period out of court. In September 1939 the Quaker philanthropist Alice, Lady Waddilove signed over £3,000 to Sir Curtis and his associates, ostensibly in aid of the Women's League of Unity, a charitable organisation under the auspices of a feminist journal called the *Women's Newspaper* – a publication that did not exist. Lady Waddilove declined to press charges, saving herself and her deceiver from public humiliation.[10]

Sir Curtis refined his talent to mislead during his late teens, under the mentorship of the most audacious con-artist of the age: Horatio Bottomley, Independent Member of Parliament, press magnate and, proverbially, 'the greatest crook in England', who, before his fall in 1922, enriched himself with four decades of scams and swindles, many operated through rigged competitions and lotteries run on the pages of his mass-circulation weekly newspaper, *John Bull*. Rich, well-connected widows were one of Bottomley's lifelong interests: the carpet beneath Lady Lampson's coffee table, therefore, was a place he was keen to put his feet. Sir Curtis presumed upon this family connection while he was engaged in his crusade to improve the wages of young women employed in the catering business. It was a post-coital conversation with a waitress from the Lyons Corner House in Holborn that awakened his social conscience. 'She spoke of the conditions under which Nippies were forced to work,' he wrote, 'long hours, remuneration totally inadequate for a normal existence from which deductions were made, and which forced many of these teenage girls, living away from home, to augment their earnings by bestowing favours upon men who were willing to pay for them.'[11] Appalled by these revelations, Sir Curtis persuaded the assistant manageress of another Lyons establishment to spend a weekend with him in a hotel in Brighton, discussing pay and conditions. Armed with this information, he employed his title to gain an interview with the secretary of the Lyons firm at Cadby Hall, the company's vast headquarters in west London, where thirty thousand staff toiled twenty-four hours a day to produce sausage rolls and fondant fancies for the nation. The Baronet was ejected with a flea in his ear.

Horatio Bottomley, however, listened with interest to his findings, ran the story in *John Bull* under the title 'Slaves in Uniform', and sent Sir Curtis to follow up this exposé with investigations into the underpayment of nurses, the misappropriation of landed estates for agricultural purposes, and the confinement of sane patients in psychiatric hospitals. *John Bull* thrived on the aggressive reporting of sharp practice by other companies and individuals; it made an excellent smokescreen for Bottomley's own illegal activities, and was sometimes useful as an aid to blackmail. Shortly after 'Slaves in Uniform' appeared on the pages of *John Bull*, the firm of J. S. Lyons put the paper's proprietor on a yearly £500 retainer – for services unspecified in the company's accounts.[12] This was the lesson that Curtis Lampson learned from Horatio Bottomley: that a good confidence trickster was not a discreet, subtle worker, but a creature of noise and bravado.

The Baronet's *Pot-Pourri* is an expression of that bravado: elements of its story may be pure fantasy, but the fact that Sir Curtis was willing to commit them to typing paper says much about what went on inside his head. Much of the material relates to his romantic life. At the age of seventeen, he writes, he began an affair with a young woman who worked behind the counter of a shop in Sloane Street that specialised in the sale of women's riding habits – and got her pregnant. 'Like father before me I scorned the use of the condom,' he explains, 'with the result that shortly after commencing cohabitation with Alice I found myself faced with a predicament, which, at first, appeared insurmountable.' His mother helped to make it more surmountable, listening silently to her son's confession, pulling the chequebook from her satinwood bureau and providing him with a hundred guineas to pay the fees of an expensive young abortionist in Hammersmith. Lady Lampson was less accommodating when, three years later, the gossip column of the *Daily Mail* speculated on her son's dalliance with a Drury Lane chorus girl called Doreen, with whom he was spotted in the Savoy Grill. A Lampson council of war was convened and ruled to pack him off to Canada with £25 in his wallet – which, thanks to a card-sharp he encountered on his crossing, did not stay there for long. Arriving penniless in the New World, he was forced to pawn his musquash-lined overcoat in order to pay his hotel bill. After a spell licking envelopes in a bank in Winnipeg, he attempted to build a career in farming – but this was cut short by a violent incident, the details of which he altered with the passage of time: he told his family that he had used a pitchfork to kill a man in self-defence; later, he informed the *Sunday Pictorial* that he had sunk a branding iron into the face of a farmhand 'who had given a venereal disease to a girl of seventeen'. Whatever the truth of the matter, he quickly abandoned agriculture in favour of property speculation – and when that venture collapsed, returned to his homeland, where his old mentor Horatio Bottomley was making a memorable contribution to the war effort. *John Bull* printed detailed accounts of fictional German atrocities, catchy slogans such as 'Hang the Kaiser!', and editorials that advised readers, 'If by chance you should discover one day in a restaurant that you are being served by a German waiter, you will throw the soup in his foul face.'[13] Still only twenty-four years old, Sir Curtis joined up – though in the course of the conflict, he seems never to have fired a shot in anger.

The Baronet's military record suggests that he considered a black mark fair exchange for whooping it up on the town. The War Office file that describes his career as a lieutenant in the transport section of the Royal Army Service Corps notes that he was acquitted of an alleged misdemeanour involving a number of dud cheques and the irate manager of the De Vere Hotel, Kensington – and also preserves his feeble excuses after an unauthorised night of drunken shore leave on Malta. ('Although the manager of the hotel told me that I had been called at an early hour,' he declared, after crashing out halfway home from a rowdy carnival night at the Maltese Royal Opera House, 'I do not remember having been called, and I did not wake until 10.30 a.m.') Sir Curtis's own account of his career in khaki, however, is at variance with the surviving records. There is, for instance, no official evidence to support his claim to have received a shrapnel-wound in Flanders. He was, however, judged unfit for duty for most of 1917 and billeted to Nashenden House, near Chatham – where, despite a doctor's suspicion that his condition was being exacerbated by the effects of secondary-stage syphilis, Sir Curtis found the strength to conduct a six-month affair with the lady of the manor, Dorothy Upton. According to Dorothy, her husband, a surgeon at the Royal Naval Hospital at Rochester, terminated the affair by pulling out his service revolver and inviting his wife to leave the house via the kitchen door.[14] Sir Curtis, it seems, stayed on for another month, eating toast and marmalade each morning at the breakfast table of the man he had cuckolded, while Mrs Upton sat forlorn in her mother's bungalow in Shoreham-by-Sea and consoled herself by seducing the lodger.

Sir Curtis's passions were focused upon factory girls, chambermaids, shop assistants and Nippies: 'Close proximity to flannel drawers aroused tense excitement,' he writes in his memoir, 'whereas a pair of frilly panties left me unmoved.' And in his choice of a wife, Sir Curtis remained true to these principles. Maud Wrigley was working as a waitress when she met the Baronet in a florist's shop on Ealing High Street. They married in October 1920, shortly before he embarked upon another new career – that of a gentleman explorer. In 1921 he tested a four-man collapsible boat in the Camberwell canal and by the following year he had raised sufficient funds to mount an expedition to West Africa – backed by a respected film producer and a former Bulgarian ambassador to Britain. Probably quite wisely, Maud – or Bunny, as she was usually known – preferred to idle in hotels on the continent while her husband spent the best part of a year travelling through equatorial regions pursuing his interests in big game, crowbar archaeology and pubescent girls. According to the *Pot-Pourri*, Sir Curtis observed the habits of the pygmy gorillas of Gabon, socialised with the Tuaregs, mounted a camel train in Egypt, and stopped for several months in the oasis settlement of Siwa, deep in the Libyan desert, where he married a twelve-year-old local, supplying her father with a dowry of a tarpaulin, six Army blankets, a case of bully beef and £10 in Egyptian currency. If this betrayal was more than a fantasy, Bunny may have returned it in kind. The couple had a daughter, Sophia, in 1935. Towards the end of her life, Bunny insisted that Sophy was the product of a fling with W. H. Auden. (This relationship has eluded any biographers of the poet.)

'My swansong' is how Sir Curtis's memoir describes the meeting in the Charing Cross Hotel that began the unravelling of his criminal career. He died before he could develop the story from his notes, but his intentions are clear. 'Prosecution [was] used for publicity purposes to stop what was known to be going on,' he affirmed. 'Will prove that I was completely innocent.' In the mid-1960s, as part of this effort to clear his name, he wrote to the Metropolitan Police to check the details of his trial. His police file is now in the public domain. But I stumbled on more material relating to the case inside documents relating to his principal accomplice. Trapped within a concertina of legal paper was a fat Scotland Yard report, sealed in an envelope marked, 'To be opened only by the official receiver.' And these documents reveal the process by which Sir Curtis met his nemesis at the Charing Cross Hotel – in the form of a short-sighted magnesite dealer called Henry.

In 1940 Henry Andreae was twenty-four years old. He wanted to serve his country, but he wanted to vault straight into the officers' mess without having to bother with any of that dreary square-bashing or floor-scrubbing. Deal-making came naturally to him. He was a salesman for a firm that supplied magnesium-rich alloys to the aeronautical industry. More importantly, he was a scion of a powerful international banking family – the most prominent of whom was his uncle Herman, a senior board member at the City firm of Kleinwort and Sons. In the square mile, Herman Andreae's uncompromising nature was legendary: in 1900 he was entirely unflapped to discover that he had arrived in China in the middle of the Boxer rebellion; in 1923 he was similarly unbothered by the flak he received after having the bad grace to beat the King in a yacht race at Cowes and then write to *The Times* congratulating himself on his achievement. His nephew was not so consistently fearless. He was, however, just as wily.

In the first weeks of 1940 Henry Andreae read that the British government was considering giving its approval to a scheme to send a brigade of British volunteers to aid the beleaguered state of Finland, which had been under attack from Soviet forces since November 1939. The Finnish cause exerted a powerful appeal for Englishmen with ideological objections to Russia. Prominent among them was Sir Curtis's cousin, Commander Oliver Locker-Lampson, a well-connected Conservative MP who enthused to Parliament about the surprisingly effective Finnish resistance to 'the Communist Colossus'. Henry Andreae put his name forward to join that resistance – and began almost immediately to regret his decision. Perhaps his romantic patriotism faded in anticipation of the experience of engaging in trench warfare at sub-zero temperatures with one of the world's best-trained armies. Perhaps he noted some of the more gloomy press assessments of Finland's prospects – the opinion that, once the winter snows had melted, the Finns would lose their natural advantage and the Red Army would march inexorably towards Helsinki. Whatever the case, by the end of the first week of February, Henry was an anxious man – and was sharing those anxieties over lunch with an old school friend, Thomas Usher. Usher agreed that marching to the defence of Finland would constitute an elaborate form of suicide, and came up with a solution to his friend's problem: Henry could not reasonably be expected to dodge Soviet bullets in the frozen wastes of the Karelian Isthmus if he were already wearing a British uniform. As German bullets were as fatal as the Russian variety, he thought it better for Henry to enter the services as a commissioned officer. Thomas had two ideas about how to achieve this. He might persuade his father-in-law, a wealthy Conservative backbencher, to have a quiet word with his friend, Victor Warrender, Financial Secretary to the War Office. Alternatively, Usher knew a business adviser in the City who had a reputation for being able to secure commissions, at a price.

Usher immediately put in a call to Isaac Abelson – a man with a plush office on Moorgate and a previous conviction for fraud, which he had earned in an attempt to swindle a colleague out of one hundred thousand valuable shares in a firm of phonograph manufacturers.[15] Abelson confirmed that it would be possible for Andreae to buy himself a pip, but that he would need to speak to the man with the power to make the deal: Sir Curtis Lampson. Usher made a quick and unflattering assessment of the Baronet. 'I would not trust him as far as I could kick him. He looks a complete blackguard.' Abelson, however, was keen to arrange a rendezvous. 'The Charing Cross Hotel is rather a haunt of his,' he explained. 'Will you meet with Sir Curtis there between six and six-thirty this evening?' Henry Andreae agreed.

Once a page and a porter had identified both parties to each other, the interview began in a quiet corner of the first-floor coffee lounge. Abelson sat silently as Sir Curtis quizzed Andreae about his age, health and military experience. The Baronet then proposed to secure Andreae a commission in the mechanised transport division of the Royal Army Service Corps by giving the nod – and £300 – to an accommodating Viscount who was a senior staff officer in the War Office. The Viscount, he said, was financially embarrassed, owing to the high rent on his flat near Sloane Square and his inadvertent impregnation of an attractive young friend. A further £300 was also required by Sir Curtis for handling the transaction, payable upon the announcement of Andreae's appointment in the *London Gazette*. Everything, it seemed, had a price. For £1,500, he said, a cadet could get through his final exams at Sandhurst. 'But don't get called up,' warned Sir Curtis. 'It will be very difficult for me to get you out of the ranks. I have just done it for someone else and it was a very difficult job. He is now an officer.' Andreae appeared unsure. 'I said that I would have to consider the matter as £600 was a lot of money and that there would be trouble if it was discovered that I had obtained a commission by this method,' he later recalled. Sir Curtis attempted to reassure him: 'It is not a question of you or myself running the risk of trouble,' he insisted. 'The Staff Officer would have to take the blame.' The Baronet affirmed that if Andreae chose to pay up, he would be a second lieutenant by the following week.

Despite appearances, the Baronet's accomplice was an equally brazen operator. Isaac Harris Abelson had a police file that declared him 'an unsavoury character', a £1,000 debt to the Inland Revenue that he had no intention of repaying, and a friendly professional relationship with the notorious gangster and share-pusher Jake 'the Barber' Factor. Abelson and Sir Curtis had been in business together since the early 1930s, when, in partnership with another of Factor's criminal associates, Jack Klein, they ran a firm of stevedores at the Surrey Commercial Docks. The pair attacked their new quarry on two fronts. Abelson worked to convince Andreae that he was getting a good deal, claiming that in the previous week the Baronet had secured commissions for two other clients: a City stock-jobber who coughed up £750, and a law student at Cambridge who scraped together £600 in order to obtain leave to sit his final examinations. 'I do not make a penny out of this,' Abelson declared. 'But if I were doing the same for Tom [Usher] I should expect a gold cigarette case or something else.' Andreae assured him he would have it.

Sir Curtis, for his part, brought an atmosphere of threatening delicacy to the negotiations. He visited Andreae in his office at Westchester House, near Marble Arch, and explained that he remained willing to help out, despite the modesty of the fee. 'Abelson should not have mentioned £600,' he reflected, 'he should have mentioned a higher figure, but now it is mentioned, I don't mind sticking to it.' They agreed to meet again the following day to hand over the bribe. Sir Curtis suggested lunch, but Andreae preferred to carry out the transaction in his own rooms at Elm Place, Kensington. He was troubled, he said, by a bout of recurrent malaria, for which he was dosing himself with quinine and ammonia. Sir Curtis sympathised, and recommended an arsenic treatment he had undergone in Berlin. He refrained, however, from extolling the virtues of Dr Paulin's Vitamina.

The following morning, once Henry Andreae's flatmate and his charwoman had left the building, Sir Curtis Lampson appeared at Elm Place in a taxi, hungry for money. Finding that his intended victim was worrying about the Army medical he would be obliged to undergo, he reassured him that he was fit enough for the RASC. 'They're terribly particular in the Air Force,' he noted, telling a story of a client who failed to conceal his dislocated shoulder from the RAF doctors. 'But you can see dozens of men wearing glasses in the Infantry.' Then it was time for the money to be handed over. Obediently, Andreae wrote a cheque for £300, made out for cash, and jotted an explanatory letter to allay any suspicion at his bank. It was not as attractive as a parcel of reassuringly fingermarked banknotes, but Sir Curtis was satisfied. 'On Friday', he breezed, 'you will have a chit from the War Office.' He slipped the cheque into his pocket and walked back through the front door of 6, Elm Place – and straight into the arms of Sergeant Albert Webb of B Division.

Sir Curtis Lampson was not arrested for the fraud that he had just perpetrated, but for a separate offence – acquiring £10 credit at Harrods without revealing his status as an undischarged bankrupt. So the Baronet would not immediately have been informed that the police and MI5 knew all about his meeting at the Charing Cross Hotel; that Dictaphone equipment had been installed in the office at Westchester House and the apartment at Elm Place; that the police had taken comprehensive shorthand notes on every stage of the deal; and that one of England's highest-born con-men had been successfully out-conned.

*

In the wartime West End, the blackout ushered in a golden age of felony. The smash-and-grab robbery flourished along the pavements of Regent Street – and was not unknown in London's hotels. In January 1943, a woman fell in an apparent faint at the top of the grand staircase of the Great Western Railway Hotel at Paddington – distracting the attention of staff and guests as her accomplices made off with the hotel safe.[16] One year later, a smartly dressed gunman grabbed a thick bundle of notes from the hands of the receptionist at the Waldorf, firing two shots and dropping his monocle on the stairs as he left.[17] A similar hold-up occurred in the lobby of the Charing Cross in March 1941 – with Lord Poullett at the business end of a service revolver.[18]

More subtle crimes were better suited to these establishments. In 1942 the hotels of the West End felt the impact of a one-man crime wave known as 'the Seal' – a jewel-thief with a liking for £25,000 pearl necklaces, who left cute little notes that read, 'Sorry to have been a bother.'[19] Offenders like Sir Curtis and Isaac Abelson were, however, a much more common problem – dubious characters who used the public spaces of hotels to practise scams and cut illegal deals. Men who picked their victims from the pages of the *Tatler* and the *Sketch*, which displayed useful photographs of Society women with loot hanging around their necks. 'Seventy per cent of the fashionable wasters who infest the cocktail bars and night clubs of Mayfair live on the proceeds of blackmail,' calculated one commentator at the end of the thirties.[20] The Metropolitan Police, however, had a strategy for dealing with them.

In 1937, mindful that the imminent coronation of George VI would fill the British capital with an unusually high volume of tourists, the Met contacted police chiefs in cities all over the world and asked them to supply the details and likenesses of confidence tricksters who might try their luck in London. The result was a list of 1,700 swindlers, classified according to the criminal taxonomies of their homelands. The Australian authorities posted a file of steerers and spielers and hotel-barbers known to be on tour in Europe. The American emphasis was on bunco men and card-sharps. The Criminal Police Office of the Reich furnished the details of the international hotel thief Martha Strunck, terror of the desk clerks of Lubeck. In London, this data was collated as *The Illustrated Circular of Confidence Tricksters and Professional Criminals*, the pages of which were populated by figures such as 'Pretty' Sid Grant, Gaiety Tom, Cocky Harvey and Manley Lucas, a stocks and shares trickster with 'noticeably small feet'. The *Circular* remained in use until the second edition was produced a decade later. In the years between, dates and places of death were inked over the mugshots of those whose careers had been terminated by divine or earthly justice, and files were maintained on those still at liberty. 'Confidence tricksters', warned the foreword to the *Circular*, 'are to be found in large cities in every country, where they seek their victims among the wealthy tourists. These criminals dress well, frequent the best hotels and restaurants, are popular with the staff (by liberal tipping), good conversationalists and generally exude an atmosphere of generosity and good feeling.'[21]

A small band of police investigators specialised in the pursuit of these figures. Detective Inspector John Capstick, an accomplished thief-taker known to the criminal fraternity as 'Artful Charlie', was billeted in the attic of the Charing Cross Hotel, the better to survey the more suspicious members of its shifting population.[22] His colleague Detective Sergeant Matthew Brinnand was celebrated as the terror of the grill rooms and coffee lounges. 'When he walked into the dining-room of one of the West End hotels where crooks like to make a splash you could feel the ripple of fear run through the room, and see anxious men rise from their unfinished meals and head for the nearest exit.'[23] In an attempt to intercept professional or habitual chancers before they incurred too much embarrassment or expense, the Hotels and Restaurants Association compiled a circular of its own: a cut-out-and-keep Court and Social column listing the engagements of nine-bob peers and phoney wing commanders. Here, fake journalist K. Evans ('rather effeminate . . . keen billiard player . . . connoisseur of wines') jostled with fake Indian princess Bashu Rani Shri ('extremely talkative and of an excitable nature') and fake businessman Peter Freeman ('camel hair overcoat . . . well-spoken').[24]

*

In wartime, hotels reported on suspicious visitors, but only if they had the bad taste to leave without settling their bill. The secret service was informed when a resident absconded from a hotel in Cardiff leaving a suitcase full of Nazi literature in his room.[25] ('We have quite a museum at MI5,' crowed one intelligence officer in a secret memorandum of 1940, 'stocked with German Nazi daggers, swastika flags, swastika badges, pictures of Hitler and other Nazi leaders, stacks of German propaganda literature etc.'[26]) When illegal activity was detected on the premises, managements did their best to persuade reporters to reveal to their readers only that a crime had taken place in that vague territory, 'a West End hotel'. They did not always succeed. Thanks to the *Daily Mirror*, Sir George Reeves-Smith could not conceal the fact that Eric Nall, a twenty-three-year-old Liverpudlian with a predilection for jewel-theft and a strong familiarity with the Borstal system, had swanked his way into an £11-a-night room at the Savoy, from which he then absconded, leaving behind a stolen gold cigarette case as security. Robert Turler, manager of the Mount Royal on Oxford Street, was unable to disguise his discomfort when, in March 1941, a guest who signed the register as Lady Campbell, surgeon-commander in the Royal Navy, was revealed as plain Wynne Campbell, a forty-two-year-old secretary with ideas above her station. (In the manner of Curtis Lampson, she had persuaded a young Belgian lieutenant that her influence with the Prime Minister and the First Sea Lord could secure him a comfortable position in the Navy.[27]) There were more managerial blushes when another energetic fantasist, Pauline Hough, a square-jawed Birmingham bus conductress who favoured pinstripes and a brilliantined side-parting, proved unable to pay the bill for the 'swagger suite' she occupied at Grosvenor House – a set of rooms decorated with photographs of royalty and film stars, autographed in Pauline's own hand. The subsequent court case revealed that she had used her diary to record a lifetime of fantasies involving the actresses and Society hostesses of her day: entries described a mythical voyage to New York on the *Queen Mary* with the gleefully saucy stage turn Frances Day; her imaginary lunches at Claridge's with Lady Newborough – a Titian-haired Serbian adventuress who had lived the kind of life of which Pauline Hough's dreams were made. (Before marrying into the British aristocracy, Denisa Newborough had danced naked in the night-clubs of Bucharest, counted Mussolini, Hitler and King Boris of Bulgaria among her admirers, and allowed an Algerian nobleman, Sheikh Ben Gana, to present her with the romantic gift of five hundred sheep.[28])

The ubiquitous presence of uniforms in wartime London proved a strong temptation for many who were hungry for the pleasures of unearned status. At the Berkeley Hotel, Rion Benson passed himself off as a lieutenant in the Manchester Regiment and was unlucky enough to do so on a night when a genuine officer of the regiment was on the premises – one who happened to know the telephone number of the deputy assistant provost marshal of the Military Police.[29] At the Savoy, a teenage Army private named Rowland Jones persuaded the management that he was a secret service officer and was permitted to run up a £400 bill.[30] Peter Blake, a newly married second lieutenant in the Somerset Light Infantry who booked into Grosvenor House in the uniform of a captain, avoided a similar arrest by going into the bathroom and shooting himself in the head, one minute before the authorities rapped at the door of his room. (Blake had told the receptionist that his batman would be bringing his luggage later in the day, then spent the afternoon before his death at the Officers' Sunday Club tea dance in the hotel ballroom.[31])

Not every confidence trickster signed in under a false name or a phoney rank. Many used Sir Curtis Lampson's trick of taking criminal advantage of social privileges to which they were genuinely entitled. According to the newspapers, London's hotels squirmed with well-connected young people with expensive lifestyles and unstable incomes – which they were forced to supplement with acts of fraud and burglary until their trust funds matured or their rich parents dropped obligingly dead. For hotel managers, therefore, the difference between a dishonest chancer and a profitable guest might only be a matter of the current state of an individual patron's bank account. Managements did refuse custom on moral grounds. Until the justice system decreed otherwise, they welcomed patrons such as Victor Hervey, an aristocratic jewel-thief and gun-runner, who organised a loose coalition of well-dressed, well-bred, privately educated thugs who were whooped up in the press as the 'Mayfair Playboys'. ('Why', hissed an anonymous letter sent to Scotland Yard in 1945, 'is he allowed to frequent such places at the Mirabell Restaurant, the Rivoli bar in the Ritz Hotel, the Mayfair, the Berkeley and other respectable establishments?'[32]) They welcomed Guy Wayte, a gossip columnist with a waxed moustache, a good pedigree and a talent for persuading rich benefactors to disgorge large amounts of cash to fund bogus journalistic enterprises, who extracted £12,000 from Lady Houston – to launch a magazine that would explore her twin interests of aeronautics and Fascism. 'The business was not bona fide,' the Old Bailey jury were told, as they were urged to believe that the magazine's editor was 'a plausible, cunning scoundrel and utter rogue [who] has lived on other people's money for years'. (Three decades later, Wayte became the proprietor of the *Tatler*, in which capacity he was also judged guilty of fraud.)

Wayte and Hervey were behind bars when war broke out. A third such miscreant – equally young, privileged, sybaritic and cash-strapped – also found himself breaking rocks in 1940. His case offers a good demonstration of how pedigree could be the sharpest weapon in the con-man's armoury. Richard Vyvyan Dudley Beaumont was the subject of a warning notice in the circular of the Hotels and Restaurants Association – 'sallow complexion; fairly long moustache . . . parts of several fingers missing' – but every fruity curlicue of his name was his by birthright: Beaumont was the favourite son of Europe's last feudal ruler, Dame Sibyl Hathaway, holder of the Seigneurate of the Channel Island of Sark. He did not, however, tell the truth about everything. Richard Beaumont's missing fingers were not the result of enemy action, but the product of a childhood prank with a rusty tin can and a freshly sharpened axe. His avowed rank – flight lieutenant – was stolen from his dead brother, Lionel 'Buster' Beaumont, a former business partner of Oswald Mosley, who had been killed during an air-raid on Liverpool in

May 1941. (Lionel's wife, Mary Lawson, an actress whom he met during an unsuccessful foray into film production, died in the same attack.) During Richard's first fraud trial – the result of using a dud cheque to pay for a three-night spree at the Berkeley Hotel in the summer of 1937 – the judge commended him on his transparency, and ruled that his behaviour had been 'on the border-line between recklessness and criminality'.[33] This leniency may have been a function of deference, but the judge could also have been swayed by some remarks Beaumont had made to the *Daily Express* a few days previously, in which he reflected, with weary disgust, on the dissipated lifestyle that he pursued with his friends, and spoke of their intention to make men of themselves by sailing a fifty-foot fishing-smack from Portsmouth to Australia. 'The fellows who lead this sort of life we're giving up all run monotonously to type,' Beaumont explained. 'They have no morals whatever. They live on credit. They are always borrowing, always in debt. It's a terrible life. You get up at twelve, breakfast on a champagne cocktail. There's a cocktail party at six, then dinner, a theatre, supper and a night club. You get to bed about three. It takes all the sap right out of you. It's not good enough. There must be something more in life. We are getting away from it for good.'[34]

Beaumont and his chums went no further than the bar of the Berkeley, but they were forgiven. However, this judicial generosity had clearly expired when, two years later, Beaumont forgot his disgust for the West End and pulled a similar trick at the London Casino on Old Compton Street. Days before he came to trial, he married a young art student, who pleaded his case in the press. 'He was fighting to make good when he was arrested,' declared Violet Copplestone. 'He has been foolish in his way of living in the past, I know that. But it is finished now, and he was settling down to a good and useful life.' Violet, however, became another of his dupes. 'Everyone remarked on how charming he was which no doubt aided him in his chosen career as a con-man,' recalls Michael Beaumont, Richard's nephew and the current holder of the Seigneurate. 'He was not above forging letters – including letters from Buckingham Palace. He wrote endlessly to proclaim himself Seigneur of Sark, and tried to con some poor American girl that as Seigneur he could marry whomsoever he chose. I had a few tearful letters about that. He certainly behaved very badly to his legitimate wife, who eventually fled to a Refuge.'

In the summer of 1940, Major Albrecht Lanz made landfall on Sark with an invasion party of three uniformed men. He and his interpreter marched into the drawing room of the Seigneurie and informed Sibyl Hathaway, Richard Beaumont's mother, that her island was under the jurisdiction of the Third Reich. While she made the best of the occupation, her son made the best of his sentence – which was spent at the Scrubs during the same period as the tenancy of Sir Curtis Lampson. I find it easy to imagine the Baronet and the Seigneur's son, leaning on their pick-axes and trading reflections on the end of the age of deference.

*

From his prison cell, Sir Curtis wrote letters declaring his desire to present information to a military tribunal that might prevent his being stripped of his rank – but it was not a full-throated campaign. He had gone quietly to his fate. The case against him was unbreakable. He had been the victim of a textbook sting operation. Andreae's illness had been a ruse to lure him to a room that could be wired for sound. Two officers from Special Branch had been crouching in the lavatory, their ears hot inside headphones connected to a microphone concealed in the sitting room next door. ('The lounge of the Charing Cross Hotel', argued Detective Inspector Quinlan, 'was quite unsuitable for overhearing a conversation with or without the aid of mechanical assistance.') As the Baronet sipped whisky and boasted about his secret influence at the War Office, Detective

InspectorMonk had scribbled a shorthand version of the conversation into his notebook. Pages of incriminating remarks, ready to be typed up and given in evidence. Outside, Detective Sergeant Albert Webb waited on the pavement of Elm Place, poised to collar Sir Curtis for his debt at Harrods – and discover him in possession of Andreae's cheque for £300.

At Chelsea Police station, Webb and Quinlan retrieved the incriminating cheque from the Baronet's pockets, along with Andreae's covering letter, a diary, five newspaper cuttings about the conscription of men of military age and a small bundle of correspondence which proved that Andreae was not the only young man to whom the Baronet had made extravagant promises. A commission in the RASC had also been dangled before Albert Douglas Heppenstall, the son of a wealthy Huddersfield furniture dealer. Overtures had also been made to Louie Sherwood – an unscrupulous moneylender who had once snared Anthony Eden's sister-in-law with a loan repayable with interest at 550 per cent – assuring him that his boy might be relieved of the tiresome business of working his way up through the ranks. Under questioning, Sir Curtis and Abelson conceded that the compromised Viscount at the heart of these schemes was a product of their imaginations; that there was no pregnant woman in a flat in Sloane Square, and that Henry Andreae would have received nothing for his £600. Their guilty pleas were accepted. Abelson's counsel argued that his client was a man of good character who genuinely believed that Sir Curtis had some lawful influence at the War Office. Sir Curtis's counsel gave a stirring speech on the subject of his client's military record, and added that the Baronet had renounced his ranch in Alberta in order to return to England to do his bit in the Great War. No evidence for the existence of the ranch was produced – nor it seems, for the good character of Isaac Abelson. The business adviser received a nine-month prison sentence, the Baronet a term twice that length. Quinlan noticed that when sentence was passed upon Sir Curtis, he seemed dazed.

The Baronet was already familiar with the interior of Worm-wood Scrubs. In the early 1920s he had turned his West African experiences into material for a lecture tour. In venues from London to Windermere, he spoke of human sacrifice, lip-expansion, the slave trade (from information divulged, he claimed, by a 110-year-old survivor); the 'sagacity of termites'; the indigenous African's surprisingly subtle sense of humour – 'Around the camp fire at night they are full of sly humour and philosophic intent.' He was also booked to lecture an audience of convicts at the Scrubs. The *Daily Express* lavished an entire page on the event. 'Sir Curtis Lampson, explorer of African deserts, traveller in many lands, penetrated on Saturday night into a hinterland he never knew existed – a walled city only five miles or so from Piccadilly-circus.' To the man from the *Express*, Sir Curtis trilled his approval at the conditions and the regime. 'When I gave my lecture,' he said, 'there was only one warder present, and the governor; yet my audience behaved perfectly. Only once was I puzzled by their behaviour.' When he projected a slide of Dakar, the Baronet explained, he was perplexed to hear a snigger ripple through the audience – until he realised that a member of his audience had also visited the city – 'Dod' Orsborne, skipper of the *Girl Pat*, a Grimsby trawler that became notorious when Orsborne stole her from her owners and embarked upon a freebooting jaunt up the coast of West Africa.

Orsborne, who was employed training Naval commandos during the Second World War, remembered that lecture. 'The only thing about being in prison that really annoyed us were the people who came to lecture us about the evils of sin and the attractions of the straight and narrow path,' he wrote. He described one speaker who was 'particularly sanctimonious'. This man, recalled Orsborne, 'was always pointing out that he was sacrificing his valuable time to come to the prison and inspire us. I took great satisfaction in discovering a few years later that

he himself had been sentenced for eighteen months to Wormwood Scrubs for selling commissions in the British Army.'[35] He
did not bother to disguise his delight.

*

Henry Andreae emerged from the affair with his reputation un-
damaged. 'I did not go to the Charing Cross Hotel with the
intention of buying a commission,' he insisted, from the witness
stand at the Old Bailey. 'Not in the world. I went there more
out of curiosity . . . I realised I was dealing with some rather
dirty people, when it became evident that someone was to be
bribed.' The jury was not invited to consider whether the matter would ever have come to the notice of the police if Sir Curtis
and his pet Viscount had been offering their services for free.
Nor were they asked to reflect upon the fact that it was not
Andreae himself who brought the matter to official attention,
but a friend of his father, Captain Albert Victor Wilberforce
Sheperd, late of the 6th Gurkha Rifles and head salesman of the
Triplex safety-glass company. After a conversation with Henry's
father on Valentine's Day 1940, the Captain put his suspicions
on paper and posted them to his friends at MI5. Four days
later, Inspector Quinlan was sitting in Henry Andreae's office,
encouraging him to invent an attack of malarial fever.

Andreae did not join the RASC, but he did serve in the armed
forces. According to his family, he became a naval commander, toured the Far East and kept a black bear as a pet – though
no record seems to have survived of the naval career, still less
the bear. He never lost his appetite for a sweet deal. In the late
1940s he married into the family of Henry Pittock, a rich industrialist who owned the *Oregonian* newspaper and a string of
industrial plants. Twenty years later he inherited his father-in-
law's property, which included a magnificent lakeside house and
one of the biggest paper mills in America. He sold the factory
but retained the water rights on the land on which it was built

– without which the mill was useless. He then sold the water rights to the mill's new owners at a hugely inflated price, and retired on the proceeds.

Sir Curtis enjoyed no such good fortune. In 1960 Maud Lampson fell asleep in bed with a cigarette that proved to be her last. Another blow fell quickly upon the Baronet. 'It was a catastrophic event which occurred immediately following my Bunny's tragic and appalling death, which terminated my sexual life,' he wrote. After taking an accidental overdose of Nembutal sleeping tablets, Sir Curtis woke up in a London hospital. 'There is only one event which I can remember during this period of unconsciousness,' he declares, somewhat paradoxically, in his memoirs. 'It was an over-keen and over-enthusiastic houseman shouting in my ear as he probed my rectal passage, "I can't help you unless you indicate the site of the pain."' Why he was investigating this part of the Baronet's anatomy is unclear. 'For reasons known only to himself . . . the houseman decided to remove one of my testicles.' Three more operations followed: Sir Curtis returned home with most of his left leg amputated. Having lost his mobility and his virility, he put his remaining energy into typing and retyping the pages that record many of the events mentioned in this chapter.

This memoir also contains a curious supernatural footnote to the affair of Henry Andreae's commission. In the *Pot-Pourri*, the Baronet attempts to suggest that dark forces from the time of the Pharaohs took revenge upon the family of the man who sent him to prison. He claims that during his travels in Egypt, he was accosted by a desiccated old man who directed him to the whereabouts of a hidden tomb: 'Harken unto me O white man from a strange land,' declared the old man, in the manner of a minor character from a Marie Corelli novel. 'By the first light of tomorrow ye shall proceed to Gabel Mutah, where on its southern side ye shall find growing a single date tree. Walk in a straight line from this tree towards our Hill of the Dead, and there before your eyes ye shall find an open tomb.' The explorer gave him a fiver for his trouble and the next day went to the spot with his guide and a gang of boys equipped with crowbars. They broke down the wall of the tomb and discovered a tunnel leading to a hidden chamber containing two sarcophagi and a nest of poisonous snakes. Inside the larger sarcophagus Sir Curtis found the embalmed body of a young woman, wearing a necklace of large gold discs. He sent the boys away, tore off a section of his shirt, lifted the necklace and wrapped it up in the cloth. A local sheik helped him to spirit the necklace out of Egypt, concealed in a leather belt with a secret pouch. On his return to London he entrusted the necklace to an antique dealer on Jermyn Street, who bought it for what its sellers considered to be a poor price. The fate of this antique dealer is described in Lampson's typescript:

A few months after Andreae had disposed of the necklace to an American Museum for eight hundred pounds, his wife was certified, and incarcerated in a mental institution. Later I read in the press that his body had been found on the floor of his bedroom, with one end of a rubber tube attached to the gas fire, lying beneath a blanket which covered his head and shoulders.

Curtis was right to suspect that the man to whom he sold the necklace was a dishonourable type. The record shows as much. During his honeymoon, the antique dealer told his new wife, Doris, that he would like to kick her to death – and that the day of her funeral would be the happiest of his life. He wore his hat during dinner, and when she remonstrated, he threw her on the sofa and hit her across the shoulders.[36] In the early 1930s, his business went into voluntary liquidation – at which point he connived to conceal the most valuable items of unsold stock in a set of empty rooms at the Osnaburgh Hotel in Kentish Town. The scam was sniffed out. Bankruptcy was inevitable. But his suicide – if it happened – went unreported. And even if the buyer of the necklace did gas himself on his hearthrug, it would not have lent credence to Sir Curtis's theory of Pharaonic vengeance. The antique dealer's name was not Andreae, but Andrade. He was utterly unrelated to the short-sighted twenty-four-year-old magnesite salesman who stitched up Sir Curtis in the spring of 1940. Perhaps Sir Curtis knew it. He was not a man who allowed the truth to spoil a compelling story: particularly if he believed that there was some cash to be had at the end of it.

In this case, there was none. By the time of his death in the summer of 1971, *A Pot-Pourri of Thoughts and Deed* remained unfinished. His daughter, Sophy Milwidsky, passed it on to her daughter, Sally, who allowed me to sit at her kitchen table, reading through its pages of self-justification and self-aggrandisement. These are Sir Curtis's remains. The legacy of a man who bequeathed little to the world but bankruptcy reports, police records, uneasy memories and a chaotic document that telegraphs the quality with which he attacked the world, but never succeeded in inspiring in his family. And that, of course, was confidence.

6

Parents

They appeared together at the door of the manager's office: the composer of a poorly received Rhapsody in F Minor, nervous and exhausted; the thin-faced plastic surgeon with the German accent and the Arthur Askey spectacles. They must have looked a little comic. The message they came to deliver, however, was grave. It concerned the woman in Room 365, who had checked in six days previously, in apparent good health. 'We have a spot of trouble to report to you,' said the man in the specs. 'A young lady has died.' He had, he said, done his best to save this woman's life; injected her with painkillers; supplied her with oxygen; taken notes on her condition. The detective who made the first search of the room soon found evidence of these efforts. The waste-paper basket contained spent ampoules of the stimulants Coramine and lobeline. A glass funnel attached to a length of rubber tubing was coiled under a table. Two metal oxygen cylinders squatted on the carpet. On the sideboard lay an empty packet of Capstan cigarettes, the back of which bore a set of scribbled figures plotting the peaks and troughs of the patient's temperature. Marooned in this sea of medical clutter was the body of a young woman, sprawled on her back across the mattress, the blankets pulled up to her chin, her face covered by a hotel towel. The bedclothes were saturated with blood. A brownish liquid seeped from her nostrils. Although the body was warm, rigor mortis had already begun to set in.[1]

The cause of death was confirmed by a pathologist of international reputation. Sir Bernard Spilsbury called into the Mount Royal Hotel on his way to the St Pancras Mortuary. According to *Time* magazine, he was 'Britain's living successor to mythical Sherlock Holmes . . . [who] specializes in macabre cases in which there seem to be no clues'.[2] The problem of Room 365, however, was elementary. Its occupant had been four months pregnant. An operation to remove a foetus had proved fatal for the mother as well as the child. Mary Pickwoad was not the first woman to die bleeding in a twenty-shilling room at the Mount Royal, and she would not be the last. The war years were good years for illegal abortionists. Legislative reform in this area had stalled; the birth rate plummeted; the police recorded a fourfold increase in unauthorised terminations; Winston Churchill, worried by a claim in the Beveridge Report that 'with its present rate of reproduction the British race cannot continue', went on the Home Service to urge Britons to be more fecund. Wartime conditions had propagated permissive attitudes that legislation had failed to accommodate and the national interest could not afford to acknowledge. Mary Pickwoad was a victim of this paradox.

After the brief examination was complete, Detective Inspector John Freshney arranged for the removal of the corpse and took the lift down to the lobby of the Mount Royal, where, waiting for him in the office of the general manageress, were the composer of a minor Rhapsody in F Minor and the thin-faced plastic surgeon in the Arthur Askey specs. They gave their names. Neil Barkla and Georges de la Vatine. They came quietly. The two suspects began their progress down the long staircase leading to the street and into a police car waiting by the kerb. The third man in the case may still have been there on the pavement, pacing and smoking and fretting. He had certainly been there an hour before, in hugger-mugger with Barkla and Vatine; discussing, in low tones, the fate of Mary Pickwoad, the reason for her death – and how he was going to break all this bad news to his wife.

*

For Nicholas Pickwoad, Mary is an unfamiliar image discovered by chance in a photograph album; a person whose missing status was unknown to him until he turned a page to find a face he didn't recognise: a woman in her twenties with a dimpled chin, thick sculpted black eyebrows and an optimistic expression. 'I asked my mother who she was,' he recalls. 'And she told me. This was Aunt Mary, who died after having an abortion. My mother was quite a direct person.' A cousin, he discovered, once asked the same question, and had been warned that Mary Pickwoad was an example of what happened to girls who were too foolish and too trusting and did not treat men with the necessary scepticism required.

The incident is a childhood one: Nicholas is now a thoughtful, good-humoured man in his sixties, and a leading authority on the history of bookbinding. He advises libraries across the world on how to protect their collections from the ravages of fungus and entropy. Over a cup of tea, he tells me his family history: the Pickwoads, he explains, were a dynasty of Empire-builders. And he produces a notebook into which, as part of his own research, he has transcribed the names of the four hundred slaves owned by an ancestor who emigrated to St Kitts. Mary's father, Howell, a lowly colonial bureaucrat in Kenya, possessed no comparable symbols of prosperity. Mary's mother, a family friend named Gracie Smallwood, was despatched from Henley-in-Arden to Nairobi to marry him. (The couple, says Nicholas, had met only once before she made the journey.) Gracie travelled the last leg of the trip on the railway from Mombasa, the construction of which had been hampered by the prodigious appetites of a pair of man-eating lions. She bore one child in Africa – William, in 1912 – but had her second, Helen Mary, two years later, at her sister's home in Hull. Mary's childhood, however, was an African one. As a toddler she rode the *gharri* – a hybrid of trolleybus and rickshaw pulled on rails through the main street of Mombasa – waving graciously at passers-by. By the end of the 1930s the family were all within a few miles of each other in Lancashire. Howell, Gracie and Mary set up home in Southport and William took a flat in Liverpool, where he acted in the city's repertory theatre company under the stage name William Mervyn. War, inevitably, changed all this: William went to the Navy recruiting office, found it shut, signed up for the Army instead and was soon despatched with the Fifth Infantry to a camp in Nigeria, where he drilled local soldiers and arranged prize-fights between promising recruits. Mary applied for war-work, too – in a government bureau known to its employees as 'the Censorship'.

*

The Censorship – codenamed MC5 – was housed in the former offices of Littlewood's Pools, a bright white art deco citadel on the eastern edge of Liverpool. Today, the building is a carcass of twentieth-century modernism, beached in an area of the city that has so far proved one of the big losers of urban regeneration. The houses in the streets nearby are blind to the light. Row upon row of windows have been sealed with steel shutters, in preparation for a road-widening project that has yet to begin. During the war years, however, two thousand workers toiled at MC5, examining mail intercepted on its progress to and from neutral countries – which in practice meant, as one employee put it, 'yawning over business letters in every language from Urdu to Chinese'.[3] Many of the staff were language students, professional translators and refugee journalists, but the workforce contained all kinds of game: an archaeologist experienced in the decryption of Minoan glyptics; an Arabist working on an introduction to Sufism; a producer of West End revues; the former private secretary to the Marquess of Londonderry; the titled wife of the former British consul in Iraq.[4] Each day they sliced open ten thousand envelopes and inspected their contents for inadmissible material. Each day about a hundred questionable letters were identified. Some contained printed propaganda

– fliers that claimed, for instance, that Polish troops were break-ing international law by using British-made poison gas against the Germans. Others aroused more abstruse suspicions, and were passed on to the cryptanalysts and chemists charged to sniff out the presence of secret codes and invisible ink. In a re-stricted area known as Room 99, a laboratory equipped with exotic chemicals and a bank of ultraviolet lamps, diplomatic and consular mail was unsealed imperceptibly – and illegally – by an expert named William Webb, known in the building as 'Steam Kettle Bill'. Nazi propaganda of the period depicted the department as a bureau of nosey parkers in which prurient young women giggled over indiscretions entrusted to the Royal Mail. MC5 examiners, however, detected enemy ciphers hidden in needlework patterns, in song lyrics, in games of postal chess – and in the green tangles of botanical drawings, spotted by an employee who knew a fictitious vegetable when she saw it.

It was in the unheated corridors of the Censorship that Mary Pickwoad first encountered Jerrard Tickell, a well-connected, well-read, well-travelled Dubliner with a neat moustache and a wife and two boys a safe 125 miles away in the Cotswolds. His married life was untroubled by passion: Renée Tickell's ardour was more theological than conjugal. His background was ex-citingly literary: his mother had been a saloneuse who invited the star turns of the Irish cultural revival to her table. W. B. Yeats came up to the nursery to read Jerrard a bedtime story. The mystic poet 'Æ' (known to the Inland Revenue as George William Russell) presented him with a bag of pippins and a copy of his *Collected Poems*. A natural with languages, Jerrard spoke fluent French, German and Hungarian. (The family, too poor to send him to university, had packed him off instead for a two-year residency in an office in Budapest.) He had been recruited to the Censorship from his desk at Coleman Prentis and Varley, a smart London advertising agency at which he had gained a flashy reputation by turning up for work with a pair of lion cubs under his arm. That reputation did not leave him at

MC5. His talkative charm inspired jealousy in some of his male colleagues, who later supplied the police with sour intelligence about his knack for acquiring the friendship of the bureau's best-connected employees – particularly if they were women.

Most impressively – as far as Mary was concerned – this smart young man from the Hungarian department was the author of three moderately successful novels: witty Wodehousian romances with cosmopolitan settings, in which plucky young people negotiated their way to self-knowledge and a happy ending. He was planning a fourth, to be entitled *Soldier from the Wars Returning*. It would be the story of a wealthy family adjusting to straitened circumstances; forsaking their customary playgrounds of the Ritz and the Berkeley Grill for poached eggs on toast in a Lyons Corner House, and gaining something better than privilege from the experience of work and war.

The winter of 1939–40 was a good one for hunkering down over a typewriter. In Liverpool, the snow fell so heavily that it clogged the gutters, flooding entire streets and then turning them into ice rinks. In December, Jerrard rented a modest flat on Canning Street, a short walk from the Anglican cathedral. His absentee landlord was Mary's brother William. Here on Canning Street, as the snow piled in eight-foot drifts, Jerrard worked on his new book as Mary kept warm in bed. She called him 'Mr Cuddle Boots'. He allowed her to read the typescript, chapter by chapter, for the next two years. She would see it from its first draft to the proofs, but she would be dead before it reached the bookshops.

Theirs was a typical wartime affair: intense, pragmatic and conditioned by the possibility of imminent transfer, secondment or death. In March 1940 it encountered its first obstacle, when Jerrard was removed from his job at the Censorship and transferred to the MC5 office in London. Until his MI5 file is declassified, it will be impossible to say for certain why this happened, but police records insist that his political views had made him obnoxious to his colleagues. Some kind of purge, it seems, did take place at MC5 in early 1940. During this period the bureau also relinquished the services of Major Harold de Laesso, an elderly Dane who had served in Rhodesia and Angola as a colonial administrator, and was employed in Liverpool for a year before anyone realised that he was the same de Laesso who had been Oswald Mosley's adviser on Africa, and therefore a prime candidate for internment. There was no Fascist colour in Jerrard Tickell's background. His loyalty to Queen and Country was as unshakeable as it was conventional. Nevertheless, by June 1940 he had been dismissed from the London branch of MC5, reportedly for proving unable to keep his objectionable views to himself.

Like Algernon Westwell, the wayward hero of *Soldier from the Wars Returning*, Jerrard Tickell volunteered for military service. He trained as a driver in the Royal Army Service Corps, moving from post to post around the country, receiving a steady stream of promotions, making dutiful, infrequent visits to his family in Oxfordshire and seeing Mary whenever it proved possible and convenient. Mary's diary for 1941 tracks the progress of the affair – and Jerrard's elevation from adjutant to second lieutenant to staff captain, attached for 'special duties' to the Quartermaster General's Department at the War Office. In the spring and summer she wrote with jittery enthusiasm about sharing champagne with him in the casino of the Palatine Hotel at the foot of Blackpool Tower; of their romantic meals of grouse and strawberries in a café in Leeds; of their 'very short and blissful night together' in a boarding house in Lytham St Annes, where the names Mr and Mrs C. Boots were inscribed in the register. 'Ecstasies and transports all over again,' she wrote, recording her post-coital glow for posterity. 'Oh how happy my Jerrard makes me sometimes. Love him more than ever before.' Such was the strength of her delight that even in the presence of her parents she sometimes felt compelled to rehearse the less intimate details of her romantic weekends, with Jerrard's part recast as a female colleague from the Censorship. ('Oh,' she reflected. 'The lies I have told . . .') These months were not free from anxiety, however, particularly when Mary found herself introduced as Jerrard's wife in some places, and his sister in others. ('Told myself I would never go again but of course I will at the first opportunity,' she confessed, returning to her parents after a weekend in Lytham, spent making love and reading the latest draft of *Soldier from the Wars Returning*. 'I have no pride.')

To Georgette Hygson, a colleague at MC5 who moved into Canning Street after Jerrard's dismissal, Mary made a more serious confession: for fear of her lover's unfavourable reaction, she was neglecting to employ any method of contraception. Georgette procured some pessaries for her friend and urged her to use them. Then, in the middle of November 1941, Georgette visited London with her husband, a sailor in the Merchant Navy. Once his leave had expired, she intended to spend a further week in the capital with Mary. Georgette was waiting at Euston for her on 12 November. Jerrard Tickell was also on the platform. The three shared a taxi from the station. During the ride Mary and Jerrard began hatching plans, and Georgette quickly understood that her role was simply to furnish her friend with a legitimate reason for being away from home. Several days later the women shared the return journey to Liverpool – and news of what had happened over the weekend. Jerrard, Mary revealed, had taken her to a cottage in Chiswick owned by his friend James Monaghan, a chemist who professed to be working on a secret government project to find a new treatment for pneumonia. Monaghan and his wife Leslie were absent from the cottage but James returned unexpectedly – like the man in *Brief Encounter* who discovers Trevor Howard and Celia Johnson sitting guiltily in his apartment. Monaghan, however, did not disapprove of the liaison. They must all have got on well, because at some point in the next two days the men persuaded Mary to pose for a series of semi-nude photographic studies. Mary stripped to the waist; Monaghan pressed the shutter; Jerrard, presumably, looked on admiringly. 'I told her this was extraordinary behaviour,' Hygson recalled, 'and she said that the man had convinced her that they were from the artistic point of view only.' Mary confided to her diary: 'Came home feeling miserable and inordinately depressed.'

As 1941 grew old, the relationship between Mary Pickwoad and Jerrard Tickell began to wither. He neglected to answer her letters; forgot to send a message on her birthday; failed to call her for a seven-week stretch. 'Wish I didn't love him so terribly much,' she wrote, concluding that the affair was as good as over. 'No-one else will ever take his place in my heart or my life.' However, just as Mary was becoming reconciled to a permanent separation, Jerrard summoned her for one last tryst. He was in Leeds, he explained, rescuing his brother, Brien, the black sheep of the family, from a spot of bother. She joined him there on the morning of 17 January 1942 and by the late afternoon the pair were on a train to London, where Jerrard produced a present: a proof copy of *Soldier from the Wars Returning*. Perhaps the fact of its material existence blinded her to some of the text's uncomfortable resonances with real life. Reading it now, I find it hard not to speculate how she might have reacted to the heroine's exclamation that 'a Jewboy offered me a cheque for a hundred quid if I'd be photographed in one of his patent transparent brassieres'.[5] I wonder whether she recognised its unflattering portrait of a family who bore the stage name of her brother, William. ('Algernon Westwell', the book's narrator notes, 'had a deep and dark contempt for the Mervyns and for the sort of people one met at the Mervyns', that forcing house of idle and self-centred neurotics.'[6]) Over the coming weeks, however, other details from the novel would acquire more painful significance. The moment, for instance, at which the heroine is asked for 'the name and address of a really good abortionist'. The assertion that a young woman who enters a nursing home with appendicitis must endure speculation 'on the paternity and future sex of the appendix'.[7] A striking simile for the queasy peace of the Munich Agreement: 'Like a guilty typist who has spent a week-end with the boss and has every reason to fear the worst, England settled down to unquiet conjecture. Nine months was a long time and anything might happen in nine months. The signs of the moon couldn't always be right.'

When Mary and Jerrard arrived at Euston, a railway porter secured them a room at the Westway Hotel, a reassuringly unfashionable establishment on Endsleigh Street. The desk clerk recorded their names in scratchy handwriting: Jerrard and Ethel Tickell. Brother and sister. Up in Room 70, they shared a bed for the last time. After a late breakfast the following morning, they went their separate ways. As Jerrard counted the weeks until *Soldier from the Wars Returning* would make its appearance on the railway bookstands, Mary Pickwoad was performing more anxious calculations. On 6 February she wrote a terse entry in her diary: 'No curse.' Four weeks later she made the same record. After another four weeks, the same two words: 'No curse.' For help and comfort she turned to a man whom she had known only for a few months. Neil Glover Barkla was not Mary Pickwoad's lover. Nothing in the record – no family suspicion – suggests that. Unlike the father of her child, however, Neil stayed with Mary to the very end. And it was this loyalty that saved him from being charged as an accessory to her manslaughter.

*

Neil Barkla was employed as a maker of scientific instruments, but he was also a published composer. Music and science were family inheritances: an uncle, Charles Glover Barkla, sang baritone in the King's College Chapel Choir and received the 1917 Nobel Physics Prize for his research into Röntgen radiation. The nephew's career was not nearly so distinguished. 'Those who have serious aims in music should hardly put into print music so unformed as this,' sniffed the man from the *Musical Times*, casting an eye over a typical Barkla score for piano. 'A man who wants to set his ideas before the public must have some sort of technique, and should deny himself the more obvious sorts of padding.'[8] For such disappointments, there was always the whisky bottle.

Neil met Mary Pickwood through his wife, Constance, who worked with her at the Censorship. She quickly became a firm family friend. The Barklas took her out for dinner and to concerts, and did not disapprove when she told them of her two-year affair with a married man. They willingly provided her with an alibi when she wanted to spend an unauthorised night away from her family home in Southport. When she became pregnant, the Barklas even proposed that the baby should be born under their roof. It might have been an elegant solution: Neil and Constance, it seems, could not have children. Mary, however, rejected the offer. Continuing with the pregnancy, she reasoned, might have some grave effect upon the fragile health of her father, Howell Pickwood. The Barklas soon learned of her alternative solution. On the evening of Tuesday 12 May 1942, the three ate together at the Derby Arms Hotel in Halewood. During the meal a call came through from Jerrard Tickell. He was speaking from the consulting rooms of a medical man with a practice on Clareville Gardens, a quiet street in Kensington that supported a small colony of fashionable artists. A room, he told her, had been booked in her name at the Mount Royal Hotel. The Barklas heard nothing more from their friend until Saturday, when Neil received a telephone message at his office. Mary's voice was strange, her tone urgent. She begged him to catch the midnight train from Lime Street to Euston. He agreed to her request – and, for the next few days, would keep agreeing, despite his qualms.

*

The Mount Royal is now known as the Thistle Marble Arch,

and its wartime topography is much changed. Its three miles of windowless corridors remain; its seven floors of modest rooms. The resident doctor and dentist have gone, however, as has the roof terrace – modelled on the deck of the *Empress of Britain* – and the unusual system of supplying room-keys to guests and tenants with a personalised security password. When it was completed in 1934, the architecture critic Nikolaus Pevsner dismissed Francis Lorne's brick-and-concrete slab of a building as a perfect example of the tiresome ugliness of much contemporary British design.[9] Since receiving this disapproving notice, the hotel has squatted above the shops of Oxford Street, unregarded by the crowds of shoppers that pass below. The main entrance is on Bryanston Street, a gloomy back road that is more an ileum than an artery of communication. Here, you'll find the dingy entrance of a multi-storey car park – built for the residents of the Mount Royal – and a row of townhouses exhibiting a shabbiness that is now rarer than rubies in central London: filthy windows, bare electric bulbs, rows of grubby net curtains, knotted. In blackout conditions, Bryanston Street would have been as anonymous as the docks. Eva Salber, a Jewish refugee from South Africa, failed to see 'anything but blackness' when her taxi drew up here on a rain-swashed night in October 1939. 'My hat dropped into the wet gutter as I got out of the cab,' she recalled, 'and I was relieved to have one less object to look after.'[10] If any visitor arrived delighted at the doors of the Mount Royal during wartime, they neglected to record the fact.

A personal connection may have influenced Jerrard's choice of the Mount Royal. In the late 1930s, his wife's second cousin, Aldous Huxley, had used the hotel as a discreet hideaway for his family, booking them into three consecutive rooms. Its anonymity was useful for those with secret purposes. In the summer of 1940, the hotel provided a marital home for the Soviet double agent Donald Maclean and his wife Melinda.[11] Between September and October 1942, it found space for the Resistance fighter Henri Frenay, editor of the underground newspaper *Vérité*.[12] That same year, the D-Day landings were planned on the premises using giant tabletop maps of Europe. After the war, the tradition persisted: in 1961 a transatlantic gang of intelligence officers booked Room 360 – five doors away from the apartment once occupied by Mary Pickwoad – to pump a Russian informer called Oleg Penkovsky full of tongue-loosening Benzedrine, an interrogation that yielded the intelligence that would trigger the Cuban Missile Crisis.[13]

Today, once through the curved sliding doors of the hotel, you pass a small souvenir store: the sole survivor of a shopping arcade that once contained a hair salon, a cigarette kiosk and a toyshop. The staircase that every guest was once obliged to climb has been augmented by a skinny escalator, which carries you past a row of metal uplighters to the reception area, a vast space untroubled by natural light. Here, a looped Glenn Miller tape plays faintly, in commemoration of the gig he played in the hotel bar shortly before he was killed in a plane crash. If the management have deliberately attempted to cultivate an atmosphere of death, then they have succeeded richly. Much of this chapter was written in the gloom of that lobby, where I tapped away at my laptop, ordered as little as seemed decently possible from the extravagantly polite waiting staff, and tried to conjure up the ghosts of the men who once scudded through the dead spaces of the hotel, engaged in the clandestine business that brought the life of Mary Pickwoad to an end. I didn't have to try too hard.

*

Neil Barkla arrived at the Mount Royal in the early morning of Sunday 17 May 1942, and went straight into breakfast. Once he had cleared his plate, he took the lift up to Room 365. The room was like all the other twenty-shilling-a-night doubles at the Mount Royal. By the door were entrances to two small anterooms – a cramped bathroom and a tiny kitchenette equipped with an electric hob and refrigerator. A striped curtain divided the space into living and sleeping areas: on one side, a functional leather armchair and a sideboard and dining table in the same shiny veneer; on the other, a boxy bedside table, black Bakelite telephone and a bed with a patternless eiderdown. Mary Pickwoad had spent most of the previous two days lying on her bed, but she was sufficiently well to open the door to Neil. She was, she explained, under the supervision of Georges de la Vatine, a specialist who had performed an abortion upon her and was now treating her to 'rectify' the after-effects. 'She told me that the operation was done without an anaesthetic,' recalled Neil, 'that it was fairly painless and that she had caught a glimpse of the child in Dr Vatine's hand, and was amazed to see a perfectly developed little child, which was a boy and about the size of a hand.' Mary, said Neil, begged him to keep her secret, in case news of the operation reached her parents or her employers. She urged him not to call the Mount Royal's resident physician, Dr Rae, and to leave everything in the hands of Vatine. Barkla complied. Perhaps, if he had resisted, Mary Pickwoad might have lived.

At midday the man overseeing Mary's case appeared. Georges de la Vatine was known to his friends as 'Grisha', to readers of the *Almanac de Gotha* as Georges Frédéric Montagu de Fossard, Comte de la Vatine, and to the Metropolitan Police as a 'cunning [and] notorious abortionist' whose activities with a curette had already earned him a prison sentence with hard labour. ('I had a fellow artist's feeling for her,' he told the court at the Old Bailey, when, in June 1931, he was accused of carrying out an illegal operation on a film extra called Mary Bird.) He had once earned his living more honestly. In England at the outbreak of the First World War, he joined the Somerset Light Infantry, from which he was honourably discharged a corporal and a naturalised Briton. In 1921 he enrolled as a medical student at King's College, London. Poverty was the apparent cause of his departure after nine months. By the early 1930s, however, he had lost his anxieties about money and gained a cook and an African butler and a double-fronted house on a quiet street in Kensington, where he sat at his grand piano, bashing out the Brandenburg Concertos and declaring, according to one witness, 'Now that is how Bach *should* be played.' This prosperity was the reward of his new career: remodelling the unsightly noses of the rich and scraping away the unwanted consequences of their sex lives. ('You may see some of my sculptures walking around Mayfair,' he was said to have boasted.) As he had no medical qualifications, Vatine's name appeared more frequently in divorce reports than it did in the *Lancet*. His first wife, a solicitor's daughter from Stroud, divorced him for having sex with a woman in a bathing hut at Rye. His second wife, Olive Metcalfe, owned a night-club on St Martin's Lane that provided him with a happy hunting ground for Society ladies in need of a discreet surgeon. Even after she abandoned him for a Russian lover who roomed in Soho, Vatine seems to have enjoyed the benefits of this patronage. 'No party in Chelsea was complete without him,' insisted one newspaper report, 'but he was always regarded as something of an enigma in Bohemian circles.'[14]

Although he knew that Neil Barkla was not the father of Mary's child, Grisha de la Vatine quickly took him into his confidence. A portion of the foetus, he explained, remained attached to the uterus and if not removed this might prove a threat to Mary's life. Between them, the two men kept her under observation for the rest of the day. By early Sunday evening Vatine concluded that her condition was not improving, and telephoned a sympathetic doctor with operating facilities on the King's Road. Neil helped Mary struggle into the lift, through the hotel lobby and down the long flight of stairs to a taxi. Vatine followed their cab on his motorbike. By nine o'clock, Mary was under the knife of Dr Ernst Blumberg, a German émigré with an interest in hypnotherapy and radium cures. Vatine administered an anaesthetic. Blumberg got to work with his curette; evacuated the patient's womb of obnoxious material; douched her with Dettol; administered a strong dose of antibiotic. To everyone's surprise, Mary Pickwoad rose from the operating table, dressed unassisted and pronounced herself ready to leave. Dr Blumberg agreed to drive Mary and Neil back to the Mount Royal. Perhaps he did not want to arouse the suspicions of a taxi-driver; perhaps he acted out of genuine compassion. Whatever the case, he was not blasé about the consequences of his work. With Vatine in his rear-view mirror, scooting behind the car, Ernst Blumberg gave Mary Pickwoad a stern lecture; told his patient that she was playing a game with life and death. In the event, it was a losing game.

Over the next forty-eight hours, a melancholy chamber drama was played out in the secret theatre of Room 365. The action was repetitive: Vatine making periodic visits, busying himself with his hypodermic; Jerrard Tickell appearing less frequently, with flowers and sharp questions about the presence of Neil Barkla; Barkla taking Mary's temperature, noting the results on the back of his cigarette packet, sharking out of the hotel to buy drugs; Mary Pickwoad rising and sinking on the bed like a drowning woman. At first she improved; then her pulse rate soared. Vatine despatched Barkla to Bell and Croyden's pharmacy on Wigmore Street to fetch lobeline and Coramine to bring down her heart rate and oxygen to ease the pressure on her lungs. With Neil out of the way, Vatine phoned Dr Blumberg. Ernst was not at home, but his father, Jacob, who assisted his son as an anaesthetist, agreed reluctantly to attend. There was little he could do. A dose of camphor failed to produce any obvious signs of recovery. Mary's pulse was uncountably high. After a violent fit of vomiting, she descended into delirium. At 6.30 a.m. on Wednesday morning, Dr Blumberg pronounced her dead. He left Barkla and Vatine alone with the body. At 8 a.m., the telephone on the bedside table rang. On the other end of the line was the man who had paid Georges de la Vatine to get to work with his instruments; the father of Mary Pickwoad's lost son. Neil Barkla met him to give him the bad news. They had breakfast together – not in the Mount Royal, but at the Cumberland Hotel, on the next street. Jerrard Tickell was overwhelmed. 'I can't possibly believe it,' he repeated. The pair walked back along Bryanston Street to the doors of the Mount Royal. Because Jerrard would not come up and view the body, Vatine went downstairs, where, on the pavement, the two men spent a few minutes straightening their story. Then it was time for Neil Glover Barkla and Georges Frédéric Montagu de Fossard to present themselves at the manager's office, announce the fate of the woman in Room 365, and put Jerrard Tickell beside them in the frame.

*

Had Detective Inspector John Freshney got his way, Jerrard Tickell would have broken rocks for the killing of Mary Pickwoad. Freshney and his colleague DI Leonard Clare hoped that by granting Neil Barkla freedom from prosecution, the composer's testimony would prove rich enough to condemn both the abortionist and the man who paid for his services. The detectives scented success. Jerrard had begun his defence badly. He lied about the nature of his relationship with Mary, claiming not to have seen her since March 1941. 'I am definitely not responsible for her condition,' he insisted, 'and in fact I did not know she was pregnant.' Mary's diary disproved these assertions and was corroborated by the register at the Westway Hotel. Jerrard's second mistake was to prevail upon his friend, Leslie Monaghan, to obfuscate the truth about his visits to Vatine's surgery. She was a poor liar, and in any case, Freshney and Clare were disinclined to trust her. 'Mrs Monaghan is of the Bohemian type and has clearly been instructed by Tickell as to what to tell the Police,' they concluded. A third nail was forged for the coffin of Jerrard's defence when the telephone call received by Mary at the Derby Arms Hotel was traced to Clareville Gardens. For me, however, the most revealing evidence uncovered by Freshney and Clare was a remark recorded in Barkla's testimony. In the week before Mary's death, Jerrard received a financial windfall: a cheque for £800 from his publishers, who were eager for three more novels featuring the characters in *Soldier from the Wars Returning*. 'Most of it will go on this business,' he told Barkla. Jerrard had paid Georges de la Vatine £15 in respect of the abortion. The cost of Mary's post-operative care could scarcely have been calculated in hundreds. By Sunday, then, Jerrard must already have decided that his lover's death was imminent, and was envisaging hiring a defence counsel, standing in the dock, and hoping that the jury would show understanding to an officer and a gentleman. He may even have discussed his predicament with his editor at Hodder and Stoughton. No sequel to *Soldier from the Wars Returning* was ever written, and after the war a rumour circulated among lawyers and Fleet Street hacks that Jerrard's publisher had paid his legal fees.[15] In the end, however, his greatest advantage in court was the extravagant foreignness of his co-defendant.

When the trial began on 4 June, the jury heard that a search of Vatine's practice at Clareville Gardens had yielded reams of suspicious paperwork. Freshney and Clare were noisily sceptical about a cache of invoices relating to appointments for hair removal. In his client's defence, Vatine's counsel contended that the operation had been performed in Liverpool, days before Mary checked into the Mount Royal. This argument was undermined by the evidence of the prosecution's expert witness, Sir Bernard Spilsbury. Spilsbury's deductions had sent Dr Crippen to the gallows; they had proved that Helen Dalrymple, who dropped dead in the hair salon at Harrods in 1909, had been killed by the fumes from a bottle of shampoo; they had hanged Patrick Mahon, who, in 1924, had chopped his lover into pieces and scattered her from the window of a railway carriage as it chugged along the coast near Eastbourne – and they had sent dozens of abortionists to jail. Spilsbury's career was littered with the corpses of women who had lost their lives in the process of ending a pregnancy. The daughter of an Indian Army colonel, dead in the Somerset Hotel in 1920; a woman found under a railway arch in Bethnal Green the same year; a teacher in Tooting in 1929; a cashier expired in Fulham and a Swiss governess in Battersea in 1935.[16] He kept index cards on doctors whom he suspected of carrying out such operations. For him, it was a crusade. Even in the notorious 1938 case of a gang of Royal Horse Guards who raped a fourteen-year-old girl after luring her into the stables with the promise of the sight of a 'horse with a green tail', Spilsbury argued for prison for the obstetrician who terminated her pregnancy. His evidence was ignored; a rare defeat that marked the beginning of a decline in the reputation and the mental health of England's greatest criminologist. This, however, mattered little to the jury in the case of Mary Pickwoad. Despite the hardening of the wartime state's attitude to abortion, judges and juries were working quietly on establishing a de facto change in the law, drawing a moral distinction between amateur and professional offenders. Husbands who widowed themselves in the attempt to limit the size of their families were often regarded mercifully. Those who charged for their services were treated with a harshness concomitant to the size of their fee. Georges de la Vatine was not as expensive as some of his colleagues on Harley Street, but he was clearly making a handsome living – and this ensured that he was given five years penal servitude with hard labour. He served his sentence at Maidstone Jail, where, in the chapel, he painted a Crucifixion scene in which the figure of Christ was an audacious self-portrait.

Much to the annoyance of John Freshney and Leonard Clare, Jerrard Tickell did not follow the Comte to the cells. He achieved this result with contrition, but not the truth. Jerrard told the court that his wife now knew the true nature of his relationship with Mary, and 'that there had been complete forgiveness on her part'. He insisted, however, that this relationship had been platonic – with the exception of one ill-judged night at the Westway. Jerrard claimed that a week before her death, Mary had complained to him of indigestion; maintained that he had simply put her in touch with Georges de la Vatine, an acquaintance he believed to be a qualified doctor; that Vatine had informed him that Mary had suffered a miscarriage, and demanded a fee to treat the after-effects. 'This surprised me,' Jerrard said, 'and when he asked me for £15 I protested because I did not think I was responsible.' Jerrard implied that Neil Barkla was the true father of Mary's child, claiming that Neil had insisted that they would be wise to 'arrange a story' to explain the death. Jerrard's defence counsel pursued the same line, asking Neil why he had come to Mary's aid alone. Neil replied that he 'did not want his wife mixed up in it'. For the jury, the doubt was sufficient. There was certainly no evidence that Jerrard had been present when the operation had taken place, or during Dr Blumberg's remedial work.

'Tickell escaped justice,' was Leonard Clare's bitter conclusion. 'There is no doubt that he secured his acquittal by his meek behaviour on arraignment and the fact that he was dressed in the uniform of a Captain of HM Army – a clever and successful ruse which can only be despised.' Despite his acquittal, Jerrard did give the detectives one crumb of satisfaction. A week after the verdict he telephoned Leonard Clare and informed him that he had been dismissed from his post at the War Office and was expecting to be sent 'to a unit in the country'. It seems, however, that the truth was less ignominious. Jerrard Tickell was not dismissed. Instead, he began to make the contacts that would advance the next and most successful stage of his literary career.

*

Sir Crispin Tickell was twelve years old and at prep school

in Shropshire when his father's name began to appear in the crime columns of the British newspapers. A career diplomat and former British Permanent Representative to the United Nations, he now advises governments and institutions on global warming, sustainable development and population issues. When I meet him in a quiet corner of the Fellows' Library at the Royal Geological Society, he describes the success with which his schoolmasters protected him from the scandal by removing the offending pages from the common-room newspapers. But he is also keen to correct any unfavourable impression of his father I might have gained from my reading of the press coverage of the case. 'My father was gregarious, he was charming, and he was a wonderful storyteller,' he enthuses. 'We always called him Tadpole – never papa or father or daddy. It seemed to suit a man who never really grew up.' And he relates two stories which illustrate the complexity of his father's personality: one describes how, as Jerrard's mother arrived to visit her son in Budapest, he disguised himself as a Magyar beggar and accosted her as she alighted from her train; another concerns Jerrard's reaction when the sixteen-year-old Crispin informed him that he intended to register as a conscientious objector. Despite his profound disagreement with his son's position, Jerrard agreed to support him. 'Which might be why', Crispin reflects, 'I changed my mind and joined the Coldstream Guards.'

Crispin saw little of his father during the war. With his mother, Renée, and his brother, Patrick, he spent the last summer of the peace at his grandmother's cottage in Oxfordshire – an extended holiday that came to an end with Chamberlain on the wireless and his grandmother's snarled remark, 'Bloody idiot.' His mother sowed the cottage lawn with potatoes, took a job as assistant postmistress at Burford, and allowed her boys to go running over the fields. It was not an ideal existence for her. Renée Oriana Haynes was born into the heart of the British intellectual establishment: her great-grandfather was Thomas Henry Huxley, 'Darwin's bulldog'; Aldous and Julian Huxley were second cousins; her father, E. S. P. Haynes, was a prominent solicitor who campaigned for the reform of the divorce laws and cluttered his living room with figures such as Hilaire Belloc and Alec and Evelyn Waugh. (Renée and Belloc once spent an afternoon careering around London in an open-top car, singing at the top of their voices.) She devoured esoteric books as a child, read Law and History at St Hugh's College, Oxford (where she edited *Fritillary*, the magazine for women undergraduates) and published her first novel shortly after graduation. After marrying Jerrard in 1929, she forsook fiction and spent a decade writing on comparative religion, ethics and philosophy, absorbing the ideas of her idol, the Anglo-Catholic mystic Evelyn Underhill, and moving inch by spiritual inch in the direction of Rome. She was relieved, therefore, that by the time her husband was being tried for manslaughter, she had exchanged the dreary routines of the Post Office counter for the more stimulating business of the British Council's wartime home at Blenheim Palace, where she shared an office with the poet John Betjeman. Renée did not attend Jerrard's trial. At its conclusion, however, she admitted him back to the family home and, temporarily, to her bed; in consequence of which, she bore him a third boy, Thomas, in the spring of 1943. Charitably, she agreed to employ the troubled daughter of an old friend, Lady Redesdale, as nursemaid to her new son. 'Unity Mitford wasn't terribly good at changing nappies,' recalls Crispin, old enough to remember this sensational presence in the household. 'She became something of a liability. She would whistle at the POWs working in the garden and talk loudly to them in German.'

*

Tom Tickell is convinced that he would have remained unborn had it not been for Mary Pickwoad's death at the Mount Royal Hotel. A former staffer on the *Guardian* newspaper, he lives in a large Victorian house in north London, where his family competes for space with the paraphernalia of his obsessions. His living room is an Aladdin's cave of ephemera. Crowding on his shelves are busts of Mao, Hitler and Stalin; a 500-piece jigsaw of the state funeral of Winston Churchill; a vanity set in pink plastic that commemorates the Coronation of Queen Elizabeth II. From time to time, perhaps to lighten the grim details of some of our conversation, he pops up to put one of his exhibits into action. A twist of the crank on a music box produces a springy approximation of George W. Bush; the flip of a switch on the plastic fish in the centre of his mantelpiece fills the room with a tinny version of Gloria Gaynor's *I Will Survive*. 'This case haunted my childhood,' he tells me. 'From about the age of five I had the sense that there was some family secret that couldn't be discussed.'

Whereas Crispin's relationship with his parents was comparatively cool, Renée held her last son close. Too close, Tom now thinks. This proximity, however, gave him an unobstructed view of his parents' marriage. He recalls the remarks with which his mother made it clear that she believed she had married a man who was neither her intellectual nor her social equal. He can remember the moment of relaxation that followed his father's customary early departure to bed; the happy relief he felt when boarding school delivered him from the atmosphere of domestic hostility. 'My mother brought me up to dislike my father,' he reflects. 'And I spent a large part of my life wishing him dead.' That wish was granted in 1966. Today, however, Tom Tickell remembers his father with sympathy, and has concluded that Jerrard's dogged infidelity was an understandable response to Renée's contempt. ('She was always bringing up the fact that he had never been to University,' he notes.) Tom has also inherited his father's impatience with Renée's supernatural interests, and speaks of her cronies from the Catholic Church and the Society for Psychical Research with a shudder of disgust. Religion, he reflects, was a point of difference between his parents. It was also, however, the glue that held their marriage together – from

Michael Barsley's *Ritzkrieg* (1940): the Old Guard prosecutes its 'Plan of Champagne'.

Ritzkrieg: 'Under the stimulus of war, Knight-Life flourished as never before'.

Waiters bring orders to the restaurant kitchen of the Savoy, months before many were interned under Regulation 18B.

August 1940: the Savoy ballroom, reinforced by scaffolding.

Phil Piratin, leader of the Savoy invasion, is carried through the streets of Stepney after winning Mile End for the Communists in the 1945 General Election.

September 1939: a firewatcher gazes down over Hyde Park from the roof of the Grosvenor House Hotel.

A boy emerges from an Anderson shelter sunk into the grounds of the Savoy.

Mary Pickwoad, who died of a botched abortion in room 365 of the Mount Royal Hotel.

Mary Pickwoad's lover, the novelist Jerrard Tickell (centre) with colleagues at Upton Farm, an army mobilisation centre in Oxfordshire.

The aristocratic jewel thief John Lonsdale enjoys his first meal after being released from prison in 1939.

The suspected Nazi double agent Stella Lonsdale. 'Much of Mrs Lonsdale's conversation,' asserted one informer, 'cannot possibly be submitted in a report owing to its indescribably filthy nature.'

Jean Platiau (seated, with his brothers) did not survive his encounter with Stella. He was executed on 22 October 1941.

The Zogs check into the Ritz. Left to Right: Queen Geraldine, King Zog, Prince Leka, Zog's sisters, Princess Myjezen and Maxhide.

Peter II of Yugoslavia and Queen Alexandra with Crown Prince Alexander, born in Suite 212 of Claridge's, declared part of Yugoslav territory for one night.

October 1946: Chefs march from the Ritz to hear a speech by Arthur Lewis MP.

George Hayim, regular at the Lower Bar of the Ritz, c. 1940.

George in 2010, in his apartment just off Kensington High Street.

October 1946: cheerful strikers picket the Savoy at the beginning of a strike that would prove long and bitter.

18 November 1947: Arthur Lewis MP throws himself in front of the oil-tankers attempting to bring fuel to the Savoy.

the time of Mary Pickwoad's death until Jerrard's own unexpected demise. 'My mother's response to the scandal was to convert to Catholicism,' recalls Tom, 'which made the possibility of a divorce much less likely.' There was a family precedent for the strategy. Renée's father was one of the most prominent divorce reformers of his day; yet he remained steadfastly married to her mother, despite the fact that his principal sexual attachment was to his butler.

*

Jerrard Tickell insulated himself from the consequences of Mary Pickwoad's death with complete success. No journalist ever alluded to the story again. (The chapter you are now reading is the first place in which the names of Tickell and Pickwoad have been coupled in print since July 1942.) Contrary to the information he gave the police, he was not demoted, but remained at the War Office under the wing of his commanding officer, Major-General Tommy Richardson, the dedicatee of *Soldier from the Wars Returning* and the inventor of 'Richardson Rations' – the packs of tinned, dried and condensed foodstuffs that kept the British Army marching on its stomach. The 'unit in the country' to which Jerrard was transferred was an Army mobilisation facility at Upton Farm, a house situated conveniently – or uncomfortably – close to his mother-in-law's cottage in Burford. Tommy Richardson's sons both recall Jerrard during this period as a charismatic and unpredictable presence at boozy parties at Upton. ('It was a very close relationship,' remembers Squadron Leader Colin Richardson. 'My father protected Jerrard Tickell when things all went wrong.') Another colourful figure on the guest list was John Nesbitt-Dufort, a gifted pilot who had earned the nickname 'Whippy' after having effected a skilful emergency landing at Whipsnade Zoo. Nesbitt-Dufort flew Black Lysander planes on moonlit missions to drop agents of the Special Operations Executive into enemy territory. Jerrard

Tickell was not a member of SOE, but his future was shaped by his proximity to those who were – and by a woman who, like Mary Pickwoad, had a close acquaintance with sickness and pain.[17]

*

In April 1945, the Red Army liberated Ravensbrück, a Nazi concentration camp at which the staff and prisoners were overwhelmingly female. Ravensbrück was of intense interest to the British authorities because it had been the place of detention and execution for a number of SOE operatives. During the summer of 1945, the War Office began gathering information on the conditions that had existed at the camp and made efforts to locate former personnel suspected of committing war crimes within its perimeter. In December, Jerrard was despatched to Hamburg to attend the trials of guards, warders and medics accused of beating prisoners with whips, subjecting them to lethal scientific experiments, and killing the newborn babies of those sufficiently unlucky to give birth behind the wire. The Ravensbrück trials were regarded by their co-ordinators as crucial for British justice and prestige: 'This will be our swan-song as far as concentration camps are concerned,' wrote Group Captain Anthony Somerhough, the British officer in charge of the investigations, 'and we all want it to end triumphantly.'[18]

As a War Office public relations officer, it was Jerrard's job to secure that triumph by managing the relationship between the reporters and the reported. But he may also have helped to bring some of the staff of Ravensbrück to the dock. He claimed to have been involved in the capture of Vera Salvequart, a Czech nurse implicated in the programme of extermination at Ravensbrück. Salvequart had administered deadly injections to those too ill to participate in slave-labour projects. She had handled the bureaucratic side of sending women to the gas chambers. One survivor, a Dutch midwife named Neeltje Epker, claimed to have watched her climb a pile of corpses loaded on the back of a lorry, knocking the gold teeth from their gums – and to have seen a woman appear at a window in the medical block, shouting, 'Save us because Vera Salvequart is murdering us!' Despite her enthusiastic work with syringe and pliers, Salvequart had been sent to Ravensbrück as a prisoner, apparently after the authorities discovered her engagement to an Italian Jew involved in espionage activities. (She also claimed to have aided the escape of five stranded Allied officers and stolen the plans for a V-2 rocket in the hope of supplying them to British intelligence.) In the middle of April 1945, as Soviet forces surrounded the camp, her own name was added to the execution list: she survived only because a lover in the neighbouring men's camp smuggled her beyond the fence disguised as a male sewage worker. Her protectors transported her around the countryside hidden in a wardrobe until they reached an American-run transit camp near the city of Schwerin, a hundred miles west of Ravensbrück, where she surrendered a list of exterminated prisoners to the commanding officer. Jerrard claimed to have been instrumental in securing her capture.

His name appears nowhere in the reams of surviving documents relating to Salvequart's case, but he may have been one of the party who tracked her from Schwerin to Hofheim (where she was accused of embezzling the funds of a charitable agency), to Cologne, where, equipped with false papers, she was discovered living under the name of Annie Markova. He was certainly present when, wrapped in a huge fluffy fur coat, she took the stand to insist that she had treated her patients to bread, butter, honey and extra blankets; that she had stolen medicines from the SS pharmacy to keep them alive, and fiddled the death figures to allow some, once recovered, to go into hiding inside the camp. 'Pretty Vera Salvequart', Jerrard remembered, 'looked with lazy carnality at the distinguished visitors.' He also observed her defence counsel attempt to discredit the evidence of Neeltje Epker by insinuating that she had held convictions in

The Hague for carrying out illegal abortions – and watched as the judge advocate sentenced Salvequart to be hanged. Crispin Tickell remembers receiving a letter from the condemned prisoner, begging him to persuade his father to intercede in her case. 'I have no idea how she got hold of my address, or how she even knew of my existence,' he reflects. 'Perhaps it was from my father. He wasn't terribly discreet.'

Jerrard's notes on the trial furnished the opening of his first book since *Soldier from the Wars Returning*. Its subject was one of the key witnesses for the prosecution, and it was written with the uneasy blessing of Colonel Maurice Buckmaster, the head of the French section of SOE. It told how a French-born mother-of-three, married to an Englishman, was despatched by Buckmaster into Occupied France; how she was detained along with her commanding officer, Captain Peter Churchill; how she refused to betray her comrades, despite having her toenails ripped out by an SS torturer; how she had spent months in solitary confinement at Ravensbrück, where she was beaten, starved and confined in the freezing dark; how, after the war, she had received the George Cross for her bravery. Jerrard's account of the war career of Odette Sansom omitted some elements of her biography too morally ambiguous for the taste of a post-war readership hungry for tales of heroism and endurance. He did not mention that she had been captured while in bed with Peter Churchill, a relationship quite against regulations. Neither did he expose her affair with Fritz Sühren, the commandant at Ravensbrück, which guaranteed her survival more surely than her stoicism in the torture chamber. *Odette* was a resounding success. The British producer Herbert Wilcox bought the film rights, and – once Ingrid Bergman had declined the offer – put his wife Anna Neagle behind the barbed wire of a concentration camp mocked up at Borehamwood. (Crispin Tickell remembers accompanying his father and Odette on a visit to the set, where the subject of the picture grumbled about the quality of Neagle's French pronunciation.) Jerrard secured one important casting coup: Maurice Buckmaster agreed to appear as himself. More importantly, he secured his literary reputation for a decade. *Odette* is still in print, and remains one of the defining memoirs of the Second World War.

British readers of the 1950s smiled upon Jerrard Tickell. His novel *Appointment with Venus* (1951), a comedy about a secret British mission to retrieve a pregnant pedigree cow from Nazi-occupied Sark, was filmed twice, once for the Rank Organisation, with David Niven in the lead, and once by a Danish production company – which cast Jerrard himself as the War Office major who co-ordinates the rescue mission. Eventually, however, his witty, middlebrow style fell from favour. 'Towards the end of his life he had ceased to be a successful writer, his youthful charm had failed, and he felt a little shipwrecked,' recalls Crispin Tickell. Their last meeting was in 1966, when father and son spent a weekend in Paris, where Crispin was serving at the British embassy. 'We went out to a night-club where there were some Hungarian singers, and he got up and sang with them in their own language. He had a beautiful singing voice.' Jerrard returned to London the next day. He died of a sudden heart attack almost as soon as he arrived home.

*

Coincidentally, Jerrard's co-defendant enjoyed modest success in the same literary field. After walking out through the gates of Maidstone Jail, Georges de la Vatine translated the memoirs of Kapitänleutnant Günther Prien, a highly decorated U-Boat commander who became a national hero after guiding his submarine into the British naval base at Scapa Flow and destroying a battleship anchored in its waters, killing 833 men. (Hitler was so pleased that he threw him a cocktail party and pinned the Iron Cross to his chest.) *I Sank the Royal Oak* (1946) was the Comte's first and last book: the rest of his career focused on portrait-painting – bishops were a favourite subject – and fraud.

In December 1950, his photograph appeared on the front page of the *Daily Mirror*, above a report on his role in a conspiracy to deprive a group of investors of £6,000 in exchange for some 'wonderful inventions' that did not exist. Vatine received another five-year sentence, though the kingpin of the conspiracy was the former head of the Agricultural School of Oxford University, who – despite the respectable achievement of having patented an innovative method of dehydrating vegetables – had already done several stretches for fraud. A decade later, the same newspaper, in amnesiac mood, spoke to Vatine for its gossip column, and asked him to reflect upon his life as an artist. 'It has been at best a bread-and-butter existence,' he concluded. 'I'm hard up.'

Fortunes were mixed for others touched by the death of Mary Pickwoad. Sir Bernard Spilsbury, lost in depression and self-doubt, killed himself in 1947 by opening the gas taps in his laboratory. Neil Glover Barkla gained a modest journalistic reputation writing music reviews for the Liverpool *Daily Post*. Although he never achieved success as a composer, his Rhapsody in F Minor received one last public performance at the Wigmore Hall in 1946. (Did he attend, I wonder, and think of his visits to Bell and Croyden's pharmacy, only a few doors down the same street?) Ernst Blumberg died in 1971, awaiting trial for carrying out illegal abortions at his practice in Chelsea, where he had once attempted to ameliorate the damage done to Mary Pickwoad by Georges de la Vatine. (His housekeeper, Greta Meier, was given a two-year suspended sentence.) Howell Pickwoad, weakened by illness and despair, died a year after the passing of his own daughter. For some forgotten reason Gracie and William Pickwoad were in Suffolk when the death occurred, and Howell's ashes were sent to them in the post. (The local postman made the delivery with elaborate ceremony, removing his hat, lowering his head, proffering the funerary parcel and declaring, 'Your father, sir!') Under the name of William Mervyn, William Pickwoad became a familiar face in

British films and television: a fruity, avuncular Establishment figure, usually seen in a cassock or pinstripes. He was the easy-going bishop in the long-running ecclesiastical sit-com *All Gas and Gaiters*; the old gentleman who waved back at Jenny Agutter and Sally Thomsett in *The Railway Children* (1970). He also took on a film role with a discomfiting connection with the man implicated in the death of his sister. *Carve Her Name with Pride* (1958) was a biopic of Violette Szabo, an SOE agent who, unlike Odette Sansom, did not leave Ravensbrück concentration camp alive. The film's director, Lewis Gilbert, cast William Mervyn as Colonel Maurice Buckmaster.

Mary Pickwoad's short life was all but forgotten. It was as if she had never lived. Unsurprisingly, Jerrard Tickell and Renée Haynes did not mention her name to their sons: it was unknown to Crispin and Tom until I spoke to them for this book. Neil and Constance Barkla did not discuss Mary with their families. William Pickwoad never mentioned her existence to his three children. Only Georges Frédéric Montagu de Fossard, Comte de la Vatine, seems to have spoken her name again – but solely to protest his innocence to his son, Nicholas, and insist that her death was caused by the incompetence of Ernst Blumberg.

If all her layers of bad luck could be peeled away; if Georges de la Vatine had used his curette with more skill; if she had not pursued an affair with Jerrard Tickell, but with some other, less entangled and obligated colleague; if the war had not pushed her into the draughty offices of MC5, Mary Pickwoad might have lived and died in happy obscurity. She might still be alive today, her place in this book taken by another. The nature of her death, however, makes her part of a long and unhappy strand of British social history, in which the victims have received little or no attention. Her story is not uncommon – not even in the corridors of the Mount Royal Hotel.

*

In the first week of January 1943, a twenty-three-year-old WAAF named Isabel Mary Barker, three months pregnant, climbed the long staircase from Bryanston Street and collected the key for Room 276, the room in which she would die. She had travelled all day from Aberdeenshire, where she worked at the Schoolhill radar station at Porthlethen. Later that day she met a visitor in the lobby: Esther Walsby, a middle-aged woman carrying a large leather handbag. On their way up in the lift, Isabel Barker spilled out her troubles; described the lover who had turned out to be married; the humiliation she had suffered in the surgeries of three Scots doctors who declined to help her terminate her pregnancy. 'I had taken a syringe and towel with me,' Walsby later recalled. 'So I gave her a douche of soap and warm water, whilst she was in a kneeling position in the bathroom. I put her on the bed and covered her with an eiderdown and told her to lie quiet.' By the following day, nothing had happened. 'You're a young healthy girl and fat inside,' said Walsby. 'I must give you a stronger injection, as the first one was not strong enough.' The second, however, proved too powerful. For two days the maids came in and out of Isabel Barker's room and changed the water in her jug without realising that she was dead.[19]

Some police officers are capable of looking unmoved upon the sight of a corpse. The detective summoned to examine the remains of Isabel Barker on the morning of 9 January 1943 was not yet one of them. He had collared a kleptomaniac who was harvesting the shelves of Foyles with the shuttered side of a specially adapted cardboard box. He had brought in a small-time swindler who sold non-existent shares from his home in Hendon. He had clapped the cuffs on an invalided colonel who had gone down to Lord's cricket ground to daub the wall with anti-Semitic slogans.[20] His first recorded glimpse of death, however, was in 1939, when he was called to a jeweller's shop behind Euston station to examine the body of a watchmaker coshed over the head in a robbery.[21] His second had been Mary

Pickwoad, whose body he found shrouded in a blood-soaked blanket in a room high above the shops of Oxford Street. His third was Isabel Barker, seven months later, in the same hotel, one floor below. Accompanied by the same police surgeon with whom he had examined Mary's body, Detective Inspector John Freshney cast a professional eye over the scene of the crime. He picked up the telephone and asked Sir Bernard Spilsbury if he would carry out the post-mortem examination, then drove to 53 Booth Road, Colindale, a semi-detached house on a cheerless street at the perimeter of Hendon Aerodrome. Hetty Walsby knew instantly why there was a policeman on her doorstep. 'I only did it to help because she pleaded with me,' she protested. 'I got no money out of it.' John Freshney took out his pad, and began writing.

7

Subterraneans

Gilbert Bradley was a gentleman. So much was obvious from his neatly cut grey hair and careful public-school vowels; from the easy assurance with which, at the age of ninety, he mixed a gin and lime, or tapped his way over the pavement with the business end of a silver-topped cane. It was obvious, too, from his strong feeling that the modern world had turned its back on the old-fashioned manners and rituals of his youth, and forgotten, in particular, how Britons pulled together during the war. 'On the first night of the blackout all the queens headed down to St James's Palace,' he recalled, conveying their migration with a fierce whistle and a sharp chop of his hand. 'The darkness made it so much easier for one to give a guardsman a blow job in the sentry box.' When making remarks like this, his eyes would become two mischievous crinkles. 'During the war years', he said, 'life was fun.'

Gilbert was one of the last survivors of the clientele of a subterranean cocktail trough that was known during the early 1940s as the Pink Sink. His life – and the lives of two other regulars I was fortunate enough to encounter – is the main business of this chapter. The bar was a hub of the homosexual geography of wartime London, conveniently situated between the all-night Turkish baths of Jermyn Street and the all-male drinking dens of Soho. It was a place where servicemen on leave could meet, make plans and exchange news – just as it had been for their counterparts in the Great War. When the poet Louis MacNeice visited the place in 1940, he registered its unusual atmosphere. 'The bar', he noted, 'is noisy and crowded with officers in uniform but all of a peculiar kind, shimmying their hips and speaking in shrill or velvety voices – "My dear! My *dear*! My DEAR!"[1] Although he never earned his pips, Gilbert was among them. 'One went to meet new faces,' he explained. 'And they had money, so one might possibly be invited to share a free meal. Or a free bed. You can't gloss over that fact. These things must be recorded. One went there to be picked up.' This pick-up joint, however, was not some backstreet dive without a sign above the door. 'It was all very above board,' said Gilbert. 'No working clothes. Collars and best suit. Officers and gentlemen only. You had to dress up for the Ritz.'

As he made this observation, a thought struck him. 'The Rivoli bar upstairs, by the way, was for the *heterosexual* group.' He pronounced the term as if it were some scandal fit only for whispers – and began to tell me about the people whom he encountered under the pavement of Piccadilly. I was sufficiently obtuse to fail to realise that he was giving me a list of his lovers.

*

Until his death in the winter of 2008, Gilbert Bradley occupied the summit of a vertiginous Georgian townhouse on the seafront at Brighton, next door to a building that bears an appropriately blue plaque for the comedian Max Miller. On the day of our first meeting, the atmosphere in the town was unbreathably thick. Clouds of little black insects bustled through the still air. I was in the process of brushing the bugs from my jacket when he opened the front door. Leading me up several flights of stairs, he explained that the house once belonged to his partner, an antique dealer who bequeathed the property to a cousin and effected Gilbert's banishment to the eaves. In his last years, this is where Gilbert lived, with his books on Derby porcelain and his fine clear views of the English Channel. To my eyes, the floors below his attic apartment looked as undisturbed as Miss Havisham's wedding breakfast. Thick drapes extinguished the daylight, to protect the contents of the room: gilt-framed Regency portraits, Victorian shell-sculptures crouching inside bell-jars, engravings of eighteenth-century pugilists, the widescreen television which, Gilbert noted, was once a source of embarrassment to a repair man engaged to unjam a porn tape from the video recorder.

Gilbert knew the historical value of the narrative of his sexual life; knew that a sexual encounter could sometimes constitute an act of historical research. One of the first men on his erotic curriculum vitae was an elderly general who had been in Moscow in the 1880s, where he, in turn, had gone to bed with an ancient officer who had been present in the city during Napoleon's retreat of 1812. The experience was not an isolated one. In his youth, Gilbert often found himself an object of desire to the mature military man. In the mid-1930s, Brigadier-General Reginald Burton, author of *Sport and Wild Life in the Deccan* (1928) and one of the most accomplished tiger-hunters in the Raj, attempted to bag him in a room at the Grand Hotel in Brighton. The officers who commanded him as a gunner during the war, however, did not share this enthusiasm. In 1942 Gilbert was stationed in the Scottish coastal town of Oban, a base for Catalina seaplanes and an important marshalling area for the Atlantic convoys. He was part of a crew operating an ack-ack gun which had been installed, so rumour maintained, at the insistence of the Aga Khan, who had been horrified when several of his horses, destined for shipping to America, were lost in the chaos of a Luftwaffe raid on the harbour. Gilbert was billeted to the Great Western Hotel, where the basement bar was out of bounds to the odd combination of naval ratings and RAF officers. There was no prohibition against men of his own rank – which is how he came to form the relationship that, once discovered, brought him before a military tribunal. He declined to discuss the details of his case, but he did describe how he was dismissed from the Army after a punitive spell on the psychiatric ward of the military barracks at Edinburgh Castle, where, in the dungeon below, guards with fixed bayonets stood watch over a gang of prisoners from the *Bismarck*. 'When I was discharged, there was only one thing for it,' he said. 'I went back to London and applied for a job as a BBC announcer.'

During the war years, the BBC had a reputation for offering sanctuary to well-spoken types whose military service had been terminated in similar circumstances. (Newspapers occasionally ran articles asking why so many apparently able-bodied young men were on its payroll.) Although Gilbert's ambition to read the news on the Home Service went unsatisfied, he was offered a post in a new department dedicated to the production of recorded talks. Eleanor Roosevelt was among the contributors he handled: he remembered her pock-marked skin and her effortless delivery of two ten-minute lectures, entirely without notes. And the Corporation's unofficial tolerance for homosexuality made the secrecy practised in the Army unnecessary. 'It meant', Gilbert said, 'that both on and off duty one could behave in a normal and natural manner. Nobody seemed to bother.'

After each seventy-two-hour shift of manipulating vinyl discs, it was Gilbert's habit to go south to Soho and Piccadilly. The evening might end in a number of what were then called 'known' establishments: the Bœuf sur le Toit at 11, Orange Street, where the door bore no sign and the lamps were supported by sculpted Nubian slaves; the Arts and Battledress, founded on the same street in 1941; the club off the Strand where, as Goronwy Rees noted, there were 'two small rooms opening off the bar in which one could, if one wished, indulge for low stakes in games of chance of a startlingly obscene nature'.[2] Each night, however, began in the same place. 'It was recognised', Gilbert asserted, 'that if you went to the Ritz bar you would always know where to go afterwards.' I asked him if that recognition extended as far as Scotland Yard, which, under the Defence Regulations and Emergency Powers Acts, could close 'disorderly' premises without going to court – and did so, in the case of at least two queer venues in Soho. 'I think', he theorised, 'a large donation to the police Christmas charity took care of that.'

Gilbert's circle included Frith Banbury, an actor and conscientious objector born into a naval family, and known to his friends, therefore, as 'the Admiral's Gifted Daughter'; Patrick Thursfield, a journalist with a comparably salty background, the heir to a crumbling medieval abbey in Norfolk and the melancholy suspicion that his parents would have preferred polio to have killed him in the place of his idolised elder brother, a first-class cricketer and Latin scholar; Kim de la Taste Tickell, doomed to be known by his school nickname, 'Testicle', who carried a respirator box that contained nothing but the Max Factor he used to maintain the tan he had cultivated on duty in North Africa. In middle age, Tickell would become notorious as the rudest publican in England, noted for attacking a customer with a mace because he disapproved of her choice of footwear, and cancelling his order for Bass beer because the drayman addressed him as 'mate' – 'an example', he raged, 'of the creeping communism which is destroying our society'.[3] Gilbert's epitaph for his friend was unsentimental. 'Kim overplayed his eccentricities and became trapped in them,' he concluded. 'He was quite stupid and malign. And also a kind of Fascist.'[4]

*

The Ritz below the Ritz was not the one conceived by the man whose name the building bore. Its topography and its decor had been transformed to suit a world in which the upper ten thousand were obliged to conduct their social lives under fire. The below-stairs Grill Room became 'La Popote', christened in the same spirit that soldiers in the Great War had given cute nicknames to the mud-slicked rat-runs and bolt-holes of the trenches. Sandbags packed the walls, kept in place by wooden props and naked metal struts. Gently smutty graffiti adorned the woodwork. Candles burned in the necks of wine bottles set on utility tablecloths. A candelabrum composed of more bottles cast light upon a modest dance floor. Behind the stage occupied by the band stretched a panoramic mural of the Western Front, circa 1914. On the wall of the adjoining bar, a painted Siegfried Line snaked past caricatures of Hitler and Göring. 'It is as if the HQ Chateau had nearly been bracketed the week before and the Louis XVI ballroom had been jacked up for the greater safety of the brass hats,' remarked the restaurant critic of the *Bystander*.[5] To support the assertion, the magazine reproduced two images of a moustached Blimp in a smart uniform: one depicted him dining near the battlefield, the other at the Ritz. The two cartoons are identical, except for the figure attending the officer: in one, an armed sentry stands to attention; in the other, a waiter proffers an ice bucket from which protrudes a bottle of chilled champagne. The Ritz, the *Bystander* decided, had transformed its basement into 'the stage setting of *Journey's End*'. Not the real thing, but a West End illusion, populated by officers who might be Equity members in military drag – which is what some of them were.

London's hotels supported a number of vigorous subcultures: aristocrats, journalists, actors, criminals, spies. The homosexual subculture included members of all these, but was, by its nature, less easy to describe – although the shiny papers made the occasional attempt. In July 1940, Bridget Chetwynd, gossip columnist of the *Tatler*, a woman whose name was listed both in *Debrett* and the state register of heroin addicts, observed Noël Coward sharing a table at Claridge's with Captain Edward Molyneux – an Irish-born couturier who had abandoned his Parisian boutique and night-club to join the British war effort – and Jacques Franck, the interior designer on whom the Rothschilds called when they wanted someone to rearrange the furniture or build a Chinese pagoda in the garden. Franck wore 'a very smart French uniform' and, nudged Chetwynd, 'other youngish men' were also gathered at their table. Chetwynd told her readers that this male clique was discussing the news that 'Howard Sturgis, an artistic wit from the Paris-American colony, is safe in Pau with various American war-workers'. Sturgis was more than a wit: he was a protégé of Henry James, and wrote novels with a distinct homoerotic flavour. *Tim: A Story of School Life* (1891), for example, was an account of a passionate attachment formed in the common room at Eton. In domestic life, Sturgis liked to spend his evenings wrapped in a shawl, doing needlework, as his companion, William 'The Babe' Haynes Smith, hunkered down over the billiard table. News of his evacuation to Pau would have been a smart little scoop for Bridget Chetwynd, had not the author of *Tim* been dead since 1920.

The Met had a sharper eye for the queer guy. Despite the drain on their resources, the wartime police were surprisingly energetic in their surveillance and prosecution of homosexual offenders. In April 1944, John Stensby-Pickford, a former naval intelligence officer and hot hand in the Manchester branch of the British Bridge League, was found guilty of slipping barbiturates into the beer of his room-mates at various officers' clubs around Piccadilly, in order that he might investigate the contents of their pyjamas. (His spree ended at the Park House Hotel when a semi-conscious, semi-hard Canadian captain pulled a gun on him before he could retreat to his own bed.[6]) Out on the street, several divisions of the Metropolitan Police maintained a pair of plain-clothes officers on permanent patrol. The men from D Division entrapped a man in a Camden urinal and charged him with indecent assault – despite the potential embarrassment of his sharing a name with the Prime Minister.[7] In November 1943, the equivalent team from C Division, PCs Benjamin Clark and Thomas Rees, fished themselves an aristocrat in the heart of the West End: Captain Ian Maitland, the fifteenth Earl of Lauderdale. Clark and Rees claimed to have watched their target pick up a hotel kitchen porter named Robert Willson at the cab shelter by the lavatories on the northeast corner of Leicester Square. A few moments later, they observed the two men in a nearby alley, engaged in furious contemplation of each other's erections. 'I would like to say that I've had a lot of worry lately,' the Earl protested, an hour or so later, from his police cell. 'My son was killed, and I thought I'd have a binge of my own. I was drunk and I didn't realise what was happening. I am happily married and I hate this sort of thing, boys and buggery, you know . . . isn't there anything you can do?' Perhaps there was. After a three-day trial, the jury accepted Maitland's protestations of innocence and the testimony of his principal character witness, Major-General John Hay Beith, director of Public Relations at the War Office, the man credited with coining the distinction between 'funny peculiar' and 'funny ha-ha'. 'I never met a more normal and natural person,' Beith insisted.[8] Robert Willson had no such defender. Instead of returning to his washing-up trough at the Savoy, he was sentenced to eighteenth months of hard labour.

Gilbert Bradley remembered the relief with which Maitland's acquittal was discussed beneath the Ritz. The Earl of Lauderdale had not been a habitué of the Lower Bar, but many who were knew they risked standing in the dock on similar charges. At least one of Gilbert's friends discovered how it felt – Paul Latham, a Conservative MP celebrated for his youth, his blondness, his cruel good looks and his marriage to the traffic-stoppingly beautiful Lady Patricia Moore. The couple's wedding in June 1933 attracted such swarms of well-wishers that they brought the cars and buses in Parliament Square to a halt, causing Herbert Morrison to miss a debate in the Commons. Further popular goodwill was generated when, in January 1938, Latham announced his intention not to seek re-election, in order to spend more time with his four-year-old son. War prevented that promise from being kept – and public favour evaporated when, in the summer of 1941, Latham was found guilty of twelve charges of 'disgraceful conduct' towards three gunners in his own regiment, the 70th Searchlight, Royal Artillery. An intercepted love-letter brought this behaviour to light, at which point Latham attempted to avoid public humili-

ation by mounting an Army motorcycle and riding it into a tree
– which obliged the court martial to find him guilty of a further
count of attempted suicide. 'In evidence,' noted *The Times*, 'it
was stated that Sir Paul had an artificial leg and that, although
he had ridden this particular motor-cycle before, he would have
difficulty in controlling it and applying the foot brake.'[9] Gilbert
Bradley bought *The Times* that day. 'I was surprised to read
about that false leg,' he told me. 'I'm not sure how I failed to
notice it.'

The identities of the gunners were not revealed. They remain
a state secret. Gilbert, for the record, insisted he was not one
of them. His own encounter with the Member for Scarborough
and Whitby began not in barracks, but with a drink in the
Lower Bar, where the nature of Latham's sexuality was common knowledge. So common, in fact, that a poisonous anecdote
circulated there, telling how Latham's young son, Richard, had
once requested a kiss from a male guest who was staying the
weekend at the family's grand home in Sussex, Herstmonceux
Castle. A peck on the forehead was dismissed as inadequate.
'No,' insisted the boy, 'kiss me like you kissed daddy.' Lady Patricia Latham was not prepared to be amused. She took public
revenge for these transgressions by divorcing her husband and
moving to America before the court martial had even convened.
Her efficient account of her husband's hypocrisies was noted by
the newspapers and consumed by the British public as a Sunday
breakfast treat. 'You bore me an heir,' he had told her. 'That's
all I want and expect. Marriage is a device to shackle a man to a
woman he is tired of. Modern women are useless to themselves
or their husbands.'

The judge unlocked those shackles without hesitation. The
Baronet's former lovers – Gilbert among them – gave thanks
that their own letters had remained unread. Old school friends
spoke of Latham's shame in the language of their shared classic-
al education. 'I suspect now', reflected the actor Godfrey Winn,
recalling the boy he had known at Eton in the early 1920s, 'that

he had been born with the seeds of arrogance in his make-up, for which the Greeks had a word which cannot be bettered. Hubris. To imagine yourself above the power of the wrath of the gods. No one is. Unfortunately, Paul Latham was to grow up believing that there was one law for him and another for his fellows. There isn't.'[10] Particularly in the Army, where, between 1939 and 1945, there were more courts martial for 'indecency between males' than for any other offence. Her Majesty's Navy, however, was more tolerant, as I learned from a second veteran of the Lower Bar.

*

Seaman George Hayim spent much of his shore leave sinking cocktails under the pavement of Piccadilly, though he had grown to love the place while still an undergraduate at Cambridge. He used it as both a source of casual sex and a venue for family conferences. He was picked up by there by the playwright Terence Rattigan, who took him to bed and made inconsiderate love to him. But he also went there on the arm of his mother, so that she might meet his lovers. (Mimi Hayim, who had been interned in Tokyo, owed her presence in wartime England to her maid, who persuaded the commandant to release her mistress on the grounds that the poor food had given Mrs Hayim intolerable constipation.)

George's London home was a ground-floor mansion flat just off Kensington High Street that he transformed into a space resembling a cavernous oriental boudoir. Ornamental parrots flocked on the wall. There was a bed in every room. The door of his enormous fridge bore a painted mural of a Chinese riverscape. A pet macaque in a fez would not have been out of place. On my first visit, he cooked lunch – a theatrical event into which people outside on the street became incorporated. With cuts of chicken sizzling on his stove, George pulled up the window and flirted with a passing policeman. 'Where have you been all my life?' exclaimed the constable, distracting George from the task in hand sufficiently long for the oil in the frying pan to edge dangerously close to its flashpoint. 'I was never afraid of the air-raids,' he breezed, letting the pan screech under the cold tap. 'Didn't bother me a bit. I don't know why. But the thought of being caught doing something by a policeman – that worried me. The shame of it, I suppose.' The capacity for shame was not George Hayim's most obvious quality. He delighted in mischief and outrage. I had not been five minutes in his apartment before he showed me a photograph of himself standing on the dining-room table, wearing nothing but a pair of feathery angel wings. Many of his stories described incidents that occurred during his lifelong quest for brutal sexual treatment at the hands of no-nonsense working-class lovers: a pursuit so dogged that it even earned the admiration of his friend Jean Genet, who gave George the nickname 'Posso' in honour of his most unusual sexual kink. Dressing a bowl of salad leaves, he told me about the barrack-room fist-fight in which he became involved after a fellow naval rating accused him of trying to steal his money as he slept. When the sailor discovered his comrade had been reaching under his blanket for another reason, he permitted George to wipe the blood from his mouth and finish what he had started. 'I hate gayness,' George said. 'I like real men.' He chose the Navy because he looked good in blue.

Between them, Gilbert Bradley and George Hayim excavated the memory of dozens of the subterranean inhabitants of the Ritz. It may not have been the most epoch-making act of historical recovery, but on my visits to these men I took down the names of their drinking companions with the same assiduity as a plain-clothes officer from C Division. The carnal geography of London has remained surprisingly static in the last hundred years, but here, in the memories of these two pleasingly frank nonagenarians, was a list of the inhabitants of a space now wiped from the map. Subterranean monsters, all – the chimeras and camelopards of a lost world of sexual dissidence.

Some of the names did not surprise. Gilbert and George had both known Brian Howard, a fading figure of inter-war bohemia who, by the 1940s, was using whisky and cocaine to assuage his gathering sense of failure. Both had encountered Harold Acton, an extravagant aesthete who had once used a megaphone to declaim *The Waste Land* from the window of his room at Christchurch – and into whose face Howard threw a Lower Bar cocktail with the words, '*A Monsieur l'Officer!*'[11] Both had met Paddy Brodie – the original for Evelyn Waugh's Miles Malpractice – who, in a state of advanced refreshment, once mistook the Ritz bar for a row of urinals. Both knew Edomie Johnson, nicknamed 'Sodomy' or just plain 'Sod' Johnson, a gin-swashed artist's model who was celebrated for her expert shoplifting, her heroic rudeness and her affinity for homosexual culture – for which she was saluted as 'the buggers' Vera Lynn'. Johnson funded her social activities by providing curious American officers with an entrée into the bohemian West End, but she was no Society beauty. Gilbert remembered her as 'podgy and grey and drunk, in shabby furs and a rattling pearl necklace'. 'Had she been a bird,' recalled the artist Michael Wishart, 'she would have been a turkey – plucked.' George thought of her as the noisiest and meatiest of the barflies that buzzed beneath the Ritz, and was glad that she usually arrived at the Ritz in possession of a naïve serviceman who might fund her feats of alcoholic endeavour.

*

Being a plutocrat's son, George was usually the one who signed the bill for his friends. Until the moment of his death in January 2011, generosity remained his defining characteristic. When you took your leave of him, his eyes darted around the room in search of a parting gift. (After my first visit I departed, somewhat reluctantly, with a bag of gunpowder tea and a painted china bauble.) His old friends worried, justifiably, that he would give everything away. At the wartime Ritz, he stood drinks for the Marchesa Casati, a vampish Venetian aristocrat famed in the 1920s for painting her servants gold and making fashion accessories of panthers and bears and boa constrictors – but who, by the 1940s, was living in shabby-genteel exile in a flat near Marble Arch, compiling lists of people who had slighted her. (George recalled her touching decrepitude: the boot polish she dabbed around her eyes when make-up proved too expensive; the atropine drops she used to keep her pupils dilated; the frocks she fashioned from brown paper, inked with leopard spots and fastened to her bony frame with pins.)

Custom, however, sometimes forced George to put his wallet away – particularly when he descended to the Lower Bar accompanied by both his mother and his principal lover of the period, Anthony Heckstall-Smith, a wiry naval lieutenant commander whom he had picked up in Hyde Park in the summer of 1941. This was not a social situation envisaged by the etiquette books of the period. However, without acknowledgement from any of the participants, Mimi Hayim treated Heckstall-Smith as any Society woman might treat a gentleman who had shown a romantic interest in her marriageable offspring. It helped that Heckstall-Smith was dashing and well connected. He had just returned from a secret submarine mission on Crete and his father had been a favourite yachting companion of George V – two facts that partly obscured his eternally impecunious status. As the host on their visits to the Lower Bar, he was required to pay for the evening. 'Fortunately', said George, 'my mother drank nothing more expensive than lemonade.'

The invitation did not extend to George's father, whom George so feared that their rare meetings made him physically sick – partly because Ellis Hayim, chief of the Shanghai stock exchange, liked to discipline his children by stabbing at their lips with a needle he kept tucked in his shirt collar for the purpose. I asked George if he thought that his father might not have accepted his relationship with Heckstall-Smith in the

same pragmatic fashion as his mother. The suggestion was outrageous. Ellis Hayim, he said, had once burst into his room
in the middle of the night in the hope of catching his son in
bed with Heckstall-Smith. George's heart raced, he said, just to
remember the moment. 'I planned to kill him, you know,' he
added, matter-of-factly, as he broke up chunks of dark chocolate into a bowl. 'I thought of running him over as he came out
of his office. Even if I'd only crippled him and he had tried to
blackmail me over it, that would have been fine.' And without
betraying any hint of a deliberate attempt to shock, George
began to fantasise his brutal revenge: 'I'd have done him in
while he sat in his wheelchair,' he said, sweetly. 'But first I'd
have brought two men home with me and made them humiliate
me sexually in front of his eyes. A way of saying thank you for
all his beatings and that business with the needle.' He pushed
the plate of chocolate into the middle of the table. The scenario
appears in his memoir, *Thou Shalt Not Uncover Thy Mother's
Nakedness* (1988), in which he concluded that he could never
have gone through with the scheme.

*

Many Lower Bar liaisons occurred between men who were not
equals either in wealth or social status. Although the element
of patronage was not always explicit, the ritual of the wartime
pick-up often included the offer of a gift from the picker to the
picked. Such gifts occasionally became Exhibit A in a criminal trial. Gilbert Bradley remembered how his friend Dick Birley
had been incriminated by a white raincoat found during a kit
inspection at the barracks of the Household Cavalry: a present
to a guardsman who had visited him in his flat next to the
Dorchester. Gilbert also recalled the night he spent in a suite at
Claridge's with a man who expressed his gratitude by presenting him with a smart pair of leather gloves. 'Then he called for
service and one of the staff came in and I was sitting on the

loo reading *The Times*,' he told me. 'It was obvious that I had stayed overnight. But fortunately there were two beds in the room, so I could go downstairs and sign in as a guest. So for many years after that I used to receive a Christmas card from the manager.' One of Gilbert's contemporaries, interviewed by Alkarim Jivani for his book *It's Not Unusual* (1997), received a £5 note after a similar encounter in the same hotel with a visiting American. 'I went down the street', recalled Chris Gotch, 'singing, "I'm a whore, I'm a whore."'[12]

To some customers of the Lower Bar, this kind of transaction remained an invisible secret. Gilbert's fondest remembrances were reserved for the memory of Captain Leycester Otter-Barry, a devastatingly handsome officer in the King's Shropshire Light Infantry, who appears to have frequented the Lower Bar without any understanding of the nature of its inhabitants. Otter-Barry's unpublished memoir, which is sufficiently comprehensive to record the moment when its author contracted ringworm from an infected hairbrush, contains no evidence that he ever enjoyed a homosexual encounter.[13] But the Otter-Barrys had a history of making unwitting incursions into London's queerer social spaces. In 1883, Leycester's grandfather had cause to complain when a young hustler named Cecil Froom stole his watch and chain at the Queen's Road baths in Bayswater. In July 1931, Leycester's cousin Francis, stuck in London and unable to find a hotel room, booked himself a cubicle at the all-night Savoy Turkish baths on Jermyn Street, where he awoke to find a naked man beside him in the bed. 'This man', heard the Public Order Committee of the London County Council, 'was attempting to force his penis which was erect into his [the complainant's] hand.'[14]

The Savoy baths brochure boasted that it had 'attracted the enthusiastic patronage of connoisseurs and those "who know"'.[15] And if the Otter-Barrys did not 'know', then they were not alone in their ignorance. The overlap between London's homosocial and homosexual cultures was sometimes difficult to detect. It was relatively simple to spot the painted boys who loitered under the boxed figure of Eros at Piccadilly – but the cafés on Panton Street in which they played pinball were not exclusively queer. The guardsmen who stood at the after-hours coffee stands on Park Lane were not necessarily in the same game as their comrades patrolling Hyde Park, who had a list of fixed fees for a range of sexual services – and sometimes took the money home to their wives. The habitués of the Ritz bar or the Savoy baths might be strangers like Leycester Otter-Barry or 'known' men like Gilbert, participants in a sexual economy that was customarily cashless, but occasionally involved the exchange of coupons or notes. In this world, it was not always easy to tell the players from the bystanders. Such ambiguity suited many who drank below the flagstones of Piccadilly – and not only those with wives and fiancées back home or unsympathetic commanding officers back in barracks. There were others standing alongside Gilbert and George for whom secrecy was more than a social convenience – it was a professional requirement.

*

In the middle of 1940, an office block around the corner from the Ritz acquired new tenants. Marie-Jaqueline Dorothea Beatrice Alexina Romaine Adriana Hope-Nicholson, a teenage girl with spectacular red hair and a sizzling typing-speed, was one of them. Her boss, Vernon Kell, had two requirements of his secretarial staff: 'I want all my girls to be well bred and have good legs.'[16] Marie-Jaqueline satisfied on both counts – and could also take shorthand in phonetic French. At the interview she was asked: 'Can you keep a secret?' She answered with a description of the complexities of her family life; how she managed the competing demands of her parents, who had parted on unfriendly terms. It was sufficient. And with that, she became a member of MI5. Not because she burned with a desire to aid the secret state, but because the weekly rate was ten shillings higher than for the equivalent job at the Ministry of Information.

Marie-Jaqueline's work for MI5 began when the organisation was briefly housed in a wing of Wormwood Scrubs – where she did all she could to avoid being allotted office space in the condemned cell and to ignore the cons who stared up her skirts as she ascended the iron staircases. (Among them was the titled burglar Victor Hervey, who, before his incarceration, had quickstepped with several of Kell's personnel at their coming-out parties.) That government spooks haunted the Scrubs was not the war's best-kept secret. As the bus rattled down Ladbroke Grove, the conductor would ting the bell and yell, 'All alight for MI5!' The organisation soon moved out. When a bomb hit the building and incinerated hundreds of intelligence files, alternative accommodation was arranged in Mayfair at 57–58 St James's Street. As a result, the Ritz Hotel became the staff canteen of the secret services and their fellow travellers. Guy Burgess breakfasted there each morning, unshaven. 'We were Ritz people,' says Marie-Jaqueline, echoing the Noël Coward song about nails and quails. 'We were in our element.'

I met Marie-Jaqueline in the spring of 2008, when she was staying in a convalescent home on the King's Road, recovering from an injury to her leg. Bored by her confinement and eager to return home, she sipped her cup of hospital tea and spoke of her past with striking candour and clarity. Before the war, she said, she was as spoilt and ignorant as any of her class. And for her, the war came late. When her parents separated in the summer of 1937, the family divided. Her mother, Jaqueline, an expert on heraldic history, remained in their house on Tite Street – a Queen Anne labyrinth with twelve bedrooms and a vast first-floor studio that could accommodate a hundred dancing couples. Marie-Jaqueline's brother, Felix, lodged with his mother. Hedley, the patriarch of the family, a passionate believer in the divinity of Charles I and proud owner of a bloody scrap of the shirt in which his idol had been executed, took Marie-Jaqueline and her elder sister Lauretta to a villa near Cannes, where, by 1939, the possibility of a Nazi invasion had made rents attractively cheap. Hitler marched into Poland; Britain declared war on Germany; Warsaw fell; the Blitzkrieg thundered westwards – and Hedley, Lauretta and Marie-Jaqueline ate buttered crevettes in half-empty restaurants and drove their huge American car along the Riviera coastline. 'In retrospect it was awful,' she reflected. 'But that was the type of man my father was. It would never have occurred to him to come back and do war-work. It didn't occur to me, either.' In November 1939, the Hope-Nicholson girls made a brief and surprisingly easy trip back to London to collect some books, records and a bundle of Alpine knitwear. On her arrival, Marie-Jaqueline was shocked by the war's sudden apparentness, and shamed by the disapproval of an official who asked her why she wasn't carrying her gas mask. She replied: 'What's a gas mask?'

For the Hope-Nicholsons, however, the absence of cash was a more pressing problem than the proximity of war. To conserve his funds, Hedley relinquished the lease on the villa at Cannes and took his daughters to lodge with his friend Matthew Smith, a painter who lived in a palatial house in the inland town of Grasse. The arrangement collapsed under a freight of bohemian complexity. The two men annoyed each other. Lauretta fell in love with Smith's son. Hedley returned to London in a fit of pique. His daughters remained defiantly in France. Then Smith was arrested and interned at Cap d'Antibes – and it was here that Marie-Jaqueline experienced a kind of awakening. Visiting the camp, she realised that only the wealthy inmates were being given sufficient food; the rest were being left to starve slowly. 'That changed me,' she said, 'seeing that injustice. Because it was the kind of injustice that, if you actually had your eyes open, was all around.' The sisters packed their suitcases and returned to London. They were not, however, the last expatriates to quit the Riviera. Some remained even after the fall of France. George Hayim remembered a friend who declined an offer of safe transit made by a Resistance group that was willing to spirit him across the Pyrenees and into neutral Spain. Michel de Buisseret explained that he had a prior engagement to play tennis. The following day he was arrested and sent to Buchenwald, where he spent the remainder of the war.

The Hope-Nicholson girls returned to Tite Street and threw themselves on the mercy of their mother. She welcomed them back, but revealed that she had rented out their rooms to lodgers – whom Marie-Jaqueline then made it her mission to dislodge. The sisters were also reunited with their brother, Felix, who became Marie-Jaqueline's companion as she explored wartime London's nocturnal possibilities. They spurned the hotels of Park Lane. ('The Dorchester', she insisted, 'was frightfully boring.') They listened to jazz at the Nest and other clubs staffed by black musicians. ('They were full of drugs and dope but they were much more fun.') They danced at the Gargoyle club, where, on one memorable night, Dylan Thomas sank seductively to the floor and, in time to the music, licked the gravy browning from Marie-Jaqueline's legs. (Guy Burgess, sitting at the table with them, was too drunk to notice.) In more respectable places, however, the Hope-Nicholsons were not always welcome. M-J recalls dancing with Felix in a night-club on Bond Street, where a middle-aged couple made several vicious attempts to elbow them from the floor. 'At first I thought they were drunk and then I realised they were doing it deliberately. I burst into tears – at which they became very embarrassed. And it served them bloody well right.' One of the advantages of the Ritz, she asserted, was that nobody minded if you were unconventional.

Felix Hope-Nicholson, however, stood out from the crowd even in the Lower Bar. With some amusement, George Hayim recalled his drainpipe trousers and long Beardsleyan hair; the pratfall he executed when he tripped drunkenly over the sleeping figure of Prince Leka of the Albanians. Gilbert Bradley remembered a story about Felix's arrival at Oxford, which told how he had tumbled onto the railway platform under the weight of eighteen of his most essential hatboxes. Some of these unconventionalities, however, were maintained in observance of family tradition. Like his mother, Felix was obsessed by heraldry and genealogy. Like his father, he was bisexual. (A scurrilous couplet by John Betjeman memorialised this inheritance: 'H is for Hedley, who lives in a Place. What he makes on his bottom, he spends on his face.') Felix also shared his father's indifference to the war, for which his family exacted a terrible penalty. After a furious row with her son, Jaqueline Hope-Nicholson reported Felix to the police as a person of anti-British sympathies. He was not interned under Regulation 18B, but admitted to a psychiatric institution in which, Marie-Jaqueline recalled, all the inmates held defeatist views and were obliged to wear a uniform consisting of a bright blue suit and a red necktie.

During Felix's confinement, M-J acquired another confidant – a waspish, well-connected MI5 officer whom she found wandering the corridors of Wormwood Scrubs in a mustard-coloured suit. Of the survivors of the Lower Bar I encountered in the course of my research, Howard was the one figure who had made an indelible impression on all three. Perhaps this was because he was already a relic of a former age; a Bright Young Person in a period when the Bright Young People were evoked as exemplars of unacceptable decadence, a pre-war phenomenon that would have no place in a victorious peace. Howard had spent much of the previous two decades attending elaborate costume parties, acidifying his conversational style, and failing to live up to the promise of the poetry he had written at Eton. By 1940 he had squandered everything but his money and his talent to offend. Those whom he had offended were baffled by his recruitment to MI5, but less baffled by his disinclination to stop talking about it. That kind of incontinence was quite in character, as was his inability to retain the job.

He was employed to spy on his friends and contemporaries, but his qualifications for the post were moral as well as social. Unlike many of his class, Howard had never felt a shiver of sympathy with Fascism. In 1931 he had dined with the novelist Thomas Mann, who convinced him of the savage nature of Hitler's ambitions. This ensured that Howard did not become one of those privileged young men who were obliged to rewrite their political histories on the collapse of the Munich Agreement. At the end of 1940 he was charged in his capacity as an 'outside contact' to detect the odour of Fascism at the breakfast tables of English country houses; to identify potential Quislings in the grill rooms and the cocktail bars of the smart West End. He also wrote a propaganda play for the BBC Home Service: *Baldur von Schirach* (1942), one of the most impassioned and perceptive denunciations of Hitler's Germany produced during the war years, not least because of its unusual and prescient emphasis on Nazi eugenics. Howard's reputation for triviality, however, remained incurably powerful. His fellow (and less successful) propagandist, Dylan Thomas, wrote a radio play called *The Art of Conversation*, in which the narrator announces, 'When the light behind my head turns pink and then green, I shall tune you into a meeting, held in the cocktail bar of the Blitz, of some of our most advanced poets. Not one of them will see twenty-one again. Some of them are sober.' Naturally, one of them is called Bryan. If Howard had been more discreet; if he had been able to resist making drunken threats about internment to disliked acquaintances; if he had not infuriated a group of Army officers by wagging a finger and teasing them about 'Dunkirky-wirky', then he might have reached August 1945 with his dignity intact and his record unblemished.[17] Instead, underneath the Ritz, he sowed the seeds of his expulsion.

Marie-Jaqueline knew the story well. It related to a gin-fuelled night in 1942. This is how she told it in her book, *Brian Howard: Portrait of a Failure*:

In that unmistakable and articulate voice of his he was deploring the state of the war, the behaviour of Churchill, the equivocal outcome of the Second Front, and so on, peppering his semi-satirical monologue with defeatist pin-pricks as only he knew how to. It was all too much for a high-ranking RAF officer sitting nearby, who got up and demanded with steely authority Brian's name, number and station. Brian broke off his private conversation just long enough to say, loudly over his shoulder, 'My name is Mrs Smith.'

A few days later Howard was surprised when a small blue four-seater car screeched to a halt in front of him on the pavement. Out leapt a furious RAF officer, who was, Howard recalled, 'tall, dark, good-looking in a disagreeable, public schoolboy way'. The officer ascertained Howard's identity and let rip: 'Unless you stop going about London talking the way you do, I shall see that you are court-martialled and posted. Repeating things you hear in work, from your boss. Spreading alarm and despondency. You know what I mean, don't you?' Howard pondered the incident in his diary:

Upon reflection it must either be the rocket-bombs, or that story I told about an Air Marshal. It was in front of Colonel 'X', and a strange Air Vice Marshal in the Ritz, when I was on leave. It was simply, 'The Army may be able to get them there' (meaning the Second Front), 'but how are they going to get them back?' I quoted this as an Air Marshal's remark (I did not say *who* it was), and also said what curious people they were, like robber barons. Could this be Colonel 'X''s revenge for my having invented the perfect nickname for him? Colonel '*Cutie*'![18]

This perfection was attested by Felix Hope-Nicholson, who recalled that the officer in question 'had a mania for meeting young Second Lieutenants'. But when Marie-Jaqueline wrote *Portrait of a Failure*, she spared the colonel his blushes by declining to name him. By the time I met her, age had robbed her of the knowledge of his identity. Colonel Cutie's secret is safe – unlike much of the classified information that circulated in the Lower Bar.

*

Brian Howard was banished behind a desk at an RAF aerodrome. And not without good reason. The Lower Bar was a security disaster waiting to happen. Jointly occupied by the homosexual subculture and that of the secret state, it was a space within which two clandestine networks coexisted and one code of silence competed with another. In the decade following the war, the combination of homosexuality and espionage would prove its volatility in a flurry of defections to the Soviet Union – defections that gave lasting notoriety to a number of men familiar to the below-stairs barmen of the West End. But the wartime secret state seems to have remained untroubled by such possibilities – even if the agents themselves were sometimes discomfited by this collision of worlds. Denis Rake was an actor who left the chorus of the Ivor Novello musical *The Dancing Years* (a work known to its cast as *The Prancing Queers*) to train as a wireless operator in the SOE. The heads of F Section recorded their concerns about Rake: a shrill performance during explosives training and his reliance on sleeping pills moved them to report him to be 'a trifle effeminate' and 'a drug addict'. They had no misgivings, however, about sending him on missions into occupied France – possibly because they did not know he had spent some of his year undercover performing in Parisian drag clubs and conducting an intense affair with an officer in the Abwehr. In London, one of Rake's duties was to entertain new recruits to SOE, many of whom were confused to hear the Ritz barman address him as 'Mr Greer' – not an SOE cover identity, but the stage name under which he performed in West End shows.

Victory in Europe signalled a kind of defeat for the inhabitants of the Lower Bar. As the barbed wire was rewound, and the used condoms and charred fragments of deck-chair harvested from the grass of Green Park, the subterranean areas of the Ritz went dark. 'It was shut on the day the war ended,' reflected Gilbert Bradley. 'For redecoration, ostensibly. That's what the sign on the door said.' For him, this was the first phase in the extinction of the world of sexual opportunity through which he had once moved; a world that was destroyed as much by the normalisation of homosexuality as the forces that sought to proscribe its acts. He listed the disappearances: queer London's Great Auks and its Euston Arches; the men-only bar of the Trocadero on Piccadilly Circus; the tube carriages that lent erotic possibilities to the thirteen-minute journey between Finchley Road and Wembley Park; the vanished conveniences of the Underground. 'Do you know,' he said, wistfully, over treacle tart in a restaurant near his flat, 'there was once a gents on almost every platform of the Circle Line? One could just buy a ticket and go round and round.' In the immediate post-war years, others discerned the same process at work: 'I have noted a great many very savage sentences for sex offences during the past year,' wrote Anatole James in a Mass Observation report for December 1945. Two months later he added: 'There is now a veritable outbreak of savagery with regard to all things sexual.'[19]

After the Pink Sink had gurgled its last, its regulars scattered. Patrick Thursfield decamped to Tangier, where he opened a restaurant, translated Hungarian fiction into English, and developed his instinct for toxic snobbery. ('You take a local boy to your bed,' he told a fellow Tangerine, 'but never, never, to the table.'[20]) Leycester Otter-Barry went into the hotel trade and fathered two girls. Denis Rake became valet to the film star Douglas Fairbanks Junior, who remained ignorant of the dazzling military record of the man who brushed the lint from his sports jackets until the day a letter arrived addressed to Major Denis Rake. Edomie Johnson switched her alcoholic allegiances to the Colony Room. Starved of her wartime supply of impressionable American servicemen, she lodged in a garret in St John's Wood with the painter Anne Dunn and a large South American fruit bat that decorated their flat with stinking orange diarrhoea. (Edomie slept not on a bed, but on the floor of a cage full of pigeons.) Paul Latham lost himself in the project of restoring Herstmonceux Castle and its gardens. He died in 1955, pitied by his servants and despised, from across the Atlantic, by the family he had betrayed.

The relationship between George Hayim and Anthony Heckstall-Smith did not survive the war. In 1945 George's boyfriend became a victim of Peter and Julius Gert, a pair of Austro-Hungarian confidence tricksters who lured him into a share-broking scam that earned the perpetrators £8,000 and a prison sentence for their dupe. The Gerts absconded to Argentina; Heckstall-Smith descended the stairs from the dock of the Old Bailey to the cells below, reflecting upon the pleasures of which he was about to be deprived. 'I reminded myself', he wrote in his prison memoir, *Eighteen Months* (1953), 'that the evening before I had been sitting in the Berkeley Hotel, drinking cocktails with two of my dearest friends. I recalled how one of them had said as we parted: "Well, tomorrow you will be coming down to stay with us in the country or a guest of Her Majesty!"'[21]

In the last year of the war Marie-Jaqueline Hope-Nicholson shortened her name by taking that of Maurice Lancaster, an American war correspondent seventeen years her senior; a man with a passion for velvet jackets and silver-topped canes, more Diaghilev than Ed Murrow. When ill-health forced him into retirement, M-J became the chief breadwinner, lavishing the efficiency she had brought to the MI5 index upon the editorships of *House Beautiful* and *Trio*, the first in-house magazine for Sainsbury's supermarket. Her brother, Felix, inherited the house in Tite Street, where, in the late 1940s, he rented his sister's old bedroom to a tenant who had spent the war in prison –

Anna Wolkoff, convicted of spying for Nazi Germany in 1940. Adrian Liddell-Hart, another Tite Street tenant, recalled her as 'a very right-wing strident lady much given to fanatical hatred of Jews and Communists'. Marie-Jaqueline died in May 2010. When I visited her in the convalescent home, we agreed to go for a cocktail at the Ritz. Both of us, I think, suspected that it would never happen.

In any case, visiting the Lower Bar would have proved impossible. In 1978 the subterranean Ritz underwent a divorce from the Palm Court and the restaurant and the sunny uplands above. It is now the Ritz Club Casino, owned by a separate company that has filled the space with roulette wheels and baccarat tables that run nightly until 6 a.m. 'Gambling may be good for you,' enthuses the casino's website, hedging its bets. Staring too long at the hideously opulent decor could not be good for anyone's health. The clientele down here are the super-rich: the customary cast of oligarchs and oil barons. Only their occasional brushes with the law reveal their identities: the two Serbs who used a concealed electronic scanner to gather a legal £1.3 million harvest at the roulette table in 2004; the Saudi Arabian arms dealer Adnan Khashoggi, who, in 1986, presented the Ritz cashiers with dud cheques for £3.2 million; the Syrian billionaire known as 'the Fat Man', whose £10 million spree at the Ritz ended with a writ from the management. Bohemian is not a word that could be used to characterise such figures.

The wartime Lower Bar was hardly a progressive environment. It was no kind of Stonewall. 'When I think of the place I think of groups of people sitting on gilt chairs sipping pink gin,' said Gilbert Bradley. But if the rules of class difference were not suspended in the place, nor were they observed with the same assiduity as was customary upstairs – and the sexuality of its clientele was surely the reason for that. 'One was always brought up with the idea that gaiety was accepted amongst the aristocracy and the working class,' noted Gilbert. 'It was that middle group, the people in between, with whom you had to be on your guard. So one was always rather afraid of bus conduct-ors.' Before I took my leave of Gilbert, I asked him what drew him to the bar beneath the Ritz, night after night after night. He answered with a mischievous narrowing of his eyes. 'One did want a bit of culture in one's life. Somebody who could speak the King's English, and could amuse you. And now when you go into a gay pub, it's full of middle-class people. And they're all so hideously ugly.'

8

Traitors

The men from MI5 knew the woman at the Waldorf was a liar. What they couldn't decide was whether she was also a Nazi spy. The story she told was certainly a wild one – the sort that prompted more questions than it satisfied. Had she really married a Russian prince in Monte Carlo? Had she really risked her life to help the network of British agents in Vichy France? Had the mark on her forehead really been made by the hot cigarette of a raging Nazi interrogator? Did she want to parachute back into France in order to aid the Allied cause – or to return to the bed of a lover in the German intelligence agency, where she could tell him all she had discovered about a new British aerial torpedo? Nobody, it seems, could be entirely sure about Stella Lonsdale.

On other matters, however, the spooks could pronounce with complete certitude. They knew she liked fur coats, champagne and money. They knew she liked the smell of a good cigar. Most of all – and to their intense embarrassment – they knew that she liked sex. They knew this because she talked about it at great length and in great detail; pushed it to the foreground of every conversation. Report after secret report commented, with a mixture of disapproval and terror, on her willingness to enumerate the complexities of her erotic career. 'Much of Mrs Lonsdale's conversation', asserted one informer, 'cannot possibly be submitted in a report owing to its indescribably filthy nature.' The officer assigned to her case from B1A, the counter-intelligence division of MI5, recorded: 'She is without any doubt at all a woman whose loose living would make her

an object of shame on any farm-yard.' Another snoop reported: 'Her mind is – simply and frankly – a cesspool. Without
going into details, she held forth for 40 minutes on the difference in love-making of a Frenchman and an Englishman. On
another day she expatiated on the theme of animals. She apparently knows not the meaning of decency or reticence. She
is sex-fanatical.'[1] During the war, it seems, the secret state was
run by a species of men easily discomfited by women like Stella
Lonsdale.

In the winter of 1941, Stella made a dramatic escape from
France via the neutral city of Lisbon. Her Imperial Airways
flight landed at Whitchurch Airport on Guy Fawkes Night. She
provided her own fireworks: a colourful and noisy narrative involving invisible ink, a tangle of lovers and a stint in a German
interrogation cell with a pistol stowed secretly in her suspender
belt. She claimed to be concerned about the ineffectual nature
of covert British operatives in Marseilles, where she had lived
for several months. She claimed to know the name of the Nazi
officer who controlled agents despatched from Paris to Britain
by the Abwehr, the German intelligence service. Most explosively, she claimed to have cultivated a pro-British *Hauptmann*
(captain) within the organisation, who was ready to turn double
agent for the Allies and reveal the name of a British Army officer
in the pay of the Axis.

Most people arriving in wartime Britain with such a story
would have been forced to reiterate it in front of a stern committee at Latchmere House, an unlovely Victorian mansion on
the edge of Ham Common in which MI5 detained and questioned its suspects. Latchmere had a motto: 'No chivalry, no
gossip, no cigarettes.' Stella Lonsdale thrived on all three. The
strategy would have yielded little from her. Her questioning,
therefore, took place in less austere surroundings: the restaurant
and the thickly upholstered lounge of the Waldorf, the massive
hotel that follows the curve of the Aldwych. Stella checked
in on the day after she touched down at Bristol. She embar-

rassed her military escort by pointing out that the name he had signed in the hotel register bore little resemblance to the one sewn into the lining of his spectacles case.[2] The men of MI5 gave the occupant of Room 519 a codename: Michael. They bugged the phone. They also picked up the bill. ('Oh!' wrote one of her handlers. 'What this might cost B1A in certain circumstances!!'[3])

*

For the next few days, a small gang of intelligence personnel circled Stella, listening to her story over coffee and lunch and sherry, eavesdropping on her telephone conversations, mingling with the press delegates assembled at the hotel to debate the Board of Trade's decision to halve the government production of corsets. Her first official assessment was made by Helenus Milmo, an Irish-born libel lawyer transformed by war into one of the toughest interrogators in the secret service. In the 1930s, Milmo had saved the reputation of a French baron fingered as a German spy by a fellow resident in a Hampstead boarding house; in the following decade he would defend the honour of a celebrated Cannes hotelier who had been forced to flee France after being accused of collaboration with the Gestapo. Milmo was so skilled at breaking down suspects that his colleagues at Latchmere House nicknamed him 'Buster'. He had arranged to meet Stella at the Waldorf on the morning of 15 November, but he was late getting to the office and asked his secretary to advise her that he would be delayed. When his secretary reported that Stella had suggested postponing their meeting until the following week, Milmo immediately suspected that his interviewee was playing for time in which to smooth out the wrinkles in her story. Without replying to her request he belted down to the Aldwych. She kept him waiting for half an hour. When she eventually appeared, she claimed to have been dressing. Ironing, suspected Milmo, might have been nearer the mark.

Stella had more than a straight story – she had a complicated plan. She said, reported Milmo, 'that she had been so impressed by the way in which the humble people in this country had stood up to German air raids last winter that she felt it was up to her to do what she could to assist the country's war effort'. To this end, she explained, an associate in Marseilles had procured her a false passport, which was waiting for collection at the Swiss consulate in the city. If she could be parachuted into unoccupied France within the next fortnight, she could use this passport to enter occupied territory, meet with her contact in the Abwehr and relay his information back to London. He had, she said, already supplied her with a codebook taken from a captured British agent and given her a masterclass in how to confect invisible ink from bird droppings. Milmo quizzed Stella about this friendly Nazi, but she was unwilling to divulge his identity, referring to him only by the codename 'René' and describing him as an aristocratic lawyer who spoke fifteen languages, had been educated at Oxford and in America, and was hungry for an opportunity to strike a blow against Hitler. 'On any view Mrs Lonsdale is an unusual woman,' reflected Milmo, 'inasmuch as any normal person having managed to get out of German clutches would have made her way to this country as quickly as possible. She did not do so and therefore she is either an intensely patriotic person or alternatively she is thoroughly bad and has been in fact working for the Germans.' His chief suspicions circulated around the rogue Abwehr officer in Stella's story. 'Everything shows', he asserted, 'that René, if he exists at all, is running her as an agent.'[4] This was not necessarily a bad thing: if Stella could spy for one side, she could also spy for the other.

*

The following week, Milmo returned to the Waldorf and introduced Stella to two of his colleagues, Mr Thompson and Mr

Martin. These were not their real names. Mr Martin was Cyril Mills, co-owner of the Bertram Mills Circus. Mills had put the resources of his business at the disposal of military intelligence. The circus offices in Dorset Square were signed over to the Special Operations Executive. The winter home of the family firm was transformed into an internment camp for 18B detainees. Vans and vehicles used for the transport of horses and tigers were earmarked for an official plan to evacuate MI5's stable of double agents to a cluster of hotels near Betws-y-Coed, in the event of a German invasion. (The name of the operation was 'Mills's Circus'.) Mills's colleague, Mr Thompson, was Major T. A. Robertson. Robertson was the architect of the Double Cross system, through which Nazi agents who had landed in Britain were persuaded to work against their original employers. 'Tar', as he was known, had come to the attention of the intelligence services after a smart performance in the witness box at the trial of Norman Baillie-Stewart, who, in 1933, was found guilty of passing military blueprints to Berlin. Baillie-Stewart received a five-year custodial sentence and the distinction of being the last con to serve his time in the Tower of London. Robertson received the offer of a job with MI5, where he flourished. By the end of 1941, he could be confident that most of the agents parachuted into Britain by German intelligence had been captured – most of them shortly after they hit the ground. Stella, however, was a different kind of opponent.

Over coffee at the Waldorf, Tar told Stella how fascinated he had been to read the reports of her imprisonment and release from the Abwehr's secret interrogation centre at Angers; how he could only admire her for the bravery she had shown. He expressed enthusiasm for her scheme to return to France, but stressed that in order to construct a plan that would guarantee the safety of her mission, he would need to know every detail of her recent history. Some of this fervour was genuine. Only five days before this meeting he had spoken optimistically to a colleague about grooming Stella as a double agent. It was, however, also a matter of policy; a way of making her feel sufficiently relaxed and complacent to make mistakes. As the meeting progressed, Robertson's hopes for Stella's useful future faded. His report, written that same day, concluded that she was 'the lowest and trickiest human being that it has ever been my misfortune to encounter . . . I still hope that she will, before very long, say something which will entitle us at least to lock her up for the duration of the war.' Cyril Mills was more cautious. 'Stella, if only on her past record, must be credited with ability as a man-charmer, and for the reason that she takes as much care to charm as to be convincing, she is difficult to assess,' he wrote. 'She is, in my opinion, an extremely clever woman – but she knows it and this very fact may indeed be her undoing.'[5] And so it would prove.

*

Of all the characters I encountered in the course of writing this book, Stella Lonsdale was the most magnetic, and the most reprehensible. Those who remember her can attest to her cleverness, her charm and her talent for manipulation. In working through the thousands of pages of official documents on her case and meeting her surviving friends, relations, supporters and detractors, I have sometimes felt that death did not rob her of these powers. I have been impressed by her pragmatism and repelled by her opportunism. I have heard evidence of her reckless bravery and her callous treachery. I have heard her described as a war heroine, a prostitute, a collaborator, a fraudster and a burglar. I have listened to her allies defending her in the language of loyalty and love. I have witnessed the outrage of the family of a young Frenchman who went before a German firing squad, and in whose death Stella is implicated.

A man named Anthony Pitt-Rivers made the shrewdest observation about her. 'Everyone you speak to will give you a different version of Stella,' he told me, over lunch at the Cavalry and Guards Club, his soft voice at war with the Piccadilly traffic.[6] 'None of them will be the same.' Pitt-Rivers knew Stella for sixty years. She was his stepmother – or at least, she would have been, had not his father, Captain George Lane Fox Pitt-Rivers, proved unable to dissolve his first marriage, obliging her to annex the family name through deed pole. 'I owe her a great debt,' Anthony reflected. 'She was a surrogate stepmother to me. She was very kind and great fun. She wasn't all good, but she certainly wasn't all bad.' Anthony is the last of the Pitt-Rivers line. When he dies, the name will die with him. He is writing a family memoir, which he will bequeath to his heirs along with the family estate in Dorset, so that they might be able to identify the figures in the canvases that line the walls of the manor house. Stella's face has no place of honour there, though she will be accorded a small part in the narrative. There may be space in the footnotes for some of the war stories she told to Anthony and his brothers: her account of the brothel in Marseilles used as a meeting-place for the escape organisation for which she professed to have worked; the tale she told of a mission to Brest, the heart of the Nazi *zone interdite*, on which she claimed to have gunned down a Gestapo officer on the orders of the French Resistance. On another occasion, I heard the same tale from the closest friend and confidant of Stella's final years, an art dealer named Kenelm Digby-Jones – only in this version, two Gestapo officers fell dead to the deck.

A more sceptical assessment came from Pauline, Lady Rumbold, who, in the 1940s, was married to Anthony's brother, Julian Pitt-Rivers. 'Stella was very intense, very overwhelming,' she recalled, when I asked her to describe their first meeting.[7] '"We must buy you a hat," she said, and she took me by the arm and off we went shopping. And she bought me a hat. It was covered in Bird of Paradise feathers and cost over a hundred pounds.' The memory caused Lady Rumbold to rattle with laughter. 'Stella had all sorts of amazing stories,' she said. 'It was always hard to know whether she was telling the truth.' On the coffee table between us was a sheaf of papers: photocopied reports of interrogations; transcripts made by the phone-tappers of MI5; letters marked 'SECRET' in bloody red; a bill from the Waldorf Hotel; some photographs of a fleshy-faced woman with a strong jaw and a lipstick pout, stepping briskly down the street, or staring coolly from behind a pair of smart round spectacles. These papers told the story of a woman named Stella – an extraordinary story, very little of which is demonstrably true.

*

The future Mrs Lonsdale was born Stella Edith Howson Clive at Olton, near Solihull, in January 1913. Her father was a confectioner who was as free with his affections as he was with his sherbet pips: he abandoned his wife and children during Stella's girlhood. Perhaps it was from him that she acquired her talent for mendacity – her mother and four older siblings were comparatively guileless. Her brother John had been diagnosed with *dementia praecox*, a psychological disorder that obliged him to submit to periodic hospitalisations. Her brother Dennis had a position with the RAF. Her sister Norah was a schoolteacher in Solihull, and lived with her mother in the family villa on Reservoir Road.

In her lifetime Stella triumphed over a small army of men: they will march through these pages, often in pairs. The first was Paul Christian Holme, a prosperous Danish food importer with an office in the centre of Birmingham and a smart home in Edgbaston that, much to his regret, was also occupied by his wife, Nancy, who would not consent to divorce him. Stella did all she could to achieve co-respondent status: in 1934 she set up home with her lover and persuaded him to give her the cash to set up the Phoenix Bureau Secretarial Agency – a business which owed its brief but apparently brilliant success to the fact that Stella maintained a heroic opposition to paying any of the bills. After the sale of the agency Stella and Paul moved to London and rented a flat in Belsize Park. She took a job with the *Encyclopaedia Britannica*, but stayed alert for more rewarding possibilities, apparently pursuing an affair with Charles Lyttelton, the aristocratic captain of Worcestershire cricket club. And then, in the summer of 1936, she went through the grey-and-rose painted doors of Irfe, a fashionable perfume shop on Dover Street. The shop was jointly owned by Felix Yusupov – the Russian prince who was part of the gang that executed Rasputin by shooting him, beating him with an iron bar and hurling him through a gash in the ice-covered surface of the River Neva – and Barbara Lithgow Smith, a wealthy Russian émigré who lived in a suite in Claridge's. Stella examined the display cabinets, which contained bottles of Yusupov's branded scent (one kind for blondes, another for brunettes) and jars of face lotion purporting to be made from a recipe favoured by Catherine the Great; then fell into conversation with a shop assistant named Nicky Sidoroff – and also, perhaps, fell a little bit in love.

*

Connivance was the principal talent of Nicholas Sidoroff – that, and his instinct for picking a winner at the dog-track. He was born in St Petersburg during the first month of the Great War, but was educated in America and France, where he ran away from every school except his last, a reformatory with very high walls. His conduct in adulthood was so monotonously dishonest that his mother stopped answering his letters – which were usually requests for her to cable him more cash. He befriended a Roman Catholic bishop in Chambery and robbed him of several thousand francs. He stole a gold watch chain from a sea captain and stowed away at Cherbourg on a ship bound for Southampton, from where he made his way to London and threw himself at the mercy of his wealthy aunt, Barbara Lithgow Smith, who put him to work in Irfe.

Sidoroff was standing behind the counter when he met Stella, but they hatched their escape plan over cocktails in the Ritz. In November, they left their respective jobs to begin a new life on the Riviera. They did not, however, go as themselves. Nor did Stella inform Paul Holme that this was, in effect, the end of their engagement. Stella and Nicholas established impressive new identities at a church wedding in Monte Carlo, inscribing two bogus names in the register: the Prince and Princess Dimitri Magaloff. (The title was in Sidoroff's family, though he had no right to it.) They lodged with Sidoroff's half-brother, a pianist who kept a flat in Monte Carlo: he had warned against the marriage on the grounds that the flat was on the first floor, and all English girls loved horses. After the ceremony the newly-weds hit the gaming tables, and lost. They continued to lose, until Stella persuaded the British consul in Nice to hand over three thousand francs, with a cabled assurance from a lovelorn Paul Holme as security.

If Holme thought that he had bought Stella back with this act of generosity, he was wrong: the Magaloffs headed for Casablanca and then back to London, where, in October 1937, Stella gave birth to a boy. The couple had, by this time, exchanged identities yet again, so the baby was registered as Felix Nikita Warner – the first name commemorating the slayer of Rasputin whose perfume Nicholas had peddled on Dover Street. The boy lived for four months. Stella found him dead in his cot. The authorities did not discover the phoney status of his name until the end of the year, and by that time Nicky Sidoroff had been picked up by the police, charged with having entered the country as an illegal immigrant, and sentenced to two months in Wandsworth prison. And here he made a fateful friendship with a fellow lag with a name that betrayed a vertiginous fall from grace: a man who would destroy his relationship with Stella.

*

John Christopher Mainwaring Lonsdale was the son of a decorated Army officer, and like Sidoroff, had been kicked out of some of the best schools in Europe. He was known to readers of the *News of the World* as a jewel-thief, who worked the hotels around Piccadilly and Park Lane as part of that gang of well-dressed, well-bred, privately educated thugs who were whooped up in the press as the 'Mayfair Playboys'. The Playboys' more civilised crimes involved spiking the drinks of suggestible married women and relieving them of their emeralds – a trick known in the trade as 'Goodnight Cinderella'. Their less civilised crimes involved bloody attacks with a black mallet – an activity for which hard labour and the cat o'nine tails was the reward. Although MI5 regarded Lonsdale as a 'born crook', he was not completely bad. For a few days in June 1936, he had briefly enjoyed the experience of occupying the moral high ground when Sir Norman Birkett represented him in a libel case against a socialite named Pamela Blake, who had silenced the bar of the May Fair Hotel by declaring that Lonsdale was afflicted with a form of syphilis inherited from his father. (The judge obliged Miss Blake to support her expressions of regret with a cheque for £500 – signed by her mother, Lady Twysden.) The rest of Lonsdale's career, however, was a mixture of fraud, violent crime and right-wing politics. He joined the RAF and was impounded in Cairo for overstaying his leave. Under an assumed name, he joined and deserted the Dorset Regiment. He canvassed on behalf of the National League of Airmen, a pressure group through which Lord Rothermere and Oswald Mosley promoted the expansion of British air power with the intention, as one of their most enthusiastic supporters put it, of joining forces with Germany and America to attack 'the enemies of the White race, or human sub-species'.[8] He set up a number of companies – one a film-production outfit – that were fronts for running guns from Finland to the forces of General Franco's National Front. Lonsdale was so passionately attached to the rightist cause in Spain that he became one of the few

Englishmen to spend the Civil War fighting for Franco's Spanish Foreign Legion.

The incident that propelled John Lonsdale behind bars and into the arms of Stella was the violent assault he helped to inflict upon a jeweller in a suite at the Hyde Park Hotel in December 1937. This attack left Etienne Bellenger, the London representative of the Cartier company, senseless and bleeding on the carpet. It ensured that Lonsdale and Nicholas Sidoroff were slopping out at Wandsworth for the same months in 1938. It allowed Lonsdale and Stella to come into contact during prison visiting hours and begin a dialogue that continued in person and by correspondence. By June 1939, the Mayfair Playboy was free to hit Piccadilly again. He took Stella to mass at the Brompton Oratory; spoke of her lost son, Felix; wooed her with condolences. Stella accepted his proposal, she said, 'on the impulse of the moment'. The couple married in a brief civil ceremony at the Kensington Registry Office on 14 July 1939. A fortnight later, the union was solemnised at the Oratory. Stella's family did not attend. Nicky Sidoroff, however, did make it to the chapel, and attempted to thwart this second ceremony by offering the impediment of the marriage he and Stella had undergone in Monte Carlo. The bride silenced his protests with a signature on a letter declaring that the Monte Carlo ceremony lacked any civil status. In any case, the Russian's objections were purely technical. The new Mrs Lonsdale spent her wedding night with the groom on one side of the bed and Nicky Sidoroff on the other. The arrangement held for about as long as the Munich Agreement.

Inevitably, this triangular relationship was volatile. John Lonsdale claimed that Sidoroff had employed 'two mysterious gentlemen', who owned a Mercedes Benz and were members of the Hurlingham Club, to beat him up on the street. (Instead, he maintained, they 'attacked someone resembling me and caused them to lose an eye'.) The presence of a third man complicated the marriage yet further. In August, Stella met Wing Commander Lewis Dew in the American Bar at the Savoy. Dew was an influential agent within the British secret services and was preparing for a dangerous mission on German territory. That's the story, at least, with which he approached women at hotel bars and employed to con them out of their valuables. In truth, he was a well-spoken fantasist who worked for an insurance company. Dew asked Stella if she would be willing to do intelligence work when the war eventually came. It is not clear what her answer was – or whether she worked out that Dew was simply a plausible charlatan – but her experiences with him may have convinced her that the next best thing to being a spy was pretending to be one.[9]

*

The war broke up the Lonsdale ménage. On the day Germany invaded Poland, John surprised Stella by taking a match, setting fire to a piece of paper and declaring, 'That is what is going to happen to the world.' The following day he enlisted in the Army. By Christmas he was in France with the British Expeditionary Force as a sapper in the Royal Engineers. The date of his mobilisation proved unfortunate for Sidoroff, who had arranged to spend the night with Mr and Mrs Lonsdale in a hotel in Guildford. The couple stood him up. According to Stella, Sidoroff waited for them until 2 a.m., after which he consoled himself by picking up a local woman, from whom he received a series of passionate embraces and a dose of venereal disease.

Stella advised Sidoroff to seek medical help for his condition, but he refused. His state of mind was not calmed when John Lonsdale fired a shot from France in his direction: a letter to Scotland Yard accusing him of blackmail. Stella waved away the accusation, but responded to the jealous impulse behind it. On 12 January 1940 she sailed from Southampton and made her way to Paris, ostensibly to attend her mother-in-law, who lived in the city and was about to undergo a difficult medical operation. (Friendship was certainly not the motive: MI5 officers who eavesdropped on Stella's calls from the Waldorf concluded that Ina Lonsdale was 'not a particularly nice woman'.) Stella stayed in Paris for as short a time as was decently possible, then took the train west to Nantes, where John was stationed. They lived uproariously in the city, telling officials that they were members of the British secret services. Stella boasted to the local chief of police that she was a cousin of the War Minister, Leslie Hore-Belisha. Her presence in the port was not appreciated by her husband's commanding officer, who, when Stella refused to take his hints about returning home, arranged for John to be transferred back to England, hoping that his troublesome wife would follow. The strategy failed. Stella stayed stubbornly put, giving the feeble excuse that in London she would be unable to escape the unwelcome attentions of Sidoroff. She remained in Nantes even after it became clear that the city was to be abandoned to the Nazis, who were marching ever closer and bombarding its citizens, by radio and in print, with their most effective propaganda slogan: 'The British will defend France to the last Frenchman.' On 17 June, a Polish seaman begged Stella to escape to England on board his ship. She refused. Four days later the Nazis marched into Nantes. They occupied the harbour and the railway stations, rounded up a gaggle of useful hostages and imposed a 9 p.m. curfew. Stella was trapped behind enemy lines.

Why did Stella refuse to budge? It's no easier to decide the question now than it was for Cyril Mills and his colleagues. Under interrogation, she claimed that her reasons were both personal and patriotic: she aimed to do something for the Allied cause that would recuperate the bad name of her jailbird husband. Given that Germany seemed, in the first year of the war, to be assured of domination of the European continent, Stella may already have concluded that her most profitable course was to make friends with the Nazis. A letter sent to her mother suggests that, weeks before the invaders arrived, she was already involved in some kind of espionage activity. Stella bragged that she 'was doing a very interesting job which it would be interesting to relate after the war'.[10] Her only legitimate employment, however, began on the very day that the occupation began. As the Germans surged through the streets, Stella took up a teaching post at the local Berlitz language school. Here, she claimed, she became an immediate object of interest. A Gestapo agent named Oswald Bendemann signed up for English lessons and – with revealingly perfect grammar – persuaded her to share a bottle of champagne. A young local named Jean Platiau booked daily four-hour tutorials, during which, Stella claimed, he declared his love for his teacher. He was just another man on Stella's list – but of all the men with whom Stella had dealings, Jean Platiau is the one who paid the highest price.

Stella's recorded remarks about Jean Platiau are vicious. He was 'not normal'. He was 'an effeminate little Frenchman', with 'the mannerisms of a pervert'. She describes how he tricked her into sharing a lunch date with him by offering the invitation in front of the school principal. She describes how he propositioned a waitress in a restaurant in order to provoke her jealousy. A photograph of him is included in one of her files. He is an owlish young man with high cheekbones, a pristine centre parting and spectacles with large round frames. He stares sharply towards the camera lens. The image survives because in 1941, the Communist Resistance assassinated a prominent German officer in Nantes, Feldkommandant Fritz Hotz. In retaliation, fifty prisoners were executed by firing squad. Jean Platiau was among them. He had four hours to prepare for death. He was twenty years old.

*

From this point, it becomes increasingly difficult to navigate the multiple versions of Stella's narrative. She was clearly exhilarated by the possibilities for intrigue offered by a city under occupation. She took on several new boyfriends, one of whom was a Spanish black marketeer with an inexhaustible supply of tinned sardines. A French contact, she said, gave her details of a plan to turn the port of Lorient into a massive submarine base: she relayed this information in a letter to her husband, encoded as some cryptic remarks about the size of the fishes in the harbour. In November, she said, the same contact supplied her with the plans of a secret petrol dump that the Germans were constructing near the town of St-Luce-sur-Loire: she claimed to have had these in her handbag when the Germans took her into custody.

Her surviving accounts of this period are riddled with inconsistencies and deviations. Sometimes her map of the petrol dump becomes a map of an airfield; the place of her arrest flickers from the front door of her lodgings to the steps of the American consulate. Each version, however, awards the figure of Jean Platiau a central role. Her most sustained and detailed account told how Platiau had come stabbing at her doorbell and pushed his way into her apartment in the middle of the night. 'He was crying,' recalled Stella, 'which is an unusual thing for a man to do. He said to me he was a German agent. He was a Frenchman but he was working for the Germans which is pretty nasty, and he had been watching me on their orders for months.' With tears streaming down his face, Stella said, he made two unwelcome confessions: he was in love with her – and he had also denounced her to the authorities as a supporter of the exiled General de Gaulle. Then, in a detail straight from *The 39 Steps*, she described how he pulled back the curtain and gestured down into the street, where two Gestapo men were waiting to apprehend her as soon as she left the building. He would send them away, he said, if she would consent to him spending the night in her lodgings. Stella said that she had told him to sleep on the divan, and locked herself in the bedroom. The next morning a German military vehicle pulled up outside the apartment. She and Jean Platiau were taken away under escort. On the journey, Platiau made a proposal. 'If you would agree to work for the Germans and if I were to say you were in love with me as well . . . they would not do anything to you,' he suggested. 'Otherwise, they may do anything to you.' Two hours later, the car arrived in Angers, home to the secret interrogation centre of the Abwehr. On arrival, however, Platiau was treated not as a dutiful Nazi operative, but as someone who shared the same doubtful status as his prisoner. According to Stella, they were confined in cells within earshot of each other – and Platiau was soon shouting his apologies across the landing.

It was Stella's account of what happened next that proved the most debated and contested part of the narrative she wove in the coffee lounge of the Waldorf: her spell of detention and questioning by the Abwehr officers at Angers. Cyril Mills listened to her tell the story over and over again, and pored over transcripts of the version she gave in bugged telephone conversations. Reading through this material, a strong sense of Stella's manipulative personality emerges. You can sense the element of sexual tease in her repeated description of what she was wearing on the day of her arrest: a light frock with a silk bolero, scant underwear and a narrow suspender belt in which a pistol was hidden. You can sense the self-pity in her enumeration of the privations of confinement: the stale, butterless bread; the burnt black coffee; the stinking broom with which she swept the floor of her cell; the chill winter wind that rattled through the open windows and made the prison uninhabitable for bugs. You can sense the element of melodrama in her account of being worked over by her interrogators. What's more or less impossible to determine from this material is the veracity of her story. As a female MI5 operative noted, 'She is a liar of such convincingness as I would not have believed existed. Unless one actually hears her make statements that appeared to bear every ring of truth, and then, shortly afterwards, gloating over the way she had put them over, one could have sworn that she was sincere.'

First, then, is Stella's version of the story. She asserted that her chief interrogator at Angers was Standartenführer Dernbach. She described Dernbach as 'so much the caricature of all the Germans you see in *Punch*'. He was, she said, a stuttering, schnapps-bibbing Bavarian officer who despised women but loved boys – almost as much as he loved his sprightly green Citroën with the front-wheel drive. In a fit of anger, claimed Stella, he had stubbed out a cigarette on her forehead, then rifled through her handbag and discovered the plans of the petrol dump at St-Luce-sur-Loire. He took the document to his superior, Hans Meissner, a suave former U-Boat captain with excellent English and, Stella noticed, surprisingly dirty fingernails. Meissner had a brutal reputation: he preferred brisk executions to lengthy interrogations. Also present in the room was another Abwehr officer, Meissner's right-hand man. Stella claimed to have recognised him instantly: she and Sidoroff had encountered him in Paris in November 1936. He did not appear to remember her. She gave nothing away. Throughout her meetings with MI5, Stella referred to this man as 'René', though she admitted that this was not his real name. She had strong reasons, she explained, to keep his identity dark.

René and Meissner, said Stella, examined the map and agreed a course of action. The British suspect would be imprisoned before being put on trial, found guilty, and executed by firing squad. The first stages of this plan were quickly implemented. A tribunal was convened, at which the star witness was Jean Platiau. Platiau attacked Stella for her promiscuity as well her politics. He declared that she had fifteen lovers in Nantes, and numbered himself among them. Under cross-examination he reduced his own claim to have slept with Stella to the more minor assertion that he had kissed her hand. His testimony was further undermined when it became clear that he meant 'admirers' rather than lovers, which, Stella argued, could not reasonably be held against her. Despite Platiau's failure as a witness, Stella's guilt was established to the satisfaction of the tribunal. She was discharged to her cell, where she lay on the wooden plank that served as a bed, gazed at the obscene graffiti chalked on the wall, shivered and despaired. A few days later, she received a visit from René. He admitted that he remembered meeting her in Paris five years previously, and had another confession to make: he was vehemently pro-British and despised the Nazis and all their works. A second tribunal was imminent. If she demonstrated her readiness to serve the German cause, he would do everything he could to push the committee's verdict in her favour. After that, he would help her to double-cross her Nazi controllers and carry vital intelligence back to Britain. He had details about a spy named Alfred Gaessler, a radio-operator who had been despatched to Nantes by the British. Gaessler, he said, had taken his suitcase wireless set straight to the Abwehr and, under Nazi supervision, was now feeding radio messages back to London – some of them accurate, some of them misleading. René also had information about German agents operating within Britain – one of them within the ranks of the armed forces – and details regarding Prince Louis of Liechtenstein, who, Stella asserted, was the spymaster co-ordinating their operations from Paris. In return for this portfolio of secrets, René demanded a British passport and, for the sake of his family, complete anonymity. He gave her a speech about his sympathies: 'I think if the Germans under the Nazis win the war then I personally shall blow out my brains, because for anyone who loves liberty this will not be a world to live in.' Stella accepted his proposal, and his condolences, too: on 12 February, the anniversary of the death of her baby, he presented her with a bunch of carnations.

At the second tribunal Stella assured the panel that she was eager to work for the Third Reich in any capacity they might desire. She sang the praises of Nazism by recycling words and phrases she had once learned when given the task of celebrating

Hitler's achievements at a meeting of the Birmingham Junior Conservative League. After three days of questioning, she was released to a room in the Hôtel de France, a requisitioned building close to the railway station at Angers.

There was a wealth of persuasively outré detail in Stella's account of the Nazi officers she met during this period: a colonel with a loyal wire-haired terrier and fond memories of Cornwall; a sub-lieutenant who had worked as a travel agent for the Hollywood film star Marion Davies. It was the smaller details that Cyril Mills found hard to swallow. If Stella was wearing such a skimpy silk dress when she was captured, why did the Abwehr not discover the pistol hidden in her underwear? Why did they not search her handbag before she arrived in prison? Why could she remember nothing about the Frenchman who told her about the military petrol dump? And if she and René had concocted a secret plan of some kind, why attract suspicion by filling her cell with carnations? Perhaps, Mills reasoned, those flowers had been received in less grim surroundings: a room at the Hôtel de France, for instance. Perhaps the story of René concealed a simpler, more ignoble tale, in which Stella was not a heroine of the German occupation of France, but the mistress of a Nazi officer – or officers – with whom she had taken a tour of the prison, in order to improve the texture of her cover story.

*

Like police constables, Stella's men tended to come in pairs – and she possessed a talent for playing one off against another. Her accounts of her ongoing relations with René and Meissner read like a sexless version of her *ménage à trois* with Lonsdale and Sidoroff. Meissner, she said, took her on trips to Paris and urged her to agree to operate in tandem with a partner agent, perhaps for a mission in Turkey or Yugoslavia. René took her to Brest and advised her only to agree to work alone, for fear of exposure. René also procured false documents that allowed her to cross France's new internal borders unescorted. He sent her on a mission to Paris to pass a message to a group of escapees: she was told she would recognise them by the beaded dragonfly badges they wore under their coat lapels. These excursions did not always go to plan: in one railway restaurant car Stella clocked a member of her tribunal at Angers, and was obliged to evade him by clinging to the outside of the carriage. Her greatest mistake, however – the error that forced her to go on the run from her Nazi handlers – was, she claimed, committed in the café of the Hôtel de France.

One afternoon early in April 1941, Stella related, a loud, unattractive sexagenarian man came bounding up to her café table. 'I understand you are an English lady,' he ventured. 'You must say hullo to me.' He introduced himself as Hermann Hyman – known as Harry, he explained, because of his twelve years in Australia, where he had been interned in the last war and where his wife, an actress, had been shot dead on stage by an assassin in the audience. Harry poured out his troubles. 'I am not on very good terms with the German authorities,' he explained, unfolding a narrative involving official persecution and confiscated property. 'I am trying to get away because I am a Jew.' He implored Stella for help. She made sympathetic noises, but regretted that she could not help him escape from France. The next day she received an angry phone call from René. Hyman was not a refugee, but a low-rent agent provocateur in the pay of the Gestapo, who had already filed a report on Stella's anti-Nazi attitudes. His advice was simple. 'You had better go at once.' He instructed her to make contact with an undercover organisation in Marseilles that could return her to London. Once in London she would make contact with Colonel Claude Dansey, head of the Secret Intelligence Service, and inform him that René was willing to parachute into England 'to discuss plans for dealing with Hitler'.[11]

Marseilles in the Vichy years was a city of refugees, runaways, adventurers, criminals and liars. It had, according to its wartime inhabitants, two kinds of black market: the good one, through which you bought a packet of cigarettes at an exorbitant price; and the bad one, through which you bought a packet of cigarettes at an exorbitant price to discover they were stuffed with straw. People on the run, however, were its principal commodity. Gangsters aided the escape of Jewish refugees and anti-Nazis: though their services did not come free, the criminal syndicates of the city, in this respect, acquitted themselves more honourably than many of its citizens. Kim Philby snooped around the dockside bars on behalf of the *Daily Telegraph* and British intelligence. At the Hôtel Splendide, Varian Fry, a foppish, Harvard-educated foreign correspondent, co-ordinated a rescue organisation from his bathroom – funded by the US government, which was keen to exploit the 'fire sale on brains' caused by the war. (Max Ernst, Hannah Arendt and Marc Chagall were among his haul of geniuses.) At the Seaman's Mission on the Rue de Forbin, an unexcitable Scotsman named Captain Ian Garrow and Albert Marie-Guérrise, a Belgian doctor, ran an escape outfit which spirited British soldiers over the Pyrenees and into the relative safety of Spain. Marie-Guérrise was known by the *nom de guerre* of 'Patrick Albert O'Leary' and gave this phoney name to what become known as the 'Pat' Escape Line. It was this organisation to which Stella Lonsdale made overtures. Frustratingly, however, they were received with little enthusiasm. Garrow, she said, failed to understand the significance of the information she had yielded to him about the secret petrol dump, the submarine base at Lorient and the rogue Abwehr officer willing to help the Allied cause. Garrow's refusal to incorporate her within the 'Pat' Line organisation, however, did allow her to begin forming the geometry of her next triangular relationship. Her two new lovers, Frank Viner and Christian

Boulanger, were unlike Meissner and René in one important respect: MI5 had proof that they both existed.

Boulanger was the most ardent and the most volatile. A well-connected businessman with his own chateau and the necessary paperwork to travel freely through France, Stella used him to relay messages to her Nazi associates in Nantes. Once she had escaped to London his scented letters began to arrive at the Waldorf, from where they were forwarded to Cyril Mills: 'I grudge you all the men that you have known,' Boulanger wrote. 'I should like you to suffer as I am suffering.'[12] Viner was a more calculating character, as sleekly amoral as Stella. A former sergeant in the Czech Army, he was a glamorous, lounge-lizardly figure who supported himself through a mixture of freelance journalism and prostitution: night-clubs were his natural environment. Like Stella, Viner came to Marseilles in order to offer his services to Garrow's escape organisation. Like Stella, he was treated with suspicion. When it became clear that Garrow intended to hold them both at arm's length, Viner began to file unflattering reports back to London: '[Garrow] is not a capable intelligence officer and gives his subordinates no guidance.' MI5's assessment of Viner was scarcely less flattering. They had been keeping tabs on him since June 1939, when, as Paris correspondent of the New York *Herald Tribune*, he had developed an overly cosy relationship with the German press attaché. Kim Philby, who had encountered Viner in Marseilles, supplied the damning phrases: 'He is an intelligent man who has lived by his wits for some time; he is, however, weak-minded and easily swayed. He has a great attraction for women, and a large part of his income probably comes from this source. He is one of the most gifted liars I have ever met, and is indiscreet in every language he knows.'[13]

Stella spent the summer and autumn of 1941 in Marseilles. What she was doing there – beyond wooing Garrow and being wooed by Boulanger and Viner – is hard to establish. It may be pure coincidence that during this period the 'Pat' Line operatives suffered a series of crises and reversals. Representatives of French military intelligence prowled around them all summer. Leading members were arrested, interrogated and released. One of them claimed that Stella was implicated in this process.[14] Garrow was forced into hiding, lying low in an apartment just around the corner from the local Gestapo HQ. His luck ran out in October, when the Vichy authorities transported him to a prison camp in the Dordogne. His compatriots assumed that these betrayals were the work of a crooked 'Pat' Line operative named Sergeant Harry Cole. Cole was a member of the Royal Engineers who claimed to have been employed before the war as a bodyguard to Wallis Simpson, but was in fact a deserter with a manslaughter charge hanging over him in Britain. In September Garrow discovered that Cole had been snuggling up to the Gestapo and supporting a mistress in Lille with money intended to fund the travels of escapees and evaders. Garrow planned to kill him with a syringe of insulin. This gave Cole a strong motive for betraying the 'Pat' Line agents, but it is entirely possible that Stella deserves some of the blame. Garrow's arrest certainly forced Pat O'Leary, who controlled the organisation in Garrow's absence, to make a swift decision about Stella's future – and Stella, for her part, claimed she had a pressing reason to leave. She had, she said, received a postcard from René warning her that the Gestapo were on the point of arresting her. They even knew that, with the help of a bottle of peroxide, she had recently gone blonde. As soon as she received the card, she went straight to the salon to have her hair returned to a darker shade. News from Nantes may also have increased her anxiety. On 21 October 1941, fifty prisoners were shot dead in retaliation for a fatal attack upon a Nazi officer in Nantes. Jean Platiau fell with them.

As October drew to a close, O'Leary sent a radio message to London, informing them that he was sending Stella out of the country. A boat would carry her to Lisbon, from where she would fly to London. Before she left, she gave Frank Viner a parting gift: the wedding ring that had been slipped on her finger by John Lonsdale. A week later she was applying her make-up in Room 519 at the Waldorf, waiting for her first softly-softly interrogation to begin, while the men of MI5 speculated about how best to crack her. 'We might put her in prison,' mused John Cecil Masterman, the cricketing Oxford don who chaired the committee that controlled MI5's stable of Nazi double agents. 'I am inclined to think . . . that the deprivation of sexual gratification alone will quickly bring her to disclose anything in order to secure her release.'[15]

Masterman was wrong. Stella Lonsdale was not a slave to her appetites. Quite the opposite: it was her ability to control and direct them that made her so formidable. During her period of surveillance she had no sexual relations with any of the old flames that smouldered around her. She drank very little, too. MI5 noted that her bills at the Waldorf were mainly for fruit juice. At her lunches with Cyril Mills, she nursed one glass of sherry through the entire meal. The tap on her phone revealed nothing incriminating, except, perhaps, the violence of her feelings towards John Lonsdale. (In a conversation with her sister-in-law, Stella reflected that it was lucky that she did not own a revolver, as she might be tempted to secure herself a divorce with a bullet.) Most frustratingly for Mills, Stella's private accounts of her activities in France tallied with the version that she had offered to her handlers. To catch her off-guard, to expose the cracks in her story, a more intense form of observation was required.

In the last week of November 1941 Mills informed Stella that she would be relocated from her room at the Waldorf to a flat in Queen's Court, a mansion block in Bayswater. The accommodation came with an incumbent flatmate called Nina Myers. Stella graciously accepted, but knew that Myers was a spy as surely as she knew that the phone in the new apartment was tapped. This new level of surveillance, however, told MI5 only what they knew already – that Stella could be as shameless and manipulative as circumstances demanded.

From her new home in Queen's Court, Stella rang the Waldorf each day to check for letters and telegrams. Sometimes she called twice a day. She rang the Dorchester for the same reason. There was little point. All of her mail – violent declarations of love from Christian Boulanger, more temperate messages from Frank Viner – was forwarded to the desk of Cyril Mills. Boulanger's letters were dabbed with Stella's favourite perfume 'Shocking', which came in a bottle formed like a dressmaker's mannequin, and was the work of Elsa Schiaparelli, an outrageous couturier who wore a hat shaped like a lamb chop and went skiing in a curly silver wig. 'Take a sniff at this paper my love,' Boulanger implored. 'It is scented with Shocking, but so slightly . . . Like our love which is fading because it is doomed.'[16]

Lovers nearer to home chose more direct means of communication. Nicky Sidoroff and John Lonsdale returned to Stella's orbit. They were both back in London and had both acquired new partners; two women who now regarded Stella with understandable suspicion. Stella did not want these men back in her bed – not even one at a time – but she was deeply interested in the contents of their wallets. Nina Myers observed her use a ferocious display of tears to extract cash from Sidoroff. 'Her histrionic powers are of the first water,' Stella's flatmate reported. 'On one occasion she indulged in violent bouts of weeping and hysteria for an hour and a quarter that seemed to shake her whole being. When the man for whose benefit they were staged departed, within one minute – in fact, instantaneously, she was laughing and congratulating herself on the success of her act.' Nina also observed her con Lonsdale out of a small bundle of notes: Stella told him she had promised to meet some business acquaintances for lunch at Claridge's, but had lost her handbag in the blackout. Lonsdale, with some reluctance, made up the loss. Nina Myers wrote: 'The whole aim of her life is to make as much money as possible, and she gives the impression that she would stick at nothing to achieve this.' Stella may have concurred. 'As long as I either earn enough money or get enough I don't care about the future,' she told Lonsdale.[17]

Stella's social life in London revived pre-war friendships made through her two husbands. Sidoroff took her to Charlton greyhound track and tea at the Savoy. Stella hit the smorgasbord at the Claridge's Causerie with Sidoroff's aunt, Barbara Lithgow Smith. She gossiped with Olga Tredegar, a White Russian émigré who had married Evan, Lord Tredegar – a disciple of the blood-drinking occultist Aleister Crowley and widely regarded as one of the worst poets in Britain. She sank cocktails at the Ritz bar with another East European refugee, Cécile, Lady Kemball-Cook, a Russian general's daughter who owned a Mayfair boutique called Xenia, and, according to a police informer, 'looked as if she were either an international jewel thief or a spy'. Cécile shared a sense of humour with Stella: on the day that her husband, Basil Kemball-Cook, was shamed by an appearance in the bankruptcy courts, she threw on a posh frock and drove to the Gaumont, Haymarket, to attend the European premiere of Frank Capra's *You Can't Take It with You*.[18]

Stella's principal confidante in this period, however, was a West End actress called Diana Vernon, John Lonsdale's married sister. Diana is remembered by her surviving relations as a glamorous good-time girl who, in her lifetime, acquired a series of rich husbands connected with the British film business.[19] MI5 regarded Vernon as 'a thoroughly disreputable person', and this was probably the basis of her friendship with Stella. Together, they rolled up the carpet at Queen's Court to truffle for concealed microphones, rifled through Nina Myers' room and stole the top pages of her notebook in the hope of detecting the ghost of a report to Cyril Mills. In return, Stella allowed her sister-in-law to use the Queen's Court flat to meet her lover, and lied on her behalf to conceal the affair from her husband. Diana's lover was Jimmy Bruce, a wing commander seconded from the RAF

to the Ministry of Aircraft Production. Stella came to know him
well. He had a gift for careless talk. He told Stella that he was
working on the prototype for an electrically driven aerial war-
head. He told her that she ought to be demanding £1,000 a year
for her services to British intelligence. He also told her that he
had a friend who would like to take her out for cocktails. Stella
was glad of the diversion. It was, however, her association with
Bruce that brought an end to her freedom, and persuaded Cyril
Mills that the state's best option was to lock her up for the duration of the war.

On 5 January 1942, the two couples – Stella, Diana, Jimmy
Bruce and his friend Dickie Shaw – went on a jaunt down to
the Hampshire coast, stopping on the way for lunch in a pub
at Tunbridge Wells. Their destination was the Aerial Torpedo
Development Unit at Gosport, a base that comprised a Victorian fortress, an aerodrome built during the last war, and a cluster
of huts in which engineers and scientists were developing the
next generation of airborne weapons. In the mid-afternoon,
the car scudded into the complex and came to a halt on the
quayside overlooking the Solent. Stella and Diana waited inside while Dickie and Jimmy went to view the latest test launch
of the new torpedo. That accomplished, the four drove back
to London. Alarm bells rang when the men of MI5 heard that
Stella, still under suspicion of being a Nazi spy, had, with casual
ease, penetrated a high-security military research establishment.
Dickie Shaw and Jimmy Bruce were hauled in for questioning
and admitted discussing the prototype torpedo with Stella. This
was just the kind of information that the intelligence agencies
were most keen to keep dark – not because the torpedo was a
fearsome new secret weapon, but because it represented a tech-
nological step backwards from an earlier, diesel-driven model.
Stella had enough evidence to demonstrate to the Germans
that, for want of materials, the British missile-development programme was going into reverse. Official peace of mind could
not have been improved when, two days after Stella's visit, a

Bristol Beaufort bomber armed with the new torpedoes suffered engine failure on take-off from Gosport and exploded on the ground, killing the three-man crew.

After this, the walls closed quickly upon Stella Lonsdale. On 17 January 1942 she was summoned to the War Office for an interrogation more aggressive than anything she had experienced in the coffee lounge at the Waldorf. Cyril Mills informed her that she was no longer being assessed for a mission for the intelligence services: the aim of the questioning was now to determine whether it would be prudent to intern her under Regulation 18B. That night she called Nicholas Sidoroff and told him that if the judgement went against her, she would commit suicide. 'And nobody and nothing will stop me,' she declared. 'Everyone has the means to kill themselves if they want to. Fingernails cut.' One week later an officer from Special Branch arrived at the flat to take her into custody. On the same day that Stella began her journey to Holloway, Tar Robertson killed the phone line at Queen's Court and arranged for Stella's letters to be redirected to the desk of his colleague Cyril Mills. Among her belongings, Robertson discovered a small wrap of blue paper that contained a fine white powder. He sent it to the laboratory for analysis. A few days later the lab wrote back to inform him that it was a packet of salt from a bag of Smith's potato crisps.

*

Stella's imprisonment endured for as long as the hostilities between the Allied and Axis powers. At first, she kept her confinement secret from everyone but Nicholas Sidoroff. She wrote to him, called him by his pet name Koliouschka, begged him to visit, and implored him to tell her friends that she had been hospitalised 'partly from shock'. (He did not visit, but his new girlfriend, Cissie Dare, sent parcels containing little delicacies: chocolate, sherry, fish and dried fruit.) The other men in Stella's life raged and roared in her absence. Christian Boulanger's scented letters continued to clog the pigeonholes of the Waldorf, but were read only by Cyril Mills. ('I hate myself for loving you . . . I have caught myself crying over the linen which you wore and which has retained the perfume of your body.'[20]) Frank Viner left messages at the desk in person. They went unanswered. John Lonsdale plotted to divorce his wife on grounds of bigamy and fired off missives to Scotland Yard, declaring that she was using her connections with the secret services to engineer a campaign of blackmail. ('I have good reason to believe that she has obtained, and may still be obtaining, money from credulous people on the strength of such stories and is also quite unscrupulous enough to trap some poor devil into an indiscretion and turn in a statement to you that would contain enough truth to damn him.'[21])

Behind the bricks and bars of Holloway, Stella kept busy by teaching herself Spanish and writing immense and emotive letters to her lovers and relations. Once the *Sunday Pictorial* had run a story about her imprisonment, written from the sexy angle of her marriage to a former Mayfair Playboy, there was little point in attempting to conceal her whereabouts. By post, she convinced John Lonsdale's maternal grandmother that she was a wronged woman – but failed to extract the enormous cheque for which she hoped. She sent soft, nostalgic letters to Nicholas Sidoroff about their lost son. 'A woman here is going to have a baby – I can't help feeling absurdly jealous of her,' she wrote. 'I loved Felix so much and so did you. Why did he have to die? It altered both our lives and separated us.' She also spoke of Felix to one of the warders, Doris Andrews. 'My little baby died,' Stella told her. 'He was a beauty. It sort of put me off my head. I went completely gay, even to an extreme . . . If my baby had lived I should have been with my husband now. Will you come up to my room sometime and see my baby's photograph?'[22] Doris Andrews filed reports of all her conversations with Stella to Cyril Mills. She did not mention whether she ever found time to accept the invitation. Perhaps her masters would not have cared. Stella had become a tiresome distraction. Mills took Sidoroff for coffee at the Piccadilly Hotel and complained to him about the amount of time that had been wasted investigating her story. 'Frankly', he admitted, 'neither I nor anyone else was willing to go on seeing her much longer to be fed with small talk and/or lies.'[23]

Conclusive dismissals of Stella's entire case had already begun to accrue in her file. 'I am more and more convinced that she is not quite normal,' noted an MI5 officer named Barton. 'I believe she hardly knows herself when she is telling the truth or lying,' observed Doris Andrews. 'Although I do not think she is certifiable, I should say she has a mental kink.'[24] MI5 released its grip on Stella and reclassified her as a problem for the Home Office Advisory Committee, along with all those right-wing cranks and Italian waiters. They had, it seems, decided that the true story of Stella Lonsdale would never be told – and that they had no appetite to hear another dishonest version of it from her.

There was one more flurry of secret-state interest in Stella before it left her in the hands of the civil authorities. In July 1942, MI5 decided to transfer her to HMP Aylesbury in Buckinghamshire and put her in a cell with a new prisoner named Mathilde Carré. Carré had been a leading Resistance co-ordinator in Paris – until November 1941, when, for a monthly fee of sixty thousand francs, she had agreed to switch her allegiance to the Nazis. In February 1942 she had travelled to London to make a report to her masters on the structure of the Special Operations Executive: her audacious plan was to become the mistress of Lord Selborne, the government minister responsible for the organisation. After reading reports of a conversation conducted between Selborne and Carré over cocktails at Claridge's, some of Selborne's colleagues were under the impression that she was on the point of succeeding. She was interned at Aylesbury on the first day of July 1942. As she could speak very little English, MI5 thought it might be fruitful to give her a cellmate who could interpret for her – a cellmate who shared a similar personal history.

Stella was encouraged to inform on her fellow internee. She spent three years confined with Carré, but little information seems to have been surrendered. A revealing incident, however, did occur on 21 July 1942, the day of Stella's transfer from Holloway – an incident that casts doubt on her boasts about having remained cool under interrogation by Standartenführer Dernbach of the Abwehr. Stella simply refused to move. The officers carried her through the door of her cell. She began to scream. She was still screaming as the warders dragged her down the metal stairs, with such violence that her dress was torn away from the waist. She was wearing nothing underneath. Miss Wilson, the deputy governor, took a dirty sheet from a pile of laundry and wrapped it around her. Stella was carried into the waiting coach, where she sat, sobbing, among a small group of fellow 18B detainees: Mathilde Krafft, who had funded the activities of German agents by laundering money through the tills at Selfridges; Josephine Eriksson and the Duchesse de Château-Thierry, who had both been in the pay of an Abwehr spymaster. An MI5 report speculated on why Stella had responded with such fear and rage. 'It is not perhaps fanciful to entertain the possibility that Mrs Lonsdale misinterpreted the transfer of this peculiarly sinister little party as a preliminary to a trial for treachery.'[25] And a preliminary, therefore, to execution.

*

The prison system spat out Stella Lonsdale in May 1945. One year later, however, she had recovered her composure and, in an unlikely turn of circumstances, reinvented herself as the director of a motor repair workshop in Shepherd's Bush. From her office overlooking the canal at the Seymour Car and Tyre Company, she wrote wistful letters to Cyril Mills, alluding to their time as prisoner and interrogator as if it were a cherished wartime love affair. Stella's living relations, friends and acquaintances can offer no clue as to how she came to acquire this business. Over the summer of 2008, I met with most of the survivors of her circle, all of whom were mystified by this short-lived career in motor engineering. They knew her instead as the consort of the man who rescued her from the job market for ever: Captain George Pitt-Rivers, anthropologist, eugenicist, author, eccentric and the little-liked landlord of dozens of tenant farmers in a vast tract of Dorset. Accounts vary as to how they met. The most popular version places them at a cocktail party at the Ritz – where Stella was serving the drinks.

To his friends – of whom he had few – George Pitt-Rivers was known as Jo. He was a notorious figure in the county, who had been imprisoned for his intimacy with the Nazis.[26] His books had a relentless theme: *The Clash of Culture and the Contact of Races* (1927) argued against racial integration; *The Czech Conspiracy* (1938) blamed the Sudeten Jews for attempting to foment a European war. ('Fight if we will if fight we must,' he declared, 'not against Germany for daring and being strong enough to look after her own sons, but against the enemy in our midst!'[27]) The latter gained excellent reviews in the Nazi press, not least because the German secret service had funded his research trip to the Sudetenland. By the time war came, his political position was firmly established. He had cheered Hitler at the 1937 Nuremberg rally. He had worn a gold swastika on his lapel and boasted of his friendships with Göring and Ribbentrop. He had hugger-muggered at the Russian Tea Room in Kensington with his friends in the Right Club, a gang of pro-German ideologues led by a Tory MP named Archibald Maule Ramsay. It is not clear whether Pitt-Rivers ever joined Ramsay in a chorus of the club's sardonic theme song – 'Land of dope and Jewry/ Land that once was free' – but he certainly went to jail with him when, in the summer of 1941, Ramsay and

Anna Wolkoff, the proprietor of the Russian Tea Room, were exposed as members of a Nazi spy ring that had stolen thousands of confidential documents from the American embassy in London. Pitt-Rivers, like many 18B detainees, drew a kind of moral sustenance from internment. In the camp at Ascot, he struck up a strong friendship with Leigh Vaughan-Henry, and the pair conspired in a campaign of awkward resistance against their captors. After his release, Pitt-Rivers took a perverse pride in his experience of detention. When his son Julian announced his intention to marry, the Captain expressed his desire to place an announcement in *The Times* describing himself as 'George Henry Lane Fox Pitt-Rivers, late of Her Majesty's Dragoon Guards and Ascot Concentration Camp'. 'That', reflected the bride, six decades later, 'was one of the arguments that I won.'

*

The former Mrs Julian Pitt-Rivers later became Pauline, Lady Rumbold. When we met in 2008, she was one of the few remaining witnesses to Stella's immediate post-war career. Before that, however, she was Pauline Tennant, the bright, beautiful and rather spoiled daughter of David Tennant, owner of the Gargoyle, a hub of bohemian Soho filled with spies and writers and cigarette smoke and Matisses. During the war years, the club was her domain. She watched over the patrons, sheltered from the V-2s, ate the free dinners and took no nonsense from the clientele. When a customer known to her father as 'that little scrounger Lucien Freud' insulted the honour of the Pitt-Rivers family, Pauline responded by flinging a glass of white wine into the offender's eyes – destroying their friendship in a stinging instant. This ferocity served her well during her first marriage. 'In this house', George Pitt-Rivers declared, on her second visit to the family mansion at Hinton St Mary, 'I exercise *droit de seigneur*!' When he attempted to invade her boudoir via the bathroom with which his bedroom shared a connecting door, he discovered that his daughter-in-law had already cased the joint and fastened the bolts. 'Let me in, my child, let me in!' boomed Pitt-Rivers, banging on the panelling and declaring that he only wished for a discussion about his latest book. 'It was rather like a scene from *East Lynne*,' reflected Lady Rumbold, who could never bring herself to read *Weeds in the Garden of Marriage* (1931).[28]

Over a pre-lunch gin in the sitting room of her cottage in Wiltshire, Pauline Rumbold told me her theory about Stella Lonsdale's entrance into the Captain's life. She was certain that Stella's career encompassed a fair amount of prostitution – and that George Pitt-Rivers had known her as a client before he installed her as head of the household. 'She lived in France for a long time where she was *sur les trottoirs*,' she told me, recalling how Stella sailed into the study one morning and greeted her husband with a shrill, '*Tais-toi, papillon!*' – an expression, she reasoned, that Stella surely used while swinging her handbag under a Gallic streetlamp. As her Siamese cat, Mr Browning, batted at the mike of my Dictaphone, I asked Lady Rumbold to assess the relationship between her in-laws. In the months after the war, she recalled, Jo Pitt-Rivers refused to acknowledge the inconvenient absence of servants at Hinton St Mary and simply said pointedly to Stella, 'Tell *them* to make some tea' – which would be Stella's cue to disappear into the kitchen for thirty-five minutes before returning with a loaded tray – or 'Tell *them* to light the fire' – which would be Stella's cue to stagger about the drawing room with an armful of logs. On balance, however, the power was Stella's. The record shows that when a French court passed a death sentence upon her old cellmate Mathilde Carré, she prevailed upon the Captain to lobby Lord Selborne to argue for clemency. (One can only imagine the discomfort felt by his lordship at being addressed by a former 18B detainee who knew how close Carré had come to ensnaring him.) 'Jo Pitt-Rivers always used to say, "I'm going to play the Jew's game," and tap his finger on his nose,' recalled Lady Rumbold, 'but he was terribly gullible.' I asked her whether he was gulled by Stella. 'Of course he was gulled by her!' she exclaimed. 'But there was no point in saying to him that she was a liar and a German spy. He wouldn't have believed it and he'd have been very angry, so we just didn't discuss it.'

I heard a more charitable assessment from Anthony Pitt-Rivers, the Captain's youngest son. He was under no illusions about Stella's unerring self-interest; acknowledged that she had, for example, packed off his father on several long foreign holidays in order to spend time alone with a lover in France – a lover whom she would marry, in secret, before the Captain's death. He regarded Stella, however, as the last and most suitable of a long string of girlfriends acquired by his father after his release from internment: a woman who took a strong maternal interest in the three Pitt-Rivers boys, a reliable presence who guided the family through the crisis that occurred in 1954, when the eldest of those boys, Michael Pitt-Rivers, was embroiled in a homosexual scandal.

The family's private museum – home of the archaeological and ethnographic treasures collected by General Augustus Lane Fox Pitt-Rivers – proved another flashpoint. In the early 1960s, Stella, afraid that the questionable status of her relationship with Jo would leave her without an inheritance, arranged for the most notable exhibits, a set of Benin bronzes, to be valued for insurance purposes by a young Sotheby's employee named Bruce Chatwin.[29] She then employed the son of the local blacksmith to copy the bronzes, and put the fakes on display in the museum – from which they were then mysteriously burgled. (A few days after the robbery, Mrs Joyce, the curator of the museum and a relation of Lord Haw-Haw, committed suicide.) The plot turned out to be supremely pointless: in early 1965 the Captain signed ownership of the collection over to Stella. He died that same summer, whereupon Stella disposed of some of the remaining exhibits in order to fund her new life in the south of France in a house she christened 'Stelladoux'. She shared her new home with her last husband, Raoul Maumen, a taxi-driver whom she had met in the bar of the Carlton Hotel in Cannes, and married in secret several months before the death of George Pitt-Rivers. Maumen presented himself as a hero of the Resistance. Stella soon learned that he had spent the war as a racketeer. The relationship ended explosively. In 1970, Raoul Maumen appeared on the doorstep of Michael Pitt-Rivers, seeking protection from Stella. Six months later, Maumen's body was discovered in the bathroom of an apartment in Cannes, awash with whisky and disinfectant. 'He might have done it on his own,' reflected Anthony Pitt-Rivers. 'But equally, he might have had help.'

The art dealer who helped Stella to disperse the Pitt-Rivers collection was more ready to theorise. 'Some Mafia acquaintance force-fed it to him,' suggested Kenelm Digby-Jones.[30] Unexcitable, unflappable, with a sleepy-eyed Mandarin courtesy, Digby-Jones has been a fixture of Cork Street salerooms since the 1960s. Marooned in a sea of empty tables, we lunched in a Mayfair restaurant that, a decade before, had been one of the most fashionable in London. The prices did not reflect the establishment's loss of status, but my guest navigated the menu with discreet consideration, ordering a modest dish of mussels, discarding the shells, returning the naked animals to their sauce and spooning up the mixture like bouillabaisse. He had granted me an interview on condition that I did not ask him about the museum, and for an hour he discoursed on the powerful maternal interest that Stella had taken in him: how she bought him presents, monitored his girlfriends, berated him for his hangovers. He told me how reticent she had been about her wartime experiences; how a mutual friend, a former member of the French Resistance, had filled him in on the details. 'She was working for the British,' he asserted, telling me a story in which Stella was despatched on a mission to Paris and was forced to shoot two Gestapo officers in cold blood. Her imprisonment under Regulation 18B, he insisted, was all for love; the consequence of her loyalty to a lover in the Abwehr. 'She refused to give his name,' he said. 'And by doing so, probably saved his life.' Another version of the truth, and quite unverifiable.

His account of Stella's last two decades, however, had the authority of first-hand experience. He spoke of rescuing her from the machinations of a parasitic acquaintance, who, he said, still sat in her home in the south of France with Pitt-Rivers' paintings on her walls. He spoke of Stella's decline into alcoholism and described how, even in this desperate state, she had aroused the romantic interests of the psychiatrist who oversaw her case. He spoke of the suspicious death of Raoul Maumen. Had Stella, I asked, been shocked or upset by her husband's death? Kenelm indicated that her principal emotion had been relief.

At this point, the waiter appeared by our table. I ordered coffee. My guest asked if the Brie was soft. The waiter shook his head apologetically. With that cheerful rudeness that is one of the defining qualities of the English upper classes, Kenelm wondered what was the bloody point in serving hard Brie and requested some Roquefort instead. It arrived swiftly. As he picked at his cheese, I asked him how he imagined Stella would have responded to my questions, had it been possible to put them to her in person. What, Kenelm wondered, would I most like to know? I made my list briskly: I would have asked about the true identity of René, whether he was more than just a figment of her imagination. I would have asked whether it was she who had denounced Jean Platiau to the Germans, rather than the other way round. 'She might have told you,' said Kenelm Digby-Jones, unsmiling. 'But she would have poisoned that coffee and you'd be dead by now.'

Thirteen fat folders on Stella's case are lodged at the National Archives in Kew: the Lonsdale version, recorded and transcribed – but largely untested – by the British security services. The Abwehr records from Angers were destroyed before the Allies took the town, though one document suggests she was as bothersome to them as she was to MI5. Stella's name remains undetected in the files of the *Bundes-Militärarchiv* in Freiburg.[31] Her story, however, can be challenged by other sources. In the summer of 2008, I paid a visit to Françoise Prévost, the niece of Jean Platiau.[32] She showed me a photograph of her uncle and his brothers: a group of boys seated around a table, groomed into premature manhood by the liberal application of hair-cream. Françoise told me the version of her uncle's story that has circulated among the family since the war. Jean Platiau, she said, was arrested near the harbour at St Nazaire, a camera in his hand, at the end of November 1940. Suspected of espionage, he was interrogated by the Abwehr and imprisoned – though his relations sometimes caught a glimpse of him through his cell window by going to a high building that overlooked the prison. The following October, the German *Feldkommandant* of Nantes was assassinated by members of the Communist Resistance. Reprisals were brutal. Fifty hostages, some in Paris, most in Nantes, were executed. Many were forced to dig their own graves and stand by them as they received a fatal bullet. The name of Jean Platiau was added to the list. He had only a few hours' notice of his death. An account of his final moments has survived, written by the priest who attended him and two fellow prisoners during the agonising wait for the firing squad. Françoise Prévost read it to me, her voice choked with emotion. 'They went to their deaths with quiet dignity,' went the priest's account. 'They did not protest.' Within days of this atrocity, Stella Lonsdale changed the colour of her hair and began her journey home.

9

Majesties

Suite 212 at Claridge's has all the standard appurtenances of luxury: the chunky brocade curtains, the mountainous four-poster, the vase of monstrous white lilies, the china illuminated inside glass-fronted wall cabinets. On the day I was permitted to snoop around inside, however, my attention was commanded by something nearer to the floor. The Hollywood actor Sharon Stone had just checked out, abandoning her lunch half-eaten on the sideboard: copper bowls of saffron rice and cold biryani. In the spirit of research I nibbled one of her poppadoms, and then hunkered down, pushing my head and shoulders into the gap between the bedstead and the carpet – the location of a unique event in diplomatic history. In this room, for one day in 1945, the conventions of cartography were suspended. The borders of England receded to the corridor outside and a new country rushed to meet its retreat – summoned by a few words from Winston Churchill and the sympathetic magic of a box of earth placed beneath the bed. A state within a state, conjured two storeys above the pavement of Brook Street, W1. A piece of Yugoslavia.

Throughout the hot hours of 17 July 1945, Suite 212 was furious with activity. Six men occupied the sitting room all day, some in three-piece suits, some in military uniform. Four royalists and two Communists: representatives of the Yugoslav government. They smoked, made uneasy conversation, insisted that the door to the bedroom be kept ajar. Beyond that door, on a high bed imported from the London Clinic, lay a twenty-four-year-old woman in the agonies of labour. Her husband,

King Peter II of Yugoslavia, two years her junior, stood at the bedside, administering gas from a rubber mask. Queen Alexandra of Yugoslavia inhaled the analgesic and clawed at King Peter's clothes as, from the end of the bed, the beetle-browed gynaecologist William Gilliat offered deferential encouragement. At 9.15 in the evening, there was a loud wail, and into the world came eight-and-a-half pounds of Slavic royalty. King Peter, his shirt in tatters and rather more dazed than his wife, crossed the threshold of the bedroom to proclaim the news to the gathered ministers. The six men filed into the bedroom to offer their congratulations. They ranged themselves around the bed, lifted the mattress from the iron frame and, with great ceremony, carried Queen Alexandra from Suite 212 through the fortuitously wide corridors of Claridge's. A nurse followed behind with the baby.

Having settled their cargo in her own room, the officials left with a bow, allowing a priest from the Serbian Orthodox Church to enter. The priest blessed mother and child, and – much to Alexandra's bewilderment – began to jump up and down on his homburg, in observance of a ritual intended to bring good luck to the newborn Prince. The charm failed. That, at least, is the judgement of history. As they passed from Suite 212, Peter and Alexandra left Yugoslav territory for the last time. The royal couple was fated to die in bitter exile, with little cash and even less equanimity. The Claridge's baby, Crown Prince Alexander Karadjordjevic, would be their only child. Born in a phantom version of his homeland raised into existence by official courtesy, he was the heir to the abolished throne of a country that would strip him of his citizenship and identify him as an enemy of the state.

*

The royal families of Europe, that great transcontinental cousinry of Hapsburgs and Saxe-Coburg-Gothas and Schleswig-

Holstein-Sonderburg-Glücksburgs, failed to insulate themselves from the traumas of world war. Some suffered more than others. King Christian X of Denmark spent the conflict under house arrest in Copenhagen, keeping his dignity and his position with small acts of discourtesy against the invaders. (An insultingly brief reply to a birthday telegram from Hitler was his most celebrated act of resistance.) After capitulating to the invading Germans, Leopold III of Belgium was interned in Austria – but became sufficiently intimate with his captors to face a charge of collaboration once he and his country were liberated. King Boris III of Bulgaria ended three years of neutrality by allowing himself to be drawn into an alliance with the Axis powers: his sudden death in the summer of 1943, shortly after a visit to the Führer, prompted a surge of conspiracy theories and the hasty coronation of his five-year-old son. Carol II of Romania and his mistress, Magda Lupescu, fled Bucharest in September 1940, escaping with nothing but five railway carriages packed with Titians, Rembrandts and Rubenses, the armorial contents of the palaces of Pelişor and Peleş, the world's most valuable stamp collection and six of their favourite dogs. Romania's indigenous Fascisti, the Iron Guard, sprayed the royal carriages with bullets, but Carol and Magda took cover in the bathtub, fled south via Spain to the Copacabana Palace Hotel in Rio de Janeiro, and spent the rest of their lives drinking tequila and ignoring the contempt of the nation they had abandoned, and more or less everyone else they encountered. ('To shake hands with him', noted one observer of Carol II, 'was like gripping hold of a piece of wet cod.'[1])

London proved a strong magnet to the crowned refugees of Europe – particularly those who hoped for post-war restoration and the official sponsorship of the Allies. King Zog and Queen Geraldine of the Albanians checked into the Ritz, where gossip declared that they paid their bills in bullion that had once constituted the gold reserves of their nation. The remainder of the pack put down at Claridge's. King George of Greece signed in as 'Mr Brown' and fooled nobody. The Duke of Windsor, Britain's royal abdicant, left Mrs Simpson behind in Barbados and made landfall at Claridge's as rumours spread that he was plotting to ascend the throne of a Nazi England. In the Causerie, the old hotel billiard room converted by the wartime management into a Scandinavian-style all-you-can-eat, King Haakon of Norway filled his plate with potato salad and pickled herring, and thought of the old country. Queen Wilhelmina of the Netherlands, imported from Holland on the deck of a British destroyer, startled fellow guests by descending the grand staircase in a flannel dressing gown, followed by a phalanx of black-clad ladies-in-waiting. More genuinely alarming activity was pursued by her son-in-law Prince Bernhard, who, looking through a window of his suite in the hotel, noticed a light burning brightly in an uncurtained penthouse somewhere in Mayfair, and, at the suggestion of Wilhelmina's bodyguard, tried to shoot out the bulb with a Tommy gun. Bernhard failed to enforce the blackout on his neighbour, but did succeed in bringing a fellow guest out onto the landing, shouting about an attack by Fifth Columnists.[2]

The force of precedent brought these regal refugees to Brook Street. James Mivart, proprietor of the first boarding house to occupy the site, had been accommodating royal guests since the time of Waterloo. In 1854 he retired to Swiss Cottage and sold his business to William and Marianne Claridge. William Claridge was a flunkey's flunkey. It was said that the depth of his bows increased by increments determined by the recipient's position in the *Almanac de Gotha*: the presence of a Royal Highness, for example, propelled his skull slightly nearer to the carpet than a mere Serene Highness. Since the union of Victoria and Albert, royal weddings, coronations and official visits had crammed the building with kings, queens, archdukes and margraves. Empress Eugenie of France wintered on the premises; Emma, Dowager Queen of the Sandwich Islands, took rooms at the expense of the British government – as did her great rival,

King Kalakaua of Hawaii, who used Claridge's as a base for a fortnight of state-subsidised larks. During the twentieth century, as monarchies began to fall to war and revolution and democracy, the human wreckage washed up on the shores of Brook Street: Manoel II of Portugal, a man who never wore a suit more than twice, arrived in 1921, having watched mutinous warships fire on the royal palace in Lisbon and taken the hint to emigrate; Amanullah Khan, the former Shah of Afghanistan, deposed in 1929, dined in exile at Claridge's, alongside King Prajadhipok and Queen Ramphai of Siam, chivvied from power in 1935. King Alfonso XIII of Spain arrived during the spring of 1931, after a diplomatic exit from a suddenly republican Madrid. When he appeared in the hotel lobby, Manoel of Portugal was waiting to offer his commiserations. In 1942, the film star Douglas Fairbanks Junior arrived late for a cocktail party supervised by a senior waiter named King. 'Finding myself drinkless,' recalled Fairbanks, 'I called out to my old livesaver of a headwaiter, "Oh King!" At that, a familiar bald-headed gent in khaki uniform turned to face me and politely said, "Yes?" It was King George of Greece.'[3] Claridge's was noted as 'the royal hostelry'; 'the annex to Buckingham Palace'. It was a Sargasso Sea of unloved majesties.[4]

When Oswald P. Milne redesigned the public spaces of the hotel in 1929, he paved the lobby with a chessboard of black and white tiles. To some of the monarchs who shuffled across its squares, it must have seemed a bitter joke – most of all, perhaps, to Peter of Yugoslavia, a king who lived most of his life as a pawn. Peter was the uncharacteristically passive scion of a dynasty restored to power by murder and sustained by uncompromising autocracy. In his short reign and long exile, Peter was manipulated by his ministers and by his mother-in-law, by British and American intelligence, by Winston Churchill and by Marshal Josip Tito. The circumstances of his first visit to Claridge's say much about his marginal status in the game of his own life. He arrived at the hotel in September 1924, shortly after his first birthday, under the assumed name of Comte d'Avala. His parents did not accompany him. The three-month trip to England was a consequence of the desire of his nanny to visit her parents in Harrogate. ('Give me the baby and I'll take him with me,' suggested Nurse Bell, and Alexander I and Queen Marie of Yugoslavia concurred without a qualm.) Peter's first steps were made over the carpets of the hotel, his hands held by two Hungarian émigrés, a Mr and Mrs Szirmay.

His return to the hotel a decade later was similarly parentless. On this trip, the Crown Prince was under the protection of his private tutor, Cecil Parrott, who had been charged to escort the boy from the Austrian border to his first term at Sandroyd, a prep school in Surrey. Parrott wrote the name 'Count of Rudnick' into the register, but the reporters who swarmed around the lobby knew better – as did the restaurant band, who struck up a Serbian folk tune as the pair sat down for dinner. The visit was not without incident. Outside the hotel, Parrott and his pupil were obliged to dodge pursuing journalists by leaping between buses and taxis. Inside his second-floor suite, Peter caused a violent explosion with a stationary steam engine bought from Hamley's toyshop on Regent Street. Eager to set the machine running, the Crown Prince rang room service and asked for alcohol: a surprised-looking valet appeared at his door with a bottle of brandy. The afternoon ended with a loud bang, the smell of burning varnish, and a soppy-stern reprimand from his maternal grandmother, Queen Marie of Romania, who had arrived for dinner. Worse explosions, however, were only weeks away.

On 9 October 1934, Peter's father, Alexander I of Yugoslavia, arrived in Marseilles aboard the destroyer *Dubrovnik*. The King, dressed in an admiral's uniform of his own preposterously tight-cut design, was received on the quayside by the French Foreign Minister, Louis Barthou. As their motorcade scudded from the harbour towards the Prefecture, a man jumped on the running board of the royal car and pointed a gun at Alexander's head. Vlado Chernozemski, a Macedonian nationalist and career assassin, pulled the trigger four times, killing both the King and his ministerial host. The assassination was one of the first to be captured on film. The footage shows Chernozemski as a menacing smear across the left-hand side of the frame. The gun is discharged; policemen and bystanders swarm over the vehicle; the sword of a mounted cavalry officer slashes down upon the gunman. The camera directs its gaze at Alexander, lying across the back seat, his eyes already glassy.

The following morning, Cecil Parrott arrived at Sandroyd to inform Peter of his bereavement and his accession. However, as their Daimler sped back towards London for a lunch of condolence hosted at the Ritz by Queen Marie of Romania, the tutor found himself quite unable to break the news to the boy. He stared out of the window, hoping his charge would not notice the newspaper hoardings blaring regicide, or the placards carrying huge colour photographs of the slain monarch lying across the blood-soaked upholstery of the royal car. Parrott's reticence ensured that for much of the journey Peter was under the impression that he had been expelled from Sandroyd for infringing the school rules regarding the possession of sweets. Boys were required to consume them on the day of purchase: Peter had stashed some under his dormitory pillow.

*

Parrott remained at Peter's shoulder for the next five years. The tutor noted the boy's placid reaction to the murder of Alexander and concluded that fear was the only emotion that the father had ever stirred in his son. He watched Peter somnambulate through the business of the state funeral and the installation of Alexander's brother, Prince Paul, as Regent of Yugoslavia. (The newsreel footage shows Alexander's coffin moving through the streets of Belgrade in a glass-sided hearse; the tiny Peter walking, stiff as Pinocchio, at the side of his thickly veiled mother;

Field Marshal Hermann Göring at the jolly centre of a knot of foreign dignitaries, exchanging a warm handshake with Marshal Pétain.)

Parrott also observed the widowed Queen's indifference to her first-born son and her displays of favour towards his younger brothers, Tomislav and Andrej – who, unlike Peter, received a maternal escort to their first term at Sandroyd. To his discomfort, the tutor's pessimistic assessments of Peter's academic abilities became ammunition in the war between those fighting for political advantage in Yugoslavia: Milan Stojadinovic, leader of Serbia's pro-Fascist Greenshirts, suggested that the tutor had filed a secret report with which Prince Paul planned to prolong his Regency by claiming that Peter was mentally unfit to rule. It might have worked: there was precedent in the case of Peter's uncle, Crown Prince George, a deranged sadist who ate rats, killed a servant during an attempt to shoot a cigarette from his mouth, and amused himself by sprinkling a school playground with broken glass. Peter, however, suffered only from an inadequate education and a mind that was more engaged by cartoons and jazz and model railways than the agonies of Yugoslav politics – a position with which Prince Paul had some sympathy. Life on the throne, the Regent confessed, was 'a dog's existence' which was scheduled for a happy ending on 6 September 1941, his nephew's eighteenth birthday. However, thanks to the clandestine efforts of British intelligence, nobody was obliged to wait that long.

As Hitler struck out into Europe, Prince Paul and his ministers struggled to keep the Axis at arm's length. Peter's mother, Marie, in a characteristic display of affection, left Belgrade with her younger sons, Tomislav and Andrej, and set up home in Bedfordshire. King Peter remained in the Royal Palace at Dedinje, kept resolutely in the dark by the ministers of the court, as Belgrade pursued a policy of hopeful neutrality. Then, in November 1940, Hungary, Romania and Slovakia signed the Tripartite Pact, leaving Yugoslavia surrounded by hostile neighbours. Bulgaria soon joined the company. Prince Paul's strategists calculated that it would take Germany thirty days to overpower the Yugoslav Army. His government concluded that they had little choice but to add their names to the Pact, and began drafting new clauses to ameliorate its impact upon Yugoslav sovereignty. In London, however, a small group of men was determined to wreck the agreement and limit Axis influence in the Balkans, primarily to prevent Hitler access to the oilfields of Romania. They convened a dinner to discuss how to put a new, more pro-British government in power and Peter on the Yugoslav throne. Inevitably, the hotel was Claridge's. Just as inevitably, the plan went horribly wrong.

*

In January 1941, Hugh Dalton, Minister of Economic Warfare, sat down at a restaurant table with Frank Nelson, director of the Special Operations Executive, the secret department dedicated to acts of subversion and sabotage behind enemy lines. They were there to brief the man they had chosen to implement a change of regime in Belgrade. He was George Taylor, an Australian banker who had been recruited to SOE after another operative had observed him ordering the same meal in the same restaurant on three consecutive nights – proof, it seems, of his reliability. SOE had several means of exerting influence in Yugoslavia. All were put at Taylor's disposal. The British Legation in Belgrade was a nest of agents, some of whom had influential friends in the Yugoslav Army and Air Force. The organisation had bought the loyalty of a number of government ministers, among them the leader of the Peasant Party, Milan Gavrilovic. It was also in possession of ten suitcases of plastic explosives. Any of these assets would be useful when the time came to foment a *coup d'état* – and on 24 March, as Prince Paul's ministers concluded a secret conference with the Germans in Vienna, a flurry of telegrams between London and Belgrade

signalled that the moment had come. Quite how much credit
SOE can take for the fall of Prince Paul is still a matter of debate among historians, but it is clear that when General Dusan
Simovic assumed power on 27 March 1941, Taylor's superiors were in the mood for self-congratulation. 'What a day!'
whooped Hugh Dalton. 'As the day goes on, we hear more detail, and it is clear that our chaps have done their part well.'[5] At
Claridge's, a gang of his colleagues toasted the coming of a new
Yugoslavia.[6]

Peter's part, however, was predictably passive. That morning,
Radenko, the royal valet, shook his employer awake to tell
him that a revolution was in progress. At nine o'clock the
King switched on the radio to hear a young man exhorting
Serbs, Croats and Slovenes to rally round the throne: the voice
claimed to be that of King Peter II of Yugoslavia. That evening
Prince Paul informed his nephew that he had renounced the Regency and was taking his family by train to exile in Greece.
A few minutes later, Peter was adding his signature to documents appointing Simovic as his new Prime Minister. The
following morning, Peter, dressed by Radenko in his general's
uniform, was sworn into office and driven through cheering
crowds for a thanksgiving service to celebrate his full accession
to the throne. He had ten days to enjoy this uneasy privilege.
On 6 April, Hitler launched Operation Punishment against
Yugoslavia. Belgrade endured three days of pitiless bombing.
Seventeen thousand corpses were pulled from the rubble. Exotic
animals, released inadvertently from the Zoological Gardens,
blundered through the burning streets. The Luftwaffe targeted
the Royal Compound, where the air-raid siren system failed to
work: Peter posted a trumpeter on the roof to warn of incoming
enemy aircraft. Bombers arrived in waves. The royal bedroom
received a direct hit. Every window in the palace was shattered.
Craters pitted the grounds. Pages from the books in the library
fluttered across the grass. The bodies of seven guards were retrieved from the peculiar underground tunnel that connected

the dining room with the palace kitchens – the seventy-foot-long architectural consequence of Alexander's aversion to the smell of frying onions. As bombs rained down, Peter and his staff were evacuated south to Niksic in Montenegro, where a plane waited to take him to Greece. Peter flew the plane himself to an airstrip at Paramythia, from which 815 Squadron of the RAF was attacking Italian shipping in the Adriatic. As the plane skidded to a halt it was surrounded by a group of armed British crewmen. Their leader, Michael Torrens-Spence, tore open the door and ordered the occupants out. 'I'm King Peter of Yugoslavia,' explained the pilot. 'And I'm Father Christmas,' replied Torrens-Spence. 'Get out!'[7]

*

The Royal Compound sprawls over the summit of a hill in the southern suburbs of Belgrade. I visited on an unseasonably warm day in February 2010. Banks of dirty snow lay defeated at the roadside. As I arrived, a uniformed guard pushed open the steel gates; gates that have admitted the motorcades of Yugoslavia's leaders from King Alexander I to President Slobodan Milosevic. The estate beyond is a palimpsest of the Yugoslav century. In the grounds are monuments that indicate where Marshal Josip Tito interred his favourite horse, his favourite dog and his favourite mistress. In the cupola of the chapel, the forehead of the portrait of Christ retains the bullet hole added at some point between the Second World War and the Civil War of the 1990s. (The gunman, it seems, lay on his back and fired upwards.) The palace basement, a vaulted, frescoed sanctum like a set from Eisenstein's *Ivan the Terrible*, contains the Whispering Room, named for its ornamental fountain – installed by Alexander I to prevent servants or spies from overhearing his conversations. The recent past has also left its mark: the seventeenth-century astral globe in the library bears the scars from the night in 1999 that a NATO bomb shattered the windows. When this was pointed out, I felt a strong urge to apologise.

'Only dictators erase history,' explained Crown Prince Alexander, the baby born in Suite 212. We met in the Blue Room of the Royal Palace: a vast field of Smyrna carpet, overlooked by a Poussin *Venus and Adonis*; with enormous French windows gazing down upon a wooded valley. The contents of my bag were a test of Alexander's assertion: copies of official files relating to his father's years in London, his destination after that long and difficult journey from his homeland; reports on King Peter's moral conduct, his emotional life, his fitness to govern, his finances; transcripts of ciphered communiqués between Churchill, Roosevelt and Stalin that suggest the Yugoslav monarchy was doomed to exile long before the Communists took power. I disgorged these documents upon the table, flustering the maids who were trying to fill the same space with coffee and plates of impossibly small sandwiches. An official photographer snapped away. Myself, the Crown Prince and Dragomir Acovic – the third member of our party, a privy councillor and president of something called the Serbian Society for Heraldry, Genealogy, Vexillology and Phaleristics – smiled for the camera over a field of papers.

Examining this material, discussing the details of King Peter's wartime exile in London, was not, I sensed, a particularly enjoyable experience for Alexander. 'My father was a very lonely individual,' he judged. 'The Second World War affected him very deeply. He was always saying, "I'm certain that this can be resolved, that we can all go back home." But homesickness killed him in the end.' And for an hour, over coffee and canapés, we discussed the slow destruction of his father's hopes.

'Imagine', began Dragomir Acovic, in a low, sonorous voice, 'the problems of any young man trying to find a place, trying to find a circle of friends in which to confide. Imagine if you take such a person from his natural environment and surround him with political opportunists, with career men, agents. A desolate feeling.' Alexander nodded in sad agreement. 'We are not an easy people. We are a complicated people, politically. And he was surrounded by some of our most complicated politicians.' The complexity of the Yugoslav government-in-exile was a source of despair to the British officials who were obliged to accommodate its discordant factions. Its members reflected the social and tribal divisions of their homeland, and were veterans of a political system in which exchanges of gunfire in Parliament were not unknown. No such outrages were committed at Claridge's, where the Prime Minister, Dusan Simovic, and his senior colleagues were accommodated, but the hotel was the scene of some eccentric and unsubtle intrigue. One prospective minister, an unwilling member of a later incarnation of the wartime royal government, found himself the victim of a political ambush. 'I was tricked into becoming a minister,' claimed Milan Martinovic. 'They invited me to a discussion, and when I had entered the room a priest was waiting to swear me in.'[8] 'They were a strange group,' pronounced Mr Acovic. 'And many of them were people of rather unstable ideas. Not the best company for a young man who has only just begun to discover his own feelings and opinions.'

When you know how it all ended – in a broken marriage, in alcoholic bitterness, in a failed liver transplant in a hospital in Denver, Colorado – it's hard to remain unmoved by the accounts of Peter's youth that filled the press after his arrival in England. Magazine profiles inventoried the cute banalities. His lapel bore the badges of the Fox Film Corporation and the Serbian Football Association. He liked detective stories and Damon Runyon and jazz and transatlantic slang. 'Traffic Jam' was his favourite Artie Shaw number. The profilers could afford to be amused. They had not set themselves the task of transforming a naïve seventeen-year-old boy into a figure of steadfast Yugoslav national unity. Those who shared this aspiration could not conceal their disappointment. George Rendel, Britain's ambassador to the Yugoslav government-in-exile, pro-

fessed himself 'profoundly shocked' after discovering Peter idly
playing darts, and diagnosed him 'mentally not more than sixteen and a half'. Sir Alan Lascelles, watching Peter participate
in a pointless flag-saluting ceremony at Buckingham Palace, dismissed Peter as 'an unimpressive little monarch', and was not
the only commentator to use such adjectives.[9] 'The King is a
funny little creature,' Hugh Dalton informed his diary. 'The
poor little chap gives me the impression of having adenoids,
and, though faintly shrewd at times, is rather unimpressive.'[10]
Dalton's opinion did not improve with better acquaintance:
'Peter, King of the Jugs . . . seems to be less and less impressive
every time I meet him.'[11] British officialdom soon concluded
that Peter's defining quality was one not particularly useful in a
political leader: he generally agreed with the opinion of the person he happened to be talking to at the time. They determined,
therefore, to remove him from his bad influences. By the middle
of 1942, they had identified the sources of those influences – a
knot of hard-drinking Serbian majors who acted as Peter's ad-
jutants, the Greek Princess with whom he was falling in love,
and his prospective mother-in-law.

*

In September 1941, at the Officers' Sunday Club gathering at
Grosvenor House, King Peter found himself seated beside a
royal refugee with a troubled past to match his own. Princess
Alexandra of Greece was two years older than the Yugoslav
King and had spent most of her life in exile. Her father, Alexander I of the Hellenes, had been killed in the winter of 1920
by an infection contracted from a monkey-bite sustained during a walk through the Royal Gardens in Athens. Alexander's
wife, Aspasia Manos, became a mother in the fifth month of
her widowhood. Her marriage and her child were at first unacknowledged by the family of her dead husband – but that
injustice became academic in 1924, when Greece was declared

a republic. Peter and Alexandra did not discuss the miseries of banishment over Grosvenor House soup; instead they explored their shared abhorrence for official engagements and fought the urge to giggle that overcame them when their hosts decided to punctuate the meal with bagpipe music. The growth of their relationship occurred under the eye of Detective Sergeant Farns, the Special Branch minder assigned to King Peter. Alexandra claimed that Farns was present in the car when Peter made his proposal of marriage; that the policeman reached forward to steer as the King removed his hands from the wheel in order to embrace his fiancée. Like many wartime courtships, theirs was swift and urgent. Unlike most wartime courtships, it was a matter of international diplomatic significance.

Queen Marie of Yugoslavia rarely got up before 7.30 in the evening and spent the daylight hours in bed, chain-smoking and replying to correspondents – but she rose early to meet Peter and Alexandra for lunch at the Dorchester, where she offered her blessing and two crocodile-skin dressing-cases. Her consent was not unconditional: the royal engagement, she insisted, must remain secret until approved by the Yugoslav government-in-exile. The young couple felt compelled to consent. Marie was unused to opposition. She was a vast, bosomy power-broker who wore her hair in a tight bob and went about town with a Sam Browne holster slung across a military uniform of her own design. She probably knew that her proviso was as good as a wrecking clause. Although the Croats and Slovenes in the Yugoslav Cabinet did not oppose the match, the Serbs insisted that it was impolitic for a monarch to marry during wartime – and were unenthusiastic about their sovereign's choice of a bride. (Prince Paul had married a Greek, and this was not regarded as the least of his mistakes.) They were also concerned that a royal wedding might alter the course of the guerrilla war being waged against the occupiers of their homeland, where the favoured resistance force, the royalist Chetniks led by General Draza Mihailovic, were losing support to the Communist Partisans, led by a dynamic newcomer called Josip Tito. Princess Aspasia, sensing that Queen Marie and her pet ministers had the potential to exert as negative effect on her family's future as the monkey that sank its teeth into Alexander of Greece, began a diplomatic counter-offensive, with the object of marrying Alexandra to Peter as quickly as possible. The British government were as divided. 'My advice to the King, if you force him on me,' declared Churchill, in a bad-tempered exchange with Anthony Eden, 'will be to go to the nearest Registry Office and take a chance.' Eden was confident that he was capable of handling 'this minor Balkan domestic imbroglio' – and reaffirmed his belief that King Peter remained the best hope for a post-war Yugoslavia unbroken by secession and unabsorbed by Communism. 'We are therefore anxious to attach to him some younger man who might be able to get on close terms of friendship and thereby obtain a real influence over him . . . Obviously any appointment of this sort must be in the nature of a gamble, but it is a gamble which, if it comes off, might have very valuable results.'[12]

Eden dismissed the first candidates for the post as 'a useless list of wooden-headed guardsmen'. Then the name of Squadron Leader Archibald Dunlop Mackenzie was proposed. Dunlop Mackenzie was twenty-nine years old, had served in Malta and the Middle East, and came with the enthusiastic approval of the secret state. As the officials of the Foreign Office considered him for the job of adjutant to King Peter, a cottage on his family's estate in a sparsely populated stretch of Argyllshire was being used for one of the most important covert missions of the war: Operation Gunnerside, which aimed to destroy the Norwegian electro-chemical production plant where German scientists were manufacturing the raw materials for an atomic bomb. Most importantly, Dunlop Mackenzie had also been one of SOE's agents in Belgrade, where he had helped to foment the coup against Prince Paul. The relationship between Archie Dunlop Mackenzie and King Peter of Yugoslavia was founded upon chilling political pragmatism, but it proved to be one of the warmest friendships that either man would enjoy, before it ended in a screaming match in Suite 212 at Claridge's.

*

When Andrew Dunlop Mackenzie asked his father what he did in the war, he usually received an evasive answer. The Squadron Leader died in 1996, taking most of his secrets with him. 'About the only thing he told me', he explained, 'was a technique for getting rid of Gestapo officers from a train during a blackout.' Among his effects, however, his son discovered a file of documents that suggest the strength of his attachment to King Peter: a thick cache of maps, a bundle of royal correspondence (which indicates that Dunlop Mackenzie went on stealing Queen Marie's letters into the 1950s), a photograph of himself lighting a cigarette for Peter, and a number of typewritten reports. One of these reports, bashed out on four pages of thin blue paper in the summer of 1944, is, in effect, a letter of resignation. 'It must not be imagined that I am myself in any way antagonistic towards His Majesty. For, although he may not at this moment fully realise it, I am still perhaps his only intimate friend.'

I met Andrew Dunlop Mackenzie several times during the course of writing this book. Our second encounter took place over breakfast at the Special Forces Club, a discreet red-brick townhouse behind Harrods, where the bell is unmarked and the walls are filled with framed portraits of SOE agents. Two elderly veterans sat at separate tables, a man and a woman, both attacking plates of bacon and eggs, and both old enough to have spent the war blowing up railway lines. In this Diogenic atmosphere, any conversation felt brash and indiscreet, but Andrew sketched out the little that his father was willing to reveal about his Yugoslav past: his last stand in the British Legation, where he manned the phones and gave out misleading information to hostile callers as German Stukas strewed Belgrade with bombs; his visits to Balmoral to meet George VI, to whom Peter always referred as 'Uncle Bertie'; his strong sense of brotherly responsibility towards King Peter, amplified by the death of his own younger sibling, Flight Lieutenant Robert Dunlop Mackenzie, whose Manchester bomber was shot down over a frozen Dutch lake in March 1942.

It was an Arctic wind that blew Archie Dunlop Mackenzie into the Yugoslav court. He had spent the long vacation of 1935 acting as surveyor to a team of Oxford University students despatched to the Svalbard archipelago to make observations and do their best to discover the fate of Herbert Schröder-Stranz's lost expedition of 1912. A frozen sleeping bag was the only trace of this German team – and Dunlop Mackenzie narrowly avoided a similar fate, leaping from floe to floe on the splintering surface of Rijps Bay. When he was not facing death, it seems, he spent most of his time firing shots at kittiwakes, tallyhoing at polar bears and learning passages of Jane Austen by heart.[13] This was his audition for SOE. When the leader of the group, the glaciologist Sandy Glen, was recruited to work for the organisation in Belgrade, he brought Dunlop Mackenzie with him. 'Archie was a curious and unexpected person,' remarked Glen, in his account of the expedition. 'Superficially, he might appear disappointing, as he was extremely reserved. It took long before one really knew him, for he would rarely reveal his inner feelings.' Glen suggested that these feelings masked something darker. 'Below this façade of supreme efficiency, he was very unsettled, being a rebel against accepted values.'[14]

This façade was a professional necessity – particularly as genuine warmth grew between the two men. For Peter, the Squadron Leader was his best source of friendly advice since the resignation of Cecil Parrott; for Dunlop Mackenzie, the King stirred memories of his younger brother – an unruly young man who had occasionally been in trouble with the police.[15]This was, however, a relationship of convenience. The state had ordered Dunlop Mackenzie to become King Peter's most trusted confidant; to keep him 'on the straight and narrow' – which, in practice, meant navigating him away from vodka, prostitutes and dissent from the official British position on the war in Yugoslavia. He was also charged to determine the strength of Peter's feelings towards Alexandra, and, if necessary, offer him a way to terminate the engagement with honour. ('If he is in doubt or wants to get out of the marriage,' cooed the Foreign Office, 'we can provide him with plenty of good excuses.') It was Princess Aspasia, however, who was identified as the greatest threat to British policy in Yugoslavia. She had made at least three attempts to 'get an official announcement of the engagement slipped into the British Press by a trick' – which had given her cause for at least one blazing row with Dunlop Mackenzie, who refused to call the small ads department of *The Times* on her behalf. ('Her Highness', reflected the Squadron Leader in a memo to his superiors, 'has never made any secret of her antipathy towards me.')

The Yugoslav government-in-exile had made it clear that a royal wedding would trigger their mass resignation. With this in mind, Anthony Eden arranged for Dunlop Mackenzie to remove the King from the orbit of Alexandra, Aspasia and Marie – the three women who had the power to turn Peter into a mirror of their own opinion. In August 1943, the Squadron Leader and his royal charge boarded a plane to Cairo, where they stayed for eight months. Here, Dunlop Mackenzie arranged for the King to take flying and shooting lessons, attend dinner parties with young officers and their wives, and participate in the debate on the wisdom of transferring official Allied approval from Mihailovic's guerrilla fighters to Tito's Communist Partisans. (There was even a suggestion from an SOE colonel that Peter should fly straight from Cairo to Yugoslavia to fight alongside Tito in the mountains.) And as the King flew and shot and made conversation, Dunlop Mackenzie reported back to

Churchill: 'Putting it even more bluntly,' he wrote, 'I think that King Peter is not in love with Princess Alexandra, though he thinks he is. Princess Alexandra is really in love with him. Her mother, Princess Aspasia, is determined that her daughter shall marry King Peter. Queen Marie of Yugoslavia dislikes the business, but the motive behind the attitude of the two mothers is in neither case simple mother love.'[16]

The Greek princesses responded to Peter's absence by leaving their flat in Grosvenor Square and taking up residence in a suite at Claridge's. It was a strategy to make their marginalisation more difficult: moving into Brook Street brought them closer to the most senior members of the European royal diaspora, to the their governments-in-exile, to Britain's decision-makers and their secret advisers. It also made the hotel the scene of the most hysterical episodes in the story of the last King and Queen of Yugoslavia.

*

There are two accounts of the psychodrama that preceded the Yugoslav royal wedding. One was produced by Alexandra in 1956, when her marriage to Peter had soured beyond recovery, the crown jewels of Yugoslavia had been sold at auction, and her first suicide attempt was three years behind her. *For a King's Love* (1956) was dictated to Joan Reeder, the royal correspondent of the *Daily Mirror*: the emphasis is on tears, palpitation and self-justification. The other account was written in the summer of 1944. Its sole author was Archibald Dunlop Mackenzie, and though intended only for the eyes of Foreign Office officials, is a product of no less fierce a passion.

The Alexandra version begins with the telephone ringing in her sitting room in Claridge's. The caller is her cousin, Princess Marina, the widow of the Duke of Kent, who has some important news: King Peter, she says, is returning from Egypt and will soon be landing at RAF Northolt. There is a snag: Marie of

Yugoslavia is despatching her allies in the government-in-exile to intercept her son and deliver him straight to her cottage. There is, however, also a solution: George VI, Marina says, has requested the presence of the Yugoslav monarch at Windsor Castle – which trumps any claim that can be made by Peter's mother. At four o'clock on morning of 11 March 1944, the Claridge's night porter brings black coffee to Alexandra and Aspasia and packs them into their car to Northolt. In the arrivals lounge of the air base, a gang of Yugoslav ministers stare stonily at the princesses – but do nothing to stop them as they run towards King Peter's plane to communicate the royal summons. By 8 a.m., Peter, Alexandra and Aspasia are back in the suite at Claridge's, where Marina rings again to inform them that King George believes that a wedding will now be possible.[17] She also advises Alexandra to raise the barricades: 'You must not go out today,' she insists, 'and do not let anyone in.'[18] Aspasia, sensing imminent victory over Queen Marie, calls room service for a bottle of champagne and three glasses. Peter, however, has other ideas. 'I can't go on like this,' he declares, 'staying virtually locked up in Claridge's, for fear she sends someone up here to inveigle me down to see her.'[19] He resolves to motor down to Cambridgeshire to confront his mother. The meeting, however, is a disaster. Marie receives them in her bed, which becomes a quilted battleground: they shout, they weep, they smoke cigarettes. Alexandra picks up the bedside telephone and calls Claridge's, allowing Aspasia to make her own, long-range contribution to the exchange of insults and recriminations. And beyond the bedroom door, Archibald Dunlop Mackenzie listens to the sound of all his good work being torn to pieces.

Dunlop Mackenzie's version of events is preserved in a report contained in the file that he bequeathed to his son. 'A somewhat stormy meeting, at which I was not present, took place in Her Majesty's room,' he wrote. 'It had the effect of reducing the Princess to tears for the rest of the day, and of making His Majesty extremely agitated.' As the royal couple stormed out,

Queen Marie summoned Dunlop Mackenzie to her bedside, and instructed him to return King Peter to her that evening. He made no promises, but, on the drive back to London, persuaded the Yugoslav King to accede to Marie's request. Alexandra cried all the way to Brook Street. By dinner time, however, Peter had changed his mind. Flanked by the two princesses, he asked the Squadron Leader to use Aspasia's phone to contact Queen Marie and tell her he was too tired to attend. It's at a moment like this that King Peter seems at his most doomed. This was a young man who hoped to unite the ethnic and political factions of his homeland, keep Tito's Partisans in alliance with Mihailovic's Cetniks, and mould the shape of post-war Yugoslavia– a young man who was afraid to telephone his own mother.

Depending on whom you believe, what followed was violence. Dunlop Mackenzie claimed that he had given his frank opinion on Peter's decision to spend the night in Suite 212, and that he had received an intransigent reply. 'He insisted that he would not change his mind,' he reported, 'and I retired in the face of considerable ill-feeling and opposition from their Highnesses.' Alexandra, however, recorded this night as one of invasion and assault. Dunlop Mackenzie, she maintained, had forced his way into the apartment. 'The door crashed with a violent jar,' she wrote. 'Peter sprang to his feet, leaping towards it. He thought mummie had slipped as she was coming in. But as he opened it quickly, the tall powerful figure of Peter's British liaison officer, Sqd. Ldr. Dunlop Mackenzie, thrust into the room. "Sir," he said. "I've come to take you to your mother, the Queen." He rapped the words out. "You're coming now, sire. With me. I've come to take you away from this princess."'[20] She does not say that he wore a black cloak, but the picture is clear.

Alexandra's account describes a physical fight between monarch and minder; Dunlop Mackenzie bracing himself against the lintel, a screaming King Peter shouldering his mentor backwards into the corridor, slamming the door and turning the key. Aspasia called a doctor, who pulled a syringe from his bag, drew some liquid sedative from a glass ampoule, and sank the needle into the arm of the sobbing Princess. A second dose made its way into King Peter's bloodstream. Two days later Dunlop Mackenzie reported to the Yugoslav Legation to find a letter from the King waiting for him. It was an offer of one week's leave, and had clearly been dictated. King Peter had chosen Alexandra over Archibald Dunlop Mackenzie. The Squadron Leader had lost the battle for Peter's heart and mind.

*

By the morning of 20 March 1944, the crying and shouting and swooning were over and the Claridge's hairdresser was sticking pins into the future Queen of Yugoslavia. Alexandra's maid, Rose Holloway, packed up the bridal wear – a veil donated by Princess Marina, the pale oyster satin gown in which Maimie Lygon had married Peter's cousin, Prince Vsevolod of Russia – and hoicked it round to the Yugoslav Legation. Anxious not to tower over her husband in the wedding photographs, Alexandra pulled on a pair of flat shoes, wrapped herself in a fur coat, stepped through the doors of the hotel's service lift and slipped out of Claridge's via the kitchens. During the ceremony the bride and groom stood side by side, their arms tied with a silk scarf, their skulls capped with the crowns of the Karadjordjevices. Afterwards the couple posed for what has became the team photograph of Allied royalty: Queen Elizabeth, smiling her tight little smile in fox fur; George VI, the best man, cast in the role of indulgent Uncle Bertie; Princes Tomislav and Andrej, the groom's younger brothers; Aspasia of Greece, her face a hard mask of triumph; the Claridge's mob, Wilhelmina and Bernhard of the Netherlands, George of Greece, Haakon of Norway; and just offstage, Anthony Eden, the Foreign Secretary, who had favoured Peter's accession partly because he had disliked his Uncle Paul when they were contemporaries at Cambridge. The groom's mother, Marie of Yugoslavia, did not attend, due to a toothache that was interpreted by the Foreign Office as a clear sign that she regarded Tomislav I as the preferred monarch of post-war Yugoslavia.

Archie Dunlop Mackenzie received news of the wedding on the day he returned from leave. For him, it represented the irrevocable triumph of Alexandra and Aspasia, who, for the remaining months of his official attachment to King Peter, ensured that the monarch was rarely alone with the Squadron Leader. Although Dunlop Mackenzie was noted for his reserve, his final report to George Rendel, written at the end of August 1944, is a document with a heartbroken tone, something between a headmaster's assessment of a favourite pupil who has gone off the rails and the thoughts of a jilted lover. 'Away from other influences he still seemed a very reasonable person,' he wrote, describing how, despite their estrangement, he put Peter's finances in order, established a trust fund to protect his money from 'other interested parties', and procured him the use of an 'advanced training aircraft'. However, the most revealing passage comes when Dunlop Mackenzie describes his own wedding, which King Peter was expected to attend. It took place on 9 August 1944 at St Mark's on North Audley Street, the same church in which Dunlop Mackenzie's ill-fated brother had married. The reception was held at Claridge's. The identity of the bride discloses much about the Squadron Leader's sense of compassion and duty, and the mutual web of SOE relationships. Ann Nicholls was the widow of Lieutenant Colonel Arthur Nicholls, who had perished five months previously on a mission with Enver Hoxha's Partisans in Albania. Nicholls died in horrible agony, starved and frostbitten after months of dodging German patrols in the mountains. ('Bare bones showed through the gangrened flesh,' said the report.) He left behind a daughter who was too young to remember a father other than Archie Dunlop Mackenzie.

Peter's non-appearance was clearly a cause of distress to the groom and to those members of the Yugoslav court who kept their promise to attend. 'Their apologies for his absence were almost embarrassing,' noted Dunlop Mackenzie, for whom the whole business was clearly a manipulative act on the part of Alexandra and Aspasia; a decisive move in their attempt to eliminate him from the game of King Peter's life. 'His entourage are in despair, and practically have no sure contact with him, except either in the passages of the hotel or in the presence of his wife and/or mother-in-law in their joint suite. He rarely if ever comes to the office in the Embassy, and appears to do no work at all. Such audiences as he grants and keeps are held in Claridge's Hotel with the Queen and the Princess hovering in the background or behind half-closed doors.' One such audience was granted on the first day of June 1944, when the last Prime Minister of Yugoslavia, Ivan Subasic, an enthusiastic supporter of Tito's Partisans, entered the royal sitting room to swear his oath of allegiance to the King. Alexandra's memoir states that Peter emerged from this brief ceremony in a state of despair. 'Sandra,' he said wearily, 'this is the beginning of the end.' According to her account, she then curtsied to her husband and declared, 'You are still King.'[21]

*

The King's estrangement from Archie Dunlop Mackenzie did not release him from the gaze of the secret state. At Claridge's, there were more spies than sommeliers. SOE and its American equivalent, the Office for Strategic Services (OSS), held joint receptions and dinners on the premises. At one of these soirées in May 1942, Lord Selborne, the minister responsible for SOE, narrowly avoided making a fool of himself with a flirtatious French double agent named Mathilde Carré. At a cocktail party in April 1944, General Henry Miller, chief supply officer of the Ninth Air Force, was overheard offering to take bets on the likely date of D-Day, and was demoted and deported in disgrace.[22] A whole synod of senior OSS figures made Claridge's their wartime address: Wallace Phillips, who survived the attack on the *Lusitania* to become the OSS Director of Special Information, in which capacity he sought detailed information on German troop movements and the amount of Château Margaux 1920 in the hotel's cellars; Moe Berg, a former baseball player assigned by OSS to investigate the German atomic programme and – if necessary – to assassinate its leading researcher, Werner Heisenberg; Major Arthur Goldberg, who was one of the first American agents to receive evidence that the Germans had made murder an industrial process in their concentration camps in the east. Above them all was the chief of the organisation, Colonel 'Wild' Bill Donovan, who once departed Claridge's on a mission to the French front line, leaving his suicide pills on the bedside table.[23]

In her memoirs Alexandra describes Donovan 'as a very good friend of ours'. He was, however, paying a number of agents to spy on her. Of those figures that were close to Peter and Alexandra during this period, most were betraying them to one of these secret authorities. The most limpet-like were a husband-and-wife team who were provided with rooms on the fourth floor directly above the royal suite. Bernard Yarrow was a Russian-born lawyer who ran the Rackets Bureau at the office of the New York district attorney. His wife, Sylvia, was a sculptor with a thriving studio on East Seventy-Fourth Street, and the principal engineer of a treacherous intimacy with Peter and his family. As Bernard intrigued to install Roosevelt's preferred candidate, Ivan Subasic, as Prime Minister of the government-in-exile, Sylvia went shopping with Alexandra and Aspasia, shared their secrets and anxieties, and made discreet visits to their rooms via the service staircase. When Peter expressed his frustrations regarding Churchill, his émigré ministers, or the progress of the guerrilla war in his homeland, the Yarrows produced a typewritten report and delivered it to the cable desk at the OSS offices on Grosvenor Street. There was a name for this way of life – the Shepherd Project. At its conclusion in March

1945, the Yarrows posted an extravagant thank-you note to Donovan, accompanied by an expenses claim for $10,488. And yet, until her death in 1993, Sylvia Yarrow's mantelpiece bore a signed photograph of the couple upon whom she had spied.

The unkindest cuts came from Robert Hayden Alcorn, who befriended the royal couple in 1944, under orders from Donovan. Twenty years later, Alcorn published a memoir of his time in the OSS which described the nights he had spent in the royal suite in Claridge's, knocking back whisky and trying to disguise his contempt for his hosts. *No Bugles for Spies* (1963) tells how its author made King Peter the present of an American Air Force flying suit: 'He immediately put it on and strutted about in it like a small boy with his first cowboy suit. It seemed to make little difference that the suit was much too large for his slender, undersized frame.' Alcorn was also present in the royal apartment when Alexandra performed one of her favourite party tricks – playing with the Yugoslav crown jewels, which had been surrendered by Queen Marie, with much ceremony and little grace. Aspasia, Alcorn claimed, informed Alexandra that she was too flat-chested to carry them off.[24]

Crown Prince Alexander expressed little sympathy for the spooks that haunted the lives of his parents. 'Everybody had their man,' he shrugged. 'Some men were loyal to the British system. Others were loyal to the Americans. They all had directives. The whole thing was quite sordid.' He dismissed my suggestion that Archie Dunlop Mackenzie enjoyed a less cynical relationship with his father. 'There were several like Dunlop Mackenzie,' he said. 'They came and went. If you're going to penetrate somebody you must have the most warm and charming attitude. Good bad manners, you might say. This was normal. And my father was used to living under surveillance. Even when he was king under the Regency, each step he made was reported. Someone made a note every time he had a stomach ache. This is how an intelligence service works.'

Alexander entered the world under state surveillance. At the moment of his birth in Suite 212 of Claridge's, that temporary outpost of his homeland, the official agents of the Yugoslav government were present in the next room. The circumstances of the birth were not auspicious. On that day in the summer of 1945, the future of the Karadjordjevic dynasty looked doubtful. Most of the ministers who had danced around King Peter since 1941 had returned to Yugoslavia, chosen exile or, in one case, committed suicide in a room at the Mount Royal Hotel on Oxford Street. A provisional coalition government was already established in Belgrade, in which Tito was the dominant personality and Communism the dominant ideology. This surprised no one – least of all Winston Churchill. At a meeting in Cairo in 1943, the Prime Minister had discussed the future of the Balkans with Fitzroy MacLean, an SOE brigadier attached to Tito's Partisans. MacLean stated his belief that support for Tito would lead inevitably to a post-war Yugoslavia on Soviet lines. Churchill asked him a question: 'Do you intend to make Yugoslavia your home after the war?' MacLean replied that he did not. 'Nor do I,' returned the man with the cigar.[25]

The final year of the war was a tough year to be King of Yugoslavia. In February 1945, Subasic and his supporters returned to Belgrade to share power with Tito. The night before their departure they held a noisy party at Claridge's. John Walters, the diplomatic correspondent of the *Daily Mirror*, was passing through the hotel when he noticed 'a forlorn-looking young man' standing on the chequered floor. 'Your king is in the lobby,' Walters informed an official. 'One does not presume to invite royalty to parties,' he was told.[26] That same year, Yugoslavia became a one-party state; the monarchy was abolished and the privileges of the Karadjordjevic dynasty revoked; Tito charged Peter with 'abandoning the Yugoslav peoples to their fate'.[27] On Crown Prince Alexander's first birthday, Draza Mihailovic, Peter's Minister of War, was executed by firing squad, having been found guilty of high treason by a tribunal in Belgrade. During the following summer, the Yugoslav National

Assembly stripped Peter and his family of their citizenship and their property rights. They would not be restored until March 2001, by which time the existences of King Peter, his Greek bride and the state of Yugoslavia had all reached their unhappy conclusions.

Crown Prince Alexander, the Claridge's baby, grew up into a successful insurance broker with his father's creased little smile and no expectation of returning to his homeland. From a little office on Park Lane he campaigned against the wars that brought bloody dismemberment to post-Communist Yugoslavia in the 1990s – and against the regime of Slobodan Milosevic. It was here, in 1997, that I first met the Crown Prince. He had just chaired a meeting of Milosevic's political opponents over coffee and biscuits at Claridge's. (The Serb state media claimed that they had gone to the pub.) We talked about Milosevic's court-ship of King Peter's brother, Tomislav, who returned to Belgrade in 1991, with the approval of the Serb government. He showed me a Serbian newspaper that had published an incendiary letter in his name, and pointed out the errors that revealed it as a mischievous forgery. Alexander had no hope of returning to live in Yugoslavia while Milosevic was in power – but the President's fall in October 2000 began the process that led to his homecoming, and his acceptance of the keys of the Royal Compound, its palaces slightly scuffed by four decades of Communism and a barrage of NATO bombs. On 12 March 2001, Alexander met with Zoran Zivkovic, the Serbian Interior Minister, who presented him with a certificate of citizenship. The ceremony took place in Suite 212 of Claridge's.

'Churchill didn't have to do it, of course,' Crown Prince Alexander volunteered, as our meeting in the Blue Room came to an end. For a moment I wasn't quite sure what he meant. 'It isn't necessary for a King of Yugoslavia to be born on Yugoslav soil. It would have had no effect on the succession.' The maids scuttered about, harvesting coffee cups, collecting salvers, sweeping crumbs. Dragomir Acovic answered a call on his mobile phone. I asked Alexander why he thought the Prime Minister had taken the trouble; why he had pursued this eccentric reorganisation of geopolitical space, transforming a suite in Claridge's into a fragment of the Balkans. 'It was a thoughtful gesture,' he reflected. 'And maybe he did it out of remorse.'

On the day in 1945 that the same set of rooms above Brook Street was subject to honorary Balkanisation, the Potsdam Conference was convened – the last great diplomatic conference of the Second World War. Here, Winston Churchill, exhausted by four years of campaigning, discussed the cartographical and political divisions that would remain intact in Europe until 1989, and larked about for the cameras with Josef Stalin and Harry S. Truman. The photographs in the press that day showed the Prime Minister shaking hands with his Russian and American counterparts, caught in the middle of a hearty guffaw, his mouth wide open like a frog about to swallow a bluebottle. He was in a hearty mood. A General Election had just taken place in Britain; crowds had cheered him as he travelled from constituency to constituency in a private train. He was anticipating a Parliamentary majority of eighty. The electorate, however, had other ideas. By the time the Potsdam Conference was over, a new Labour Prime Minister, Clement Attlee, had taken Churchill's place at the negotiating table. On the day after the election Clementine Churchill made a mournful telephone call to Hugh Wontner, managing director of the Savoy Group. 'We have nowhere to go,' she said. Wontner collected her in his car with the intention of finding the couple accommodation at the Savoy, where he imagined that the former Prime Minister, a keen painter, would appreciate the river view that had inspired Claude Monet. In order to give the couple a choice, however, he brought Clementine first to Claridge's, where they ascended the curved private staircase that led up to the penthouse, with its grand sitting room and French windows gazing south towards the Thames. The view was magnificent – except, perhaps, for the tactless prominence of the Houses of Parliament. 'That'll do,' she said. On 27 July 1945, the hotel became their London home.

A month after moving into Claridge's, Churchill arranged a private dinner for a small group of Tory ministers. During the meal the Prime Minister's private secretary, John Colville, bowled into the room with a note from Attlee, bringing news of the surrender of Japan. One of the guests, Alan Lennox-Boyd, located a radio, around which the defeated ministers gathered to hear the new Prime Minister announce the conclusion of five years of bitter conflict. Years later, Lennox-Boyd recalled the moment:

. . . on a borrowed wireless set in a hired room in Claridge's, Winston heard of the end of the war, and I think that there wasn't a single of his former colleagues who wasn't near to tears at the irony of the situation. Then he went out into the rain and there were three old ladies under an umbrella who had heard he was there and gave him a cheer. Well, that was the end of war co-operation.[28]

10

Strikers

The sheik was having a yard sale. Prince al-Waleed bin Talal, owner of the Savoy since 2005, had decided to close his hotel for refurbishment and was therefore obliged to rid himself of three thousand unwanted knick-knacks. And for three chilling days in the week before Christmas 2007, we came scavenging for *plafonniers* and occasional tables: pin-striped men with over-the-collar hair; antique-shop speculators; Russian women with unusual ideas about make-up; a man in a mesmerising ginger toupee and stringed glasses – and me, nursing the hope of looting a souvenir from the greatest hotel in the world. We sat in ranks, clutching our thick glossy catalogues and numbered paper paddles, under the ballroom's *trompe l'œil* ceiling: plaster moulded to mimic the ripples of a marquee.

The lots offered a smattering of starry items – a twelve-panel painted screen by Lincoln Taber, depicting a hunt galloping across parkland; the parquet dance floor of the Lancaster Room, jemmied up in a hundred oaken pieces; the electric chandelier that had once lit the way down to the River Room. But most of the lots were undistinguished tat: Regency-style TV cabinets; pink-and-white console tables; 1980s sofas in eye-watering patterns. A standard lamp, harvested from a room once occupied by Fred Astaire, went for a measly £50. (We were smart enough to guess that the contents of the room may have altered somewhat since Fred tripped around the carpet in the 1920s.) The objects that caused genuine excitement were the ones allotted the lowest status by the valuers from Bonhams. Simple circles of chromium-plated steel for hanging a hand towel, bonded by a stylised 'S', like the lightning-flash emblem of the British Union of Fascists. Estimated at £40 each, few left the building for less than £700. As every rail found a new home, there came one of those nervous titters or warm eddies of applause that customarily follow a sale that rises above the estimated price, as if the buyer had performed some minor admirable act, like catching a cricket ball or rescuing a cat from a tree. An auction-room correspondent explained the phenomenon to me. 'If I've been after a particular lot then I may well have something rather like it at home. A Damien Hirst. A Picasso. A relic of some grand hotel. So even if you outbid me, I still applaud because your bid has raised the market value of such pieces. That applause is the sound of the rich making each other richer.' In the circumstances, I had to content myself with stealing a flannel from the gents.

Whenever the Savoy is bought or sold, or marks an important anniversary, or decides to change the colour of its lampshades, there is one man on whom the journalists call for a quote – usually with the encouragement of the hotel's public relations officer. The Savoy management loves Joe Gilmore not just because he is as much part of the history of the building as its stainless-steel canopy, but because, unlike others who have held the venerated office of head barman at the American Bar, he has never been tempted to betray his employers. Joe's successor, for instance, came out against Prince al-Waleed's refurbishment plan and declared that the hotel had sold its soul at the auction. (The Savoy, rather tactlessly, said that it was only disposing of items that were 'in poor repair or of little to no value' – an admission found nowhere in the auction catalogue.[1]) Such controversies, however, are anathema to Joe. Just as he kept the secrets of the actors and aristocrats and politicians who unburdened their late-night thoughts at his upstairs confessional, he has stayed loyal to the Savoy, a quiet, soft-spoken man in a neat white jacket, shaking his customers' Martinis, supplying them with crisps and nuts, sympathising with their woes, and embodying the spirit of discretion.

During the war years, Joe Gilmore poured drinks for de Gaulle and Eisenhower and Jan Masaryk. He confected vokda rickeys for Alice Faye and something tall and non-alcoholic for George Bernard Shaw. (Joe once made this for me, a sweet-and-sour combination of fruit cordial and celery sticks.) After the war, he popped champagne for Marlene Dietrich and Judy Garland and became the Joe whom Frank Sinatra exhorted to 'set 'em up' in 'One for My Baby'. In 1969, he created a cocktail called the Moon Walk in honour of Neil Armstrong, a flask of which was despatched to Cape Canaveral and consumed by the astronauts as they emerged from quarantine. From behind his place at the bar, Joe observed disputes industrial and personal; watched managements deal with hostile and friendly takeovers; witnessed programmes of restoration and ripping-out. And throughout all these, he has kept his opinions to himself. One of his most enduring creations, a combination of apple brandy and vermouth called the Savoy Corpse Reviver, was named for its remedial effect upon the hangovers of his clients – but surely also because its inventor knew where all the bodies were buried.

Seeing Joe Gilmore beyond the walls of the Savoy was a faintly disorienting experience. In the week that the hotel closed its doors, I visited him in his flat high above Great Ormond Street. It seemed odd to be sitting with him in a room undominated by soda siphons or optics. His wife, Marie, trundled into the sitting room with a trolley bearing Earl Grey and cakes and neatly cut finger sandwiches – a domesticated version of a Savoy tea. She remained in the kitchen throughout our conversation. Joe was in blazer and tie, and slicked with hair-cream as if ready for a military inspection. He talked like a man who preferred to listen. I did, however, learn something about his background. He was born in Belfast in 1922, one of ten children brought up by teetotal parents. 'My father owned shops and he had an idea that his sons would run them,' he said, 'but we had different ideas.' Joe's struck him at the age of sixteen. In the summer of 1938 he boarded a boat to Liverpool, made his way to London and found work in the Sanderson's wallpaper factory on Oxford Street. (The building, fittingly, is now a luxury hotel.) Among his friends were boys apprenticed elsewhere as kitchen porters and waiters, who made him envious by describing the food they consumed on the job. It was war that gave Joe the entrée he required – in the form of the cull of hotel staff effected by the demands of the military and the exigencies of Regulation 18B. In 1940, he became the new trainee barman at the Savoy.

Almost immediately, he was transferred to the Perroquet bar of the Berkeley, the Piccadilly outpost of the D'Oyly Carte empire. He was working the night that a bomb slipped through the body of the Rialto cinema and into the subterranean space of the Café de Paris – and like all who witnessed the aftermath of that event, he retained strong memories of the dazed and dust-covered figures of the walking wounded. He assisted them in his own way. When one bruised survivor leaned on the bar and asked for something with a sting, Joe filled the cocktail-shaker with brandy and crème de menthe and concocted a form of liquid shock therapy now known as the Berkeley Stinger.

Joe's wartime recollections, however, were dominated by one man: Winston Churchill, who elevated the barman to a unique position of trust – designated keeper of the private prime ministerial bottle of Black & White whisky, from which his glass would be filled whenever he dined at the Savoy. Joe served him when he dined with members of the Other Club, a fortnightly political gathering in the Pinafore Room, and devised three cocktails in his honour – the Blenheim, the Fourscore and the Churchill. The Prime Minister had little cognisance of Joe's life beyond the hotel. He once spotted the barman having lunch in a restaurant on his day off, and demanded to know why he wasn't at the Savoy. But Joe's loyalty to the man was intense and unquestionable. Talking to him six decades after the 1945

election, he seemed unable to comprehend why the British electorate had spurned their war leader in the peace. 'It was such a
shock,' he whispered, as if still reeling from the news. His disbe-
lief put me in mind of a much-repeated story that is sometimes
claimed for the Savoy, sometimes for Claridge's; sometimes told
of a Society woman standing by the ticker-tape machines on
election night, sometimes of a Society gentleman rising from
bed on his first morning in Attlee's Britain. 'They have elected a
Labour government,' goes the punchline, 'and the country will
never stand for it.'

Joe was not a member of Society, but he respected it. He
mixed its drinks and accepted its patronage. He spent the late
1940s commiserating with those beyond the post-war con-
sensus, listening to them rail against the new government's high
rate of income tax. 'It's only a sixpence to you,' said one customer, snapping a coin on the bar, 'but it's a pound to me.' He
remembered how many habitués of the American Bar talked
of moving to Franco's Spain to escape socialism, rationing and
the freezing weather of 1947. He also recalled an incident that
demonstrates what is often identified as the most profound cultural shift of the post-war period: the end of deference. For Joe,
the moment came when a diner in the Savoy restaurant attempted to attract the attention of a waiter by clicking his fingers.
'The waiter turned to him and said, "I'm sorry, sir – have you
lost your dog?"' The words were burned into Joe Gilmore's
memory. Sixty years after hearing them, he had yet to decide
whether they indicated progress or disaster.

Deference was the business of the grand hotel. Inequality was
a commodity in which it traded. Its hierarchies had been shaped
after military models. Orders were obeyed. Uniforms were inspected. Shoes gleamed. Democracy had no obvious place in the
kitchen or the grill room. Escoffier's academy system reigned in
the hot subterranean parts of the hotel, other militarisms elsewhere. At the Savoy, no waiter was permitted to wear a watch,
a ring, spectacles or false teeth. At Claridge's, the restaurant

staff were obliged to carry a white cloth at all times and stand precisely two yards apart from each other. Sackings for coughing, sneezing or nose-blowing were not unknown. Trade unions were unrecognised. Most waiters, receptionists and porters received a nominal wage or no wage at all, and obtained the bulk of their money through the *tronc* system, under which tips were pooled and then distributed among the staff – a fund from which the management also took its cut. When, in March 1948, the government attempted to reform this practice, the Savoy's response was to bill some of its employees for the right to work on the premises.

It was at this moment that James Townsend, the seventy-two-year-old chief attendant of the gentleman's cloakroom at the Savoy, found himself in the office of Arthur Collard, the assistant general manager. 'He informed me that I should be required to pay a sum of money each year to the Company in order to be in full charge of the gentleman's cloakrooms and gentleman's toilets,' Collard told an industrial tribunal.[2] 'The sum finally agreed upon was £250 to be paid every two weeks.' (An extraordinary £6,500 in today's money.) The management got their way. By the time Townsend was having this argument with his employers, the Savoy had been at war with its staff for over two years – a war that it had won.

*

Clement Attlee's Britain was virtually bankrupt. Rationing persisted, and in tighter forms than during the war. Spivs loitered in the shabby streets. Willowherb colonised the bombsites. And yet a sense of imminent utopia is what this period has bequeathed to the cultural memory: pipe-smoking doctors tearing up their account books and joining the NHS; the nationalisation of the coal, gas and electricity industries; the birth of a post-war progressivism of which even the new young Queen seemed part. This was a Britain starved of wealth but rich in

ambition, aspiration and the determination to build a more just
and equal society. Nowhere in our collective memory of this
period is there a place for the image that greeted visitors to the
Savoy during the cold months of 1947: a group of pickets lining
the pavements outside the hotel, shouting 'Fuck the police!'

The *Daily Mirror* called it 'War in the West End' and began
leading the cheers. 'Why, belatedly, have the drums of democracy sounded behind the green baize doors?' asked the paper's
business correspondent, George McCarthy, in October 1946.
'Why is it that the waiters and chefs and cooks, the chambermaids and the valets of London's West End hotels are organ-
ising strike action? The truth is that the object is to revolutionise
life in the luxury hotels.' The campaign began on 7 October
1946, on a bench in Thames Embankment Gardens, where
a committee of Savoy employees met to discuss how to ob-
lige the hotel to recognise the Catering Branch of the General
and Municipal Workers' Union, of which five hundred of their
colleagues were members. They met under the leadership of
the union's London district organiser, Arthur Lewis, a chubby,
ruddy-faced, publicity-hungry, twenty-nine-year-old MP propelled into Parliament by the Labour landslide. At midnight,
the committee pinned up a notice in the staff quarters, headed
'The time has come'. In the following days, the strike spread
speedily from hotel to hotel, and beyond. The meat porters of
Smithfield came out in sympathy and caused rejoicing among
the housewives of East Acton and North Hammersmith, where
the butchers' shops were suddenly and miraculously filled with
offal.[3] At the Berkeley, heads of department served dinner as
waiters stood on the pavements of Piccadilly. At Claridge's,
three loyal kitchen staff and a boy struggled to marshal abandoned ovens full of roasting partridges, chickens and joints of
beef.[4] (Only two chefs remained at the Ritz.) At the Dorchester,
guests ate bread and cheese with their coffee. ('How tiresome it
all is,' moaned a dinner-jacketed young man to the hack from
the *Mirror*.) At the Connaught Rooms, Manny Shinwell, the

Minister of Fuel and Power, found that the lobster and pears on the menu of his dinner-dance had been cancelled in favour of a cold buffet. (The *Express* photographed him gnawing at a chicken drumstick and quoted him declaring, 'It's the best function I've been to for a long time.'[5]) An interviewer from the Mass Observation project spent a day canvassing opinion around the Strand and Piccadilly and taking notes at a gathering of two thousand catering workers at the Victory Hall on Leicester Square. 'We're working in terrible conditions,' confessed a kitchen hand at the Ritz. 'What we get to eat wouldn't feed a chicken.' She took tea at the Park Lane Hotel, where she heard the views of an 'old waiter who had no teeth, and spoke without moving his lips, because he was afraid anyone might hear him'. 'Do you know we don't have enough to buy ourselves a glass of beer after the day's tips have been divided?' he asked. 'Look at my shoes! They're just falling off me. And they want 26 coupons for a new uniform, but how could I get some more socks if they take all my coupons? What a life, eh!'[6]

At the end of the first week of the strike, a Savoy chef named Arturo Ravera, dressed in his kitchen whites, marched beside Arthur Lewis MP, two kilted pipers, a fife band and a crowd of five thousand supporters. They processed from the Savoy's Embankment entrance and past the Strand Palace Hotel, where guests leaned out of their windows to wave them on. ('What about a Vienna steak?' called a passer-by in Trafalgar Square. 'We've no sausage meat!' replied Ravera.) When the marchers reached Hyde Park, E. V. Watering, the London district secretary of the GMWU, railed against the 'dictatorial pro-Fascist' bosses of the hotel trade and issued a wary cry to their employees. 'Arise, ye hotel workers, from your slumbers. Get off your bellies, boys. You have been cringing and crawling to the duchess long enough. Let the duchess cook her own kipper. Let her make her own bed.'[7]

On the eighth day, the Hotel Employers' Association acceded to the strikers' principal demand – the official recognition of the

GMWU. During a prickly meeting at the Ministry of Labour, an agreement was drawn up between union members, hotel directors and government officials. That, however, was not the end of the business. There were other issues that would prove much more difficult to resolve. Other forces, too, that would attempt to exploit this discord.

*

The most detailed published account of the strikes was written by Jean Nicol, the publicity manager of the hotel, in an otherwise enjoyably frothy memoir, *Meet Me at the Savoy* (1952). Nicol was a former journalist at the *Mirror*, where she had assuaged the heartsickness of her readers under the nom de plume of Dorothy Dix. After five years at the Savoy, she married a fellow journalist, Derek Tangye, which may be one of several reasons to treat her version of events with caution. Tangye was a gossip columnist who was sacked from the *Mirror* after he proved too squeamish for the job. Ferreting quotes from film stars and celebrities embarrassed him, it seems. However, he had no qualms about repeating the private conversations of his colleagues. As MI5's man on Fleet Street, he delivered weekly reports to Guy Liddell throughout the 1940s. He was still on duty when the pickets and the police arrived at the Savoy.

Mrs Tangye's account of the strikes is passionately faithful to the public image of her workplace. 'I knew the Savoy had a just cause, and to beat these extremists and trouble-makers was something of the most far-reaching importance,' she argues, 'not only from the point of view of the hotel which I loved, but from the point of view of all those good, hard-working loyal people.'[8] Hers is the story of a harmonious institution disrupted by a small band of Communist dissenters determined to bring the management to its knees and London to a standstill. Harmonious, unfortunately, hardly describes the Savoy of the 1940s. Theft from the kitchens was endemic; most of the bar staff diluted the alcohol and drank their own stock; the *tronc* was a constant source of tension; chefs used deliveries from the continent to pursue their own illegal rackets, stuffing bundles of currency inside boxes of French beans. Nicol, however, was right about the Reds turning over the beds. A small cell of agitators had indeed joined the staff in order to radicalise their colleagues. They were led by Francesco Piazza, a *chef de rang* in the Grill Room. He was twenty-eight and from Catford, southeast London, and he wanted to smash the state.

*

Joe Gilmore remembered Frank Piazza with a shudder, and would only speak of him with the Dictaphone dead on the table between us. The authorities on the Isle of Man, where Piazza had been interned under Regulation 18B, took the view that he was 'ugly [and] rather coarse-looking, [but] exceptionally honest'. Jean Nicol recalled him as 'a fuzzy-haired Italian waiter . . . a stormy agitator'. Hugh Wontner thought him 'very able, a clever chap' who headed 'a little nucleus of people who were infiltrated into the Savoy'. The spymaster Maxwell Knight, considering the matter from behind his desk on Dolphin Square, concurred: 'Piazza was deliberately introduced there', he reasoned, 'with the object of creating strife.'9

But introduced by whom? In 1940, in the Palace internment camp on the promenade at Douglas, Piazza denied he was a member of the Communist Party. By 1943, however, he had been appointed propaganda secretary of the Feltham branch of the CPGB, distributing circulars that posed questions such as 'Could we have a revolution now?' In late 1947, Special Branch officers detected his presence in the lives of two prominent British Communists known to be conduits for information back to Moscow.10 But Piazza's security file is curiously unburdened by evidence of activism. He never speaks as a Communist, never owns a Party card, never makes a public utterance on any subject other than his career at the Savoy. The most suggestive document the file contains is a photographed copy of a letter addressed jointly to Frank and his elder brother, Guerrino, which was intercepted, copied and filed by MI5 in the summer of 1940. It is from a man called Maurie, who is about to marry the eldest sister of the Piazza boys. 'I see by the paper that there has been a little scrap at your place of study,' he breezes, referring to press reports of a disturbance in a camp at Douglas. 'It wasn't by any chance you, was it, Francis? I have a sneaking feeling that you have been having a cut at causing another strike. It's funny but whenever I read of trouble my thoughts always wander to my delightful, good-natured brother in law.' More innuendo follows. Maurie writes that he has passed Frank and Guerrino's offshore address to a mutual friend 'who still has the same ideas in life, if you get what I mean'. This prompts a question, and a little flight of fancy. 'Are your views still the same?' he asks. 'If they are, I only wish you were here with me. Boy, could we do things. Why don't you two try and get out? It would be a lot better for all concerned. You remember that little talk that you and I had once, walking home from the West End? Well, what a time the present is.' Maurie might have been talking about a minor criminal opportunity – a little bit of theft in the blackout. But that mention of a strike, that heavy-handed enquiry about his views, suggests the possibility of some political objective.[11]

Frank Piazza joined the staff of the Grill Room on the third day of October 1946. Four days later the building was paralysed by industrial action. The Savoy's managers did not consider this coincidental. It was immediately apparent, their legal representative claimed, that the new recruit was 'not of the type or up to the standard required for the Grill Room'. Fomenting a strike, implied Gilbert Paull KC, was simply a ruthless exercise in avoiding dismissal. Piazza's unsuitability may have been a consequence of the waiter's noticeable limp or the permanent rattle of his catarrh, but the most likely explanation lay

in his attitude to authority. During the campaign for union recognition, the waiter quickly appointed himself as the Savoy's
principal union spokesperson – a role he performed with such
aggressive enthusiasm that the hotel's lawyers served him with a
writ forbidding him to advocate his cause on the premises. Once
the Savoy had been obliged to recognise the union, the tables
were turned. Piazza became almost unsackable, as any attempt
to dislodge him from his job could have been construed as victimisation. He now presented himself as chairman of a new and
muscular shop stewards' committee, whose members included a
Swiss chef named Ronald Kaufmann and Marion Lunt, a thirty-
eight-year-old waitress from Liverpool. Piazza now had weight,
and he proceeded to throw it about.

At the beginning of evening service on 11 March 1947,
Vokes, the manager of the plate room, reported a rebellion: the
gang of men who scrubbed plates and scoured cutlery were refusing to work under him, apparently because he had denied
them one of the traditional perks of the job – eating the leftovers
that clung to the plates. In response, Luigi Pellosi, the assistant
manager of the Grill Room, had ordered the commis waiters
to transport the dirty crockery down to the plate room – a
duty customarily performed by the plate-room workers themselves. Piazza, in a state of great excitement, marched from the
Grill Room to voice his objections. According to a report filed
by MI5, 'He threatened the staff manager; he told the juni-
or waiters to disobey an order properly given by the manager
of the Grill, and generally behaved in an insubordinate manner.' When Piazza arrived for work the following morning, he
was informed of his suspension. Ronald Kaufmann presented a
letter to the staff manager, Cecil Toye, demanding the reinstatement of 'Brother Piazza'. The demand was ignored. Although
technically barred from the premises, the man at the centre of
the affair stood on a table in one of the banqueting suites and
laid out his plans. 'Well, comrades,' he declaimed, 'you have decided to strike and now we must increase the picket line and

stop all supplies to the hotel. Get everybody out and bring the place to a standstill.' Cecil Toye hurried from this meeting to bring the bad news to the boardroom. To his surprise, he found two senior figures from the General and Municipal Workers' Union closeted with his superiors – men who seemed equally miserable to hear that Francesco Piazza had brought their members out again. One of them was E. V. Watering, who had raised cheers in Hyde Park by professing his belief that duchesses should fry their own kippers. The union for whom the first Savoy strike had been fought was losing control of the second.

It is possible that the impetus for this action lay entirely with the unruly *chef de rang*, who preferred being photographed by the newspapers to sitting at home in south-east London, tending his tomato plants. But there are other possibilities. In the summer of 1947, the Revolutionary Communist Party (RCP) – a marginal but ambitious organisation dedicated to the political ideas of Leon Trotsky – published its annual organisational report. A friendly mole ensured that a copy was collected by the security services. This now resides in the National Archives. Towards the end of the document is a section that deals with the Party's attempts to influence the progress of industrial disputes across the country: those of dockers in Liverpool, bin-men in Glasgow, bus drivers in London – and waiters and kitchen staff at the Savoy. 'In this strike', concluded the report, 'our activities were inevitably affected by the level of the workers involved. These workers were drawn into the struggle for the first time, and the nature of the discussions, contact, etc., were conditioned accordingly.' In retrospect, the leadership of the RCP judged that the approach taken at the Savoy was unnecessarily subtle. 'The maximum gains for the Party were not obtained from this activity owing to the mistake made by the comrades in presenting themselves only as trade unionists, and not in a more positive sense as Trotskyists. However, the comrades subsequently took steps to rectify this. In the dispute of March this year which involved the Savoy group, closer relations were established.'[12]

The RCP was led by Jock Haston, a charismatic former merchant seaman, and funded, incongruously and fitfully, by Jacques Spreiregen, the owner of a successful hat-manufacturing business in Cumbria. (His firm, Kangol, was the principal supplier of berets to the British Army in the Second World War, and still thrives today.) The RCP positioned itself considerably further to the left than the Communists who had marched through the Savoy's front doors during the Blitz. It dismissed its more mainstream rivals as 'His Majesty's Loyal Communist Party' – but Phil Piratin's comrades had something that their Trotskyist rivals lacked: measurable public support. Haston's organisation possessed only three hundred members and lost every election it contested. However, it claimed many more undeclared sympathisers – including sixty seeded in the body of the Labour Party.

'In the post-war period', concluded the RCP conference of 1945, 'capitalism can only offer a "hell on earth" for the industrial working class of Britain.' For the delegates, however, this was a Hades with possibilities: 'Increasing attacks on wages . . . the victimisation of trade union militants under the cloak of redundancy; increasing unemployment – all these factors are producing but one effect – the development of a profound molecular process of an essentially revolutionary character among the masses.'[13] With nerveless optimism, this tiny party aimed to catalyse that process by offering advice and assistance to strike committees and talking up their campaigns on the pages of its newspaper, Socialist Appeal – a publication that could comfortably shift ten thousand copies each fortnight, and which, in the spring of 1947, was being read in the staff room of the Savoy. One of those readers, Marion Lunt, even made it to the cover, placard in one hand, and handbag in the other, a broad smile spanning her face. She also wrote an article for the newspaper in which she accused the management of the Savoy of cheating its workforce by 'arrogantly refusing' to carry the decisions of the tribunal appointed to investigate Piazza's dismissal and obstructing the legitimate work of the union on its premises. Lunt's prominence on these pages was an example of editorial favouritism. She had been a member of the Revolutionary Communist Party since its foundation and joined the staff of the Savoy with revolution on her mind. Her appearance on the pages of *Socialist Appeal*, however, proved to be one of the causes of her Party's dissolution.

*

The third and most bitter act of the Savoy strikes began on the first Thursday of November 1947, a week before one of that year's most significant national events – the wedding of Princess Elizabeth and Prince Philip of Greece. It is the only drama of British social history to have allocated roles to Bob Hope, Margaret Lockwood, a future monarch and a knot of indigenous Trotskyists. It was a grim business. The holiday atmosphere of the previous October was utterly gone. The national leaders of the GMWU had lost their enthusiasm for shaking up the Savoy and now wanted to end the business as painlessly as possible. They censured Piazza's rowdy interference in the plate room and approved his suspension. As committees wrangled over the rights and wrongs of his case, tired and frustrated employees of the Savoy drifted away from the union. Those who had voted for action began to suffer the consequences. Norman Phillips, a waiter in the restaurant, discovered that the terms of his employment had been revised: the new arrangement added two hours and subtracted ten shillings from his working week. The hotel began stockpiling food and hiring casual workers without GMWU cards. Days before a National Arbitration Tribunal was due to issue its verdict on whether Piazza was to be permitted to return to the Grill Room, the Savoy gave the waiter his notice. Without reference to his superiors, Arthur Lewis called a third strike. 'We will fight to the finish!' he declared. When the Savoy announced the automatic dismissal of any employee who did not turn up for work at 6 a.m. on Saturday 8 November, the union was obliged to give the strike action its official backing. What followed, in the words of Hugh Wontner, was 'a kind of war. Guerrilla warfare.'[14]

Jean Nicol was one of its generals. She conducted her campaign through the *Sunday Express*, which cleared a swath of its front page to print a letter from a member of the Savoy's staff who was opposed to the strike: Angel Ferroll, head waiter, military hero, disaffected member of the catering union, and an Italian who had been sufficiently patriotic to anglicise his name by deed poll at the beginning of the war. 'We are heartily sick of strikes,' he complained. 'We are threatened with physical violence and the prospect of no work in the future if we do not support the strike. Some of the staff have had their clothing soaked with water. Lockers in the dressing rooms have been interfered with; even kitchen machinery has been tampered with. As a result of that, a member of staff lost a finger during the last few days.' (The finger, severed at the knuckle, belonged to a man known as 'Darkie', the foreman of the plate room, and became Exhibit A in Jean Nicol's argument against the agitators – though no report of the incident was made to the police.)

'We see no reason for this unpleasantness,' continued Ferroll. 'We have always looked on the Savoy – and still do – as a very well-managed hotel. We have very good remuneration and conditions, and believe ourselves to be the best hotel and restaurant staff that any hotel can have in England or anywhere else. We think the strikes really have another motive . . .' With that, he announced his intention to resign from the union. On reading this, Arthur Lewis retorted that he had nobody named Angel Ferroll on the books. Jean Nicol, who kept her publicity office open all hours for just such eventualities, invited the photographers to the restaurant to snap close-ups of the waiter's membership card, which was due to expire in January 1948.

Policing the Savoy also became a twenty-four-hour operation. The senior officers, Chief Inspector Barnes and Superintendent Arthur Rowlerson, posted a round-the-clock patrol of the hotel. Plain-clothes men haunted the Embankment and the surrounding courts and alleys. Uniformed officers stood guard at the entrances and exits and obliged the demonstrators to pace the pavement at thirty-foot intervals. According to Barnes, the pickets 'consisted mainly of students at the School of Economics, a number of fanatical communists and other trade unionists with a very small number of Savoy Hotel strikers'. As support for the action deteriorated within the hotel, Lewis was forced to swell the depleted ranks of pickets with bright-eyed young recruits from the Socialist Society of the London School of Economics, roused readers of the *Daily Worker*, supportive members of the Revolutionary Communist Party, and more dubious figures who came along simply for the aggro. Lewis and his deputies flagged down taxis and urged their drivers to turn back from Savoy Court. They persuaded the porters of Smithfield, Billingsgate and Covent Garden to withhold deliveries of meat, fish, fruit and vegetables. They knew, however, that there was only one commodity that the Savoy was incapable of doing without. The hotel was unconnected to the electricity grid. It made its own power. A bank of generators kept its lights burning, its radiators glowing, its sewage pumps thrumming. The building ran on oil, which was pumped weekly into the capillaries of its system through an inlet pipe sunk into the ground opposite the staff entrance. If the Savoy were denied oil, then it would soon lose its identity as a cosy Thameside fairyland and become a dark, chilly place full of the smell of food waste and unflushed toilets. Under such circumstances, it would be impossible for the hotel to play its role in the nuptials of Princess Elizabeth and Prince Philip: the Floral Charity Ball scheduled for the Wednesday before the wedding; the cocktail party for British and American film stars attending the royal premiere of *The Bishop's Wife*, a comedy starring Cary Grant. 'The government said that the honour of England was at stake; crowned heads must lie cosy and warm,' observed John Platts-Mills, the young Labour MP who acted as legal adviser to the strikers. 'Arthur [Lewis] said the honour of the NUGMW was at stake; crowned heads must share the discomforts of the common people.'[15] At a meeting of the London Trades Council, a delegate declared, 'We will stop their meat, we will stop their fish, their milk, their beer, and their oil. And oil is the red light for the Savoy.'[16] The expression was duly painted up on placards.

On the evening of 11 November, two tankers rumbled into the access road on the west side of the Savoy and prompted the strikers to action: a self-conscious re-enactment of the Battle of Cable Street. Vernon Fung, a clerk from Maida Vale, described in the police files as 'a man of colour', stepped out in front of the first lorry, waving his hands in the air and declaiming, 'It shall not pass,' the old anti-Franco slogan memorably employed by the Communists who resisted Mosley's march through the East End. It, however, did pass. A group of constables formed a protective cordon around the tanker as its driver attached the outlet pipe and loosed his cargo into the Savoy's fuel store. But by the time the second tanker was manoeuvring into position, the strikers had formulated a more effective strategy of obstruction. They threw themselves down on the road in the path of the vehicle and pressed their backs to the tarmac. When the police dragged them back to the pavement, they flopped down again. The irrepressible Vernon Fung crawled beneath the lorry and occupied a suicide position in its undercarriage: lying across the back axle with his legs posted through the spokes of the wheel. Two constables pulled him out, but the job was done. The driver had lost his appetite for confrontation. The lorry roared backwards. The pickets cheered. The police sent for reinforcements. So did the strikers. A group of around 250 women and men appeared, some wooed from a dance at Victory House on Leicester Square, some from a Communist Party meeting at the Kingsway Hall, where Harry Pollitt had been speaking on the thirtieth anniversary of the founding of the USSR. They formed quartets, linked arms and walked slowly up and down outside the Embankment entrance of the hotel shouting, 'Down with the rich!' and 'Squeeze the idle rich!' In a spirit of something other than solidarity, the Savoy's guests began dropping coins from their windows. They may only have been sixpences to the strikers, but they were a pound to the patrons who let them fall. Arthur Lewis and his supporters, it was claimed, nudged the money into the gutters.

Sufficient oil was delivered that night to keep the Savoy illuminated and sanitary for a further seven days. During this time, the strikers maintained a presence outside the building, withdrawing only to allow the unembarrassed passage of Princess Elizabeth into the ballroom, where she accepted flowers from a chorus line of young ballerinas. In Whitehall, the Cabinet listened to Ernest Bevin worry aloud about the possibility that the Savoy strikes were being fomented by the Soviet Union, keen to punish the Labour government for deviating from the Moscow line and keener still to make a heavily bugged Savoy a useful means of gathering intelligence. Hugh Wontner, meanwhile, acquired two tankers from the RAF and bought oil straight from the ships in Liverpool docks, bypassing fuel companies who were nervous about the political implications of doing business with him. Superintendent Rowlerson must have got wind of this: he convened a meeting with the Savoy's assistant manager and chief engineer, in order to satisfy himself that the hotel was not procuring oil on the black market. They assured him that the generators were powered by 'sludge' – a recycled form of motor oil not subject to government controls. But Rowlerson was also worried about the closeness of the relationship that was developing between his officers and the management of the Savoy, warning his colleagues of 'the need for the avoidance of any possibility of it being suggested that the police were not being impartial'. The events of the following Sunday morning did nothing to assuage his fears.

At 6 a.m. on 16 November – four days before the royal wedding was due to take place – eighty police officers, ten of them mounted, all of them authorised to use their truncheons, appeared at the Savoy to clear a path for three tankers from the Strand Power Company. Arthur Lewis was at home in bed. Fifty bleary-eyed strikers stood in the darkness to greet the delivery. 'Fuck the police!' shouted one. 'No oil is coming into the Savoy!' The first vehicle to break through the human barricade bore a suited passenger, the hotel's business manager. 'Some [strikers] jumped onto my tanker and tried to interfere with the driver and myself,' reported James Maxwell Hannay. 'They adopted a most menacing manner.' As the lorry chugged towards its objective, its headlamps failed. 'If you hadn't cleared that bloody mob,' said the driver, Sydney Robinson, 'I should have run over them.' Under police protection, all three tankers made their way to the fuel store and discharged their loads of sludge. From the other side of a ring of uniformed officers, the third driver barracked Lewis and his supporters. 'I'm paid a bloody good wage by my guv'nor and I'm bloody well going to deliver it,' declared Godfrey Wright. 'For your information I shall be back in two or three days with some more bloody oil.'

And he bloody was. In the week that Britain celebrated the wedding of its future Queen – an event described by Winston Churchill as a 'bright ray of colour on the hard grey road we have to travel' – the streets and courts around the Savoy became a theatre of noise, protest, violence and retribution. Alf Salisbury, a veteran of the International Brigades, threw himself in front of a tanker, declaring his willingness to die for the trade unionist cause. Jock Haston, the leader of the Revolutionary Communist Party, attacked an oil outlet pipe with a pair of bolt-cutters. Ernest Pole, a clerk from the accounts department, was beaten up on his way from the office by a drunken colleague. Mary Mackie, a casual worker in the housekeeping department, was left limping after an assault, and refused to name her attackers. Robert Cunningham, a bruiser with a taste for street fighting, tossed a camera flash-bulb under the hooves of a police horse and was spotted handing out fistfuls of galvanised one-inch nails and exhorting his comrades to scatter them in front of the tankers. ('He is a man who advocates violence', noted the plain-clothes policeman on his tail, 'and seizes every opportunity of causing trouble.') Leslie Bohringer, a junior waiter in the restaurant, gave the guests a fright by setting off a firework under the ballroom window. ('I don't care what you do,' he told the police officer who cuffed him. 'They are all a lot of rats in there.') Olive Ross, the wife of the national treasurer of the RCP, suffered a fatal seizure on the picket line. No inquest was ordered. Rumours swashed around the building: it was claimed that a constable from E Division had grabbed a striker by the throat and declared, 'I'd like to fuck you . . .' before breaking her arm with a blow of his truncheon. An eye-witness asserted that she had seen a police officer split the lip of a young lecturer from the LSE.[17] A picket called Alice Hadley appeared at the Charing Cross Hospital and reported that a uniformed officer had sent her reeling with a blow across the shoulders. The *Daily Mirror* ran a picture of her on the front page – not realising, it seems, that Alice Hadley was Frank Piazza's sister.

Anonymous communiqués arrived at Scotland Yard: 'Lay off our pickets, you rats, or bombs will be forthcoming,' warned the writer of one threatening postcard. 'Don't think we Communists will lie down to your Fascist ways.' A letter, signed 'Englishman' and purportedly the work of a Savoy employee, charged that 'Lewis and his gang of communist troublemakers' were 'simply out to create disorder and chaos so that they can seize power in this country'. The strike committee issued its own bulletin. 'The flowing tide is with us! Nothing can beat us! Provided our people remain sound and refuse to listen to Rumourmongers and alarmists, who more often than not are the mouthpieces of the Savoy directors . . . with every day our prospects of success become brighter. All together for the final effort which will spell the doom of those who are the enemies of Catering Workers and of all working people.' Doom, however, had other names to transcribe.

*

Interviewed late in his life, Hugh Wontner remembered the moment at the height of the strike when he went to the House of Commons to seek the advice of Winston Churchill, the refugee whom he had rehoused at Claridge's the day after Labour's landslide victory. The former Prime Minister listened to his story, picked up the phone and put a call through to the Home Secretary, Chuter Ede. Churchill advised Ede not to allow the Savoy to fall dark – people lived there, slept and ate there, and if the pumps failed, he warned, the Thames would reoccupy the hotel basement. In her memoirs, Jean Nicol wrote that during the strike, Churchill had told one of her colleagues, 'Watch the Savoy – a beacon is being lit which may shine all over England.' Perhaps it was as this meeting that those words were used. Certainly, when Wontner returned to his desk, he found a message from the Home Secretary reassuring him that the oil would be delivered.

Just before midnight on 17 November, the police strategy towards the strikers underwent a sudden revision. Instead of dragging the defiantly recumbent pickets from the path of the oil tankers and towards the kerb, they loaded them from the road into police vans, drove them off to Bow Street police station and charged them with obstruction of the highway. Twenty-five bodies were netted that freezing Monday night. Among them were Norman Phillips – the striking waiter who had his hours increased and his wages cut – and Ronald Kaufmann, the cook and committee member who had delivered the message demanding the reinstatement of Brother Piazza. Marion Lunt was in the van, too – and added another line to her charge sheet when she slammed her handbag across the face of her arresting officer. Christian Darnton, a blond, bellicose giant of a man known to concertgoers for his avant-garde compositions, was also driven to Bow Street, in the company of Eric Paice, a wireless student from the LSE, who, ten years later, would become script editor of the BBC police series *Dixon of Dock Green*. The biggest fish in the catch, however, was Arthur Lewis MP, whose arrest added a touch of farce to the event. 'As soon as Lewis was arrested,' said one eye-witness, 'he behaved like a complete hooligan. He commenced to struggle and cried out, "Press! Press!" and "I am an MP!" He then tripped up Chief Inspector Barnes, with whom he crashed to the pavement, exclaiming, "Press! Press! Oh, my head!"' The final flourish, however, came from the magistrate: for those arrested, keeping away from the picket line was made a condition of bail. The noisiest demonstrators had been silenced – just in time for the royal wedding.

The following night, a £500 cocktail party for British and American film stars was held in the Lancaster Room of the Savoy. To increase the depleted waiting staff, Greta Hofflin, the wife of the assistant manager, and Honor Bannerman, the hotel florist, shimmied around with trays of cocktails. Loretta Young, the star of *The Bishop's Wife*, appeared in an ankle-length New Look dress, and caused a frenzy. Bob Hope, who had checked in with his wife, his manager and three gag-writers, acted as host. Among this starry crowd, in his best suit, was Robert Cunningham, the picket with the pockets full of one-inch nails. As Hope stood on the platform to introduce the band, Cunningham rushed to join him, pulled the microphone from his hand and told Patricia Roc, Phyllis Calvert, Margaret Lockwood, Googie Withers and their colleagues that they ought to have stayed at home – before a pair of liveried doormen bundled him from the room. '*I* didn't cross the picket line,' protested Bob Hope. 'I flew in by helicopter.' Everybody laughed. The next day, Leslie Sayer, the Savoy's chief engineer, installed a large television set in the River Room, before which were arranged ranks of gilt chairs. In the afternoon, the hotel's guests and residents sat drinking champagne, eating nuts and watching Princess Elizabeth and Prince Philip promise to love, honour and obey.

There were more arrests, more allegations of police brutality, more accusations of dirty tricks – but by the day of the royal wedding, the strike was all but defeated. John Platts-Mills, defending the pickets in court, used the occasion to accuse the police of accepting bribes from the Savoy management, but the story was not taken seriously. The Revolutionary Communist Party also lost interest in the battle on the Strand, preferring to focus its energies on the battle against itself. One faction favoured dissolving the organisation and fighting their campaigns from within the Labour Party. The other argued for the maintenance of an official, open presence in British politics. The debate had been rumbling on for years, but in October 1947, the Party began the formal process of disarticulation. It had also suddenly acquired a reason not to antagonise the management of the Savoy: a writ relating to an article in the October 1947 edition of *Socialist Appeal*, in which Marion Lunt had attacked her employers in language that her editor, Ted Grant, had come to regret. Too impecunious to fight the case, Grant conceded defeat and settled out of court, paying the Savoy £100 in damages and costs. A small amount, but quite enough to deprive *Socialist Appeal* of its future. A plea for donations was printed on the back page of the May 1948 edition, placed by the treasurer, Arthur Ross, whose wife had died on the picket line. 'Mark the envelope "Savoy Case",' he implored.

The national leaders of the GMWU brought the hotel strikes to an end by going over the head of Arthur Lewis and negotiating their own settlement with the Savoy. They set about finding employment for Frank Piazza somewhere far from the Grill Room. After turning down offers of a job in a jam factory and an Italian restaurant in Soho, he accepted a position in the buffet car on the line between Euston and Liverpool. That done, the union then came for Arthur Lewis, expressing dismay and embarrassment at the tactics that he had employed against the hotel. They examined the literature that he had been circulating at the picket line, found it in breach of their regulations and removed him from his job. Lewis spent the rest of his long Parliamentary career asking awkward questions in the Commons, particularly when Winston Churchill was standing at the despatch box. When, in July 1954, the restored Conservative Prime Minister announced his decision to dissolve the wartime Ministry of Materials, Lewis raised so many objections that *Punch* suggested 'it seemed as if he might end by adopting his old Savoy Hotel tactic and lying down on the floor of the House to obstruct its progress'.[18] In 1981, Lewis denounced his own constituency party as '100 per cent Trotskyist, Militant Tendency, Communist and IRA supporters', and was promptly deselected.[19] He may only have been out by a few percentage points.

The Savoy strike ended officially on the second day of December 1947. Jean Nicol and Hugh Wontner celebrated with champagne. On the third day, Christmas came early to the Savoy – or at least, to those employees who had not participated in the dispute. All those waiters, waitresses, chambermaids, chefs, receptionists, engineers and carpenters who had remained at their posts found themselves in receipt of a gift of £10 worth of shares in the Savoy group. Mr Boot in stocktaking, Mr Spilling in supplies, Mr Beale in the bill office, Hansen the head porter, James Townsend, the chief cloakroom attendant, 'Darkie', foreman of the plate room, and a young man from Belfast who had become a fixture behind the American Bar. 'It was a generous gift,' said Joe Gilmore. 'They were "B" shares, the kind that came with voting rights. But we were just glad to get back to work. To get back to normal.'

This was the kind of attitude that Jean Nicol considered to be the essence of the hotel. 'It was always present, this candle-flame of devotion, but it took the inflammability of a crisis for it to break forth into the great glowing beacon that shone now through the Savoy,' she wrote. 'And so the strike ended in an atmosphere of sentimental loyalty and affection. Everyone loved everybody and worked harder than ever . . .' Except, of course, the six hundred employees who had gone on strike, many of whom, dispirited, drifted on to other jobs.

A few months after these events, Joseph Vecchi, the manager of the Hungaria restaurant, published a memoir entitled *The Tavern Is My Drum* (1948). 'We hear a lot about the "rights" of catering staff,' he wrote. 'They have a right to be popular with the public; as they invariably are if they do their job well . . . Some are born to serve, and others to be served. There are two sides of the counter, and while some wait others bestow largesse. The world has always been like that and always will.' Vecchi was one of those who believed that London's grand hotels could insulate their paying guests from the social changes taking place beyond the revolving doors, just as their thick walls had protected their clients from the wartime bombs. Perhaps, in 1948, he was right.

Conclusion

Ghosts

There was the echo of war in the moment chosen for the re-opening of the Savoy. Ten minutes past ten, on the tenth day of the tenth month of the tenth year of the century. A moment fit for an Armistice or a two-minute silence.

It had been a long time coming. The Savoy's refurbishment was eighteen months late and £120 million over budget. Nobody cared, however – not the journalists who swooned over the Midas-touched surfaces of the new Beaufort bar, not the first guest, the actor Stephen Fry, who twittered his approval online, not even Prince al-Waleed bin Talal, the man who paid for the work in the middle of a global financial crisis. The project was, he said, 'a gift to the British monarchy and the British people' – though as it allowed him to increase the average price of a room by a third, he could hardly have been said to have neglected his own interests. Three weeks later, a real live British royal appeared on the hotel doorstep to inspect this offering. Prince Charles nodded to the doorman, made approving noises about craftsmanship and Spanish mahogany, and reminisced about the cherry-brandy cocktail that Joe Gilmore had created for his investiture, four decades ago. His Saudi host expressed the wish that the work of two dark years would secure the hotel an illuminated future for the next fifty. What nobody asked was how such a place had survived for so long.

Grand hotels rarely make grand profits. Historically, they have done the opposite and often require the financial support of rich individuals or consortia that are content to own them as expensive trophies. In the post-war period, the shared story of such establishments was one of apparently terminal decline. 'After the war financially things were bad at the Ritz,' Victor Legg told me. 'They couldn't do refurbishing. And we were plagued with rats. If I was on night duty I could hear them squeaking away.' He remembered receiving a call from the Greek shipping magnate Basil Goulandris who complained that there were 'six mice doing ballet in front of the fireplace of Suite 318'. (At the Savoy, stray cats were more of a problem.)

Victor also recalled the hotel's faintly suicidal policy towards prospective guests. 'I have been in this hotel in the middle of winter,' he said, jabbing the air for emphasis, 'and the place has been starving, half-empty, and a very flamboyant man has walked in, obviously *nouveau riche*. He's gone to the reception and they've given him one look and said, "I'm very sorry, we're full up." They refused the man because he didn't have a title. They'd rather have a man with a title who couldn't pay the bill.' To counterpoint the story, he told me of another guest who signed in with a plausibly aristocratic name and then vanished after several weeks without settling his account. 'After a couple of days we went up to the suite and there was a Louis Vuitton suitcase on the floor. And we tried to lift it but we couldn't. When we forced it open we found it had been screwed to the floor.' The Dorchester also operated a similar policy, preferring to accommodate aristocrats at discount rates than give rooms to less elevated figures with full wallets. And yet, the big four institutions described in this book – the Dorchester, the Ritz, the Savoy and Claridge's – are still here. Oddly, it is the less grand establishments that have been erased.

*

As the carpenters and glaziers and wranglers of gold leaf refreshed and remodelled the spaces of the Savoy, the wrecking balls slammed against the hotel that was designed to supplant it: the Regent Palace, a ten-storey triangular prism of steel girders and terracotta tiles that, when it was raised in the second year of the Great War, instantly became the largest hotel in Europe. Its owners, J. S. Lyons and Co., were the people whose Corner Houses had brought lunch and dinner and afternoon tea into the era of mass production. They had democratised the restaurant meal with a relaxed dress code, the abolition of service charges and the aggressive exploitation of the economy of scale. At the Piccadilly branch, two thousand customers could be served at one sitting – and none were obliged to wear a tie or leave an extra shilling with the bill. Prices and products were standardised throughout the country: a French cream sandwich or a gammon steak cost the same on the Strand as it did on Sauchiehall Street. The Regent Palace was built upon the same principles: it had no en suite bathrooms, but ran hot and cold running water into all of its 1,280 electrically heated rooms. Its telegraphic address, UNTIPPABLE PICCY, signalled that neither guests nor employees would feel tyrannised by the *tronc* system. The purpose of the place, avowed Lyons, was 'to make the luxuries usually available to the very rich open to the less well-off'.[1] The company had created an economy-class version of the grand hotel. A wipe-clean Ritz. A bargain-bucket Savoy.

The Second World War changed its reputation for the worse. Around the boxed statue of Eros, the battalion of prostitutes known as Piccadilly Commandos made their patrols, advertising themselves by playing the beam of a pencil torch over their stockinged legs. Wally Hoffman, a B-17 bomber pilot, remembered 'a girl in a parted overcoat revealing a very short skirt and a pair of nice legs in high heels', who cooed 'Owbout it, love? Around the corner for a pound?' Hoffman claimed that he and his friends 'weren't that desperate', but many were. The newspaper vendors provided the prophylactics; the Regent Palace provided the bed. The poet Emanuel Litvinoff had endured 'a tremendously terrible honeymoon' on the premises, thanks to two GIs, a pair of Commandos and one thin wall. ('You could hear every wretched word,' he recalled.) The hotel's receptionists, it was said, were happy to procure prostitutes for guests who rang down and requested an extra pillow. (When the revue writer David Climbe took his wife to the hotel, just after the war, a colleague suggested that he might be charged for 'corkage'.[2])

The hotel also suffered a more literal form of damage. At lunchtime on the last day of June 1944, a V-1 rocket-bomb sliced through the staff annex of the Regent Palace, killing a chambermaid as she dozed in her bed between shifts. Joanne Shipway, a young nurse who was walking through Piccadilly, saw the body blown through a top-floor window and down to the pavement below. 'I ran to help the casualties as did a doctor who, luckily, had his bag with him,' she recalled. 'We did what we could for the chambermaid but the doctor was fairly sure she had broken her back. In the absence of splints, we were trained to use rolled up newspapers.' She dashed into the hotel, collected an armful of abandoned copies of the *Evening Standard*, and ran back to her patient. As she lost the battle to save the woman's life, she was suddenly struck by an odd anomaly of the bombing. 'A pub had its windows blown out,' she remembered, 'but all the drinking glasses and optics behind the bar were still intact.'[3] The impact was also felt two streets away at the notorious Windmill Theatre, where the principal attraction was the series of nude *tableaux vivants* formed by its resident chorus of dancers and models. The Lord Chamberlain permitted the exhibition on condition that this display of nudity remained static – something that proved impossible when the blast disgorged a dead rat from the rafters and onto the stage.

The day before the doors were locked and the men with hard hats and sledgehammers arrived, I took a valedictory walk around the carcass of the Regent Palace. It was like exploring the corridors of an abandoned ocean liner. For years, few significant repairs had been carried out. Broken doors were patched with board. Wires spilled from electrical fittings. Carpets suffered from bald patches and dirty grey gum-spots. But the dead still seemed populous. Here was the reception area, through which the young Quentin Crisp had once trolled in a black silk dress – his only outing in drag. It was here, also, in 1925, that Captain Leslie Bligh Barker, a Regent Palace concierge and a member of the National Fascisti, was arrested on bankruptcy charges and, after a medical examination in Brixton Prison, discovered to be Valerie Arkell-Smith, a mother of two and the estranged wife of a lieutenant in the 20th Australian battalion. (The contents of Captain Barker's staff locker contained some dress clothes, an eyebrow pencil, a powder puff, safety pins, two pieces of ribbon and a razor.[4])

I took the lift up to the second floor. Here was Room 201, from which a mechanic named Herbert Turner and his married lover Mabel Hill went on a spree in October 1932, splashing out on theatre tickets and expensive dinners and spending cash like there was no tomorrow – which, for Mabel at least, there wasn't. ('I cannot think of any other way out for a bad girl,' she wrote, before climbing into bed and toasting her lover with prussic acid.) Here was Room 293, where a chambermaid called Lily Sargent was pinned to the bed by Mervyn Brown, a trilby-wearing rapist from Toronto. ('You'll be alright, kiddy,' he assured her, 'I am a Canadian.') Here was Room 266, where, during the Great War, Dr John Henderson Bell had jiggered a syringe into the knees of his clients, servicemen hungry for the painful arthritic inflammation of synovitis – a complication of both dysentery and chlamydia, and therefore a plausible battlefield complaint. ('After I have finished with you,' Dr Henderson reassured Sergeant-Major Howard Hawkins, 'you will do no more military service.') The walls that might have told their stories have now been atomised – and with their demise, it is now no longer possible to find a hotel room in central London for less than £50 a night. Wealthier travellers can, of course, still check into the Dorchester, the Ritz, the Savoy or Claridge's.[5]

*

It is the job of a grand hotel to protect its patrons from the world beyond its doors, from the discontent of its employees and from the unhappiness of fellow guests. It is a city within the city; a gated community that offers food, softness, music and pleasure behind an entrance guarded by uniformed officers. These buildings do not gaze out upon the street. The Ritz has eyes only for Green Park. The Savoy turns its back on the Strand and looks longingly out over the Thames. On the ground-floor coffee lounge of the Dorchester, the light is as indeterminate as in a Las Vegas casino. But the grand hotel also bears a more occult responsibility: to ensure that the occupants of its rooms remain untroubled by the ghosts of their predecessors. True, a few of the most dazzling are permitted to materialise: Winston Churchill at the Savoy, General Eisenhower at the Dorchester, Crown Prince Alexander at Claridge's. Other manifestations, however, are not encouraged. And yet almost every night of the week, someone snores easily in the bedroom at the Mount Royal where Mary Pickwoad and her baby died by slow degrees. Someone loses consciousness in the suite at the Ritz where Baron Pierre de Laitre and his secretary hanged themselves from the light fittings. Someone sleeps calmly in the bedroom at the Charing Cross Hotel where Barbara Devonshire took a seven-barrelled revolver purchased from Banghams of the Strand and shot her sleeping ten-year-old daughter, before putting the gun to her own temple.[6]

Stories of actual haunting are rare, but not unknown. Lucy, Lady Phillimore, a Society hostess installed at the Ritz at the state's expense to hold informal dinner parties for the lost souls of governments-in-exile, found the atmosphere of her top-floor suite miserable and oppressive. A waiter, taking pity on her, informed her that the son of an admiral had recently tipped himself from the window-ledge. As a leading spirit of the Society for Psychical Research, Lucy Phillimore knew exactly what to do: she had the room exorcised by a gang of priests from the

Brompton Oratory, then moved into another suite, just to make sure.[7]

Atrocities are inevitable in any building that is such a generous provider of warm baths, comfortable beds and lockable doors. As long as a hotel remains a hotel, it will never be free to memorialise such events; never be compelled to narrate the stories from its history of strife or violence. How many people, taking coffee on the chequered floor of Claridge's, want to be reminded of the day in the summer of 1940, when its Italian waiters were removed to guano-encrusted cells in a Liverpool jail? How many diners, cracking the fabulous sugar-basket that encases their Peach Melba, want to be reminded of the long cold nights of November 1947, when the Savoy was besieged by demonstrators who shouted words such as 'Rats' and 'Parasites' up at the windows? To do so would be to destroy the dream that is theirs for the price of admission; and without that dream, few would be willing to pay.

When Britain feels divided and unequal, London's grand hotels can still provide a concrete symbol of the social and economic differences between us. On 26 March 2011, student protestors bombarded the former workplace of Victor Legg with paint and smoke bombs, and hefted an uprooted road sign through one of the plate-glass windows. The following day, the front page of the *Mail on Sunday* captured the attack in a word: 'Ritzkrieg'. The event seems unlikely to be mentioned in any of the hotel's publicity material. The Dorchester, the Ritz, the Savoy and Claridge's must remain like amnesiac patients: able to conjure the pleasant generality of a great and glittering past, but with recall of only a handful of celebrated names. Let this book be the memorial to all those unacknowledged employees and guests, during the years when these buildings seemed more important, closer to the centre of things, than they are today. The men and women of the original Ritzkrieg. Gilbert Bradley, who committed acts of gross indecency in Claridge's and was rewarded with a Christmas card from the management.

Edomie Johnson, the most celebrated shoplifter of 1940s London, shameless at the bar of the Ritz. Phil Piratin, who brought the reproach of the bombed East End to the heart of the West End. Neil Barkla, watching the slow death of his wife's best friend, and telling her all would be well, when it was not. They are the ghosts that pass us on the stairs and in the bedrooms and in the hallways; the revenants of a war on the edge of living memory.

Notes

1 A vicious circle: as a result, the youngest, newest and poorest members of staff were the ones charged to deliver his soup to the table. Churchill was so embarrassingly rude that his cousin, Clementine Mitford, once forced him to apologise to a waiter in the Savoy Grill at whom Randolph had sworn. See Anita Leslie, *Cousin Randolph* (London, 1985), p. 44.

2 Savoy brochure. Quoted in Stanley Jackson, *The Savoy: The Romance of a Great Hotel* (London, 1964), p. 21.

3 Although the claim is often made, and a blue plaque has been affixed to the building erected on the site, there is no documentary evidence to support the story. See Sophie Quinn-Judge, *Ho Chi Minh: The Missing Years 1919–1941* (Berkeley, CA, 2002), p. 24. This doubtless nails Mae West's assertion that she seduced Ho Chi Minh in a corridor of the Carlton – for which, see Gavin Young, *A Wavering Grace: A Vietnamese Family in War and Peace* (London, 1997), p. 44.

4 A common occurrence, according to one such young man, George Hayim.

5 See *Hansard* (16 November 1937), vol. 329, cc. 243–307.

6 'Safe return to dear old London', *Daily Express* (1 September 1939), p. 5.

7 See 'News in Brief', *The Times* (7 November 1939), p. 5.

8 'Foreign News: Up Labor!', *Time* (21 October 1940).

9 See Jackson, *Savoy*, p. 174.

10 Letter, *The Times* (14 September 1939), p. 6.

11 See 'Commandeering of Hotels, "Ruthless" Methods Alleged', *The Times* (22 September 1939), p. 5.

12 See 'Requisitioned Hotels', *The Times* (26 September 1939), p. 5.

13 See 'Commandeered Hotels', *The Times* (23 September 1939), p. 4.

14 William Hickey, 'Chit-Chat', *Daily Express* (14 September 1939), p. 8.

15 'Night-Life Cure for Black Out Blues', *Daily Mirror* (14 September 1939), p. 5.

16 'Secret Rooms', *Tatler and Bystander* (18 December 1940), p. 471.

17 William Hickey, 'Gas for the Blimps?', *Daily Express* (19 October 1939), p. 4.

18 Robert Rhodes James (ed.), *Chips: The Diaries of Sir Henry Channon* (London, 1967), p. 221.

19 The Ritz claims to be the first building in Britain to be constructed with these techniques. (Its owners have, historically, preferred to ignore the fact that the Grand Hotel in Folkestone had beaten them to it.)

20 See 'The Ritz Hotel', *Builder's Journal* (22 March 1905), pp. 148–56.

21 Jean Nicol, *Meet Me at the Savoy* (London, 1952), p. 69.

22 See 'The West End Front', *Tatler*, (3 January 1940), p. 27.

23 Michael Barsley, *Ritzkrieg* (London, 1940), pp. 8, 12, 37.

24 Observe, for instance, the correct way for a minion to approach Ming the Merciless in *Flash Gordon Conquers the Universe* (1940).

25 When the photojournalist Ruth Mitchell rolled up in Tirana for Zog's wedding, her thoughts were drawn irresistibly to the camp excesses of the West End stage: 'Whenever a writer of musical comedy wants to prepare his audience for something utterly improbable and absurd,' she noted, 'he sets his scene in "a kingdom in the Balkans". But no extravaganza could surpass the improbability, the absurdity of this real wedding. It exhibited every stock character, every stock comic situation, besides special phantasia of

its own.' See Ruth Mitchell, *The Serbs Choose War* (New York, 1943), p. 12.

26 See National Archives file FO 371/37139.

27 *Ritzkrieg*, p. 59.

Chapter One: Aliens

1 See HO 45/23695.

2 Arnold Bennett, *Imperial Palace* (London, 1930), p. 82.

3 See, among many, 'Today's Gossip', *Daily Mirror* (5 January 1928), p. 7.

4 Seymour Hicks, *Between Ourselves* (London, 1930), p. 198.

5 'Tales They Tell of Santarelli', *Daily Mail* (12 October 1944), p. 3.

6 See HO 45/23695.

7 See HO 45/25561.

8 John Boswell, *Daily Mirror* (27 April 1940).

9 See Midge Gillies, *Waiting for Hitler* (London, 2006), p. 141.

10 See 'Questions to Ministers', *Manchester Guardian* (31 May 1940), p. 11.

11 Nicol, *Savoy*, p. 32.

12 Nigel West (ed.), *The Guy Liddell Diaries*, vol. 1 (Abingdon, 2005), p. 71.

13 See Lucio Sponza, 'The British Government and the Internment of Italians' in *Immigrants and Minorities* 11 (1992), pp. 125–144.

14 Harold J. Laski, 'Government in Wartime', in *Where Stands Democracy?* (London, 1940), p. 35.

15 Interview with Ettore Emanuelli, 6 February 2008.

16 HO 45/23691. See also 'The Sabini Gang', *The Times* (24 August 1922), p. 5.

17 HO 45/24729.

18 Letter from Ezra Pound to Leigh Vaughan-Henry (12 August 1934), Ezra Pound Collection, University of Victoria, British Columbia, EPC 3/47.

19 See Arnold Leese, 'Toreador in Teesdale', *Country Life* (15 June 1945).

20 See 'British Union Organisation at Ascot Camp, October 1940', pp. 32–3, Frederick Wiseman Papers IWM 86/1/1.

21 See Graham D. Macklin, '"Hail Mosley and F—— 'Em All": Martyrdom, Transcendence and the "Myth" of Internment', *Totalitarian Movements and Political Religions* 7 (2006), pp. 1–24.

22 For the case against Braybrook, see MEPO 3/2385. Also 'Alleged Thefts from Aliens', *The Times* (18 April 1941), p. 2.

23 HO 45/23695 Sir Guy Hambling to the secretary of the Home Office Advisory Committee (5 September 1940). Other testimonials were received from Sir Gordon Campbell; E. B. McInenry, manager of the Royal Bank of Canada; J. Hirst of the General Electric Company; W. Balfour, MP for Hampstead; Sir William Fraser, director of the Anglo-Iranian Oil Company.

24 Letter from Harry Beckett Overy to Winston Churchill (16 November 1937), Churchill College archive, CHAR 28/146B/22.

25 H. Montgomery Hyde, *Norman Birkett: The Life of Lord Birkett of Ulverston* (London, 1964), p. 134.

26 Letter from Norman Birkett to E. B. Stamp (23 November 1941), HO 283/25.

27 Letter from MacLeod to Norman Birkett (5 February 1940), HO 283/25.

28 For a portrait of Hickson see J. Wentworth Day, *Lady Houston: The Richest Woman in the World* (London, 1958), p. 227.

29 Hyde, *Birkett*, p. 470.

30 Albert Pam, *Recollections and Adventures* (Oxford, 1945), p. 149.

31 Interview with Hugh Wontner in the National Sound Archive.

32 James M. Langley, *Fight Another Day* (London, 1974), p. 126.

Chapter Two: Reds

1 Drew Middleton, *The Sky Suspended* (London, 1960), p. 167.

2 See Ernie Pyle, *Ernie Pyle in England* (New York, 1941), p. 30.

3 Constantine FitzGibbon, *The Blitz* (London, 1957), p. 109.

4 Basil Woon, *Hell Came to London* (London, 1941), pp. 156–9.

5 FitzGibbon, *Blitz*, p. 120.

6 Ibid., p. 110.

7 Middleton, *Sky Suspended*, p. 181.

8 See advertisement, Royal Asylum of St Anne's Society, *The Times* (13 June 1903), p. 10; Basil Woon, *Eyes West* (London, 1940), p. 35.

9 Constantine FitzGibbon, *Random Thoughts of a Fascist Hyena* (London, 1963), p. 28.

10 C. Kent Wright, *ARP and All That* (London, 1940), p. 38.

11 Woon, *Hell Came*, p. 157.

12 Randall Swingler, 'Sheltering in London Tubes', *Daily Worker* (14 September 1940), p. 4.

13 'He Offers To Be Bombed', *Daily Mirror* (25 July 1939), p. 14.

14 Haldane employed a number of Communist Party members to serve alongside him as guinea pigs in the *Thetis* experiments. Among them was Donald Renton. Among the men who died on board the *Thetis* was Richmond Temple's son-in-law.

15 Wright, *ARP*, p. 234.

16 Ibid., p. 221.

17 Wal Hannington, *Ten Lean Years* (London, 1940), p. 241.

18 'Dole Men Demand Tea at the Ritz', *Daily Mirror* (23 December 1938), p. 1.

19 'Onlookers Applaud Unemployed', *Daily Mirror* (18 January 1939), p. 19.

20 Phil Piratin, *Our Flag Stays Red* (London, 1948), p. 73.

21 Jack Dash, *Good Morning, Brothers!* (London, 1969), p. 42.

22 Piratin, *Our Flag*, p. 74.

23 Interview with Alf Minto, 29 April 2006; correspondence with Alice Hitchin; for Shapiro on Piratin, see Neil Redfern, 'Michael Shapiro in China', *Communist History Network Newsletter* (Autumn 2001); Special Branch quote from National Archive file KV 2/2033.

24 Woon, *Hell Came*, p. 25.

25 Ibid., p. 159.

26 Hugh Montgomery-Massingberd, *The London Ritz: A Social and Architectural History* (London, 1981), p. 92.

27 See FitzGibbon, *Blitz*, p. 109; Bernard Gray, 'Rich Hotels Turn People Away During Air Raids', *Sunday Pictorial* (22 September 1940), p. 4; James Reston, 'London Homeless Camp in Subway', *New York Times* (16 September 1940), p. 3; George Orwell, *A Patriot After All* (London, 1998), p. 263.

28 See 'Churchills Verbrechen an Londons Müttern', *Völkischer Beobachter* (18 September 1940), p. 1; Tony McEnery, *Swearing in English* (2006), p. 119; West (ed.), *Guy Liddell Diaries*, vol. 1, p. 129.

29 The initiative was Anderson's, but Morrison made sure it was carried out.

30 The allegations are listed in MEPO 3/2357 – though the only offence for which Davis was ever committed was for riding on the tube without a ticket.

31 See N. A. Rose (ed.), *Baffy: The Diaries of Blanche Dugdale* (London, 1973), p. 175.

32 'Nation Awaits Wendell's Report', *Life* (17 February 1941), p. 21.

33 *The Times*, 30 January 1941; Jackson, *Savoy*, p. 187.

34 Rene MacColl, 'The Day MacColl Insulted Winnington', *Daily Express* (9 March 1955), p. 4.

35 Surprisingly, this did not shake his belief in Maoism, nor that of his family. In February 2010, I wrote to Michael's brother, Jack, to request an interview. He died with the letter unopened on his kitchen table. At his funeral, tributes were offered by representatives of the governments of China and North Korea, and by the Communist Party of Great Britain (Marxist-Leninist), a minuscule group of diehards of which he was honorary president. At the time of writing, it is still possible to view Jack Shapiro on YouTube, denouncing Khrushchev's revisionism.

36 See 'Chinese Journalists Win Shapiro Prize', *China People's Daily* (14 June 2000), p. 2.

Chapter Three: Players

1 See Mark Mazower (ed.), *The Policing of Politics in the Twentieth Century: Historical Perspectives* (Oxford, 1997), p. 241.

2 See HO 45/23800.

3 Sir Francis Towle, 'A Brief History of a New Enterprise', in Michael Arlen, *A Young Man Comes to London* (London, 1932), p. 27.

4 Quoted in Philip M. Taylor, *British Propaganda in the Twentieth Century: Selling Democracy* (Edinburgh, 1999), p. 74.

5 According to a report filed to the KGB by Anthony Blunt, Pollock's principal targets were figures called Brooks and Hiddedus, and Bertil von Wachenfeldt, a Swedish journalist and former Oylmpic athlete. Hungarians were a Dorchester speciality. André Deutsch, the future head of a distinguished publishing house, did a stint on the reception desk before he was packed off to an internment camp on the Isle of Man. Baron Anton Dirsztay, a twenty-two-year-old listed in the small print of the *Deutsches Adelslexikon*, toiled, incongruously, in the Dorchester's kitchen storeroom, where he learned pages of *Debrett* by heart in the hope of acquiring sufficient familiarity with his British equivalents to be promoted to the reception desk. The war photographer Robert Capa was asked to leave the hotel when the management became disturbed by the quantities of women seen entering and leaving his room at all hours of the night. (He took his bags to the less fastidious environment of the Savoy.)

6 See KV 2/2839.

7 Jebb's theory is quoted by Hugh Dalton. See Ben Pimlott (ed.), *The Second World War Diary of Hugh Dalton 1940–45* (London, 1986), p. 75.

8 See Cecil Beaton, *The Years Between: Diaries 1939–44* (London, 1965), p. 53.

9 See Bridget Chetwynd, 'The Social Roundabout', *Tatler and Bystander* (27 November 1940), p. 360; Charles Ritchie, *The Siren Years* (London, 1974), p. 78.

10 Sir Malcolm McAlpine, 'Some Facts and Figures about the Dorchester', in Arlen, *Young Man*, p. 42.

11 D. F. Karaka, *Then Came Hazrat Ali* (Bombay, 1972), p. 194.

12 Cecil King, *With Malice Toward None* (London, 1970), p. 75.

13 See Ritchie, *Siren Years*, pp. 73, 78.

14 See Beaton, *Years Between*, p. 49.

15 Robert Rhodes James, *Victor Cazalet: A Portrait* (London, 1976), p. 241.

16 Andrew Roberts, *The Holy Fox* (London, 1991), p. 247.

17 *Hansard* Debates (6 March 1940), vol. 358, cc. 452–3.

18 Juliet Gardiner, *The Blitz* (London, 2010), pp. 368–9; quoted in Gardiner, *Blitz*, p. 369; quoted in Simon Garfield, *Our Hidden Lives* (London, 2004), p. 430.

19 See King, *Malice*, p. 75; Beaton, *Years Between*, p. 53; Ritchie, *Siren Years*, pp. 68, 48.

20 See *Daily Mirror* (29 October 1940), p. 3.

21 Kenneth Schuyler Lynn, *Hemingway* (Cambridge, MA, 1995), p. 510; Tom Buchanan, *Britain and the Spanish Civil War* (Cambridge, 1997), p. 6.

22 See Stephen Spender, 'Waiting for the Bombers', *Guardian* (11 February 1989).

23 Igor Lukes & Erik Goldstein (eds), *The Munich Crisis, 1938: Prelude to World War II* (London, 1999), p. 259.

24 Frederic Morton, *The Rothschilds: Portrait of a Dynasty* (New York, 1998), p. 9.

25 See A. G. MacDonnell, 'The Passing Hour', *Bystander* (29 May 1940), p. 250.

26 West (ed.), *Guy Liddell Diaries*, vol. 1, p. 188.

27 The Plugges were the parents of twins, both of whom died in tragic circumstances. Their son Creville was killed in a road accident in 1973. Their daughter, Gale Ann, came under the influence of the Black Power activist Hakim Jamal and followed him to a commune in Trinidad, where, on the order of the commune's leader, Michael X, she was buried alive. Leonard Plugge owned the house occupied by Mick Jagger's character in *Performance*.

28 As revealed by documents in the KGB archives. See Nigel West &
    Oleg Tsarev, *Crown Jewels: The British Secrets at the Heart of the
    KGB Archives* (London, 1998), p. 152.

29 *Bystander* (21 February 1940), p. 224.

30 See KV 2/1696.

31 'People in War News', *Time* (11 September 1939).

32 Sylvia Schweppe, *The Story of the Officers' Sunday Club* (Lon-
    don, 1945), p. 15.

33 John Wells, 'A Long Course to Remember' in *Naval Review*
    (October 1990), p. 376.

34 See 'Dorchester Party: The Sunday Club for Officers', *Tatler* (24
    April 1940), p. 131.

35 See KV 2/2388.

36 Diary held at the University of Victoria, Canada. This page online
    at http://graves.uvic.ca/graves/site/xscan.xq?id=gro1_1008_000.

37 See Basil Kentish, *This Foul Thing Called War* (Lewes, 1997), p.
    106.

38 Kentish, *Foul Thing*, p. 109.

39 John Paddy Carstairs, *Vinegar and Brown Paper* (London, 1939),
    pp. 8–9.

40 See D. N. Pritt, *Forward to a People's Government* (London,
    1941), p. 3.

41 See George Orwell, *The Collected Essays, Journalism and Letters
    of George Orwell: As I Please* (London, 1968), p. 113.

42 Pritt, *People's Government*, p. 5.

43 'BBC May Ban Show People', *Daily Express* (22 January 1941),
    p. 5.

44 Quoted in Robert Mackay, '"An Abominable Precedent": The
    BBC's Ban on Pacifists in the Second World War' in *Contemporary
    British History* (December 2006), p. 498.

45 *Sunday Express* (16 March 1941).

46 E. M. Forster, *Civil Liberty* (8 December 1940).

47 Cassandra, *Daily Mirror* (17 March 1941), p. 4.

48 Cassandra, *Daily Mirror* (6 March 1941), p. 2.

49 Quoted in Mazower (ed.), *Policing of Politics*, p. 233.

50 Bob Graham, 'World War Two's First Victim', *Daily Telegraph* (29 August 2009).

Chapter Four: Brigades

1 Interview with Jean Kent, 7 August 2009.

2 See 'Hotel Chef's Purchase of Horse Flesh', *The Times* (28 April 1942), p. 2.

3 Nicol, *Savoy*, p. 70.

4 Clement Freud, *Freud Ego* (London, 2001), p. 35.

5 Interview with Leslie Amos, 27 February 2007.

6 See Brian Connell, *Knight Errant: A Biography of Douglas Fairbanks, Jr* (London, 1955), pp. 178–9.

7 See Bee Wilson, *Swindled* (London, 2008), p. 215. For a comprehensive account of the role of food in the Second World War, see Lizzie Collingham, *The Taste of War: World War Two and the Battle for Food* (London, 2011).

8 *Herald*, November 1917. See John Burnett, *England Eats Out* (Harlow, 2004), p. 179.

9 Earl of Woolton, *The Memoirs of the Rt Hon. the Earl of Woolton* (London, 1959), p. 191.

10 Duff Hart-Davis (ed.), *King's Counsellor: Abdication and War: The Diaries of Sir Alan Lascelles* (London, 2006), p. 68.

11 John J. Abt, *Advocate and Activist* (Illinois, 1993), p. 110.

12 'Slanguage', *Daily Express* (13 September 1939), p. 7.

13 See *Hansard* (10 November 1942).

14 Freud, *Ego*, p. 45.

15 'And a pound of macon, please', *Daily Express* (7 December 1939), p. 4.

16 Ben Pimlott (ed.), *The Political Diary of Hugh Dalton 1918–40, 1945–60* (London, 1986), p. 316.

17 'West End Chefs try their art on Macon', *Daily Express* (21 November 1939), p. 7.

18 'KC turns judge to try rashers of macon', *Daily Express* (14 December 1939), p. 3.

19 'Great Britain: Fight to the Finish?', *Time* (25 December 1939).

20 'Macon, Salty, Wins Longer Drink Hours', *Daily Express* (30 November 1939), p. 7.

21 'A Macon and Mam Menu', *The Times* (7 December 1939), p. 10.

22 'Government "Macon" to Cease', *The Times* (26 February 1940), p. 4.

23 'Macon MP Is Dead', *Evening Standard* (1 March 1940), p. 1.

24 'An Ounce of Practice', *The Times* (23 September 1944), p. 5.

25 Grace Wyndham Goldie, 'Roar without Lion', *Listener* (27 March 1941), p. 464.

26 Cassandra, *Daily Mirror* (17 October 1941), p. 2.

27 Freud, *Ego*, p. 35.

28 'News in Brief', *The Times* (17 August 1966), p. 1.

29 Jackson, *Savoy*, p. 176.

Chapter Five: Cons

1 See *The Times* (31 January 1866), p. 7; (2 February 1866), p. 5; (5 February 1866), p. 12; (14 February 1866), p. 7.

2 Information from her nephew, the late Geoffrey Gwilliam.

3 Ian Bisset, *The George Cross* (London, 1961), pp. 147–8.

4 See 'Middlesex Sessions', *The Times* (18 July 1871), p. 11; 'Police', *The Times* (16 February 1903), p. 3.

5 See 'A Very Extraordinary Story', *The Times* (10 February 1872), p. 5.

6 See 'The End of a Long Adventure', *The Times* (2 May 1914), p. 7.

7 See *Daily Mirror* (3 May 1938), p. 25.

8 See 'Conditions of Baltic States', *The Times* (23 April 1926), p. 5.

9 See '36 in Three Groups Indicted on Charges of Liquor Violation', *Washington Post* (1 April 1924).

10 See 'Baronet Sued for Fares by Railway Company', 'Law of Platform Tickets', *The Times* (30 July 1930), p. 9; 'Charge Against Sir Curtis Lampson', *The Times* (6 May 1936), p. 4; 'Warrant

Against Sir Curtis Lampson', *The Times* (17 April 1936), p. 7; 'After a Party', *Daily Express* (17 September 1936), p. 5.

11 Sir Curtis Lampson, *A Pot-Pourri of Thoughts and Deed*, unpublished memoir. His use of the term 'Nippie' is anachronistic in this context. In 1906 or thereabouts, the nickname for a woman who worked in a Lyons Corner House was a 'Gladys'.

12 For Bottomley and J. S. Lyons, see Julian Symons, *Horatio Bottomley* (London, 2001), p. 72.

13 Alan Hyman, *The Rise and Fall of Horatio Bottomley* (London, 1972), p. 160.

14 See PRO WO 339/1161.

15 See 'New Trial of a Shares Case', *Daily Express* (19 May 1931), p. 7.

16 *News of the World* (9 January 1943).

17 'Monocled Gunman', *Daily Mirror* (3 January 1944), p. 1.

18 *Sunday Pictorial* (16 March 1941), p. 4.

19 'London Jewel Thefts', *Chicago Evening Post* (29 September 1942), p. 5.

20 Claude Swain Kastinole, *Mayfair with the Lid Off* (London, 1938), p. 92.

21 *The Illustrated Circular of Confidence Tricksters and Professional Criminals*, p. 3.

22 John Capstick, *Given in Evidence* (London, 1960), p. 46.

23 John Gosling, *The Ghost Squad* (London, 1959), p. 16.

24 MEPOL 2/5015.

25 See West (ed.), *Guy Liddell Diaries*, vol. 1, p. 30.

26 HO 283/8.

27 'Woman Is Said To Have Posed as a Naval Surgeon', *Daily Express* (19 March 1941), p. 3.

28 'Fairy Tale Life of "Society Struck" Woman Ends in Prison's Cold Reality', *Daily Mirror* (14 September 1944), p. 3.

29 'Ex-Officer Fined for Misrepresentation', *The Times* (4 October 1940), p. 9.

30 'Private Gave Savoy Party', *Daily Mirror* (18 April 1940), p. 5.

31 'Death Beat Police by 60 Sec.', *Daily Mirror* (19 June 1941), p. 5.

32 See MEPO 3/2030.

33 See 'A Young Man's Cheques', *The Times* (3 September 1937), p. 9.

34 '£100-a-week Mayfair Playboy Starts a Man's Life', *Daily Express* (21 August 1937), p. 3.

35 Dod Orsborne, *Master of the Girl Pat* (New York, 1949), p. 172.

36 See 'A Wife's Unhappy Honeymoon', *The Times* (14 October 1920), p. 5.

Chapter Six: Parents

1 Case details are quoted from MEPO 3/2219.

2 'Sherlock Spilsbury',*Time* (2 July 1934).

3 Eric Maschwitz, *No Chip on My Shoulder* (London, 1957), p. 128.

4 They were Edith Eccles, John Arberry, Eric Maschwitz, H. Montgomery Hyde, Lady Honor Fowle.

5 Jerrard Tickell, *Soldier from the Wars Returning* (London, 1942), p. 109.

6 Ibid., p. 81.

7 Ibid., p. 114.

8 *Musical Times* (1 February 1932), p. 129.

9 *The Burlington Magazine* (April 1984), pp. 234–7.

10 Eva J. Salber, *The Mind Is Not the Heart: Recollections of a Woman Physician* (Durham, North Carolina, 1989), p. 43.

11 Robert Cecil, *A Divided Life: A Biography of Donald Maclean* (London, 1990), p. 104.

12 Henri Frenay, *The Night Will End* (London, 1976), pp. 190–8.

13 See Jeffrey T. Richelson, *A Century of Spies* (Oxford, 2007), p. 274.

14 For the case of Mary Bird, see 'Film Actress's Escape', *News of the World* (28 June 1931), p. 11. Other quotations from *News of the World* (5 July 1942), p. 5; *Daily Express* (1 December 1950), p. 5.

15 The story was told by the High Court judge Sir Stephen Tumim.

16 'Murder Verdict Against a Doctor', *The Times* (27 February 1920), p. 11; 'Death of Colonel's Daughter', *The Times* (3 December 1920), p. 9; 'Woman Teacher's Death', *The Times* (11 January 1929), p. 9; 'Swiss Woman's Death', *The Times* (7 August 1935); 'Girl Cashier's Death', *The Times* (19 October 1935), p. 4.

17 Jerrard told Betty Box, the producer of the film adaptation of his novel *Appointment with Venus*, that he was 'with British Intelligence all throughout World War Two'. See Betty Box, *Lifting the Lid* (Lewes, 2000), p. 57.

18 Letter from Group Captain Anthony Somerhough, PRO WO 311/1158. For the political background to the trials, see 'The Scars of Ravensbrück' in Patricia Heberer and Jürgen Matthäus (eds), *Atrocities on Trial* (Lincoln, Nebr., 2008), pp. 123–58.

19 See National Archives CRIM 1/1479.

20 'Boxes Fitted with Shutters', *The Times* (2 January 1935), p. 15; 'Illegal Offer of Shares', *The Times* (30 October 1937); 'Colonel Who Wrote on Wall Remanded', *Daily Mirror* (15 June 1940), p. 11.

21 'Attacked Man Died a Natural Death', *Daily Mirror* (23 February 1939), p. 27.

Chapter Seven: Subterraneans

1 Louis MacNeice, 'Blackouts, Bureaucracy & Courage', in *Selected Prose* (1990), p. 101.

2 Goronwy Rees, *A Bundle of Sensations* (London, 1960), p. 111.

3 Pete Bunten, 'Literary Drinkers', *Innspire* (February 2008), p. 28.

4 Allan Ramsay, 'Patrick Thursfield: The Last Tangerine', *Contemporary Review* (April 2004).

5 'London Nights', *Bystander* (21 February 1940), p. 'A'.

6 See CRIM 1/1586.

7 See CRIM 1/1150.

8 'Lord Lauderdale Acquitted', *The Times* (24 November 1943), p. 2.

9 'Court Martial of Sir Paul Latham', *The Times* (5 September 1941), p. 2.

10 Godfrey Winn, *The Infirm Glory: The Green Years* (London, 1967), p. 112.

11 M. J. Lancaster, *Brian Howard: Portrait of a Failure* (London, 1968), p. 431.

12 Quoted in Alkarim Jivani, *It's Not Unusual: A History of Lesbian and Gay Britain in the Twentieth Century* (London, 1997), p. 69.

13 See Leycester Otter-Barry, *Memoirs of Major Leycester Otter-Barry, MC* (unpublished, deposited in Shropshire County Archive 94/1364).

14 *Minutes of the London County Council*, vol. 41 (1931), p. 1108.

15 *The Savoy Baths: A Guide* (London, *c.*1910), p. 12.

16 See Anthony Masters, *The Man Who Was M: The Life of Maxwell Knight* (Oxford, 1984), p. 77.

17 Lancaster, *Howard*, p. 431.

18 Ibid., pp. 459–60.

19 All that Anatole got for his trouble was porridge – his second serving since 1918 – but his criminal convictions did not preclude him from becoming one of the most tireless contributors to the Mass Observation project. His diary entries, written under the pseudonym B. Charles, are quoted at length in Simon Garfield, *Our Hidden Lives* (London, 2004).

20 Interview with Dennis Dewsnap, 19 January 2010.

21 Anthony Heckstall-Smith, *Eighteen Months* (London, 1954), p. 11.

Chapter Eight: Traitors

1 See KV 2/732.

2 The incident is recounted in Langley, *Fight Another Day*.

3 See KV 2/728.

4 See KV 2/728.

5 See KV2/730.

6 Interview with Anthony Pitt-Rivers, 20 June 2008.

7 Interview with Pauline, Lady Rumbold, 28 February 2008.

8 C. C. Grey, quoted in Stephen Dorril, *Blackshirt* (London, 2006) p. 329.

9 Dew was sentenced to nine month's hard labour in 1941.

10 See KV 2/731.

11 Stella's words, according to her escort to the Waldorf, James Langley. See Langley, *Fight Another Day*, p. 182.

12 See KV 2/729.

13 See KV 2/728.

14 The accusation, noted in Stella's file, was made by Elisabeth Furse, a British woman involved with 'Pat' Line activities in Marseilles. Her memoirs contain an account of the affair, but do not name Stella. See Elisabeth Furse, *Dream Weaver* (London, 1993), pp. 122–39. Furse, by coincidence, was continuity girl on the Arthur Askey picture *Miss London Ltd* (1943).

15 See KV 2/731.

16 See KV 2/729.

17 MI5 phone tap, 17 December 1941.

18 After the death of her husband, Lady Kemball-Cook lived on in genteel poverty in their flat in Queen's Gate. As the years went by her poverty became more obvious than her gentility – one relation remembers her single-bar electric fire and the single mattress on which she slept in the hallway – but her life was not without its pleasures. She is reported to have been a good friend of the singer Freddie Mercury, who often visited the flat and played her grand piano. Correspondence with Geoffrey Kemball-Cook.

19 Interview with Jane Cairns, 28 August 2008.

20 See KV 2/734.

21 See KV 2/734.

22 See KV 2/734.

23 Stella seems to have sensed that her captors were becoming less tolerant. At the beginning of 1942 she agreed to reveal the true identity of René on condition that it remain a secret between herself, Mills and Tar Robertson. She wrote it down on a piece of paper, which was then placed inside an envelope marked 'NOT

TO BE OPENED WITHOUT THE PERMISSION OF MAJOR ROBERTSON', which was then sealed with two blobs of hot red wax bearing the impression of Tar's signet ring. It remained unread until August 1942, when Mills broke the seal and pulled out the name: Gerhardt Gunther du Pöel. They made no attempt to ascertain the truth of this statement. By the time that the liberation of France had made it possible to despatch an officer to Angers and Nantes to check the details of her story, Stella had changed her mind again. René was now Dr Siegfried Rauch, a lawyer with teeth as perfect as his English. 'It can be said at once that there was in fact at the material time a junior officer called Siegfried Rauch serving in the German intelligence headquarters in Angers,' reported the intelligence officer assigned to make enquiries in France, 'but from this point onwards all attempts to verify and check the identification break down and indeed tend to disprove it.' His conclusion was a shrug: 'In short, MI5 are driven to the conclusion that, in this as in other instances, Mrs Lonsdale has taken a piece of the truth and placed it in a false setting.'

24 See KV 2/734.

25 See KV 2/734.

26 Pitt-Rivers had acquired the loyalty of his most trusted stooge, a man named Trelawney Darrell Reed, by pressuring a jury to find him innocent of a murder he had committed on the estate. (Reed shot down and killed the pilot of an aeroplane he claimed was unsettling his heifers – the jury at his trial was composed mainly of Pitt-Rivers tenants, who ignored the instructions of the judge in favour of those of their landlord.)

27 Capt. George Henry Lane Fox Pitt-Rivers, *The Czech Conspiracy* (London, 1938), p. 88.

28 Not everyone possessed such strength. George Pitt-Rivers had his sister, Marcia, committed to a psychiatric institution after her son was killed in action and she, as a ritual of grief, took to camping out in a stretch of woodland near the house. (The final straw came on a car journey during which Marcia tore off her clothes and threw them through the window of his yellow Bentley.) He

strong-armed his eldest son, Michael, into motoring around the family estate obliging tenants to sign a petition against evacuees being billeted in the area, on the grounds that they would probably be Jews from the East End of London.

29 Nicholas Shakespeare, *Bruce Chatwin* (London, 2000), pp. 182–6.

30 Interview with Kenelm Digby-Jones, 12 June 2008.

31 According to the historian Peter Geiger, these records have, however, yielded the tantalising information that Prince Louis of Liechtenstein – the man whom Stella fingered as the spymaster controlling German agents operating in Britain – was indeed an Abwehr officer stationed at Angers during her period in France.

32 Interview with Françoise Prévost, 24 May 2008. I was able to make contact with Françoise thanks to information provided by Charles Platiau, a well-regarded photojournalist who is the unofficial historian of the Platiau family.

Chapter Nine: Majesties

1 Frank Giles, *Sundry Times* (1984), p. 26.

2 Noel F. Busch, 'Queen Wilhelmina', *Life* (16 April 1945), p. 15. See Sefton Delmer, *Black Boomerang* (London, 1962), p. 23.

3 Douglas Fairbanks Jnr, *A Hell of a War* (London, 1995), p. 146.

4 For Manoel's suits see Joseph Vecchi, *The Tavern Is My Drum* (London, 1948), p. 21.

5 Pimlott (ed.), *Political Diary of Hugh Dalton*, p. 176.

6 Leo Amery, *Empire at Bay* (London, 1988), p. 667.

7 Obituary, Michael Torrens-Spence, *Daily Telegraph* (9 November 2001), p. 29.

8 See Vladimir Dedijer, *The War Diaries of Vladimir Dedijer*, vol. 3 (Ann Arbor, Michigan, 1990), p. 173.

9 Hart-Davis (ed.), *King's Counsellor*, p. 30.

10 Pimlott (ed.), *Second World War Diary of Hugh Dalton*, p. 499.

11 Ibid., p. 579.

12 Quotations from official sources in this chapter are from docu-

ments contained in National Archives files PREM 3/511/2; PREM 3/511/9; PREM 3/511/10; PREM 3515; FO 371 33480; FO 271 37625; FO 371 37626.

13 See A. R. Glen, *Under the Pole Star: The Oxford University Arctic Expedition*, 1935–6 (London, 1937); A. S. T. Godfrey, *The Cradle of the North Wind* (London, 1938); 'Youth in the Arctic', *The Times* (15 July 1935), p. 15.

14 Glen, *Pole Star*, p. 14.

15 In 1936 Robert was involved in a violent assault at their mother's cottage near Preston Crowmarsh in Oxfordshire: when two ramblers – a schoolmaster and a Justice of the Peace – attempted to use a public right-of-way across the garden of Ferry Cottage, Robert backed his car into them and kicked the schoolmaster in the chest. See 'Right of Way Dispute', *The Times* (28 September 1936), p. 9; 'Schoolmaster's Appeal Allowed', *The Times* (6 January 1937), p. 14.

16 Letter from Archibald Dunlop Mackenzie to Winston Churchill (18 February 1944), Dunlop Mackenzie family archive and PREM 3515.

17 This royal enthusiasm for the wedding is not reflected in King George's correspondence with Churchill, in which he expressed doubts about Alexandra's suitability: 'I am not at all sure that the girl is fitted to be his wife or to give King Peter the assistance he will require in the very difficult times he will have to face . . .'

18 Queen Alexandra of Yugoslavia, *For a King's Love* (London, 1956), p. 100.

19 Ibid., p. 102.

20 Ibid., p. 103.

21 Ibid., p. 124.

22 Stephen Ambrose and Richard H. Immerman, *Ike's Spies: Eisenhower and the Espionage Establishment* (New York, 1981), pp. 91–2.

23 'Solicitous for the health of Claridge's personnel,' recalled a colleague, 'he told me to wireless as soon as we returned to the ship

that any medical supplies left in his room should be gathered carefully together and deposited with the hall porter.'

24 See Robert Alcorn, *No Bugles for Spies* (London, 1963), pp. 145–7.

25 Fitzroy MacLean, *Eastern Approaches* (London, 1949), p. 402.

26 John Walters, 'The Lonely King', *Daily Mirror* (10 February 1945), p. 1.

27 'Yugoslavia a New Republic', *The Times* (30 November 1945), p. 4.

28 See Philip Murphy, *Alan Lennox-Boyd: A Biography* (London, 1999), p. 74.

Chapter Ten: Strikers

1 Bo Wilson, 'Savoy has been stripped of its soul, says retired head barman', London *Evening Standard* (23 July 2010).

2 See LAB 16/311.

3 'Musicians are told "join the hotel strikers"', *Daily Mirror* (11 October 1946), p. 1.

4 'Strike at 3 Mayfair Hotels', *Daily Express* (9 October 1946), p. 1.

5 'The man who came to dinner', *Daily Express* (10 October 1946), p. 1.

6 See Angus Calder, *Speak for Yourself* (Oxford, 1985), pp. 231–6.

7 'Hotel Workers on the March', *Manchester Guardian* (14 October 1946).

8 Nicol, *Savoy*, p. 189.

9 See KV 2/1864; Nicol, *Savoy*, p. 186; Hugh Wontner interview in the National Sound Archive, British Library; KV 2/1864.

10 Bob Stewart (1877–1971), the spymaster of the CPGB, and Jimmy Shields (1900–49), a former editor of the *Daily Worker*, who were both involved in the maintenance of a secret radio transmitter in Wimbledon.

11 For the details of the Piazza case and its consequences see files LAB 10/630, LAB 10/ 731, KV 2/1864 and MEPO 3/2805 – the

sources of quotes in this chapter from government and police documents, unless otherwise indicated.

12 See HO 45/254486.

13 *Revolutionary Communist Policy* (London, 1945), pp. 28–9.

14 Hugh Wontner interview in the National Sound Archive.

15 John Platts-Mills, *Muck, Silk and Socialism* (Wedmore, 2001), p. 253.

16 'London Trades Council Backs Savoy Strikers', *Daily Worker* (14 November 1947), p. 3.

17 Kenneth Sykora, who would go on to be a respected jazz guitarist and BBC broadcaster.

18 'Impressions of Parliament', *Punch* 227 (21 July 1954), p. 127.

19 Richard Heffernan and Mike Marqusee, *Defeat from the Jaws of Victory: Inside Kinnock's Labour Party* (London, 1992), p. 18.

Conclusion: Ghosts

1 Quoted in John Edzard, 'People's palace threatened with demolition', *Guardian* (16 April 2004).

2 Wally Hoffman's reminiscences are archived at www.storyhouse.org/wally7.html; interview with Emmanuel Litvinoff, Museum of London archives; author's interview with Ned Sherrin, 19 January 2006.

3 Joanne Shipway's letters, photographs and reminiscences are preserved at http://London.allinfo-about.com/features/joanneblitz.html.

4 See Quentin Crisp, *The Naked Civil Servant* (London, 1968), p. 82; Rose Collis, *Colonel Barker's Monstrous Regiment* (London, 2001), p. 141.

5 Files from these cases; see 'The Charge against a Doctor', *The Times* (1 June 1917), p. 3; 'The Synovitis Case', *The Times* (6 July 1917), p. 3.

6 For Baron Laitre, see Hugh Montgomery-Massingberd, *The London Ritz: A Social and Architectural History* (London, 1981),

p. 125; for Barbara Devonshire, see 'Inquests', *The Times* (15 August 1906), p. 6.

7 Elias Canetti, *Party in the Blitz* (London, 2005), p. 130.

Acknowledgements

The origins of this book lie in an article I wrote in 1997 for the *Independent on Sunday* about the deposed kings of Eastern Europe. I owe thanks to Andrew Tuck and Ruth Metzstein for commissioning it, and to HM King Leka of the Albanians for agreeing to be its principal subject, despite his displeasure with the result. Peter Sweasey, with whom I made a Channel Four television series called *Checking into History*, had a similarly formative influence. During the production of that series, Gerrie Pitt and Stephen Boxall at the Ritz, Susan Scott at the Savoy and Mia Josephs and Graham Copeman at Claridge's kindly allowed me to ferret in the archives and loiter in the hallways of their respective hotels. Tom Woolfenden provided exemplary research assistance. Petra Falkenberg worked on my behalf at the Berlin State Library. Staff at the National Archive, the British Library, the Imperial War Museum, the London Library, the Marx Memorial Library, the Bancroft Library, and Shropshire County Archive gave expert help.

I owe thanks to over a hundred interviewees and correspondents, many of whom answered impertinent questions about painful episodes from their personal or family histories. Ettore Emanuelli and Robert Rietti shared their experiences of internment; Joan Blair-Richley, Yolande Knight, Joan Lambert, Ann Manno and Fernando and Francesco Santarelli told me stories of the Santarelli family. It was a privilege to listen to the reminiscences of Max Levitas, last of the Savoy protestors. Michael and Danny Lee were generous with memories of Phil Piratin – which were supplemented by the recollections of Alice Hitchin,

Alf Minto and Bertha Sokoloff. Rosalind Davy, Louella Frankel, Alan Klotnick, Michael Rosen, Anna Shepherd and Chris Woon all provided fruitful thoughts on the Savoy invaders. The world of their inheritors, the Savoy strikers of 1946–7, was illuminated by Ray Bohringer, Barney Platts-Mills and Duncan Sykora. Joyce Stone brought the Dorchester's dance-band years to dazzling life, with further details furnished by Seth Cardew, the late Lady Mairi Bury, Prince Franzi von Hohenlohe and Herbert Lom. Leslie Amos, Barry Crugten and Nora Pakenham told me what happened below stairs; Martin Macquisten and Jean Kent about what was eaten above. Sophy and Sally Milwidsky generously allowed me to read the *Pot-Pourri* of Sir Curtis Lampson. Additional information was furnished by Henry Andreae, Seigneur Michael Beaumont of Sark, David Hill CBE, Sir Michael Peat KCVO, George and Gill Usher, Patricia Webb and David and Colonel Gervas Wells-Cole. The late Marie-Jaqueline Lancaster brought the subterranean Ritz to life, as did the late George Hayim, and the late Gilbert Bradley, who was kindly introduced to me by Chris Horodyski, who hosted our afternoon in Brighton. More stories about the figures from the Ritz below the Ritz came from Dennis Dewsnap, Anne Dunn, Bevis Hillier and Janetta Otter-Barry. Norman Barrett, Edward Bourke, Michael Buckmaster, Jane Cairns, Richard Carlyle-Clarke, Vivien Chapman, Nicholas Gibbs, Anthony Haden-Guest, Dr Geoffrey Kemball-Cook, Louis Oury, Charles Platiau, Francoise Prevost, the late Pauline, Lady Rumbold, David Lithgow Smith and Andy Spallek helped me to navigate the world of Stella Lonsdale and her lovers, victims, friends and enemies. Tom and Sir Crispin Tickell, Michael and Professor Nicholas Pickwoad and Claire Barkla spoke to me with astonishing generosity and candour about the tragic episode shared by their disparate family histories. Additional information was provided by David and Martin Barkla, Professor Susan Benedict, Professor Susan Blackmore, Eric Davidson, Professor M. R. D. Foot, Dr Ronald de Fossard, Dr Alison

Acknowledgements

O'Donnell, Michael Pickwoad, Major-General Tony Richardson, Squadron Leader Colin Richardson and Roy Smith. HRH Crown Prince Alexander of Yugoslavia was kind enough to receive me at his palace, Andrew Dunlop Mackenzie to receive me at his club – and share his father's papers and journals. The world of Yugoslav diplomacy was also illuminated by His Excellency Dragomir Acovic. Other insights and tips were furnished by Crispin Blunt MP, David R. Bon, Barbora Cowle, Professor J. W. Dumbrell, Sir Clement Freud, Kenneth Kendal, Lord Killearn, Rob Lemon, Leigh Smith and the Friends of the Regent Palace Hotel, and Raine, the Dowager Countess Spencer. Above all, I consider myself very lucky to have spoken to two of the greatest figures of the London hotel world, Joe Gilmore and the late Victor Legg.

Draft chapters of this book were read by Matthew Beaumont, Roger Clarke, Juliet Gardiner, Matt Houlbrook, Peter Sweasey, David Sweet, Phil Tinline and Kenith Trodd, who saved me from many blushes. Remaining sources of embarrassment are, of course, my responsibility. Joanna West and Rebecca Lee brought order to the text. The errors and misapprehensions that remain are all my own work. My editor Walter Donohue and agent Simon Trewin remained enthusiastic and showed saintly patience as deadline after deadline expired. My greatest debts, however, are to my wife, Nicola – and to our daughters Gracie and Connie, who have barely known life without this book.

Index

Unless otherwise specified, all establishments are in London.

Index

Autori (cartoonist), 23
Aylesbury, HMP, 247–8

Baillie-Stewart, Norman, 221
Banbury, Frith, 194
Bannerman, Honor, 309
Barker, Isabel Mary, 188, 189
Barker, Capt. Leslie Bligh, 317
Barkla, Charles Glover, 167
Barkla, Constance, 168, 187
Barkla, Neil Glover, 159, 167–8, 170–1,
    172–4, 177, 186, 187
Barnes, Ch. Insp., 303, 309
Barriteau, Carl, 84
Barsley, Michael, 15, 21
Barthou, Louis, 261
Barton (MI5 officer), 247
Bauer, R. J., 131
BBC: blacklist, 106, 107–8;and homo-
    sexuals, 193;ignores Savoy invasion,
    68–9;Legg's call, 3;radio plays,
    210;and USSR, 109;war announced,
    4
Beacon Hotel, Bristol, 35
Beaton, Cecil, 82, 91, 95, 96
Beaumont, Lionel 'Buster', 149
Beaumont, Michael, 150–1
Beaumont, Richard Vyvyan Dudley,
    149–51
Beaverbrook, Lord, 70
Beckett, Joe, 36
Beecham, Thomas, 132
Beith, Maj.-Gen. John Hay, 197
Belgrade: British Legation, 264,
    272–3;German bombing, 265–6,
    273;Royal Palace, 263, 265–7
Bell, Dr John Henderson, 317
Bellenger, Etienne, 228
Belloc, Hilaire, 126, 179
Bendemann, Oswald, 231
Bennett, Arnold, 23
Benson, Rion, 148
Berg, Moe, 281

Bergen-Belsen concentration camp, 128
Berkeley Hotel: band at war's outset,
    11;Beaumont's spree, 150;fake lieu-
    tenant at, 148;Gilmore at Perroquet
    bar, 290;Heckstall-Smith on,
    214;Legg works at, 2;rations scandal,
    122;Santarelli at, 23;strike at, 293
Berlin, Isaiah, 97
Berly, Harry, 86–7
Bernhard, Prince of Lippe-Biesterfeld,
    259, 278
Bertram Mills Circus, Ascot, 22, 32–3,
    34–6, 38–41, 221, 250
Betjeman, John, 209
Bevin, Ernest, 305
Bigio, Edna, 102
Bird, Mary, 171
Birkett, Sir Norman, 44, 227
Birley, Dick, 203
blackouts: and crime, 144, 297;and ho-
    mosexuality, 190;at Mount Royal
    Hotel, 169;at Savoy, 9
Blake, Pamela, 227
Blake, 2nd Lt Peter, 148
Blitz: ARP wardens, 9–10;Ascot camp as
    Luftwaffe marker, 38;Café de Paris
    hit, 290;Charing Cross Hotel hit,
    130;dancing at Dorchester, 20,
    83;Docklands, 54;Dorchester's solid-
    ity, 89–90;preparations for, 8–9;and
    Santarelli's 'anxiety', 43;see also air-
    raid shelters; blackouts
Blumberg, Dr Ernst, 172–3, 177, 186,
    187
Bœuf sur le Toit (nightclub), 193
Bohringer, Leslie, 307
Bon, Anton, 80, 99, 111
Boris III, King of Bulgaria, 258
Bottomley, Horatio, 135, 136, 137
Boulanger, Christian, 238–9, 242
Bowlly, Al, 85, 108
Bowman, Frederick, 36–7
Bowyer, Padre, 101

Index

Index

Index

Index

ff

Faber and Faber is one of the great independent publishing houses. We were established in 1929 by Geoffrey Faber with T. S. Eliot as one of our first editors. We are proud to publish award-winning fiction and non-fiction, as well as an unrivalled list of poets and playwrights. Among our list of writers we have five Booker Prize winners and twelve Nobel Laureates, and we continue to seek out the most exciting and innovative writers at work today.

Find out more about our authors and books
faber.co.uk

Read our blog for insight and opinion on books and the arts
thethoughtfox.co.uk

Follow news and conversation
twitter.com/faberbooks

Watch readings and interviews
youtube.com/faberandfaber

Connect with other readers
facebook.com/faberandfaber

Explore our archive
flickr.com/faberandfaber